The Book of Christian Prayer and Devotion

Congregant's 1ˢᵗ Edition

All prayers and praises—with the exceptions mentioned below—were written right from the scriptures, but no specific translation was maintained in the bulk of the text. Many different translations were referred to, as well as the Hebrew, Aramaic, and Greek used in the original manuscripts. Any version or texts referenced were altered at the discretion of the author for the sake of prose.

Some of the Jewish Siddur prayer book was incorporated into the text of this book and was altered for the sake of doctrine and prose at the discretion of the author.

Some of the Book of Common Prayer was incorporated into the text of this book and was altered for the sake of doctrine and prose at the discretion of the author.

The complete volume of the classic work of Oswald Chambers, My Utmost for His Highest, has been included in this book for daily devotions 365 days of the year. Its inclusion does not assume the author's theological agreement.

BOCP = Taken—or altered—from the Book of Common Prayer, Episcopal, Amended in 2015.
Siddur = Taken—or altered—from the Jewish Siddur prayer book.

Copyright © 2024 Arlyn Satanek, all rights reserved

Dedicated to Anchored Fellowship, Uniontown, PA
May this book be your second most used book for the purposes of personal spirituality; the first being the Bible. May it bless you in your times of prayer and devotion, however you make use of it, and may it teach you more about praying the way the people of the Bible prayed.

Introduction

This book was born out of my own frustrations with an unstructured prayer life. The demanding work of ministry was always vying for my time and causing me to feel rushed in my private time with the Lord. I always had those thoughts in the back of my mind: "well, I better hurry this along, because I have this and that to get done for the Lord." I was feeling the need to become more structured and deliberate about my praying. But, how?

As a very unreligious person, I had always reveled in my liberty from formality and liturgical spirituality—and still do! But much to my surprise, I was inspired when researching various Judeo-Christian groups and observing as they prayed and worshiped through more structured methods. I admit that most of it was very undesirable to me and felt dry and lifeless. But there was definitely something there; something that I could learn from; something that I could leverage in my walk with Christ.

One inspiration behind this book would be the orthodox Jews. The majority of their prayers come from reciting Old Testament scriptures that were collected and categorized in a prayer book known as the Siddur. I was shocked at how their liturgical prayer life was putting my free-from-form prayer life to shame. They prayed about everything, and they did it in the beautiful language of the scriptures! How could that be a bad thing, right? For example, when something good happens to me, or when I hear some really good news, I say, "thank You, Lord." But, in the same circumstances, an orthodox Jew recites from memory, "Blessed are You Lord our God, King of the Universe, Who is good and does good." That's better. Much better. It's not that they use more words, and not only that they use better wording, it's that they intentionally take more time to more appropriately acknowledge God. That began to help me see room for personal improvement, and I knew it would require more intention and forethought.

I can hear the argument now: "aren't free-from-form prayers better than canned and recited prayers?" Well, they can be, for sure, and should be used regardless. But I have heard many a prayer that caused me to think, "it might have been better if they had just read an already written prayer." Like as in everything, the human element is the limitation to free-from-form praying. If we are praying "off-the-cuff," we are drawing from our spiritual reservoir, and that can be a deep well or a shallow one. We can only pray from our own knowledge, memory, and thoroughness. And that's where recited prayers can shine and be a benefit. Recited prayer eliminates much of that by being planned, researched, and developed right out of the Bible. And that's always what I mean when I refer to recited prayer in this introduction. Those are the only recited prayers that I can personally approve of. That does not mean that they have to be in exact scriptural wording, but they do need to come from truths in the Bible.

The power behind recited prayer—if there is power behind it—is no different than the power behind free-from-form prayer. In either instance, it is only when we say our prayer words from our heart, with our faith added to them, that we are effectively praying. And that can be done just as well through recited prayers as with free-from-form prayers.

There is another benefit of recited prayers: because we are praying from God's scriptures, it allows us to be more confident that we are praying according to God's will. And that will be the explanation for some of the prayers that seem to be missing from this book. If it's not in the Bible, I don't want it in here. I can attempt what I wish in my free-from-form praying. But I won't try to build a recited prayer around it if the Bible hasn't already specified it.

Yet another benefit would be that it offers the person praying the confidence to pray out loud. Many are too timid to pray out loud, because they think they are only allowed to pray "off the cuff (sometimes confused with: from the heart)," and that is a most vulnerable and nerve-racking thing for some. Whereas recited prayer adds confidence to the person praying. They know the prayer is solid, thorough, and beautiful and all they have to do is mean it when they pray it. That's helpful.

I can also anticipate the argument, "but didn't Jesus teach us not to use repetition when we pray?" Or course not! That wasn't at all what He said in Matthew 6:7. First of all, Jesus was talking about the praying of the gentiles (or, heathens), not Jews. Secondly, his issue wasn't with repetition, His issue was with vain repetitions—vain being the operative word. In fact, the ESV doesn't even translate it that way. It translates it to say, "empty phrases." In other words, the heathens were praying to false gods, so their phrases—whether repetitious or not—were empty. Prayer to Yahweh is never empty, not when the heart is behind it and faith is added to it. Jesus knew the Jews had always prayed recited prayers from the scriptures, and He was definitely okay with that, seeing that He had given the Jews the very first prayer book ever written: the Book of Psalms!

But, as far as repetition is concerned, repetition will always be a part of our praying, whether we desire it or not. That's just the truth! We human creatures will naturally fall into our own repetitious words and ways over time—yes, even in our prayers and worship. Test this for yourself: attend a church for a few months and critically observe (without being critical) the way its leaders do what they do and say what they say. You'll notice all the repetition they use. Or eat with a Christian for a few months and listen to them pray for their meals. You'll hear essentially the same prayer every time. They can't help it! Again, that's because we human creatures naturally fall into repetition over time, no matter how free-thinking we think we are.

So, if we're going to naturally fall into repetition, wouldn't it be beneficial to accept it to some degree and improve upon it where we can, so that we can be more efficient and thorough, at least for a time? That was the question in mind that formed the early stages of my idea for this book. For me, the answer was, yes, at least for a time, as I intentionally broaden my reservoir for prayer and worship using the scriptures themselves. And that's what I have sought to create in The Book of Christian Prayer and Devotion. If it's nothing else, it's something to review in order to broaden our reservoirs for prayer and stick us more closely to the scriptures when we pray free-from-form.

I'm not done fleshing out of the benefits of this book's approach just yet. Here's another one: our negative human emotions can oftentimes get so oppressive that we cannot think of what to pray and we cannot motivate ourselves to even try. For example: when deeply grieving, to pray for comfort and peace; or when boiling angry, to pray forgiveness, kindness, and temperance. Having the prayer words already structured is a great solution to this problem. The words that would otherwise be clouded and crowded out by our complex feelings are already available to you, and all you have to do is locate the prayer in the book and pray it from your heart by faith. That is far easier. I learned this lesson years ago when going through unthinkable heartbreak. I just did not have the wherewithal to pray in a free-from-form manner most of the time. So, I simply started reading through the book of Psalms, and that became my praying. I highlighted sections of Psalms that dealt specifically with the way I was feeling and recited (prayed) them out loud to the Lord and meditated on them. It was a powerful experience. When we can't come up with the words on our own, thank God, He already handled that for us... in the Bible.

To take a step backwards, the Siddur was not my only inspiration for this resource—far from it. I also found inspiration in how the Catholic, the Anglican, and the Episcopal congregant makes use of various versions of The Book of Common Prayer for daily prayer time and devotions. To a lesser extent, I found a little inspiration among the Amish. Though odd, and definitely further removed from modernity, it had a certain appeal to what few religious cells I have in my body. But, without a doubt, The Book of Common Prayer became the backbone for my attempt at creating something to personally assist me—and perhaps others—in my own structuring of prayer and devotion time. I really liked the idea of The Book of Common Prayer, but—of course—its language is grievously repetitious and somewhat dated. It just wasn't for me. But... what if I rebuilt it from the ground up? What if I improved upon it—for me and for others like me? The Book of Christian Prayer and Devotion is my first attempt at that. And, yes, God willing, this release is just the beginning.

Unless I lose my spiritual fervor for this, I plan to continue to improve upon it with subsequent releases—as many as are needed, to build a more extensive prayer library, and get it to a state that accomplishes my goal. This first edition seems to fall short of that in my own heart. But it is a giant move in the right direction for me, and that is why I am releasing it to others. I have already used the content of this book for my own private time

7

with the Lord, and I have been overwhelmed at how it has blessed me; I have been overwhelmed at my overall increase in perceived spirituality; I have been overwhelmed at how powerful my praying now feels to me; I have been overwhelmed at how this has built my faith in my prayers; I am overwhelmed at how—like never before—I walk away from my prayer sessions feeling satisfied and fulfilled, as though I had really accomplished something. And I am overwhelmed by how it has improved my free-from-form praying, in private and in public gatherings. Using this book has unlocked something in me that my own habits and repetitions had once locked up. Using this book has taught me to become a better prayer, because I have actually put conscious effort into it.

I believe that if you too use this book (for a while, or indefinitely), that it will also teach you how to pray better. Do you need to be taught how to pray better? Do we? The answer to that question will vary among individuals, depending on my factors. But—to cut to the chase—I believe we can all stand to gain something beneficial from being taught to pray better. To an infinitely greater degree, it must have felt the same way to the disciples, as they listened to the Master pray. They thought (or so I speculate), "wow, we want to be able to pray like that!" So, they asked Jesus, "teach us to pray." And He did so, without condemnation. And Jesus gave them a liturgical prayer (the Lord's Prayer). But it wasn't just liturgy to repeat. More precisely, it was form; form that could be learned from and built upon. And that is the ultimate aim of this book. It's to be a steppingstone into greater free-from-form praying, by –yes, you guessed it—first learning from form!

Let me give you one more very strong reason for this book. As a Pastor, it is my constant observation, that most Christians don't maintain any kind of scheduled and consistent prayer and devotion time. Their reasons usually fall somewhere within the arguments I've already stated in this introduction. Structuring and ordering it, in the way that I have done here, eliminates all of that. It sets the daily schedule. It holds the individual to remember everything that is necessary to both read (yes, there is a daily Bible reading guide in this book and a complete devotional for every day of the year) and pray daily, and it even gives them the words (or direction) needed to do so.

Stick with this prayer and devotion guide for one month and I believe you will notice a significant improvement in your spiritual well-being. Stick with it for three months, and I believe you will notice the Holy Spirit bubbling up torrents of living water in you. Stick with it for one year and you may explode! Just kidding. But if you'll use it in the right way for you, I believe it will transform your praying and your whole person.

My highest wish is that you will cherish this book (or more complete future editions of it) second to the Bible, or maybe third to a good commentary, and always have it nearby and ready to be put to use. But my realistic prayer is that you will own this book, learn something from it, and use it in whatever way it can be helpful to you. Special thanks to the Lord Who—I believe—has inspired and helped to bring this first edition to fruition. May—by the grace of Christ—future editions be all the better!

How to Use This Book

The Table of Contents will be your best friend when using this book. You will first find section XIII, the **Daily Prayer Sessions**, and flip through the four different session numbers to find the right session for you. These are your guides for daily prayers, and they will require you to look up prayers or readings from other sections of this book. So, you'll want to hop back to the Table of Contents to look those all up. I find that little bit of lookup fun, but if you don't like even slight delays during your praying, then it's a good idea to begin your prayer time by browsing ahead and bookmarking any sections you'll need to reference during your prayer time.

Once you are ready to go with your daily prayer sessions, you can approach this a handful of different ways. You can follow the daily plans exactly, and pray the written prayers verbatim, and you will have prayed thoroughly and biblically each day. Or you can use the prayers as more of a general guide, and first read the prayers to call to mind what you need to pray about and the things you should include when you pray about them, and then pray for that particular topic in your own words. Or you can pray the prayers and elaborate with your own words as your heart leads you.

Whichever approach you take to praying with this book, there are a couple of suggestions I want to make right up front. The first thing I want to say is that—for the most part—I have tried to do a thorough job of indicating within each prayer when the prayer calls for you to state the specific names of the people that you are praying a prayer for, or the individual needs that may fall within a category of prayer, but by all means, any time you are praying any of these prayers, if any specifics come to mind when you are praying—whether names or things—then call them out to the Lord and then continue with the prayer.

Also, I want to let you know that, for the most part, regular text that is not bold or italicized should be thought of as reading, instruction, or explanation to read silently, and on occasion out loud. For example, the devotional is written in regular text, and you can choose whether you want to read that silently or out loud. Italicized text is mostly reserved for all of the scripture or material references, and you will not bother to read those unless you are wanting to really pick apart the prayers and check out the origins behind them. And Bold text, for the most part, will be prayed either silently or out loud, except for the titles of this book. You will not say section titles or prayer titles, you will only read them.

Another way to use this book is simply as a library of prayers. You do not have to follow the daily prayer sessions if you don't want. You can just sit down with the book at any time, browse through the already extensive prayer library and pray through the prayers you choose.

Finally, a quick word about how to use Amen in this book. Obviously, this would be a matter of preference. If you are praying one prayer from this book individually, it is proper to conclude that prayer by saying, "in Jesus Name, Amen." But, during your prayer session, that closure on your prayer time really isn't necessary until ending your prayers. So, you may choose to exclude Amens altogether until your final prayer for the session, and end it with, "in Jesus Name, Amen." Or you may opt to say "Amen" after each individual prayer, and conclude your prayer time with, "in Jesus Name, Amen." Again, this is a matter of preference, and whatever seems best to you in your praying.

For a more thorough online tutorial and example on how to get the most from this book:

*Go to YouTube and search: How to Use The Book of Christian Prayer and Devotion.

*Or go to anchoredfellowship.com, click on the resources tab, and then click on: How to Use The Book of Christian Prayer and Devotion.

Table of Contents

I. Prayers to Memorize 14

II. Me and My House 18

III. My Family & Loved Ones 34

IV. The Whole World 51

V. Public Prayers 57

VI. Praises 59

VII. Collects from the BOCP – Holy Days 68

VIII. Collects from the BOCP – Reg. Days 72

IX. Collects from the BOCP - Extra/Misc. 78

X. Self-Benedictions 81

XI. Group-Benedictions 83

XII. Bible Reading 84

XIII. Daily Prayer Sessions 95

XIV. Devotions 123

I. Prayers to Memorize

These prayers may be needed daily, and oftentimes more than once daily. I recommend that you put prayer 1, 4, 5, 6, 7, & 8 to memory.

---

1. For Waking Gratitude   *Immediately upon waking*
I am thankful before You, living and enduring King *(Da. 6:26; Jg. 8:23)*, for you have mercifully preserved my soul within me and graciously awakened me to life and health *(Ps. 3:5)*. Great is Your faithfulness *(Siddur, Modeh Ani; La. 3:23)*.

2. For My Morning
God Most High, Possessor of Heaven and Earth *(Ge. 14:22)*, this morning, my prayer comes before You *(Ps. 88:13)*. You have said, "Seek my face." So, my heart says to You, "Your face, LORD, do I seek *(Ps. 27:8)*." That I may know You *(Ex. 33:13)*, and keep Your Word *(Ps. 119:101)*. That I may serve You this day with gladness *(Ps. 100:2)*. For You are God, You made me, and I am Yours *(Ps. 100:3)*. In You, I live, move, and have my being *(Ac. 17:28)*. And through Your Son, Jesus, I have obtained Salvation *(He. 2:3)*; which is guarded by Your power and through my faith *(1 Pe. 1:5)*. I give thanks to Your holy Name *(Ps. 106:47)*, for Your love for me never ceases, and Your mercies are new every morning *(La. 3:23)*. Guide me *(Ps. 73:24)*, that I may do Your will *(Mt. 26:42)*. Provide for me *(1 Ti. 6:17)*, that I may live for You. Protect me *(Ps. 59:1)*, that I may dwell safely *(Pr. 1:33)*. Grant to me escape from every temptation and trouble; or else strengthen me to bear it *(1 Co. 10:13)*. And now, fill me with Your Holy Spirit *(Lk. 11:13)*, to make me useful to You, and ready for every good work *(2 Ti. 2:21)*, that I may be witness of You in the world *(Ac. 1:8)*, and bring glory to Your name upon the earth *(Mt. 5:16)*. (Amen)

3. For Confession
Loving and merciful God, be gracious to me and hear my prayer *(Ps. 4:1)*. I acknowledge my sins and iniquities and do not hide them *(Ps. 32:5)*. I confess that I have sinned against You in thought, word, and deed, by what I have done, and by what I have left undone *(BOCP)*. *[State sins]* Father, forgive me of my sins, and cleanse me from all my unrighteousness *(1 Jn. 1:9)*.

Wash me thoroughly and I shall be whiter than snow *(Ps. 51:7)*, through the blood of Your Son *(Re. 7:14)*. (**Amen**)

4. For Blessing a Meal   *If eating alone*
I am grateful before You, merciful and gracious God. You give sun and rain upon the earth *(Mt. 5:45)*, and cause food and drink to come forth *(Ps. 104:15)* to satisfy the hearts of mankind *(Siddur; Mt. 5:45; Ps. 104:15)*. I receive it from Your hand with thanksgiving *(1 Ti. 4:4)*. To Your glory, I eat, I drink, and I live *(1 Co. 10:31)*. Bless and sanctify this meal *(1 Ti. 4:5)*. In the Name of Jesus, Amen

(Or)   *If praying for a group meal, or all reciting together*
We are grateful before You, merciful and gracious God. You give sun and rain upon the earth *(Mt. 5:45)*, and cause food and drink to come forth *(Ps. 104:15)* to satisfy the hearts of mankind *(Siddur; Mt. 5:45; Ps. 104:15)*. We receive it from Your hand with thanksgiving *(1 Ti. 4:4)*. To Your glory, we eat, we drink, and we live *(1 Co. 10:31)*. Bless and sanctify this meal *(1 Ti. 4:5)*. In the Name of Jesus, Amen

5. For a Drink Blessing   *If drinking any liquid alone*
I am grateful before You, merciful and gracious God. You give sun and rain upon the earth *(Mt. 5:45)*, and cause drink to come forth *(Ps. 104:15)* to gladden the hearts of mankind *(Siddur; Ps. 104:15)*. I receive it from Your hand with thanksgiving *(1 Ti. 4:4)*. To Your glory, I drink *(1 Co. 10:31)*. Bless and sanctify it *(1 Ti. 4:5)*. In the Name of Jesus, Amen

(Or)   If praying for group liquids, or all reciting together
We are grateful before You, merciful and gracious God. You give sun and rain upon the earth *(Mt. 5:45)*, and cause drink to come forth *(Ps. 104:15)* to gladden the hearts of mankind *(Siddur; Ps. 104:15)*. We receive it from Your hand with thanksgiving *(1 Ti. 4:4)*. To Your glory, we drink *(1 Co. 10:31)*. Bless and sanctify it *(1 Ti. 4:5)*. In the Name of Jesus, Amen

6. For My Travel
My God, in Whom I trust *(Ps. 91:2)*, I will rejoice and sing for joy, because You spread Your protection over me *(Ps. 5:11)*. I humbly ask, command Your angels concerning me, to guard me in all my ways *(Ps. 91:11)*. Keep me from all harm, and protect my life, my

coming and going, from this time forth and forevermore *(Ps. 121:7,8)*. **(Amen)**

7. For Good News or Occurrence
Gracious Lord, You are good *(Ps. 106:1)* and You do all things well *(Siddur; Mk. 7:37)*.

8. For Bad News or Occurrence
Merciful Father, in You I will trust *(Ps. 25:2)*. You will work all things for my good (Siddur; *Ro. 8:28*). **(Amen)**

9. The Lord's Prayer
Our Father in heaven, Hallowed be Your name. Your kingdom come. Your will be done On earth as *it is* in heaven. Give us this day our daily bread. And forgive us our debts, As we forgive our debtors. And do not lead us into temptation, But deliver us from the evil one. For Yours is the kingdom and the power and the glory forever. Amen *(Mt. 6:9-13-NKJV)*.

10. For My Afternoon
O Lord, support me the rest of this day, until the shadows lengthen, and the evening comes, and the busy world is hushed, and the fever of this day is over, and our work is done. Then, in Your mercy, grant me a safe time of dwelling, and a holy rest, and peace at the last *(BOCP)*. **(Amen)**

11. For My Evening
Let my prayer be set forth in Your sight as the incense, and let the lifting up of my hands be an evening sacrifice *(Ps. 141:2)*. Morning and evening, I bring my life as a consecration offering to You *(2 Ch. 31:3)*. For the day is yours, O God, and also the night. You have established the sun and the moon *(BOCP; Ps. 74:15,16)*. **(Amen)**

12. For Bedtime
Lord Almighty, grant me a perfect day's end, and a peaceful night *(Ps. 74:15,16)*, that I may lie down in peace, and at once fall asleep. For only You, Lord, make me dwell in safety, and give Your beloved rest *(Ps. 127:2)*. Be my light in the darkness and defend me from all the perils of this night. Visit this place and drive far from it all snares of the enemy. Give Your holy angels

charge over me to preserve me and guard my dreams. For into Your hands, I commend my spirit. Let Your blessing be upon me always; as waking, so sleeping *(BOCP, Compline)*. (**Amen**) (or, **In the Name of Jesus, Amen**)

II. Me and My House

These prayers may or may not be needed daily. Become familiar enough with them that you can be ready to locate and use them as needed.

13. For My Time in God's Word

God of all truth, Your Word is lamp to my feet and a light to my path *(Ps. 119:105)*. It is breathed out by You and profitable for my learning, correction, and training in righteousness *(2 Ti. 3:16)*. Teach me, that I may walk in Your truth *(Ps. 86:11)*. Teach me to do Your will, for You are my God *(Ps. 143:10)*. Give me knowledge, understanding, discretion, and wisdom *(Pr. 2:6; 8:12)*. And bless me as I store up Your Word in my heart, that I might not sin against you *(Ps. 119:11)*. (Amen)

14. From a Husband

God my Father, from Whom every family on earth is named *(Ep. 3:15)*, I have found favor with You, for You have given me a wife *(Ge. 2:22; Pr. 18:22)*. Today, I will work to provide for her *(1 Ti. 5:8)*. I will fight to protect her *(1 Co. 13:7)*. I will honor her *(1 Pe. 3:7)*. I will be loyal to her *(He. 13:4)*. I will be the head of our home *(1 Co. 11:3)*, and gently lead her in Your ways *(1 Pe. 3:2)*. I will make time for her. I will listen to her. I will render the affection that is due her *(1 Co. 7:3)*. And I will endeavor to love her selflessly and sacrificially, even as You have loved Your church *(Ep. 5:25)*. (Amen)

15. For My Wife/Marriage

Heavenly Father, thank You for the wife You have given me *(Ge. 2:22)*. May she be like a tree planted by streams of water and may all that she does prosper in Your sight *(Ps. 1:3)*. May she fear You, Lord *(Pr. 31:30)*, walking in the way of righteousness with firm footing *(Pr. 8:20; Ps. 17:5)*. May she be clothed with strength and dignity and laugh without fear of the future. May her work inside and outside the home be industrious and blessed. *(Pr. 31:11-31)*. Grace our marriage with health, that her prayers be not hindered *(1 Pe. 3:7)*, guiding her in the way of wisdom and leading her along straight paths *(Pr. 4:11)*, and fill her with the knowledge of Your will in all spiritual wisdom and understanding, so that she may walk in a manner worthy of You,

fully pleasing to You, bearing fruit in every good work and
increasing in all godly knowledge *(Cl. 1:9,10)*. (**Amen**)

16. From a Wife

God my Father, from Whom every family on earth is named *(Ep. 3:15)*, You have answered my longing and have brought me to a husband, giving me to him as his wife *(Ge. 2:22)*. Today, I will stay by his side, and support and help him *(Ge. 2:18)*. I will honor him. I will be loyal to him *(He. 13:4)*. I will respect him. I will endeavor to be patient, as he leads our home *(1 Pe. 3:2)*, and will submit to him whenever necessary, as to You, Lord *(Ep. 5:22)*. I will make time for Him. I will listen to him. I will render the affection that is due him *(1 Co. 7:3)*. I will love him *(Tt. 2:4)* and be loved by him *(Ep. 5:25)*. (**Amen**)

17. For My Husband/Marriage

Heavenly Father, thank You for giving me as wife to my husband. May he be like a tree planted by streams of water and may all that he does prosper in Your sight *(Ps. 1:3)*. Strengthen him to be watchful, to stand firm in the faith, to act like a man, and to be strong *(1 Co. 16:13)*. Grace our marriage with health, that his prayers be not hindered *(1 Pe. 3:7)*, guiding him in the way of wisdom and leading him along straight paths *(Pr. 4:11)*. Lord, let Your favor rest upon him and establish the work of his hands *(Ps. 90:17)*, and fill him with the knowledge of Your will in all spiritual wisdom and understanding, so that he may walk in a manner worthy of You, fully pleasing to You, bearing fruit in every good work and increasing in all godly knowledge *(Cl. 1:9,10)*. (**Amen**)

18. For My Child*(ren)*

God my Father, I have been given reward and heritage from You through my child*(ren)* *(Ps. 127:3)*. *[State names]* I pray that they may grow in wisdom and stature, in Your favor, and in the favor of mankind *(Lk. 2:52)*. Make them blameless and innocent, Your children without blemish in the midst of this cooked and perverted generation *(Ph. 2:15)*. Show them that Your ways give more life than the ways of the world, and that following You is better than chasing after selfish goals *(BOCP)*. Guard their heart*(s)* and mind*(s)* from every evil way and influence *(Ph. 4:7; Pr. 8:13)*, and set their thoughts on what is true, honorable, just,

pure, lovely, commendable, and excellent in Your sight *(Ph. 4:8)*. (Amen)

19. From a Child
God my Father, from Whom every family on earth is named *(Ep. 3:15)*, thank You for giving me Godly parents *(Ep. 6:2)*. I will obey them, even as I obey You *(Ep. 6:1)*. (Amen)

20. For My Household
Master and Lord, as for me and my house, we will serve You *(Jn. 24:15)*. We will seek Your kingdom first *(Jn. 24:15; Mt. 6:33)*. That which we need, you will provide according to Your good will *(Mt. 6:33; Mt. 6:8)*. That which we have, you have graciously given *(Ja. 1:17)*, and our household rejoices in You *(Dt. 14:26)*. Be gracious to protect and prosper all things pertaining to us: our physical health, our spiritual health, our home, our land, our possessions, our provisions, and our finances. Grant us grace that we may honor You with all of our thriving, and as we remember the account we must one day give, may we be faithful stewards of our bounty *(BOCP)*. (Amen)

21. For My Basic Needs
Gracious Lord, who gives good gifts to those who ask of you *(Mt. 7:11)*, and who opens his hand to satisfy the desire of every living thing *(Ps. 145:16)*. you know my needs before I ask *(Mt. 6:8)*, yet desire my petitions *(Mt. 7:7; Ja. 4:2)*: Provide the things that are necessary: my food, my drink, my clothing; a dry and safe place to dwell, that is cool in the summer and warm in the winter *(Siddur)*. Give me not poverty, lest I steal and profane Your Name. Give me not riches, lest I be full and deny You *(Pr. 30:7-9)*. *[State additional needs]* I will trust that, according to Your promise, You will supply all my needs *(Mt. 6:33; Ph. 4:19)*. (Amen)

22. For My Gratitude/Thankfulness
I will give thanks to You, Lord, with all my heart, and will recount all Your wonderful deeds *(Ps. 9:1)*. My heart leaps for joy, and with my song I give thanks to You *(Ps. 28:7)*. For every good and perfect gift is from You, the Father of Lights from above *(Ja. 1:17)*. *[State any special gratitude]* Lord, You are good and Your love endures forever; and Your faithfulness extends to all

generations *(Ps. 100:4,5)*. May the fruit of my lips always give thanks to Your Name *(He. 13:15)*. And may my ultimate expression of gratitude be the offering up of my body as a living sacrifice that is holy and pleasing to You *(Ro. 12:1)*. (Amen)

23. For My Learning from Creation
O Heavenly Father, who has filled the world with beauty, open my eyes to behold your gracious hand in all Your works. That, rejoicing in Your whole creation, I may learn to serve You with gladness; for the sake of Him through Whom all things were made, Your Son, Jesus. *(BOCP)* (Amen)

24. For God's Will/Guidance for Me
Sovereign Lord, You alone know the plans You have for my future *(Je. 29:11)*. Grant me help to trust in You with all my heart, not leaning on my own understanding, but submitting all my ways to You, that You might make my path clear to me *(Pr. 3:5,6)*. *[State specific will/guidance needed]* Lord, if in anything, I seem to lack the knowledge of Your will for me, may I be ever mindful of what You have already shown me—that which is good, and that which is required of me—to act justly, to love mercy, and to walk humbly with You *(Mi.6:8)*. Now may, You, God, equip me to do Your will, and work in me what is Pleasing to You. *(He. 13:20,21)*. (Amen)

25. For My Knowledge, Wisdom, Understanding, Discernment
All knowing and all wise God, grant me that wisdom which only You can give, and that knowledge and understanding which comes only from Your mouth *(Pr. 2:6)*, For godly wisdom is better than gold, and spiritual understanding preferrable to silver *(Pr. 16:16; Cl. 1:9)*. Let Your wisdom come into my heart, and your knowledge bring pleasure to my soul *(Pr. 2:10)*, that I may discern between good and evil *(1 Ki. 3:9)*, and that my days may be multiplied, with years added to my life *(Pr. 9:10-12)*. (Amen)

26. For My Personal Holiness
Holy Lord God Almighty, You chose me before the foundation of the world, that I should be holy and blameless before You *(Ep. 1:4)*. You foreknew me and predestined me to be conformed to

the image of Your Son *(Ro. 8:29)*, as an obedient child, not being conformed to my previous passions *(1 Pe. 1:14)*, but that I might be holy in all my conduct, because You are holy *(1 Pe. 1:15,16)*. For without holiness, no one will see You *(He. 12:14)*. Grant it today, that I be crucified with Christ, that Christ might live in me *(Ga. 2:20)*, and strengthen me by Your grace to flee lusts and pursue righteousness, along with those who call on You from a pure heart *(2 Ti. 2:22)*. (Amen)

27. For My Calling
Sovereign Lord, the One Who called me, You are faithful. Graciously confirm, in me, Your calling for my life *(1 Th. 5:24; 2 Pe. 1:10)*. Open my eyes to see the work You have prepared in advance for me to do, that I may serve You faithfully *(Ep. 2:10)*. You chose me and appointed me, to Your own glory and excellence, that I should go and bear fruit and that my fruit should remain *(Jn. 15:16; 2 Pe. 1:3)*. Therefore, I desire, with all holy desire, to lead the life that You have assigned to me, to which You have called me *(1 Co. 7:17)*, and that I might walk in a manner worthy of the calling I have received, with all humility and gentleness, with patience, bearing with others in love *(Ep. 4:1,2)*. Now, Lord, do so graciously fulfill my every resolve for every work of faith by Your power *(2 Th. 1:11)*. (Amen)

28. For My Witness
God our Savior, let me be a light for You, that the world may see my good works and give You glory. *(Mt. 5:14, 16)*. Send me out as Your ambassador, as though You were making Your appeal to others through me, that I may implore them on behalf of Your Son to be reconciled to You *(2 Co. 5:20)*. Fill me with Your Spirit, so that I may boldly proclaim this mystery *(Ep. 6:19)*. Let me not be ashamed of the gospel, for in it is the power of Your salvation *(Ro. 1:16)*. Lord, help me to always be prepared to make a defense to anyone who asks for a reason for the hope that is in me *(1 Pe. 3:15)*. May my life be above reproach *(Cl. 1:22)*, and may my speech always be gracious, seasoned with salt, so that I may know how to answer each person *(Cl. 4:6)*. (Amen)

29. For My Job
Lord God Almighty, I commit my work to You *(Pr. 16:3)*. Whatever I do today, help me to do so heartily, as for You and not for men

(Cl. 3:23-24). Let Your favor, Lord God, be upon me, and establish the work of my hands *(Ps. 90:17)*. Help me to do all things without grumbling or disputing, that I may be blameless and innocent in the midst of a crooked and twisted generation *(Ph. 2:14-15)*, always conducting myself in a manner worthy of the gospel of Your Son *(Ph. 1:27)*. Give me wisdom to understand the times and to know what to do *(1 Ch. 12:32)*. And keep me from harm and from the evil one *(2 Th. 3:3)*. (Amen)

30. For My Financial Blessing
Lord of all, I ask for Your blessing on my finances. May You supply every need of mine according to Your riches in glory in Christ Jesus *(Ph. 4:19)*. Help me to honor You with my money and with the firstfruits of all my increase, that my barns may be filled with plenty and my vats bursting with wine *(Pr. 3:9-10)*. And teach me to be content with what I have *(He. 13:5)*. Let Your favor rest upon me and establish the work of my hands (Psalm 90:17). May I prosper in all things, even as my soul prospers *(3 Jn. 1:2)*. (Amen)

31. For My Future
Sovereign God, I trust in Your plans for me, plans for welfare and not for evil, to give me a future and a hope *(Je. 29:11)*. Guide me and make my paths straight as I acknowledge You in all my ways *(Pr. 3:6)*. Strengthen me to be courageous, knowing that You are with me wherever I go *(Js. 1:9)*. I place my future in Your hands, confident that You will bring Your good work in me to completion *(Ph. 1:6)*. (Amen)

32. For the Fruit of the Spirit
Holy Lord, perfect in all Your ways, I ask that Your Holy Spirit would produce His fruit in my life. May love, joy, and peace abound in me, as I walk by the Spirit and exhibit these qualities. Fill me with patience, kindness, and goodness, so that I may reflect Your character and be a light to others. Help me to be faithful, gentle, and self-controlled in all my interactions. Let these virtues grow in me *(Ga. 5:22-23)*, as I yield to the Spirit and live in a manner worthy of Your calling *(Ep. 4:1)*. May my life be marked by these fruits, glorifying You and bearing witness to Your grace. (Amen)

33. For My Increased Faith
All-knowing and all-powerful God, I ask for increased faith that comes through hearing your Word *(Ro. 10:17)*. As I learn of you, may I believe and trust in You more deeply, knowing that faith as small as a mustard seed can move mountains *(Mt. 17:20)*. Let me be fully convinced that You are able to do far more abundantly than all that I ask or think *(Ep. 3:20)*. Increase my faith that I may live by it, walking confidently in your promises and trusting in your provision *(2 Co. 5:7; He. 11:1)*. And as I believe, Lord, help my unbelief *(Mt. 9:24)*, with growing faith that is rooted in the knowledge of Your grace and truth *(Cl. 2:7; Jn. 1:17)*. (Amen)

34. For My Spiritual Strength
Mighty God, strengthen me with all power for Christian endurance, according to Your glorious might *(Cl. 1:11)*. You know my frame, that I am dust *(Ps. 103:14)*, for my flesh is weak, but my spirit is willing. Draw me to watch with You *(Mk. 14:38)*, and teach me to wait upon You, that my strength might be renewed *(Is. 40:31)*. Where I am weak—and will be weak—let your strength be made perfect in me *(2 Co. 12:9)*, that I may say that I am strong *(Jl. 3:10)*, and do all things through Christ as He strengthens me *(Ph. 4:13)*. (Amen)

35. For My Spiritual Maturation
Holy Father, I seek the growth that comes from Your grace and from the knowledge of Your Son *(2 Pe. 3:18)*, that I would not be childish, tossed and carried by waves and winds of misdirections, but that I may grow up in Christ in every way *(Ep. 4:14-15)*. Teach me to put away childish things and pursue godly things in righteousness *(1 Co. 13:11; 1 Ti. 6:11)*. Conform me to the image of Jesus *(Ro. 8:29)*, and guide me to walk in a manner that is worthy of You and fully pleasing to You, bearing fruit in every good work *(Cl. 1:9,10)*. (Amen)

36. For Me to be Filled with the Holy Spirit
Holy and Almighty God, graciously fill me with Your Holy Spirit *(Lk. 11:13)*, and empower me to be a witness and a worker for You. May Your Spirit impart giftings into my life, giftings that I earnestly desire. *[Review the spiritual gifts in Ro. 12:4-8; 1 Co. 12; 1 Co. 13; 1 Co. 14:1-5; Ep. 4:11-16; 2 Ti. 1:6&7; 1 Pe. 4:10&11]*

Grant it, Lord, in order that I may use my spiritual gifts to reveal
You to others and bring You glory. (**Amen**)

37. For My Boldness in Christ

All-powerful God, help me to be strong and courageous,
steadfast and immovable, not terrified or discouraged, for you
are with me wherever I go *(Js. 1:9; 1 Co. 15:58)*. And, seeing that
my state and future is surpassing glory, let this hope make me
very bold *(2 Co. 3:12)*. Grace me with strength to never be
ashamed of your testimony, or those bearing your testimony.
Give me boldness that remains, even if I be subject to suffering
for it *(2 Ti. 1:8)*. (**Amen**)

38. For My Humility

Awesome God, as I learn from Jesus, who was lowly in heart,
may I find rest from my pride; physical, mental and spiritual *(Mt.
11:29)*. Clothe me with humility, for You oppose the proud but
give grace to the humble *(1 Pe. 5:5)*. Teach me not to think of
myself more highly than I ought *(Ro. 12:3)*, and to do nothing
from conceit, counting others more significant than myself *(Ph.
2:3)*. (**Amen**)

39. For My Selflessness

God my Deliverer, deliver me from my selfish ambition *(Ph. 2:3)*.
See that I not seek my own good first, but the good of my
neighbor *(1 Co. 10:24)*, nor look to my own interests first, but to
the interests of others *(Ph. 2:4)*, nor insist on my own way, or be
irritable or resentful *(1 Co. 13:5)*, but give me the same mind as
Christ *(Ph. 2:5)*, who came not to be served, but rather to serve
(Mt. 20:28), and give me the same heart as Christ, who laid
down His life for me, that I would also lay down my life for
others. *(Jn. 15:12-13)*. (**Amen**)

40. For Me to Overcome Temptation

God, my rock and my fortress *(Ps. 31:3)*, my strong tower that I
run to for safety *(Pr. 18:10)*, deliver me from the desires of the
flesh, the desires of the eyes, and the pride of life, which are not
godly, but worldly *(1 Jn. 2:16)*. Quicken my willing spirit, to
crucify my weak flesh, to resist the devil, and to submit myself to
You *(Mt. 26:41;Ja. 4:7)*, taking every thought captive to obey
Christ *(2 Co. 10:5)*. Sharpen my mind, to be set on things above

and not on things that are on earth *(2 Co. 10:5)*, and to think on things that are true, honorable, just, pure, lovely, commendable, and excellent *(Ph. 4:8)*. Lead me not into temptation, but deliver me from evil *(Mt. 6:13)*, and keep me from stumbling *(Jd. 1:24)*. **(Amen)**

41. For My Self-Discipline

Holy Father, I thank You that You hear me always, and grant me the requests that I ask of You *(1 Jn. 5:15)*. I come now confidently before Your throne of grace, that, in Your mercy and grace *(He. 4:16)*, You might give me a powerful and self-controlled spirit *(2 Ti. 1:7)*. My great desire is to be diligent in all that I do, not slothful in zeal, but fervent in spirit, serving You *(Ro. 12:11)*. Strengthen me to live a life that is self-disciplined, upright, and godly in this present age, as one who waits for the appearing of the glory of our great God and Savior Jesus Christ *(Tt. 2:12-13)*. Train me to discipline my body and keep it under control *(1 Co. 9:27)*, and work in me, both to will and to do for Your good pleasure *(Ph. 2:12-13)*. **(Amen)**

42. For Greater Obedience/Faithfulness

Lord God, ever Faithful and trustworthy *(Ps. 111:7)*, give me an undivided heart *(Ps. 86:11)*, and write Your law within it, that I would delight to do Your will *(Ps. 40:8)*. Let me not be deceived as one who only hears Your Word, yet doesn't do it *(Ja. 1:22)*; for those who love You will keep Your commandments *(Jn. 14:15)*, and Your commandments will never be burdensome to them *(1 Jn. 5:3)*. Keep me from the voice of strangers and tune my ear to the voice of the Good Shepherd, Who laid down His life for His sheep *(Jn. 10:3-5,11)*. Uphold me with a willing spirit *(Ps. 51:12)*, as I obey Your voice *(Ex. 19:5)*, and faithfully follow You *(Jn. 10:5;)*. **(Amen)**

43. For My Attitude/Words

Lord, You are good and upright *(Ps. 25:8)*, righteous in all Your ways and kind in all Your works *(Ps. 145:17)*, giving the Word of life to mankind *(1 Jn. 1:1)*. Renew a right spirit within me and set a guard over my mouth *(Ps. 141:3)*, that my attitude and my words may always be acceptable in Your sight *(Ps. 19:14)*. Teach me to be kind and tenderhearted to others *(Ep. 4:31,32)*, and keep my mouth from corrupt talk, that my words may be edifying, giving grace to those who hear me *(Ep. 4:29)*. (Amen)

44. For My Choices/Decisions

Eternal God, Who declares the end from the beginning *(Is. 46:10)*, order all my steps *(Ps. 37:23)* and establish my plans *(Pr. 16:3)*. Life on earth is but a vapor that appears for a little while and then vanishes away *(Ja. 4:14)*, so teach me to number my days *(Ps. 90:12)*, and to trust in You, involving You in all my ways, instead of leaning on my own understanding. Make my paths straight *(Pr. 3:5,6)*, so that I walk—not unwisely—but wisely, making the best use of my time in this present evil world *(Ep. 5:15,16)*. (Amen)

45. For My Protection

God, my refuge and fortress, my God, in Whom I trust *(Ps. 91:2)*, I will rejoice and sing for joy, because You spread Your protection over me *(Ps. 5:11)*. Let not disaster overtake me *(Ge. 19:19)*, nor deadly pestilence, nor any weapon forged against me, for You promise this as my heritage because I am Your servant. *(Is. 54:17)*. Those who spread a net for me, Lord, catch them in their own trap *(Ps. 35:7,8)*, and let all the devil's schemes against me fail *(Ep. 6:11)*. I humbly ask, command Your angels concerning me, to guard me in all my ways *(Ps. 91:11)*. Keep me from all harm, and protect my life, my coming and going, from this time forth and forevermore *(Ps. 121:7,8)*. Let Your angels guard me in all my ways, lifting me up so that I come to no harm *(Ps. 91:11-12)*. (Amen)

46. For God's Help for Me

All-knowing and all-powerful God, who has pity on the weak and needy, and saves them, I lift up my eyes to look for help, and my help will come from You, Lord, Who made heaven and earth *(Ps. 121:1,2)*. God, be my strength, a very present helper in times of trouble *(Ps. 54:4; Ps. 46:1)*. I will cast my burden on You, Father. Please sustain me. And help my feet to never be moved *(Ps. 55:22)*. (Amen)

47. For God's Comfort for Me

Father of mercies and God of all comfort *(2 Co. 1:3,4)*, I cry out from a painful heart and wail from a broken spirit *(Is. 65:14)*. For the pain that gnaws me takes no rest *(Jb. 30:17)*. Comfort me as a child is comforted and give me rest in Your embrace *(Is. 66:13)*. May Your consolations cheer my soul *(Ps. 94:19)*. I will draw near to You—not just with my mouth, but with my heart—Lord *(Is. 29:13)*. Please draw near to me in return *(Ja. 4:8)*. Give me rest from my pain and turmoil *(Is. 14:3)*. Cause me to sing for gladness of heart again *(Is. 14:3)*. (**Amen**)

48. During Trial/Hardships

Sovereign LORD, I am hard-pressed on every side *(2 Co. 4:8)*, having met with trial*(s)*. Help me to be constant in prayer and patient in this trouble—even to the point of joy—knowing that this tests my faith and produces stability in me *(Ja. 1:2-4)*. Father, I am called according to Your purpose, and I know that You will work all things out for the good *(Ro. 8:28)*. Now, graciously strengthen me with all the power I need, according to Your glorious might, that I might not grow weary and give up, but that I may endure and reap in due season *(Cl. 1:11; Ga. 6:9)*. (**Amen**)

49. For My Sickness/Unwellness

Heavenly Father, have mercy on me *(Ps. 6:2)*, for I am afflicted and in pain *(Ps. 69:29)*. I cry out to You *(Je. 17:14)*, for the restoration of my health and the healing of my wounds *(Je. 30:17)*. Strengthen me during the days of my illness and help me to learn from it *(Is. 41:10; Ps. 119:71)*. And may my prayer be a prayer of faith, and may You mercifully hasten to save me from this sickness and graciously hasten to raise me up *(Ps. 70:5; Ja. 5:15)*. (**Amen**)

50. For My Stress/Worry/Anxiety/Fears

Lord God, my stronghold and deliverer *(Ps. 18:2)*, my spirit faints within me, my heart within me is distressed *(Ps. 143:4)*, and I am visited with panic *(Le. 26:16)*. Give ear, O Lord; listen to my plea for grace *(Ps. 86:6)*. I cast all my anxieties on You because You care for me *(1 Pe. 5:7)* and can rescue me *(Ps. 22:8)*. Secure in me an undivided devotion *(1 Co. 7:35)*, a singleness of heart, and an undivided mind *(Ja. 4:8)* that is stayed on You and trusting in You. And may you keep me in that perfect peace that surpasses understanding and guards my thoughts and emotions in Your Son, Jesus *(Is. 26:3; Ph. 4:7)*. (**Amen**)

51. For My Depression
God of all hope *(Ro. 15:13)*, who comforts the downcast *(2 Co. 7:6)*, my soul is depressed and in turmoil within me *(Ps. 42:11)*, my heart aches and throbs, and the light of my eyes has gone from me *(Ps. 38:10)*. Be the strength of my heart and my portion forever *(Ps. 73:26)* and fill me with all joy and peace in believing, that I may abound in hope, through the power of the Holy Spirit *(Ro. 15:13)*. That I shall again praise You, my salvation and my God *(Ps. 42:11)*, with a glad heart and a cheerful face *(Pr. 15:13)*. (**Amen**)

52. For My Grieving/Loss
God my Helper, the upholder of my life *(Ps. 54:4)*, be gracious to me *(Ps. 31:9)*, for my joy is gone, and my heart is sick within me *(Je. 8:18)*. My eyes are weak because of grief; my soul and my body also *(Ps. 6:7; Ps. 31:9)*. Have compassion according to the abundance of Your steadfast love *(La. 3:32)*. Lord, heal this broken heart and crushed spirit, and bind up my wounds *(Ps. 34:18; Ps. 147:3)*. (**Amen**)

53. For My Addictions/Bad Habits
Almighty Deliverer, Who led Your people Israel out of cruel bondage and into freedom *(Ex. 3; Js. 3)*, deliver me *(Ps. 39:8)*! *[State bondage/addiction/bad habit]* I do not want to be mastered by this *(1 Co. 6:12)*. My spirit is willing, but my flesh is weak *(Mt. 26:41)*. I am as a city broken into and left without walls. I have no self-control *(Pr. 25:28)*. Father, through Your Son, set me free, that I might be free indeed *(Jn. 8:36)*. And rebuild me again, from the spirit up, with power and self-control *(2 Ti. 1:7)*. (**Amen**)

54. For My Persecutions and Oppositions
Lord, You are my Rock and my fortress *(Ps. 71:3)*. Let me not be distressed or shamed because of those who persecute me *(Je. 17:18)*. Their quarrel is with You. They persecuted You, Jesus, the Master; so shall they persecute me, Your servant *(Jn. 15:20)*. I will bless them and not curse them *(Ro. 12:14) [State names]*. And may they be ashamed when, because of my good works and sound speech, they no longer have anything evil to say about me *(Tt. 2:7,8)*. (**Amen**)

55. For My Innocence in Opposition
Be not silent, O God! The wicked and deceitful speak lies against me. They surround me with words of hate and attack me without cause. *[State names]* As they accuse and hate me, even so will I endeavor to love them. As they reward me with evil, even so will I endeavor to reward them with good *(Ps. 109:1-5)*. Be not silent, O God, but bring them to silence *(Ps. 109:1; Tt 1:11)*. (Amen)

56. For My Marital Crisis
God Who restores and redeems, calamity has struck, like a terror attack, against us. And though we are mocked by our lack of wisdom *(Pr. 1:20,33)*, we ask of You, God, Who gives wisdom generously to all without reproach *(Ja. 1:5)*. You will teach us Your way *(Ps. 27:11)*, and in great compassion You will gather us *(Is. 54:7)*. Heal our broken hearts and bind up our wounds *(Ps. 147:3)*. Help us to bear with one another in our complaints against each other *(Cl. 3:13)*, and to be kind, tenderhearted, and forgiving of one another, as You in Christ forgave us *(Ep. 4:32)*. And let the peace of Christ referee between our two hearts, since we were called to peace in one union *(Cl. 3:15)*. (Amen)

57. For My Divorce
God my redeemer, we have failed to enter into the full promise of what could have been *(He. 4:1)*. Father, forgive us *(Mt. 6:12)*. Heal our broken hearts and bind up our wounds *(Ps. 147:3)*. Help us to bear with one another in our complaints against each other *(Cl. 3:13)*, and to be kind, tenderhearted, and forgiving of one another, as You in Christ forgave us *(Ep. 4:32)*. And let the peace of Christ referee between our two hearts, since we were called to peace *(Cl. 3:15)*. (Amen)

58. For My Forgiveness of Others
Loving and merciful Father of all, Your Son commanded us to love even our enemies *(BOCP)*. *[State names]* You have loved me, so I will love them. You have been merciful to me, so I will be merciful to them *(Lk. 6:36)*. You have forgiven me, so I will forgive them *(Ep. 4:32)*. You have reconciled me, so I will minister reconciliation to them *(2 Co. 5:18)*, bearing with them *(Cl. 3:13)*, in kindness and tenderheartedness *(Ep. 4:32)*. Let me not repay evil for evil *(1 Th. 5:15)*. Bless me to be a peacemaker *(Mt. 5:9)*.

And in Your good time, enable us to stand reconciled before You (BOCP). *(*Amen)

59. For My Anger/Temper
Holy Father, Who deferred Your own anger for the sake of Your praise *(Is. 48:9)*, be my example. Teach me the foolishness of being hot tempered, and the wisdom of being slow to anger *(Pr. 14:29)*. Help me to put off my old self, and be renewed in the spirit of my mind, putting on the new self that is created after Your likeness in true holiness *(Ep. 4:22-24)*. That I may be quick to hear, slow to speak, and slow to anger, knowing that the anger of man does not produce the righteousness of God *(Ja. 1:19-20)*. Train me to respond with love that is not easily agitated *(1 Co. 13:5)*, and with gentleness and self-control, bearing the fruit of the Spirit *(Ga. 5:22-23)*. And if I must be angry, grace me to sin not. *(Ps. 4:4)*. *(*Amen)

60. For My Loneliness
God my Father, I am afflicted by loneliness. Turn to me and be gracious to me *(Ps. 25:16)*. Be continually with me. Never leave me nor forsake me. Hold my right hand. I have no one in Heaven but You. And there is none on earth besides You. You are the Strength of my heart *(Ps. 73:23-26; He. 13:5)*. You are my portion forever, says my soul. Therefore, I will hope in You *(Ps. 73:26; La. 3:24)*. (Amen)

61. For My Fruit of the Womb
Creator of all the living, Who opens and closes the womb *(Ge. 29:31; 1 Sa. 1:5)*, bless our union that we may be fruitful and multiply *(Ge. 1:28)*, for children are a heritage from You, and the fruit of the womb a reward from You *(Ps. 127:3)*. We bring open hearts filled with hope and trust in You *(He. 6:11; Pr. 3:5)*. We ask for a child from You, Lord *(1 Sa. 1:20)*. We will be still before You, hope for what we do not yet see, and wait patiently for it *(Ps. 37:7; Ro. 8:25)*. That in the right season *(Ec. 3:2)*, You might grant our petition and give us the desire of our hearts *(1 Sa. 1:27; Ps. 37:4)*. (Amen)

62. For My Childlessness
See Prayer **44. For God's Comfort for Me**
Also, Prayer **48. For My Depression**

63. For My Adoption of a Child
Creator of all the living, Who opens and closes the womb *(Ge. 29:31; 1 Sa. 1:5)*, bless our union that we may be fruitful through adoption and multiply *(Ge. 1:28)*, for children are a heritage and a reward from You *(Ps. 127:3)*. We bring open hearts filled with hope and trust in You *(He. 6:11; Pr. 3:5)*. We ask for an adopted child from You, Lord *(1 Sa. 1:20)*. We will be still before You, hope for what we do not yet see, and wait patiently for it *(Ps. 37:7; Ro. 8:25)*. That in the right season *(Ec. 3:2)*, You might grant our petition and give us the desire of our hearts *(1 Sa. 1:27; Ps. 37:4)*. (Amen)

64. For My Aging
O Lord, be to me a rock of refuge. Do not cast me off in the time of old age, nor forsake me when my strength fails. Be not far from me, and be quick to help me. From my youth you have taught me and may I still proclaim your awesome deeds and righteous acts every day. So even to old age and gray hairs, O God, do not forsake me, until I declare Your might to this generation, and your power to the generation to come. I will remind them of your righteousness—and Yours alone. You have subjected me to many troubles and calamities, but You will revive me again. You will lift me up from the depths of the earth *(Ps. 71)*.

65. For My Leisure
O God, in the course of this busy life, give us times of refreshment and peace. And grant that we may so use our leisure and hobby, to rebuild our bodies and renew our minds, that our hearts may be ever more aware of the goodness of the life that You have given to us *(BOCP)*. (Amen)

66. For My Before-Church Preparedness
God of all glory, prepare my heart to enter Your gates with thanksgiving, and Your courts with praise *(Ps. 100:4)*. May I be sensitive to Your Holy Spirit, not grieving or quenching You *(Ep. 4:30; 1 Th. 5:19)*, but keeping in step *(Ga. 5:16)*, worshiping You in Spirit and in truth *(Jn. 4:24)*. And may I receive Your Word with joy *(Lk. 8:13)*, that it might take root and bear fruit in me *(Mk.*

4:20), **that I might encourage and edify others in the same** *(1 Th. 5:11)*. **(Amen)**

III. My Family & Loved Ones

67. For Their Salvation
Blessed be the God of Salvation *(Ps. 68:20)*, Who desires all people to be saved and come to the knowledge of the truth. *[State names]* My heart's desire and prayer for them is that they may be saved *(Ro. 10:1)*. Lord Jesus, stand at their door and knock, that perhaps they may bid you entry *(Re. 3:20)*. And, if it be Your will, open the door to me, that I may share the Word, and declare the mystery of Christ to them *(Cl. 4:3)*. (Amen)

68. For My Local Church
God and Father, You have arranged each member in our local body as You have chosen *(1 Co. 12:18)* and we give thanks to You for all of them *(1 Th. 1:2)*. Grant that we may continue steadfastly in sound doctrine, and in prayer, and in fellowship, and in the breaking of bread *(Tt. 2:1; Ac. 2:42)*; united in the same mind and judgment *(1 Co. 1:10)*, continuing stable and steadfast in the faith, not shifting from the hope of the Gospel *(Cl. 1:23)*. Lord, cause our love to abound more and more, with knowledge and all discernment *(Ph.1:9,10)* and let us bear one another's burdens *(Ga. 6:2)* and encourage and edify one another *(1 Th. 5:11)*, seeking to spur one another on toward love and good deeds *(He. 10:24)*; that we may be a city set on a hill, whose light cannot be hidden *(Mt. 5:14-16)*, declaring Your glory and Your marvelous works to those outside *(Ps. 96:3)*, making disciples and baptizing them in the name of the Father and of the Son and of the Holy Spirit *(Mt. 28:19)*, teaching them to observe all that You have commanded. (Amen)

69. For My Local Church Workers/Spouses
Lord, we thank You that You give pastors after your own heart *(Je. 3:15)*, and evangelists, and teachers, along with those gifted for service and activities by the Spirit *(1 Co. 12:4-11)*, to equip us for the work of ministry and build up our local church body *(Ep. 4:11,12)*. We pray for them and the spouses that assist and support them, that they may be steadfast, immovable, always abounding in Your work, never growing weary of doing good, knowing that their labor is not in vain, and that in due season

they will reap, if they do not give up *(1 Co. 15:58; Ga. 6:9)*. **Lord, we ask that You strengthen them with all power, according to Your glorious might, for all endurance and patience with joy** *(Cl. 1:11)*, **granting them wisdom and understanding as they present themselves to You as workers without shame** *(2 Ti. 2:15)*. (**Amen**)

70. For Our Upcoming Church Meeting/Service

God of all glory, prepare our hearts to enter Your gates with thanksgiving, and Your courts with praise *(Ps. 100:4)*. **May we be sensitive to Your Holy Spirit, not grieving or quenching You** *(Ep. 4:30; 1 Th. 5:19)*, **but keeping in step** *(Ga. 5:16)*, **worshiping You in Spirit and in truth** *(Jn. 4:24)*. **And may we receive Your Word with joy** *(Lk. 8:13)*, **that it might take root and bear fruit in us** *(Mk. 4:20)*, **that we might be encouraging and edifying to one another in these things** *(1 Th. 5:11)*. (**Amen**)

71. For My Friendships/Church Family

Creator and Lord, thank You for the gift of human friendship. *[State names]* **Grace me with agape-love for them, that is patient and kind, not envious or boastful, not arrogant or rude** *(1 Co. 13:4-5)*. **Teach us to better bear one another's burdens, and so fulfill the law of Christ** *(Ga. 6:2)*. **Let us be devoted to one another in love, outdoing one another in showing honor** *(Ro. 12:10)*. **Help us to sharpen one another as iron sharpens iron, so that we may grow in wisdom and strengthen each other** *(Pr. 27:17)*. **And grant us grace to forgive one another as You have forgiven us, that Your peace might dwell among us** *(Cl. 3:13-15)*. (**Amen**)

72. For Those I Love

Almighty God, I entrust all who are dear to me to Your never-failing care and love, for this life and the life to come, knowing that You are doing for them better things than I can desire or pray for *(BOCP)*. (**Amen**)

73. For Their Marriage

Heavenly Father, I lift up the marriage of my friends before You, asking for Your divine blessing and guidance. *[State names]* **Help them be kind to one another, tenderhearted, forgiving one another, as God in Christ forgave them** *(Ep. 4:32)*. **May their love be genuine, and may they abhor what is evil and hold fast to**

what is good *(Ro. 12:9)*. May they bear with one another in love, eager to maintain the unity of the Spirit in the bond of peace *(Ep. 4:2-3)*. May they be rooted and built up in Christ and established in the faith, abounding in thanksgiving for each other *(Cl. 2:7)*, submitting to one another out of reverence for Christ, and that their relationship be filled with all the fullness of God *(Ep. 5:21; 3:19)*. Above all, that they might put on love, which binds everything together in perfect harmony *(Cl. 3:14)*. And finally, I ask that the peace of Christ referee in their hearts, to which they were called in one union *(Cl. 3:15)*. (**Amen**)

74. For Their Household*(s)*
Master and Lord, I ask of You for my friends *(and/or, family)* and their household*(s)*, that they may serve You *(Js. 24:15)*, and seek Your kingdom first *(Jn. 24:15; Mt. 6:33)*. *[State names]* That which they need, You will provide according to Your good will *(Mt. 6:33; Mt. 6:8)*. That which they have, You have graciously given *(Ja. 1:17)*, and may their household rejoice in You *(Dt. 14:26)*. Be gracious to protect and prosper all things pertaining to them: their physical health, their spiritual health, their home, their land, their possessions, their provisions, and their finances. Grant them grace that they may honor You with all of their thriving, remembering the account they must one day give, may they be faithful stewards of their bounty *(BOCP)*. (**Amen**)

75. For Their Child*(ren)*
God my Father, from Whom every family on earth is named *(Ep. 3:15)*, my friends *(and/or, family)* have been given reward and heritage from You through their child*(ren) (Ps. 127:3)*. *[State names]* I pray that their child*(ren)* may grow in wisdom and stature, in Your favor, and in the favor of mankind *(Lk. 2:52)*. Make them blameless and innocent, Your child*(ren)* without blemish in the midst of this cooked and perverted generation *(Ph. 2:15)*. Show them that Your ways give more life than the ways of the world, and that following You is better than chasing after selfish goals *(BOCP)*. Guard their heart*(s)* and mind*(s)* from every evil way and influence *(Ph. 4:7; Pr. 8:13)*, and set their thoughts on what is true, honorable, just, pure, lovely, commendable, and excellent in Your sight *(Ph. 4:8)*. (**Amen**)

76. For Their Basic Needs

Gracious Lord, who gives good gifts to those who ask of you *(Mt. 7:11)*, and who opens his hand to satisfy the desire of every living thing *(Ps. 145:16)*. you know the needs of my loved ones before I ask *(Mt. 6:8)*, yet desire my petitions *(Mt. 7:7; Ja. 4:2)*: Provide the things that are necessary: their food, drink, clothing; a dry and safe place to dwell, that is cool in the summer and warm in the winter *(Siddur)*. Give them not poverty, lest they steal and profane Your Name. Give them not riches, lest they be full and deny You *(Pr. 30:7-9)*. *[State names]* May they seek Your Kingdom first, and trust that, according to Your promise, You will supply all their needs *(Mt. 6:33; Ph. 4:19)*. **(Amen)**

77. For the Poor

God our Provider, I pray for those who are in need of food, shelter, and clothing. *[State names]* May they find comfort and provision in you, and may you provide for their every need *(BOCP)*. **(Amen)**

78. For the Elderly

Look with mercy, God our Father, on those whose increasing years bring them weakness, distress, or isolation. *[State names]*. Provide for them homes of dignity and peace; give them understanding helpers, and the willingness to accept help; and, as their strength diminishes, increase their faith and their assurance of Your love *(BOCP)*. **(Amen)**

79. For God's Will/Guidance for Them

Sovereign Lord, I pray for my friend*(s) (and/or, family)*. *[State the names]* You alone know the plans You have for their future *(Je. 29:11)*. Grant them help to trust in You with all their heart, not leaning on their own understanding, but submitting all their ways to You, that You might make their path*(s)* clear to them *(Pr. 3:5,6)*. *[State specific will/guidance needed]* Lord, if in anything, they seem to lack the knowledge of Your will, may they be ever mindful of what You have already shown them—that which is good, and that which is required of them—to act justly, to love mercy, and to walk humbly with You *(Mi.6:8)*. Now may, You, God, equip them to do Your will, and work in them what is Pleasing to You, through Your Son *(He. 13:20,21)*. **(Amen)**

80. For Their Knowledge, Wisdom, Understanding, Discernment

All knowing and all wise God, I pray for my friend(s) (and/or, family). [State names] Grant them that wisdom which only You can give, and that knowledge and understanding which comes only from Your mouth (Pr. 2:6), For godly wisdom is better than gold, and spiritual understanding preferable to silver (Pr. 16:16; Cl. 1:9). Let Your wisdom come into their heart(s), and your knowledge bring pleasure to their soul(s) (Pr. 2:10), that they may discern between good and evil (1 Ki. 3:9), and that their days may be multiplied, with years added to their life (or, lives) (Pr. 9:10-12). (**Amen**)

81. For Their Personal Holiness

Holy Lord God Almighty, I make petition for my friend(s) (and/or, family). [State the names] You chose them before the foundation of the world, that they should be holy and blameless before You (Ep. 1:4). You foreknew them and predestined them to be conformed to the image of Your Son, Jesus (Ro. 8:29), as obedient children, not being conformed to their previous passions (1 Pe. 1:14), but that they might be holy in all their conduct, because You are holy (1 Pe. 1:15,16). For without holiness, no one will see You (He. 12:14). Grant it today, that they be crucified with Christ, that Christ might live in them (Ga. 2:20), and strengthen them by Your grace to flee lusts and pursue righteousness, along with those who call on You from a pure heart (2 Ti. 2:22). (**Amen**)

82. For Their Calling

Sovereign Lord, the One Who called my friend(s) (and/or, family), You are faithful. [State the names] Graciously confirm Your calling to them (1 Th. 5:24; 2 Pe. 1:10). Open their eyes to see the work You have prepared in advance for them to do, that they may serve You faithfully (Ep. 2:10). You chose them and appointed them, to Your own glory and excellence, that they should go and bear fruit and that their fruit should remain (Jn. 15:16; 2 Pe. 1:3). May they desire, with all holy desire, to lead the life that You have assigned to them, to which You have called them (1 Co. 7:17), and that they might walk in a manner worthy of the calling they have received, with all humility and gentleness, with patience, bearing with others in love (Ep. 4:1,2). Now, Lord, do so graciously fulfill their every resolve for every work of faith by Your power *(2 Th. 1:11)*. (**Amen**)

83. For Their Witness
God our Savior, on behalf of Your servant*(s)*, *[State names]* let them be a light for You, that the world may see their good works and give You glory. *(Mt. 5:14, 16)*. Send them out as Your ambassador*(s)*, as though You were making Your appeal to others through them, that they might implore others on behalf of Your Son to be reconciled to You *(2 Co. 5:20)*. Fill them with Your Spirit, so that they may boldly proclaim this mystery *(Ep. 6:19)*. Let them not be ashamed of the gospel, for in it is the power of Your salvation *(Ro. 1:16)*. Lord, help them to always be prepared to make a defense to anyone who asks for a reason for the hope that is in them *(1 Pe. 3:15)*. May they be above reproach *(Cl. 1:22)*, and may their speech always be gracious, seasoned with salt, so that they may know how to answer each person *(Cl. 4:6)*. (**Amen**)

84. For Their Job
Lord God Almighty, I pray for my friend*(s)* *(and/or, family)*. *[State the name]* That they might commit their work to You *(Pr. 16:3)*. Whatever they do today, that they do so heartily, as for You and not for mankind *(Cl. 3:23-24)*. Let Your favor, Lord God, be upon them, and establish the work of their hands *(Ps. 90:17)*. Help them to do all things without grumbling or disputing, that they may be blameless and innocent in the midst of a crooked and twisted generation *(Ph. 2:14-15)*, always conducting themself *(or, themselves)* in a manner worthy of the gospel of Your Son *(Ph. 1:27)*. Give them wisdom to understand the times and to know what to do *(1 Ch. 12:32)*. And keep them from all harm and from the evil one *(2 Th. 3:3)*. (**Amen**)

85. For Their Financial Blessing
Lord of all, I come on behalf of my friend*(s)* *(and/or, family)*. *[State the names]* I ask for Your blessing on their finances. May You supply their every need according to Your riches in glory in Christ Jesus *(Ph. 4:19)*. Help them to honor You with their money and with the firstfruits of all their increase, that their barns may be filled with plenty and their vats bursting with wine *(Pr. 3:9-10)*. And teach them to be content with what they have *(He.*

13:5). Let Your favor rest upon them and establish the work of their hands *(Ps. 90:17)*. And may they prosper in all things, even as their soul prospers *(3 Jo. 1:2)*. **(Amen)**

86. For Their Future
Sovereign God, I come on behalf of my friend*(s) (and/or, family)*. *[State names]* That they trust in Your plans for them, plans for welfare and not for evil, to give them a future and a hope *(Je. 29:11)*. Guide them and make their paths straight as they acknowledge You in all their ways *(Pr. 3:6)*. Strengthen them to be courageous, knowing that You are with them wherever they go *(Js. 1:9)*. And that they might place their future in Your hands, confident that You will bring Your good work in them to completion *(Ph. 1:6)*. **(Amen)**

87. For Their Fruit of the Spirit
Holy Lord, perfect in all Your ways, fulfill all my petitions *(Ps. 20:5)*, for the blessing of my friend*(s) (and/or, family)*. *[State names]* I ask that Your Holy Spirit would produce His fruit in their life *(or, lives)*. May love, joy, and peace abound in them, as they walk by the Spirit and exhibit these qualities. Fill them with patience, kindness, and goodness, so that they may reflect Your character and be a light to others. Help them to be faithful, gentle, and self-controlled in all their interactions. Let these virtues grow in them *(Ga. 5:22-23)*, as they yield to the Spirit and live in a manner worthy of Your calling *(Ep. 4:1)*. May their life *(or, lives)* be marked by these fruits, glorifying You and bearing witness to Your grace. **(Amen)**

88. For Their Increased Faith
Lord, on behalf of my loved one, I ask for increased faith that comes through hearing your Word *(Ro. 10:17)*. *[State names]* Help them, as they learn of you, to believe and trust in You more deeply, knowing that faith as small as a mustard seed can move mountains *(Mt. 17:20)*. May they be fully convinced that You are able to do far more abundantly than all that we ask or think *(Ep. 3:20)*. Increase Their faith that they may live by it, walking confidently in your promises and trusting in your provision *(2 Co. 5:7; He. 11:1)*. And as they believe, Lord, help their unbelief *(Mt. 9:24)*, with growing faith that is rooted in the knowledge of Your grace and truth *(Cl. 2:7; Jn. 1:17)*. **(Amen)**

89. For Their Boldness in Christ
All-powerful God, I ask that boldness be given to the household of faith. *[State names]* Help them to be strong and courageous, steadfast and immovable, not terrified or discouraged, for you are with them wherever they go *(Js. 1:9; 1 Co. 15:58)*. And, seeing that their state and future is surpassing glory, let this hope make them very bold *(2 Co. 3:12)*. Grace them with strength to never be ashamed of your testimony, or those bearing your testimony. Give them boldness that remains, even if they be subject to suffering for it *(2 Ti. 1:8)*. (Amen)

90. For Their Spiritual Strength
Mighty God, I implore You on behalf of my friend*(s) (and/or, family)*. *[State names]* Strengthen them with all power for Christian endurance, according to Your glorious might *(Cl. 1:11)*. You know our frame, that we are dust *(Ps. 103:14)*, for our flesh is weak, but our spirits are willing. Draw them to watch with You *(Mk. 14:38)*, and teach them to wait upon You, that their strength might be renewed *(Is. 40:31)*. Where they are weak—and will be weak—let your strength be made perfect in them *(2 Co. 12:9)*, that they may say that they are strong *(Jl. 3:10)* and do all things through Christ as He strengthens them *(Ph. 4:13)*. (Amen)

91. For Their Spiritual Maturation
Holy Father, I lift my friend*(s) (and/or, family)* to You in prayer. *[State names]* I seek for them the growth that comes from Your grace and from the knowledge of Your Son Jesus *(2 Pe. 3:18)*, that they would not be childish, tossed and carried by waves and winds of misdirections, but that they might grow up in Christ in every way *(Ep. 4:14-15)*. Teach them to put away childish things and pursue godly things in righteousness *(1 Co. 13:11; 1 Ti. 6:11)*. Conform them to the image of Jesus *(Ro. 8:29)* and guide them to walk in a manner that is worthy of You and fully pleasing to You, bearing fruit in every good work *(Cl. 1:9,10)*. (Amen)

92. For Them to be Filled with the Holy Spirit
Holy and Almighty God, graciously fill with Your Holy Spirit, those I love *(Lk. 11:13)*. *[State names]* Empower them to witness and work for You. May Your Spirit impart giftings upon them,

giftings that they earnestly desire. *[Review the spiritual gifts in Ro. 12:4-8; 1 Co. 12; 1 Co. 13; 1 Co. 14:1-5; Ep. 4:11-16; 2 Ti. 1:6&7; 1 Pe. 4:10&11]* **Grant it, Lord, in order that they may use their spiritual gifts to reveal You to others and bring You glory.** (**Amen**)

93. For Their Humility
Awesome God, I pray for my friend(*s*) (*and/or, family*). *[State names]* **As they learn from Jesus, who was lowly in heart, may they find rest from their pride; physical, mental and spiritual** *(Mt. 11:29)*. **Clothe them with humility, for You oppose the proud but give grace to the humble** *(1 Pe. 5:5)*. **Teach them not to think of themself** (*or, themselves*) **more highly than they ought** *(Ro. 12:3)*, **and to do nothing from conceit, counting others more significant than themself** (*or, themselves*) *(Ph. 2:3)*. (**Amen**)

94. For Their Selflessness
God our Deliverer, deliver from selfish ambition those whom I love *(Ph. 2:3)*. *[State names]* **See that they not seek their own good first, but the good of their neighbor** *(1 Co. 10:24)*, **nor look to their own interests first, but to the interests of others** *(Ph. 2:4)*, **nor insist on their own way, or be irritable or resentful** *(1 Co. 13:5)*, **but give them the same mind as Christ** *(Ph. 2:5)*, **who came not to be served, but rather to serve** *(Mt. 20:28)*, **and give them the same heart as Christ, who laid down His life for us, that they would also lay down their life** (*or, lives*) **for others.** *(Jn. 15:12-13)*. (**Amen**)

95. For Them to Overcome Temptation
God, our rock and our fortress *(Ps. 31:3)*, **strong tower that that the righteous run to for safety** *(Pr. 18:10)*, **deliver my friend**(*s*) (*and/or, family*) **from the desires of the flesh, the desires the eyes, and the pride of life, which are not godly, but worldly** *(1 Jn. 2:16)*. *[State names]* **Quicken their willing spirit**(*s*), **to crucify their weak flesh, to resist the devil, and to submit themself** (*or, themselves*) **to you** *(Mt. 26:41; Ja. 4:7)*, **taking every thought captive to obey Christ** *(2 Co. 10:5)*. **Sharpen their mind**(*s*), **to be set on things above and not on things that are on earth** *(2 Co. 10:5)*, **and to think on things that are true, honorable, just, pure, lovely, commendable, and excellent** *(Ph. 4:8)*. **Lead them not into**

temptation, but deliver them from evil *(Mt. 6:13)*, and keep
them from stumbling *(Ju. 1:24)*. **(Amen)**

96. For Their Self-discipline
Holy Father, I thank You that You hear my prayers for my friends
and family, and grant the requests that I ask of You *(1 Jn. 5:15)*.
[State names] On their behalf, I come now confidently before
Your throne of grace, that, in Your mercy and grace *(He. 4:16)*,
You might give them a powerful and self-controlled spirit *(2 Ti.
1:7)*. My great desire for them is that they be diligent in all that
they do, not slothful in zeal, but fervent in spirit, serving You *(Ro.
12:11)*. Strengthen them to live a life that is self-disciplined,
upright, and godly in this present age, as one who waits for the
appearing of the glory of our great God and Savior Jesus Christ
(Tt. 2:12-13). Train them to discipline their body and keep it
under control *(1 Co. 9:27)*, and work in them, both to will and to
do for Your good pleasure *(Ph. 2:12-13)*. **(Amen)**

97. For Their Greater Obedience/Faithfulness
Lord God, ever Faithful and trustworthy *(Ps. 111:7)*, I petition You
on behalf of my friend(s) (and/or, family), *[State names]* give
them an undividedness in their heart(s) *(Ps. 86:11)*, and write
Your law within them, that they would delight to do Your will
(Ps. 40:8). Let them not be deceived as those who only hear Your
Word, yet do it not *(Ja. 1:22)*; for those who love You will keep
Your commandments *(Jn. 14:15)*, and Your commandments will
never be burdensome to them *(1 Jn. 5:3)*. Keep them from the
voice of strangers and tune their ear(s) to the voice of the Good
Shepherd, Who laid down His life for His sheep *(Jn. 10:3-5,11)*.
Uphold them with a willing spirit *(Ps. 51:12)*, as they obey Your
voice *(Ex. 19:5)*, and faithfully follow You *(Jn. 10:5;)*. **(Amen)**

98. For Their Attitude/Speech
Lord, You are good and upright *(Ps. 25:8)*, righteous in all Your
ways and kind in all Your works *(Ps. 145:17)*, giving the Word of
life to mankind *(1 Jn. 1:1)*. Renew a right spirit within my
friend(s) (and/or, family), and set a guard over their mouth(s) *(Ps.
141:3)*, *[State names]*. By Your grace, may their attitude(s) and
their words always be acceptable in Your sight *(Ps. 19:14)*. Teach
them to be kind and tenderhearted to others *(Ep. 4:31,32)*, and

keep their mouth*(s)* from corrupt talk, that their words may be edifying, giving grace to those who hear them *(Ep. 4:29)*. (Amen)

99. For Their Choices/Decisions
Eternal God, Who declares the end from the beginning *(Is. 46:10)*, I come to You on behalf of my friend*(s) (and/or, family)*. *[State names]* Order all their steps *(Ps. 37:23)* and establish their plans *(Pr. 16:3)*. Life on earth is but a vapor that appears for a little while and then vanishes away *(Ja. 4:14)*, so teach them to number their days *(Ps. 90:12)*, and to trust in You, involving You in all their ways, instead of leaning on their own understanding. Make their paths straight *(Pr. 3:5,6)*, so that they walk—not unwisely—but wisely, making the best use of their time in this present evil world *(Ep. 5:15,16)*. (Amen)

100. For Their Protection
God, our refuge and fortress, our God, in Whom we trust *(Ps. 91:2)*, Let us rejoice and sing for joy as You spread Your protection over us *(Ps. 5:11)*. *[State names]* Let not disaster overtake them *(Ge. 19:19)*, nor deadly pestilence, nor any weapon forged against them, for You promise this as their heritage because they are Your servant. *(Is. 54:17)*. Those who spread a net for my friends *(and/or, family)*, Lord, catch them in their own trap *(Ps. 35:7,8)*, and let all the devil's schemes against them fail *(Ep. 6:11)*. I humbly ask, command Your angels concerning them, to guard them in all their ways *(Ps. 91:11)*. Keep them from all harm, and protect their life *(or, lives)*, their coming and going, from this time forth and forevermore *(Ps. 121:7,8)*. (Amen)

101. For Their Help from God
All-knowing and all-powerful God, who has pity on the weak and needy, and saves them, I lift up my eyes to look for help for my friend*(s) (and/or, family)*, and their help will come from You, Lord, Who made heaven and earth *(Ps. 121:1,2)*. *[State names]* God, be their strength, a very present helper in times of trouble *(Ps. 54:4;Ps. 46:1)*. Bid their heart to cast all burdens upon You, Father. Please sustain them. And help their feet to never be moved *(Ps. 55:22)*. (Amen)

102. For Their Comfort

Father of mercies and God of all comfort *(2 Co. 1:3,4)*, I pray for those who cry out from a painful heart and wail from a broken spirit *(Is. 65:14)*. *[State names]* For the pain that gnaws them takes no rest *(Jb. 30:17)*. Comfort them as a child is comforted and give them rest in Your embrace *(Is. 66:13)*. May Your consolations cheer their soul*(s)* *(Ps. 94:19)*. May they draw near to You—not just with their mouth*(s)*, but with their heart*(s)*—Lord *(Is. 29:13)*. Please draw near to them in return *(Ja. 4:8)*. Give them rest from their pain and turmoil *(Is. 14:3)*. And cause them to sing for gladness of heart again *(Is. 14:3)*. (**Amen**)

103. For Their Trials/Hardships

Sovereign LORD, hear my prayer of intercession for my friend*(s)* *(and/or, family)*. *[State names]* They are hard-pressed on every side *(2 Co. 4:8)*, having met with trial*(s)*. Help them to be constant in prayer and patient in this trouble—even to the point of joy—knowing that this tests their faith and produces stability in them *(Ja. 1:2-4)*. Father, they are called according to Your purpose, and I know that You will work all things out for the good *(Ro. 8:28)*. Now, graciously strengthen them with all the power they need, according to Your glorious might, that they might not grow weary and give up, but that they may endure and reap in due season *(Cl. 1:11; Ga. 6:9)*. (**Amen**)

104. For those Sick/Unwell

Heavenly Father, have mercy on my friend*(s)* *(and/or, family)* *(Ps. 6:2)*. *[State names]* for they are afflicted and in pain *(Ps. 69:29)*. They cry out to You *(Je. 17:14)*, for the restoration of their health and the healing of their wounds *(Je. 30:17)*. Strengthen them during the days of their illness and help them to learn from it *(Is. 41:10; Ps. 119:71)*. May my prayer be a prayer of faith, and may You mercifully hasten to save them from this sickness and graciously hasten to raise them up *(Ps. 70:5; Ja. 5:15)*. (**Amen**)

105. For Their Stress/Worry/Anxiety/Fears

Lord God, our stronghold and deliverer *(Ps. 18:2)*, I pray for my loved one*(s)*. *[State names]* Their spirit*(s)* faint*(s)* within them, their heart*(s)* are distressed *(Ps. 143:4)*, and they are visited with panic *(Le. 26:16)*. Give ear, O Lord; listen to my plea for Your grace toward them *(Ps. 86:6)*. That they learn to cast all their anxieties on You, knowing that You care for them *(1 Pe. 5:7)* and can rescue them *(Ps. 22:8)*. Secure in them **undivided devotion** *(1 Co. 7:35)*, **singleness of heart,** and *(an)* **undivided mind**(*s*) *(Ja. 4:8)* that is *(or, are)* stayed on You and trusting in You. And may you keep them in that perfect peace that surpasses their understanding and guards their thoughts and emotions in Christ *(Is. 26:3; Ph. 4:7)*. **(Amen)**

106.   For Their Depression
God of all hope *(Ro. 15:13)*, **who comforts the downcast** *(2 Co. 7:6)*, I pray for my loved one(*s*). *[State names]* **Their soul**(*s*) **is** *(or, are)* **depressed and in turmoil within them** *(Ps. 42:11)*, **their heart aches and throbs, and the light of their eyes has gone from them** *(Ps. 38:10)*. Be the strength of their heart and their portion forever *(Ps. 73:26)* and fill them with all joy and peace in believing, that they may abound in hope, through the power of the Holy Spirit *(Ro. 15:13)*. That they shall again praise You, our salvation and our God *(Ps. 42:11)*, with a glad heart and a cheerful face *(Pr. 15:13)*. **(Amen)**

107.   For Those Grieving/Suffering Loss
God our Helper, the upholder of our lives *(Ps. 54:4)*, be gracious to my friend(*s*) *(Ps. 31:9)*. *[State names]* **For their joy is gone, and their heart**(*s*) **is** *(or, are)* **sick within them** *(Je. 8:18)*. **Their eyes are weak because of grief; their soul**(*s*) **and their body** *(or, bodies)* **also** *(Ps. 6:7; Ps. 31:9)*. Have compassion according to the abundance of Your steadfast love *(La. 3:32)*. Lord, heal their broken heart(*s*) and crushed spirit(*s*), and bind up their wounds *(Ps. 34:18; Ps. 147:3)*. **(Amen)**

108.   For Their Addictions/Bad Habits
Almighty Deliverer, Who led Your people Israel out of cruel bondage and into freedom *(Ex. 3-Js. 3)*, deliver my friend(*s*) *(Ps. 39:8)*. *[State names and addictions/bad habits]* **Help them to not be mastered by this** *(1 Co. 6:12)*. **Their spirit is willing, but their flesh is weak** *(Mt. 26:41)*. **They are as a city broken into and left without walls. They have no self-control** *(Pr. 25:28)*. Father, through Your Son, set them free, that they might be free indeed *(Jn. 8:36)*. And rebuild them again, from the spirit up, with power and self-control *(2 Ti. 1:7)*. **(Amen)**

109.   For Their Persecution/Opposition

Lord, You are our Rock and our fortress *(Ps. 71:3)*. I pray for my friend(s) *(and/or, family)*. *[State names]* Let them not be distressed or shamed because of those who persecute them *(Je. 17:18)*. The quarrel of their enemy is with You. They persecuted You, Jesus, the Master; so shall they persecute Your servant(s) *(Jn. 15:20)*. May they bless their enemy *(or, enemies)* and not curse them *(Ro. 12:14)*. And may their enemy *(or, enemies)* be ashamed when, because of good works and sound speech, they no longer have anything evil to say *(Tt. 2:7,8)*. (**Amen**)

110. For Those in Cults

God of all truth, there are many who are insubordinate, empty talkers and deceivers, whose mouths must be stopped. They have subverted whole households, even the households of my friends. *[Name names]* Their leaders teach things they shouldn't, fables and commandments of men, that turn people from the truth. They profess to know You, but in works they deny You, being abominable, disobedient, and disqualified for every good work. May You rebuke them sharply, through myself or others, that they may be sound in the faith. And, if it be Your will to reach them through me, that I might be able to cling to the faithful Word, to exhort and convince them by sound doctrine. *(Tt 1:9-16)*. (**Amen**)

111. For the Marital Crisis of Others

God Who restores and redeems, calamity has struck, like a terror attack, against my friends *(and/or, family)*. *[State names]* And though they are mocked by their lack of wisdom *(Pr. 1:20,33)*, I ask of You, God, to give them wisdom generously and without reproach *(Ja. 1:5)*. You will teach them Your way *(Ps. 27:11)*, and in great compassion You will gather them *(Is. 54:7)*. Heal their broken hearts and bind up their wounds *(Ps. 147:3)*. Help them to bear with one another in their complaints against each other *(Cl. 3:13)*, and to be kind, tenderhearted, and forgiving of one another, as You in Christ forgave them *(Ep. 4:32)*. And let the peace of Christ referee between their two hearts, since they were called to peace in one union *(Cl. 3:15)*. (**Amen**)

112. For Their Divorce

God my redeemer, I pray for my friends *(and/or, family)*. *[State names]* They have failed to enter into the full promise of what could have been *(He. 4:1)*. Father, forgive them *(Mt. 6:12)*. Heal their broken hearts and bind up their wounds *(147:3)*. Help them to bear with one another in their complaints against each other *(Cl. 3:13)*, and to be kind, tenderhearted, and forgiving of one another, as You in Christ forgave them *(Ep. 4:32)*. And let the peace of Christ referee between their two hearts, since they were called to peace *(Cl. 3:15)*. (Amen)

113.   For Them to Forgive

Loving and merciful Father of all, Your Son commanded us to love even our enemies *(BOCP)*. *[State names]* You have loved them, help them to love others. You have been merciful to them, help them be merciful to others *(Lk. 6:36)*. You have forgiven them, help them forgive others *(Ep. 4:32)*. You have reconciled them, help them minister reconciliation to others *(2 Co. 5:18)*, bearing with others *(Cl. 3:13)* in kindness and tenderheartedness *(Ep. 4:32)*. Let them not repay evil for evil *(1 Th. 5:15)*. Bless them to be a peacemaker *(or just, peacemakers) (Mt. 5:9)*. And in Your good time, enable them all to stand reconciled before You (BOCP). *(*Amen)

114.   For Their Anger/Temper

Holy Father, Who deferred Your own anger for the sake of Your praise *(Is. 48:9)*, be the example for my friend*(s) (and/or, family)*. Teach them the foolishness of being hot tempered, and the wisdom of being slow to anger *(Pr. 14:29)*. Help them to put off their old self *(or, selves)*, and be renewed in the spirit of their mind*(s)*, putting on the new self *(or, selves)* that is created after Your likeness in true holiness *(Ep. 4:22-24)*. That they may be quick to hear, slow to speak, and slow to anger, knowing that the anger of man does not produce the righteousness of God *(Ja. 1:19-20)*. Train them to respond with love that is not easily agitated *(1 Co. 13:5)*, and with gentleness and self-control, bearing the fruit of the Spirit *(Ga. 5:22-23)*. And if they must be angry, grace them to sin not. *(Ps. 4:4)*. *(*Amen)

115.   For Someone Else's Loneliness

God my Father, I intercede on behalf of the one*(s)* afflicted by loneliness. Turn to them and be gracious to them *(Ps. 25:16)*. *[State names]* Be continually with them. Never leave them nor forsake them. Hold their right hand. They have no one in Heaven but You. And they have none on earth besides You. Be the Strength of their heart *(Ps. 73:23-26; He. 13:5)*, and their portion forever. May they hope in You *(Ps. 73:26; La. 3:24) (BOCP)*. (**Amen**)

116. For Those Traveling/Absent

Lord God, whose fatherly care reaches the utmost parts of the earth, and whose presence we find wherever we go: I humbly pray that You graciously watch and bless those whom I love, now absent from me. *[State names]* Defend them from all dangers of soul and body; and bring them in safety to their journey's end. *(BOCP)*. (**Amen**)

117. For Their Fruit of the Womb

Creator of all the living, Who opens and closes the womb *(Ge. 29:31; 1 Sa. 1:5)*, bless the union of my loved ones. *[State names]* That they may be fruitful and multiply *(Ge. 1:28)*, for children are a heritage from You, and the fruit of the womb a reward from You *(Ps. 127:3)*. I seek You with an open heart filled with hope and trust in You *(He. 6:11; Pr. 3:5)* and ask you to open and fill her womb *(Ge. 29:31)*. I ask You to give them a child, Lord *(1 Sa. 1:20)*. May they be still before You, hope for what they do not yet see, and wait patiently for it *(Ps. 37:7; Ro. 8:25)*. That in the right season *(Ec. 3:2)*, You might grant all of our petitions and give them the desire of our hearts *(1 Sa. 1:27; Ps. 37:4)*. (**Amen**)

118. For Their Childlessness

See Prayer **44. For God's Comfort for Me**
Also, Prayer **48. For My Depression**

119. For Their Adoption of a Child

Creator of all the living, Who opens and closes the womb *(Ge. 29:31; 1 Sa. 1:5)*, bless the union of my friends *(and/or, family)* that they may be fruitful through adoption and multiply *(Ge. 1:28)*, for children are a heritage and a reward from You *(Ps. 127:3)*. I bring an open heart filled with hope and trust in You *(He. 6:11; Pr. 3:5)*. I ask that they be granted an adopted child from You, Lord *(1 Sa. 1:20)*. May they be still before You, hope for what they do not yet see, and wait patiently for it *(Ps. 37:7; Ro. 8:25)*. That in the right season *(Ec. 3:2)*, You might grant all of our petitions and give them the desire of their hearts *(1 Sa. 1:27; Ps. 37:4)*. **(Amen)**

120. For Their Birthday
God, our times are in Your hand: Look with favor, we pray, on Your servant *[State name]*, as they begin another year. Grant that they might grow in wisdom and grace, and strengthen their trust in Your goodness all the days of their life *(BOCP)*. **(Amen)**

121. For Their Aging
O Lord, be to my friend*(s) (and/or, family)* a rock of refuge. *[State names]* Do not cast them off in the time of old age, nor forsake them when their strength fails. Be not far from them, and be quick to help them. From their youth you have taught them and may they still proclaim your awesome deeds and righteous acts every day. So even to old age and gray hairs, O God, do not forsake them, until they declare Your might to this generation, and your power to the generation to come. May they remind others of your righteousness—and Yours alone. You have subjected them to many troubles and calamities, but You will revive them again. You will lift them up from the depths of the earth *(Ps. 71)*.

122. For Their Leisure
O God, in the course of this busy life, give my friend*(s) (and/or, family)* times of refreshment and peace. *[State names]* Grant that they may so use their leisure and hobby, to rebuild their bodies and renew their minds, that their heart*(s)* may ever more be aware of the goodness of the life that You have given to them *(BOCP)*. **(Amen)**

IV. The Whole World

123. For the Global Church
Lord, our God, Father of Jesus Christ, Who is the Head of the body, I pray for Your Church worldwide; that it may be so guided and governed by Your holy Word and Your good Spirit, that all who profess themselves to be Christians may be led into the way of truth, and hold the Faith in the unity of the Spirit, in the bond of peace, and in all holy living *(BOCP)*. (Amen)

124. For the Church's Global Mission *Adapted from BOCP*
Ever-living God, Whose will it is that all should come to You through Your Son Jesus, inspire our witness to Him. That all may know the power of His forgiveness and the hope of His resurrection, Who lives and reigns with You and the Holy Spirit. One God, now and forever *(BOCP)*. (Amen)

125. For Humankind
O God, You made us in Your own image and redeemed us through Jesus Your Son. Look with compassion on the whole human family. Take away the arrogance and hatred which infects our hearts. Break down the walls that separate us. Unite us in bonds of love. And work through our struggle and confusion to accomplish Your purposes on earth. That, in Your good time, all nations and races may serve You in harmony around Your heavenly throne *(BOCP)*. (Amen)

126. For Our Country/Government
Almighty God, Who has given us this good land for our heritage, we humbly ask Your help, that we may always prove ourselves a people mindful of Your favor and glad to do Your will. Bless our land with honorable industry, sound learning, and pure manners. Save us from violence, discord, and confusion, from pride and arrogance, and from every evil way. Defend our liberties, and form into one united people, the multitudes brought here out of many kindreds and tongues. Endue with the spirit of wisdom, those to whom—in Your Name—we entrust the

authority of government, that there may be justice and peace at home. And that, through obedience to Your Law, we may show forth Your praise among the nations of the earth. In the time of prosperity, fill our hearts with thankfulness. And in the day of trouble, suffer not our trust in You to fail *(BOCP)*. (Amen)

127. For Local Government

Almighty God, our heavenly Father, send down upon those who hold office in this County, City, and State, the spirit of wisdom, love, and justice; that with steadfast purpose they may faithfully serve in their offices to promote the well-being of all people *(BOCP)*. (Amen)

128. For an Election

Almighty God, to whom we must account for all our powers and privileges: Guide the people of the United States *(or, of this community)* in the election of officials and representatives; that, by faithful administration and wise laws, the rights of all may be protected and our nation be enabled to fulfill Your purposes. *(BOCP)*. (Amen)

129. For Our Armed Forces

Almighty God, we commend to your gracious care and keeping, all the men and women of our armed forces at home and abroad. Defend them day by day with your heavenly grace; strengthen them in their trials and temptations; give them courage to face the perils against them; and grant them a sense of your abiding presence wherever they may be. *(BOCP)*. (Amen)

130. For World Peace

Eternal God, in Whose perfect Kingdom no sword is drawn but the sword of righteousness, and no strength is known but the strength of love. Mightily spread abroad Your Spirit, that all people may be gathered under the banner of the Prince of Peace, as children of one Father; to Whom be dominion and glory, now and forever *(BOCP)*. (Amen)

131. For the Nations

Almighty God, our Heavenly Father, guide the kingdoms of this world in the way of justice and truth, and establish among them that peace which is the fruit of righteousness, that they may become the Kingdom of our Lord and Savior *(BOCP)*. **(Amen)**

132. For Conflicts of Worldview

O God, You have bound us together in a common life. Help us, in the midst of our struggles for justice and truth, to confront one another without hatred or bitterness, and to work together with mutual forbearance and respect; through Jesus Christ our Lord *(BOCP)*. **(Amen)**

133. For Cities

Heavenly Father, in Your Word You have given us a vision of that holy City to which the nations of the world bring their glory: Behold and visit, we pray, the cities of the earth. Renew the ties of mutual regard which form our civic life. Send us honest and able leaders. Enable us to eliminate poverty, prejudice, and oppression, that peace may prevail with righteousness, and justice with order, and that men and women from different cultures and with differing talents may find with one another the fulfillment of their humanity; through Jesus Christ our Lord *(BOCP)*. **(Amen)**

134. For Towns and Rural Areas

Lord Christ, when You came among us, You proclaimed the Kingdom of God in villages, towns, and lonely places: Grant that You presence and power may be known throughout this land. Have mercy upon all of us who live and work in rural areas; and grant that all the people of our nation may give thanks to You for food and drink and all other bodily necessities of life, respect those who labor to produce them, and honor the land and the water from which these good things come. All this we ask in Your holy Name *(BOCP)*. **(Amen)**

135. For Our Planet

Almighty God, in giving us dominion over things on earth, You made us fellow workers in Your creation: Give us wisdom and reverence so to use the resources of nature, that no one may suffer from our abuse of them, and that, if You tarry, generations yet to come may continue to praise You for Your bounty. *(BOCP)*. **(Amen)**

136. For Our Agriculture
Almighty God, we thank You for making the earth fruitful, so that it might produce what is needed for life: Bless those who work in the fields; give us seasonable weather; and grant that we may all share the fruits of the earth, rejoicing in Your goodness. *(BOCP)*. (**Amen**)

137. For Rain
Heavenly Father, You have promised to all those who seek Your Kingdom and its righteousness all things necessary to sustain their life; Send us, we pray, in this time of need, such moderate rain and showers, that we may receive the fruits of the earth, to our comfort and to Your honor. *(BOCP)*. (**Amen**)

138. For the Unemployed of the World
Heavenly Father, we remember before You those who suffer want and anxiety from lack of work. *[State names]* Guide the people of this land so to use our public and private wealth that all may find suitable and fulfilling employment, and receive just payment for their labor; through Jesus Christ, our Lord *(BOCP)*. (**Amen**)

139. For Our Schools/Education Systems
Eternal God, bless all our schools, colleges, and universities, that they may be lively centers for sound learning, new discovery, and the pursuit of wisdom; and grant that those who teach and those who learn may find You to be the source of all truth. *(BOCP)*. (**Amen**)

140. For the Poor and Neglected of the World
Almighty and most merciful God, we remember before You all the poor and neglected persons whom it would be easy for us to forget; the homeless and the destitute, the old and the sick, and all who have none to care for them. Help us to heal those who are broken in body, or spirit, and to turn their sorrow into joy. Grant this, Father, for the love of Your Son, who for our sake became poor, Jesus our Lord. *(BOCP)*. (**Amen**)

141. For the Oppressed of the World

Look with pity, heavenly Father, upon the people in this land who live with injustice, terror, disease, and death as their constant companions. Have mercy upon us. Help us to eliminate our cruelty to these our neighbors. Strengthen those who spend their lives establishing equal protection of the law and equal opportunities for all. And grant that every one of us may enjoy a fair portion of the riches of this land. *(BOCP)*. (Amen)

142. For Our Prisons and Correctional Institutions

Lord Jesus, for our sake you were condemned as a criminal: Visit our jails and prisons with Your pity and judgment. Remember all prisoners, and bring the guilty to repentance and amendment of life according to Your will, and give them hope for their future. When any are held unjustly, bring them release; forgive us, and teach us to improve our justice. Remember those who work in these institutions; keep them humane and compassionate; and save them from becoming brutal or callous. And since what we do for those in prison, Lord, we do for You, constrain us to improve their lot. All this we ask for Your mercy's sake. *(BOCP)*. (Amen)

143. For Global Christian Influencers

Almighty God, You proclaim Your truth in every generation through many voices: Direct, in our time, we pray, those who speak where many listen and write what many read; that they may do their part in making the heart of this people wise, its mind sound, and its will righteous. *(BOCP)*. (Amen)

144. For Israel/Jerusalem

God of Abraham, Isaac, and Jacob, Your blessing be upon Your people Israel, the Holy Land, and the Holy City of Jerusalem. Protect them from their enemies, and let Your peace reign among them. And grant it, Lord, that the Jewish nation come to know the Salvation that is their Messiah, Jesus. (Amen)

145. For Caretakers and Public Servants

Abba Father, I pray for those who are caring for the sick, wounded, and needy, and for our public servants who keep us safe and defend justice. May they be filled with your strength and compassion, and may they be a source of fairness, comfort, encouragement, and healing to those they serve. (Amen)

146. The Prayer of St. Francis

Lord, make us instruments of Your peace. Where there is hatred, let us sow love; where there is injury, pardon; where there is discord, union; where there is doubt, faith; where there is despair, hope; where there is darkness, light; where there is sadness, joy. Grant that we may not so much seek to be consoled as to console; to be understood as to understand; to be loved as to love. For it is in giving that we receive; it is in pardoning that we are pardoned; and it is in dying that we are born to eternal life *(BOCP)*. (Amen)

V. Public Prayers

147. For a Worship Team Practice
Awesome God, pour Your blessing over us as we prepare to serve You with gladness and offer up a sacrifice of praise. Bless and increase the giftings You've already given to us, that we might play skillfully, singing and making melody to You first in our hearts, and then from the fruit of our lips and our instruments of praise *(Ps. 100:1,2; Ps. 33:3; Ps. 150:3-5; He. 13:15)*. (In Jesus Name, Amen)

148. For Service Opening/Worship Time
Lord and God, You are worthy to receive all our glory and honor and energetic worship *(Re. 4:11)*. Let our songs of praise and the exaltations of our hearts be acceptable in Your sight *(Ps. 95:2; Is. 25:1; Ps. 19:14)*. For You are blessed forever *(Ps. 89:52)*, and we will bless Your glorious Name until the whole earth is filled with Your glory *(Ps. 72:19)*. Send help and give support to those who cry to You in this sanctuary *(Ps. 20:2; Ps. 28:2)* and fill this sanctuary with Your power and glory as we behold You *(Ps. 63:2)*. May we do all things through You and for You in this place *(Cl. 1:16)*. (In the Name of Jesus, Amen)

149. For the Teaching of God's Word
God of all truth, thank You for Your gracious Spirit and the giving of the gifts of preaching and teaching *(Ro. 12:7)*. Bless the one who speaks, that he may edify the whole church *(1 Co. 14:4)*. Bless the ones who hear, that we might understand *(Mt. 13:13)*, and bless the hearts that receive, that the Word might take root and bear fruit in us *(Mk. 4:20)*. Your Word is living and active *(or, powerful)*, send it forth to accomplish what You purpose *(Is. 55:11)*. (In the Name of Jesus, Amen)

150. For Collection of Tithes/Offerings
Creator and Ruler of the universe, we honor You with our money by giving You the firstfruits of our increase, trusting that You will provide for all of our needs *(Pr. 3:9)*. We give the whole tithe, that which is rightfully Yours *(Mt. 3:10)*, and we bring our

offerings, above and beyond the tithe, as we have decided in our hearts, proportional to how You have blessed each one of us, giving cheerfully, not reluctantly or by compulsion, that there might be food in Your house *(Dt. 16:17; 2 Co. 9:7)*. Multiply it to its intended use *(Mt. 14:19)*. (In the Name of Jesus, Amen)

151. For Service Closure

Holy Father, as we depart Your sanctuary, send us into the world to shine as lights, but keep us from the world's influences and the schemes of the evil one *(Mt. 5:14; Jn. 17:15,18; Ep. 6:11)*. And let the Word of Christ, which we have heard, continue to dwell in us richly, impacting all that we say and do *(Cl. 3:16,17)*, for the glory of the Lord Jesus Himself *(2 Co. 8:19)*. (In the Name of Christ, Amen)

152. For a Special Meeting/Time of Fellowship

Heavenly Father, we thank You for the gift of fellowship and the opportunity to gather together in Your name. May we share in one another's joys and burdens as members of Your body *(Ro. 12:15)*, encouraging and edifying one another *(1 Th. 5:11)*, and spurring one another on toward love and good deeds *(He. 10:24)*, as we serve one another through love *(Ga. 5:13)* and maintain the unity of the Spirit in the bond of peace *(Ep. 4:3)*. (In Jesus Name, Amen)

153. For a Small Group Bible Study

God of all truth, Your Word is lamp to our feet and a light to our path (Ps. 119:105). It is breathed out by You and profitable for our learning, correction, and training in righteousness *(2 Ti. 3:16)*. Teach us, that we may walk in Your truth (Ps. 86:11). Teach us to do Your will, for You are our God (Ps. 143:10)! Give us knowledge, understanding, discretion, and wisdom (Pr. 2:6; 8:12). And bless us as we store up Your Word in my heart, that we might not sin against you (Ps. 119:11). (In Jesus Name, Amen)

VI. Praises

154. 1st Day of the Month
Lord, I praise You, for You are my refuge and strength, a very present help in trouble. Therefore I will not fear, though the earth gives way and the mountains be moved into the heart of the sea. You are in my midst, and I shall not be moved; You will help me when morning dawns. The nations rage, the kingdoms totter; You utter Your voice, the earth melts. The Lord of hosts is with me; the God of Jacob is my fortress. Be exalted, O God, above the heavens! Let Your glory be over all the earth! *(Ps. 46:1-3, 5-7; Ps. 57:5)*.

155. 2nd Day of the Month
I will extol You, my God and King, every day I will bless You and praise Your name forever and ever. Great are You Lord, and greatly to be praised, and Your greatness is unsearchable. One generation shall commend Your works to another and shall declare Your mighty acts. On the glorious splendor of Your majesty, and on Your wondrous works, I will meditate. They shall speak of the might of Your awesome deeds, and I will declare Your greatness. My mouth will speak the praise of the Lord, and may all flesh bless Your holy name forever and ever *(Ps. 145:1-6, 21)*.

156. 3rd Day of the Month
Bless the Lord, O my soul, and all that is within me, bless His holy name! Bless the Lord, O my soul, and forget not all His benefits, who forgives all my iniquity, who heals all my diseases, who redeems my life from the pit, who crowns me with steadfast love and mercy. You Lord are merciful and gracious, slow to anger and abounding in steadfast love. For as high as the heavens are above the earth, so great is Your steadfast love toward those who fear You. As far as the east is from the west, so far do You remove my transgressions from me. Bless the Lord, all His works, in all places of His dominion. Bless the Lord, O my soul!" *(Ps. 103:1-4, 8, 11-12, 22)*.

157. 4th Day of the Month

I will give thanks to You Lord with my whole heart; I will recount all of Your wonderful deeds. I will be glad and exult in You; I will sing praise to Your name, O Most High. You have rebuked the nations; You have made the wicked perish; You have blotted out their name forever and ever. You sit enthroned forever; You have established Your throne for justice, and You judge the world with righteousness; You judge the peoples with uprightness. Lord, You are a stronghold for the oppressed, a stronghold in times of trouble. I sing praises to You Lord, who sits enthroned in Zion! I will tell among the peoples Your deeds! *(Ps. 9:1-4, 7-9, 11)*.

158.   5th Day of the Month

I will shout for joy to You God, with all the earth; and sing the glory of Your name; I will give to You glorious praise! I will say to You, "How awesome are Your deeds! So great is Your power that Your enemies come cringing to You. All the earth worships You and sings praises to You; they sing praises to Your name." May others come and see what You have done: You are awesome in Your deeds toward the children of man. I bless You God, and may the peoples let the sound of Your praise be heard. May they come and hear, all who fear You, and I will tell what You have done for my soul. Blessed be You God, because You have not rejected my prayer or removed Your steadfast love from me! *(Ps. 66:1-5, 8, 16, 20)*.

159.   6th Day of the Month

Lord, You reign; let the peoples tremble! You sit enthroned upon the cherubim; let the earth quake! You are great in Zion; You are exalted over all the peoples. Let them praise Your great and awesome name! Holy are You! I Exalt You, Lord my God; I worship at Your footstool! Holy are You! I exalt You Lord my God, and worship at Your holy mountain; for You, Lord my God are holy! I will sing of steadfast love and justice; to You, O Lord, I will make music *(Ps. 99:1-3, 5, 9; Ps. 101:1)*.

160.   7th Day of the Month

I will bless You Lord at all times; Your praise shall continually be in my mouth. My soul makes its boast in You; let the humble hear and be glad. May others magnify You with me, and may we exalt Your name together! I sought You, and You answered me and delivered me from all my fears. Those who look to You are radiant, and their faces shall never be ashamed. This poor man cried, and You heard him and saved him out of all his troubles. May others taste and see that You are good! Blessed is the man who takes refuge in You!" *(Ps. 34:1-6, 8)*.

161.   8th Day of the Month
The heavens declare Your glory, God, and the sky above proclaims Your handiwork. Day to day pours out speech, and night to night reveals knowledge. There is no speech, nor are there words, whose voice is not heard. Their voice goes out through all the earth, and their words to the end of the world. In them You have set a tent for the sun, which comes out like a bridegroom leaving his chamber, and, like a strong man, runs its course with joy. Your Law is perfect, reviving the soul; Your testimony is sure, making wise the simple. Let the words of my mouth and the meditation of my heart be acceptable in Your sight, O Lord, my rock and my redeemer *(Ps. 19:1-5, 7, 14)*.

162.   9th Day of the Month
O Lord, our Lord, how majestic is Your name in all the earth! You have set Your glory above the heavens. Out of the mouth of babies and infants, You have established strength because of Your foes, to still the enemy and the avenger. When I look at Your heavens, the work of Your fingers, the moon and the stars, which You have set in place, what is man that You are mindful of him, and the son of man that You care for him? Yet You have made him a little lower than the heavenly beings and crowned him with glory and honor. O Lord, our Lord, how majestic is Your name in all the earth! *(Ps. 8:1-5, 9)*.

163.   10th Day of the Month
I lift up my eyes to the hills. From where does my help come? My help comes from You Lord, who made heaven and earth. You will not let my foot be moved; You keep me and never slumber. You keep Israel and neither slumber nor sleep. You are my keeper; You are my shade on my right hand. You will keep me from all evil; You will keep my life. You will keep my going out and my coming in from this time forth and forevermore. Blessed be Your name, Lord, from this time forth and forevermore! *(Ps. 121:1-5, 7-8; Ps. 113:2)*.

164. 11th Day of the Month

I give thanks to You Lord, for You are good, for Your steadfast love endures forever! May the redeemed of the Lord say so, whom You have redeemed from trouble. I cried to You in my trouble, and You delivered me from my distress. You brought me out of darkness and the shadow of death, and burst my bonds apart. I will thank You for Your steadfast love, for Your wondrous works to the children of man! I will offer sacrifices of thanksgiving and tell of Your deeds in songs of joy! Whoever is wise will attend to these things; and consider Your steadfast love *(Ps. 107:1-2, 6, 14-15, 21-22, 43)*.

165. 12th Day of the Month

I praise You Lord! I praise Your name, Lord! Blessed be Your name from this time forth and forevermore! From the rising of the sun to its setting, Your name is to be praised! You are high above all nations, and Your glory above the heavens! Who is like You, Lord my God, who is seated on high, who looks far down on the heavens and the earth? You raise the poor from the dust and lift the needy from the ash heap, to make them sit with princes, with the princes of His people *(Ps. 113:1-8)*.

166. 13th Day of the Month

I praise You Lord! I praise You Lord, with my soul! I will praise You as long as I live; I will sing praises to You while I have my being. I will say to others, "put not your trust in princes, in a son of man, in whom there is no salvation. When his breath departs, he returns to the earth; on that very day his plans perish." Blessed is he whose help is in You, the God of Jacob, whose hope is in You, Lord my God, who made heaven and earth, the sea, and all that is in them, who keeps faith forever *(Ps. 146:1-6)*.

167. 14th Day of the Month

I praise You Lord! For it is good to sing praises to You, my God; for it is pleasant, and a song of praise is fitting. You build up Jerusalem; You gather the outcasts of Israel. You heal the brokenhearted and binds up their wounds. You determine the number of the stars; You give to all of them their names. Great are You Lord, and abundant in power; Your understanding is beyond measure. You lift up the humble; You cast the wicked to the ground. I will sing to You with thanksgiving and make melody to You on the lyre! *(Ps. 147:1-7)*.

168. 15th Day of the Month
I praise You Lord! They praise You from the heavens! They praise You in the heights! All Your angels praise You! All Your hosts praise You! The sun, moon, and shining stars praise You! The highest heavens praise You! The waters above the heavens praise You! Let them praise Your name, Lord! For You commanded and they were created. You established them forever and ever; You gave a decree, and it shall not pass away. May everything that has breath praise You Lord! Praise the Lord! *(Ps. 148:1-6; Ps. 150:6)*.

169. 16th Day of the Month
I will forever sing of Your steadfast love, Lord; with my mouth I will make known Your faithfulness to all generations. For I said, 'Steadfast love will be built up forever; in the heavens You will establish Your faithfulness.' Let the heavens praise Your wonders, O Lord, Your faithfulness in the assembly of the holy ones! For who in the skies can be compared to You? Who among the heavenly beings is like You, a God greatly to be feared in the council of the holy ones, and awesome above all who are around Him? O Lord God of hosts, who is mighty as You are, O Lord, with Your faithfulness all around You? *(Ps. 89:1-2, 5-8)*.

170. 17th Day of the Month
I will give thanks to You, O Lord, with my whole heart; I will recount all of Your wonderful deeds. I will be glad and exult in You; I will sing praise to Your name, O Most High. The Lord is a stronghold for the oppressed, a stronghold in times of trouble. And those who know Your name put their trust in You, for You, O Lord, have not forsaken those who seek You. Sing praises to the Lord, who sits enthroned in Zion! Tell among the peoples His deeds! I will recount Your praises, that in the gates of the daughter of Zion I may rejoice in Your salvation *(Ps. 9:1-2, 9-11, 14)*.

171. 18th Day of the Month
I will forever sing of Your steadfast love, Lord; with my mouth I will make known Your faithfulness to all generations. The

heavens praise Your wonders, O Lord, Your faithfulness in the assembly of the holy ones! For who in the skies can be compared to You? Who among the heavenly beings is like You, a God greatly to be feared in the council of the holy ones, and awesome above all who are around Him? O Lord God of hosts, who is mighty as You are, O Lord, with Your faithfulness all around You? Blessed be the Lord forever! Amen and Amen *(Ps. 89:1, 5-8, 52)*.

172.   19th Day of the Month

Lord, the earth is Yours and the fullness thereof, the world and those who dwell therein, for You have founded it upon the seas and established it upon the rivers. Who shall ascend Your hill? And who shall stand in Your holy place? He who has clean hands and a pure heart, who does not lift up his soul to what is false and does not swear deceitfully. He will receive blessing from You and righteousness from the God of his salvation. May the gates lift up their heads! And the ancient doors be lifted up, that You, King of glory, may come in. Who is this King of glory? You Lord, strong and mighty, You Lord, mighty in battle! Lord of hosts, You are the King of glory! *(Ps. 24:1-5, 7-8, 10)*.

173.   20th Day of the Month

Bless the Lord, O my soul! O Lord my God, You are very great! You are clothed with splendor and majesty, covering Yourself with light as with a garment, stretching out the heavens like a tent. You lay the beams of Your chambers on the waters; You make the clouds Your chariot; You ride on the wings of the wind; You make Your messengers winds, Your ministers a flaming fire. O Lord, how manifold are Your works! In wisdom have You made them all; the earth is full of Your creatures. May Your glory, Lord, endure forever; may You rejoice in Your works *(Ps. 104:1-4, 24, 31)*.

174.   21st Day of the Month

Lord, You are my light and my salvation; whom shall I fear? You are the stronghold of my life; of whom shall I be afraid? One thing have I asked of You, that will I seek after: that I may dwell in Your house all the days of my life, to gaze upon Your beauty and to inquire in Your temple. For You will hide me in Your shelter in the day of trouble; You will conceal me under the cover of Your tent; You will lift me high upon a rock. And now my head shall be lifted up above my enemies all around me, and I will offer in Your tent sacrifices with shouts of joy; I will sing and make melody to You, Lord *(Ps. 27:1, 4-6)*.

175.   22nd Day of the Month

May the heavenly beings ascribe to You, Lord, ascribe to You glory and strength. I will ascribe to You the glory due Your name and worship You in the splendor of holiness. Your voice is over the waters; You, the God of glory, thunders over many waters. Your voice is powerful; Your voice is full of majesty. You sit enthroned over the flood; You sit enthroned as king forever. May You give strength to Your people! May You bless Your people with peace! *(Ps. 29:1-4, 10-11)*.

176.   23rd Day of the Month

You are my shepherd; I shall not want. You make me lie down in green pastures. You lead me beside still waters. You restore my soul. You lead me in paths of righteousness for Your name's sake. Even though I walk through the valley of the shadow of death, I will fear no evil, for You are with me; Your rod and Your staff, they comfort me. You prepare a table before me in the presence of my enemies; You anoint my head with oil; my cup overflows. Surely goodness and mercy shall follow me all the days of my life, and I shall dwell in Your house forever *(Ps. 23:1-6)*.

177.   24th Day of the Month

Lord, You are my rock and my fortress and my deliverer, my God, my rock, in whom I take refuge, my shield, and the horn of my salvation, my stronghold. I call upon You, who is worthy to be praised, and I am saved from my enemies. For who is God, but You? And who is a rock, except my God? God—Your way is perfect; Your word proves true; You are a shield for all those who take refuge in You. Lord, You live, and blessed be You, my rock, and exalted be the God of my salvation! For this I will praise You, O Lord, among the nations, and sing to Your name *(Ps. 18:2-3, 31-32, 46, 49)*.

178.   25th Day of the Month

May all the earth make a joyful noise to You, Lord, and serve the Lord with gladness! I will come into Your presence with singing!

Lord, I know that You are God! It is You who made us, and we are Yours; we are Your people, and the sheep of Your pasture. I will enter Your gates with thanksgiving, and Your courts with praise! I will give thanks to You and bless His name! For You are good; Your steadfast love endures forever, and Your faithfulness to all generations *(Ps. 100:1-5)*.

179. 26th Day of the Month

Give ear, O heavens, and I will speak, and let the earth hear the words of my mouth. May my teaching drop as the rain, my speech distill as the dew, like gentle rain upon the tender grass, and like showers upon the herb. For I will proclaim Your name, Lord and ascribe greatness to You, my God! You are the Rock, Your work is perfect, for all Your ways are justice. A God of faithfulness and without iniquity, just and upright are You. Sing aloud, O daughters of Zion; shout, O Israel! Rejoice and exult with all your heart, O daughter of Jerusalem! The Lord has taken away the judgments against you; He has cleared away your enemies. The King of Israel, the Lord, is in your midst; you shall never again fear evil" *(Ps. 32:8, 40:16-17, 50:14-15)*.

180. 27th Day of the Month

I will bless You, Lord, at all times; Your praise shall continually be in my mouth. My soul makes its boast in You, Lord; I am glad because of You. I will magnify You, Lord, and exalt Your name together with Your people! I sought You, Lord, and You answered me and delivered me from all my fears. When I look to You, I am radiant, and my face shall never be ashamed. Your angel encamps around me because I fear You and He delivers me. I have tasted and have seen that You are good! And I am blessed because I take refuge in You! *(Ps. 34:1-5, 7-8)*.

181. 29th Day of the Month

I love You, O Lord, my strength. You are my rock and my fortress, my deliverer, my God in whom I take refuge. You are my shield and the horn of my salvation, my stronghold. I call upon You, Lord, for You are worthy to be praised, and You save me from my enemies. When the cords of death encompassed me and the torrents of destruction assailed me, when the snares of death confronted me, in my distress I called upon You, Lord. I cried to

You for help, and from Your temple, You heard my voice, and my cry reached Your ears *(Ps. 18:1-6)*.

182.   30th Day of the Month
Give ear, O Lord, to my prayer; listen to my plea for grace. In the day of my trouble, I call upon You, for You answer me. There is none like You among the gods, O Lord, nor are there any works like Yours. All the nations You have made shall come and worship before You, O Lord, and shall glorify Your name. For You are great and do wondrous things; You alone are God. Teach me Your way, O Lord, that I may walk in Your truth; unite my heart to fear Your name. I give thanks to You, O Lord my God, with my whole heart, and I will glorify Your name forever *(Ps. 86:6-12)*.

183.   31st Day of the Month
Lord, You are my light and my salvation; whom shall I fear? You are the stronghold of my life; of whom shall I be afraid? When evildoers assail me to eat up my flesh, my adversaries and foes, it is they who stumble and fall. Though an army encamp against me, my heart shall not fear; though war arise against me, yet I will be confident. One thing have I asked of You Lord, that will I seek after: that I may dwell in Your house all the days of my life, to gaze upon Your beauty and to inquire in Your temple. For You will hide me in Your shelter in the day of trouble; You will conceal me under the cover of Your tent; You will lift me high upon a rock *(Ps. 27:1-5)*.

VII. Collects from the Book of Common Prayer – Holy Days

184.   For the First Week of Advent
Almighty God, give us grace to cast away the works of darkness, and put on the armor of light, now in the time of this mortal life in which your Son Jesus Christ came to visit us in great humility; that in the last day, when he shall come again in his glorious majesty to judge both the living and the dead, we may rise to the life immortal. (Amen)

185.   For the Second Week of Advent
Merciful God, who sent your messengers the prophets to preach repentance and prepare the way for our salvation: Give us grace to heed their warnings and forsake our sins, that we may greet with joy the coming of Jesus Christ our Redeemer. (Amen)

186.   For the Third Week of Advent
Stir up your power, O Lord, and with great might come among us; and, because we are sorely hindered by our sins, let your bountiful grace and mercy speedily help and deliver us. (Amen)

187.   For the Fourth Week of Advent
Purify our conscience, Almighty God, by your daily visitation, that your Son Jesus Christ, at his coming, may find in us a mansion prepared for himself. (Amen)

188.   For Christmas Eve
O God, you have caused this holy night to shine with the brightness of the true Light: Grant that we, who have known the mystery of that Light on earth, may also enjoy him perfectly in heaven. (Amen)

189.   For Christmas Day
O God, you make us glad by the yearly festival of the birth of your only Son Jesus Christ: Grant that we, who joyfully receive

him as our Redeemer, may with sure confidence behold him
when he comes to be our Judge. (Amen)

or this

Almighty God, you have given your only-begotten Son to take
our nature upon him, and to be born this day of a pure virgin:
Grant that we, who have been born again and made your
children by adoption and grace, may daily be renewed by your
Holy Spirit. (Amen)

190. For the Week Following Christmas Day

Almighty God, you have poured upon us the new light of your
incarnate Word: Grant that this light, enkindled in our hearts,
may shine forth in our lives. (Amen)

191. For Palm Sunday

Almighty and everliving God, in your tender love for the
human race you sent your Son our Savior Jesus Christ to
take upon him our nature, and to suffer death upon the cross,
giving us the example of his great humility: Mercifully grant
that we may walk in the way of his suffering, and also share
in his resurrection. (Amen)

192. Passion Week

O God, who before the passion of your only-begotten Son
revealed his glory upon the holy mountain: Grant to us that
we, beholding by faith the light of his countenance, may be
strengthened to bear our cross, and be changed into his
likeness from glory to glory. (Amen)

193. For Good Friday

Almighty God, we pray you graciously to behold this your
family, for whom our Lord Jesus Christ was willing to be
betrayed, and given into the hands of sinners, and to suffer
death upon the cross. (Amen)

194. For Easter Day

O God, who for our redemption gave your only-begotten
Son to the death of the cross, and by his glorious resurrection
delivered us from the power of our enemy: Grant us so to die

daily to sin, that we may evermore live with him in the joy of his resurrection. (Amen)

or this
Almighty God, who through your only-begotten Son Jesus Christ overcame death and opened to us the gate of everlasting life: Grant that we, who celebrate with joy the day of the Lord's resurrection, may be raised from the death of sin by your life-giving Spirit. (Amen)

195. For the Week Following Easter
O God, who by the glorious resurrection of your Son Jesus Christ destroyed death and brought life and immortality to light: Grant that we, who have been raised with him, may abide in his presence and rejoice in the hope of eternal glory. (Amen)

196. Ascension Day
Almighty God, whose blessed Son our Savior Jesus Christ ascended far above all heavens that he might fill all things: Mercifully give us faith to perceive that, according to his promise, he abides with his Church on earth, even to the end of the ages. (Amen)

or this
Grant, we pray, Almighty God, that as we believe your only-begotten Son our Lord Jesus Christ to have ascended into heaven, so we may also in heart and mind there ascend, and with him continually dwell. (Amen)

197. The Day of Pentecost
Almighty God, on this day you opened the way of eternal life to every race and nation by the promised gift of your Holy Spirit: Shed abroad this gift throughout the world by the preaching of the Gospel, that it may reach to the ends of the earth. (Amen)

or this
O God, who on this day taught the hearts of your faithful people by sending to them the light of your Holy Spirit:

Grant us by the same Spirit to have a right judgment in all things, and evermore to rejoice in his holy comfort. (Amen)

VIII. Collects from the Book of Common Prayer – Regular Days

198. 1st Day of the Month
Remember, O Lord, what you have wrought in us and not what we deserve; and, as you have called us to your service, make us worthy of our calling. (Amen)

199. 2nd Day of the Month
Almighty and merciful God, in your goodness keep us, we pray, from all things that may hurt us, that we, being ready both in mind and body, may accomplish with free hearts those things which belong to your purpose. (Amen)

200. 3rd Day of the Month
Grant, O Lord, that the course of this world may be peaceably governed by your providence; and that your Church may joyfully serve you in confidence and serenity; through Jesus Christ. (Amen)

201. 4th Day of the Month
O God, your never-failing providence sets in order all things both in heaven and earth: Put away from us, we entreat you, all hurtful things, and give us those things which are profitable for us. (Amen)

202. 5th Day of the Month
O God, from whom all good proceeds: Grant that by your inspiration we may think those things that are right, and by your merciful guiding may do them. (Amen)

203. 6th Day of the Month
Keep, O Lord, your household the Church in your steadfast faith and love, that through your grace we may proclaim your truth with boldness, and minister your justice with compassion. (Amen)

204. 7th Day of the Month
O Lord, make us have perpetual love and reverence for your holy Name, for you never fail to help and govern those whom you have set upon the sure foundation of your loving-kindness. (Amen)

205. 8th Day of the Month
Almighty God, you have built your Church upon the foundation of the apostles and prophets, Jesus Christ himself being the chief cornerstone: Grant us so to be joined together in unity of spirit by their teaching, that we may be made a holy temple acceptable to you. (Amen)

206. 9th Day of the Month
O God, you have taught us to keep all your commandments by loving you and our neighbor: Grant us the grace of your Holy Spirit, that we may be devoted to you with our whole heart, and united to one another with pure affection. (Amen)

207. 10th Day of the Month
O Lord, mercifully receive the prayers of your people who call upon you, and grant that they may know and understand what things they ought to do, and also may have grace and power faithfully to accomplish them. (Amen)

208. 11th Day of the Month
Almighty God, the fountain of all wisdom, you know our necessities before we ask and our ignorance in asking: Have compassion on our weakness, and mercifully give us those things which for our unworthiness we dare not, and for our blindness we cannot ask. (Amen)

209. 12th Day of the Month
O God, the protector of all who trust in you, without whom nothing is strong, nothing is holy: Increase and multiply upon us your mercy; that, with you as our ruler and guide, we may so pass through things temporal, that we lose not the things eternal. (Amen)

210. 13th Day of the Month

Let your continual mercy, O Lord, cleanse and defend your Church; and, because it cannot continue in safety without your help, protect and govern it always by your goodness. (Amen)

211. 14th Day of the Month

Grant to us, Lord, we pray, the spirit to think and do always those things that are right, that we, who cannot exist without you, may by you be enabled to live according to your will. (Amen)

212. 15th Day of the Month

Almighty God, you have given your only Son to be for us a sacrifice for sin, and also an example of godly life: Give us grace to receive thankfully the fruits of his redeeming work, and to follow daily in the blessed steps of his most holy life. (Amen)

213. 16th Day of the Month

Grant, O merciful God, that your Church, being gathered together in unity by your Holy Spirit, may show forth your power among all peoples, to the glory of your Name. (Amen)

214. 17th Day of the Month

Lord of all power and might, the author and giver of all good things: Graft in our hearts the love of your Name; increase in us true religion; nourish us with all goodness; and bring forth in us the fruit of good works. (Amen)

215. 18th Day of the Month

Grant us, O Lord, to trust in you with all our hearts; for, as you always resist the proud who confide in their own strength, so you never forsake those who make their boast of your mercy. (Amen)

216. 19th Day of the Month

O God, because without you we are not able to please you, mercifully grant that your Holy Spirit may in all things direct and rule our hearts. (Amen)

217.   20th Day of the Month
Grant us, Lord, not to be anxious about earthly things, but to love things heavenly; and even now, while we are placed among things that are passing away, to hold fast to those that shall endure. (Amen)

218.   21st Day of the Month
O God, you declare your almighty power chiefly in showing mercy and pity: Grant us the fullness of your grace, that we, running to obtain your promises, may become partakers of your heavenly treasure. (Amen)

219.   22nd Day of the Month
Almighty and everlasting God, you are always more ready to hear than we to pray, and to give more than we either desire or deserve: Pour upon us the abundance of your mercy, forgiving us those things of which our conscience is afraid, and giving us those good things for which we are not worthy to ask, except through the merits and mediation of Jesus Christ our Savior. (Amen)

220.   23rd Day of the Month
Lord, we pray that your grace may always precede and follow us, that we may continually be given to good works. (Amen)

221.   24th Day of the Month
Almighty and everlasting God, in Christ you have revealed your glory among the nations: Preserve the works of your mercy, that your Church throughout the world may persevere with steadfast faith in the confession of your Name. (Amen)

222.   25th Day of the Month

Almighty and everlasting God, increase in us the gifts of faith, hope, and charity; and, that we may obtain what you promise, make us love what you command. (Amen)

223. 26th Day of the Month
Almighty and merciful God, it is only by your gift that your faithful people offer you true and laudable service: Grant that we may run without stumbling to obtain your heavenly promises. (Amen)

224. 27th Day of the Month
O God, whose blessed Son came into the world that he might destroy the works of the devil and make us children of God and heirs of eternal life: Grant that, having this hope, we may purify ourselves as he is pure; that, when he comes again with power and great glory, we may be made like him in his eternal and glorious kingdom. (Amen)

225. 28th Day of the Month
Blessed Lord, who caused all holy scriptures to be written for our learning: Grant us so to hear them, read, mark, learn, and inwardly digest them, that we may embrace and ever hold fast the blessed hope of everlasting life, which you have given us in our Savior Jesus Christ. (Amen)

226. 29th Day of the Month
Almighty and everlasting God, whose will it is to restore all things in your well-beloved Son, the King of kings and Lord of lords: Mercifully grant that the peoples of the earth, divided and enslaved by sin, may be freed and brought together under his most gracious rule. (Amen)

227. 30th Day of the Month
Set us free, O God, from the bondage of our sins, and give us the liberty of that abundant life which you have made known to us in your Son our Savior Jesus Christ. (Amen)

228. 31st Day of the Month
O God, the strength of all who put their trust in you: Mercifully accept our prayers; and because in our weakness

we can do nothing good without you, give us the help of your grace, that in keeping your commandments we may please you both in will and deed. (Amen)

IX. Collects from the Book of Common Prayer - Extra/Misc.

Use these collects at will, in place of, or in addition to, use of the daily collects.

---

229. Extra/Misc. 1
O Lord, you have taught us that without love whatever we do is worth nothing; Send your Holy Spirit and pour into our hearts your greatest gift, which is love, the true bond of peace and of all virtue, without which whoever lives is accounted dead before you. (Amen)

230. Extra/Misc. 2
Most loving Father, whose will it is for us to give thanks for all things, to fear nothing but the loss of you, and to cast all our care on you who care for us: Preserve us from faithless fears and worldly anxieties, that no clouds of this mortal life may hide from us the light of that love which is immortal, and which you have manifested to us in your Son. (Amen)

231. Extra/Misc. 3
Almighty God, whose blessed Son was led by the Spirit to be tempted by Satan: Come quickly to help us who are assaulted by many temptations; and, as you know the weaknesses of each of us, let each one find you mighty to save. (Amen)

232. Extra/Misc. 4
O God, whose glory it is always to have mercy: Be gracious to all who have gone astray from your ways, and bring them again with repentant hearts and steadfast faith to embrace and hold fast the unchangeable truth of your Word. (Amen)

233. Extra/Misc. 5

Almighty God, you know that we have no power in ourselves to help ourselves: Keep us both outwardly in our bodies and inwardly in our souls, that we may be defended from all adversities which may happen to the body, and from all evil thoughts which may assault and hurt the soul. (Amen)

234. Extra/Misc. 6

Almighty God, you alone can bring into order the unruly wills and affections of sinners: Grant your people grace to love what you command and desire what you promise; that, among the swift and varied changes of the world, our hearts may surely there be fixed where true joys are to be found. (Amen)

235. Extra/Misc. 7

We thank you, heavenly Father, that you have delivered us from the dominion of sin and death and brought us into the kingdom of your Son; and we pray that, as by his death he has recalled us to life, so by his love he may raise us to eternal joys. (Amen)

236. Extra/Misc. 8

Almighty and everlasting God, who in the Paschal mystery established the new covenant of reconciliation: Grant that all who have been reborn into the fellowship of Christ's Body may show forth in their lives what they profess by their faith. (Amen)

237. Extra/Misc. 9

O God, whose blessed Son made himself known to his disciples in the breaking of bread: Open the eyes of our faith, that we may behold him in all his redeeming work. (Amen)

238. Extra/Misc. 10

O God, whose Son Jesus is the good shepherd of your people; Grant that when we hear his voice we may know him who calls us each by name, and follow where he leads. (Amen)

239. Extra/Misc. 11

Almighty God, whom truly to know is everlasting life: Grant us so perfectly to know your Son Jesus Christ to be the way, the truth, and the life, that we may steadfastly follow his steps in the way that leads to eternal life. (Amen)

240. Extra/Misc. 12

O God, you have prepared for those who love you such good things as surpass our understanding: Pour into our hearts such love towards you, that we, loving you in all things and above all things, may obtain your promises, which exceed all that we can desire. (Amen)

241. Extra/Misc. 13

O God, the King of glory, you have exalted your only Son Jesus Christ with great triumph to your kingdom in heaven: Do not leave us comfortless, but send us your Holy Spirit to strengthen us, and exalt us to that place where our Savior Christ has gone before. (Amen)

242. Extra/Misc. 14

Almighty and everlasting God, you have given to us your servants grace, by the confession of a true faith, to acknowledge the glory of the eternal Trinity, and in the power of your divine Majesty to worship the Unity: Keep us steadfast in this faith and worship, and bring us at last to see you in your one and eternal glory, O Father. (Amen)

X. Self-Benedictions

243. *The Priestly Blessing*
Lord, Bless me and keep me; Lord, make Your face to shine upon me and be gracious to me; LORD, lift up Your countenance upon me and give me peace (Nu. 6:24 & 25). **(In the Name of Jesus, Amen)**

244. *The 1st Thessalonian Blessing*
Now may the God of peace Himself sanctify me completely, and may my whole spirit and soul and body be kept blameless at the coming of the Lord Jesus Christ *(1 Th. 5:23)*. **(In the Name of Jesus, Amen)**

245. *The Corinthian Blessing:*
The grace of the Lord Jesus Christ and the love of God and the fellowship of the Holy Spirit be with me. **(In the Name of Jesus, Amen)**

246. *The Roman Blessing:*
May the God of hope fill me with all joy and peace in believing, so that by the power of the Holy Spirit I may abound in hope *(Ro. 15:13)*. **(In the Name of Jesus, Amen)**

247. *The 2nd Thessalonian Blessing*
May the Lord direct my heart to the love of God and to the steadfastness of Christ *(2 Th. 3:5)*. **(In the Name of Jesus, Amen)**

248. *The Ephesian Blessing:*
(Glory) to (You, God), Who is able to do far more abundantly than all that (I) ask or think, according to the power at work within me, to (You, Lord) be glory in the church and in Christ Jesus throughout all generations, forever and ever (Eph 3:20-21). **(In the Name of Jesus, Amen)**

249. *The 3rd Thessalonian Blessing*

May the Lord of peace Himself give me peace at all times in every way. The Lord be with me *(2 Thessalonians 3:16)*. **(In the Name of Jesus, Amen)**

XI. Group-Benedictions

250. *The Priestly Blessing*
The Lord bless you and keep you; may the Lord make His face to shine upon you and be gracious to you; may the Lord lift up His countenance upon you and give you peace" *(Nu. 6:24-26)*. (In the Name of Jesus, Amen)

251. *The 1st Thessalonian Blessing*
Now may the God of peace Himself sanctify you completely, and may your whole spirit and soul and body be kept blameless at the coming of our Lord Jesus Christ *(1 Th. 5:23)*. (In the Name of Jesus, Amen)

252. *The Corinthian Blessing:*
May the grace of the Lord Jesus Christ and the love of God and the fellowship of the Holy Spirit be with you all *(2 Co. 13:14)*. (In the Name of Jesus, Amen)

253. *The Roman Blessing:*
May the God of hope fill you with all joy and peace in believing, so that by the power of the Holy Spirit you may abound in hope *(Ro. 15:13)*. (In the Name of Jesus, Amen)

254. *The 2nd Thessalonian Blessing*
May the Lord direct your hearts to the love of God and to the steadfastness of Christ *(2 Th. 3:5)*. (In the Name of Jesus, Amen)

255. *The Ephesian Blessing:*
Now to Him who is able to do far more abundantly than all that we ask or think, according to the power at work within us, to Him be glory in the church and in Christ Jesus throughout all generations, forever and ever. Amen *(Ephesians 3:20-21)*. (In the Name of Jesus, Amen)

256. *The 3rd Thessalonian Blessing*
May the Lord of peace Himself give you peace at all times in every way. The Lord be with you all *(2 Thessalonians 3:16)*. (In the Name of Jesus, Amen)

XII. Bible Reading *(2-year plan)*

Year 1

January

1 Ge 1; John 1
2 Ge 2; John 2
3 Ge 3; John 3
4 Ge 4; John 4
5 Ge 5; John 5
6 Ge 6; John 6
7 Ge 7; John 7
8 Ge 8; John 8
9 Ge 9; John 9
10 Ge 10; John 10
11 Ge 11; John 11
12 Ge 12; John 12
13 Ge 13; John 13
14 Ge 14; John 14
15 Ge 15; John 15
16 Ge 16; John 16
17 Ge 17; John 17
18 Ge 18; John 18
19 Ge 19; John 19
20 Ge 20; John 20
21 Ge 21; John 21
22 Ge 22; Romans 1
23 Ge 23; Romans 2
24 Ge 24; Romans 3
25 Ge 25; Romans 4
26 Ge 26; Romans 5
27 Ge 27; Romans 6
28 Ge 28; Romans 7
29 Ge 29; Romans 8
30 Ge 30; Romans 9
31 Ge 31; Romans 10

February

1 Ge 32; Romans 11
2 Ge 33; Romans 12
3 Ge 34; Romans 13
4 Ge 35; Romans 14
5 Ge 36; Romans 15
6 Ge 37; Romans 16
7 Ge 38; Catch Up
8 Ge 39; Luke 1
9 Ge 40; Luke 2
10 Ge 41; Luke 3
11 Ge 42; Luke 4
12 Ge 43; Luke 5
13 Ge 44; Luke 6
14 Ge 45; Luke 7
15 Ge 46; Luke 8
16 Ge 47; Luke 9
17 Ge 48; Luke 10
18 Ge 49; Luke 11
19 Ge 50; Luke 12
20 Catch Up; Luke 13
21 Ex 1-2; Luke 14
22 Ex 3; Luke 15
23 Ex 4; Luke 16
24 Ex 5; Luke 17
25 Ex 6; Luke 18
26 Ex 7; Luke 19
27 Ex 8; Luke 20
28 Ex 9; Luke 21

March

1 Ex 10; Luke 22
2 Ex 11; Luke 23
3 Ex 12; Luke 24
4 Ex 13; Acts 1
5 Ex 14; Acts 2
6 Ex 15; Acts 3
7 Ex 16; Acts 4
8 Ex 17; Acts 5
9 Ex 18; Acts 6
10 Ex 19-20; Acts 7
11 Ex 21; Acts 8
12 Ex 22; Acts 9
13 Ex 23; Acts 10
14 Ex 24; Acts 11
15 Ex 25; Acts 12
16 Ex 26; Acts 13
17 Ex 27; Acts 14
18 Ex 28; Acts 15
19 Ex 29; Acts 16
20 Ex 30; Acts 17
21 Ex 31; Acts 18
22 Ex 32; Acts 19
23 Ex 33; Acts 20
24 Ex 34; Acts 21

25 Ex 35; Acts 22
26 Ex 36; Acts 23
27 Ex 37; Acts 24
28 Ex 38; Acts 25
29 Ex 39; Acts 26
30 Ex 40; Acts 27
31 Catch Up; Ac 28

April

1 Le 1; Catch Up
2 Le 2; Matt 1
3 Le 3; Matt 2
4 Le 4; Matt 3
5 Le 5; Matt 4
6 Le 6; Matt 5
7 Le 7; Matt 6
8 Le 8; Matt 7
9 Le 9; Matt 8
10 Le 10; Matt 9
11 Le 11; Matt 10
12 Le 12; Matt 11
13 Le 13; Matt 12
14 Le 14; Matt 13
15 Le 15; Matt 14
16 Le 16; Matt 15
17 Le 17; Matt 16
18 Le 18; Matt 17
19 Le 19; Matt 18
20 Le 20; Matt 19
21 Le 21; Matt 20
22 Le 22; Matt 21
23 Le 23; Matt 22
24 Le 24; Matt 23
25 Le 25; Matt 24
26 Le 26; Matt 25
27 Le 27; Matt 26
28 Catch Up; Matt 27
29 Nu 1; Matt 28
30 Nu 2; Hebrews 1

May

1 Nu 3; Hebrews 2
2 Nu 4; Hebrews 3
3 Nu 5; Hebrews 4
4 Nu 6; Hebrews 5
5 Nu 7; Hebrews 6
6 Nu 8; Hebrews 7
7 Nu 9; Hebrews 8
8 Nu 10; Hebrews 9
9 Nu 11; Hebrews 10
10 Nu 12; Hebrews 11
11 Nu 13; Hebrews 12
12 Nu 14; Hebrews 13
13 Nu 15; Catch Up
14 Nu 16; Mark 1
15 Nu 17; Mark 2
16 Nu 18; Mark 3
17 Nu 19; Mark 4
18 Nu 20; Mark 5
19 Nu 21; Mark 6
20 Nu 22; Mark 7
21 Nu 23; Mark 8
22 Nu 24; Mark 9
23 Nu 25; Mark 10
24 Nu 26; Mark 11
25 Nu 27; Mark 12
26 Nu 28; Mark 13
27 Nu 29; Mark 14
28 Nu 30; Mark 15
29 Nu 31; Mark 16
30 Nu 32; 1 Cor 1
31 Nu 33; 1 Cor 2

June

1 Nu 34; 1 Cor 3
2 Nu 35; 1 Cor 4
3 Nu 36; 1 Cor 5
4 Catch Up; 1 Cor 6
5 Dt 1; 1 Cor 7
6 Dt 2; 1 Cor 8
7 Dt 3; 1 Cor 9
8 Dt 4; 1 Cor 10
9 Dt 5; 1 Cor 11
10 Dt 6; 1 Cor 12

11 Dt 7; 1 Cor 13
12 Dt 8-9; 1 Cor 14
13 Dt 10; 1 Cor 15
14 Dt 11; 1 Cor 16
15 Dt 12; 2 Cor 1
16 Dt 13; 2 Cor 2
17 Dt 14; 2 Cor 3
18 Dt 15; 2 Cor 4
19 Dt 16; 2 Cor 5
20 Dt 17; 2 Cor 6
21 Dt 18; 2 Cor 7
22 Dt 19; 2 Cor 8
23 Dt 20; 2 Cor 9
24 Dt 21; 2 Cor 10
25 Dt 22; 2 Cor 11
26 Dt 23; 2 Cor 12
27 Dt 24; 2 Cor 13
28 Dt 25; Catch Up
29 Dt 26; Gal 1
30 Dt 27; Gal 2

July

1 Dt 28; Gal 3
2 Dt 29; Gal 4
3 Dt 30; Gal 5
4 Dt 31; Gal 6
5 Dt 32; Eph 1
6 Dt 33; Eph 2
7 Dt 34; Eph 3
8 Jsh 1-2; Eph 4
9 Jsh 3; Eph 5
10 Jsh 4; Eph 6
11 Jsh 5; Catch Up
12 Jsh 6; Phil 1
13 Jsh 7; Phil 2
14 Jsh 8; Phil 3
15 Jsh 9; Phil 4
16 Jsh 10; Col 1
17 Jsh 11; Col 2
18 Jsh 12; Col 3
19 Jsh 13; Col 4
20 Jsh 14; Catch Up

21 Jsh 15; 1 Thess 1
22 Jsh 16; 1 Thess 2
23 Jsh 17; 1 Thess 3
24 Jsh 18; 1 Thess 4
25 Jsh 19; 1 Thess 5
26 Jsh 20; 2 Thess 1
27 Jsh 21; 2 Thess 2
28 Jsh 22; 2 Thess 3
29 Jsh 23; Catch Up
30 Jsh 24; 1Tim 1
31 Jdg 1-2; 1 Tim 2

August

1 Jdg 3; 1 Tim 3
2 Jdg 4; 1 Tim 4
3 Jdg 5; 1 Tim 5
4 Jdg 6; 1 Tim 6
5 Jdg 7; 2 Tim 1
6 Jdg 8; 2 Tim 2
7 Jdg 9; 2 Tim 3
8 Jdg 10; 2 Tim 4
9 Jdg 11; Catch Up
10 Jdg 12; Titus 1
11 Jdg 13; Titus 2
12 Jdg 14; Titus 3
13 Jdg 15; Philemon
14 Jdg 16; James 1
15 Jdg 17; James 2
16 Jdg 18; James 3
17 Jdg 19; James 4
18 Jdg 20; James 5
19 Jdg 21; Catch Up
20 Ruth 1-2; 1 Peter 1
21 Ruth 3-4; 1 Peter 2
22 Catch Up; 1 Peter 3
23 1Sa 1; 1 Peter 4
24 1Sa 2; 1 Peter 5
25 1Sa 3; 2 Peter 1
26 1Sa 4; 2 Peter 2
27 1Sa 5; 2 Peter 3
28 1Sa 6; Catch Up
29 1Sa 7; 1 John 1

30 1Sa 8; 1 John 2
31 1Sa 9; 1 John 3

September
1 1Sa 10; 1 John 4
2 1Sa 11; 1 John 5
3 1Sa 12; 2 John
4 1Sa 13; 3 John
5 1Sa 14; Jude
6 1Sa 15; Rev 1
7 1Sa 16; Rev 2
8 1Sa 17; Rev 3
9 1Sa 18; Rev 4
10 1Sa 19; Rev 5
11 1 Sam 20; Rev 6
12 1 Sam 21; Rev 7
13 1 Sam 22; Rev 8
14 1 Sam 23; Rev 9
15 1 Sam 24; Rev 10
16 1 Sam 25; Rev 11
17 1 Sam 26; Rev 12
18 1 Sam 27; Rev 13
19 1 Sam 28; Rev 14
20 1 Sam 29; Rev 15
21 1 Sam 30; Rev 16
22 1 Sam 31; Rev 17
23 Catch Up; Rev 18
24 2 Sam 1; Rev 19
25 2 Sam 2; Rev 20
26 2 Sam 3-4; Rev 21
27 2 Sam 5; Rev 22
28 2 Sam 6; Catch Up
29 2 Sam 7; Psalm 1
30 2 Sam 8; Psalm 2

October
1 2 Sam 9; Psalm 3
2 2 Sam 10; Psalm 4
3 2 Sam 11-12; Psalm 5
4 2 Sam 13; Psalm 6
5 2 Sam 14; Psalm 7
6 2 Sam 15; Psalm 8
7 2 Sam 16; Psalm 9
8 2 Sam 17; Psalm 10
9 2 Sam 18; Psalm 11
10 2 Sam 19; Psalm 12
11 2 Sam 20; Psalm 13
12 2 Sam 21; Psalm 14
13 2 Sam 22; Psalm 15
14 2 Sam 23; Psalm 16
15 2 Sam 24; Psalm 17
16 Catch Up; Psalm 18
17 1Ki 1; Psalm 19
18 1Ki 2; Psalm 20
19 1Ki 3; Psalm 21
20 1Ki 4; Psalm 22
21 1Ki 5; Psalm 23
22 1Ki 6; Psalm 24
23 1Ki 7; Psalm 25
24 1Ki 8; Psalm 26
25 1Ki 9; Psalm 27
26 1Ki 10; Psalm 28
27 1Ki 11; Psalm 29
28 1Ki 12; Psalm 30
29 1Ki 13; Psalm 31
30 1Ki 14; Psalm 32
31 1Ki 15; Psalm 33

November
1 1Ki 16-17; Psalm 34
2 1Ki 18; Psalm 35
3 1Ki 19; Psalm 36
4 1Ki 20; Psalm 37
5 1Ki 21; Psalm 38
6 1Ki 22; Psalm 39
7 Catch Up; Psalm 40
8 2Ki 1; Psalm 41
9 2Ki 2; Psalm 42
10 2Ki 3; Psalm 43
11 2Ki 4; Psalm 44
12 2Ki 5; Psalm 45
13 2Ki 6; Psalm 46
14 2Ki 7; Psalm 47
15 2Ki 8; Psalm 48

16 2Ki 9; Psalm 49
17 2Ki 10; Psalm 50
18 2Ki 11; Psalm 51
19 2Ki 12; Psalm 52
20 2Ki 13; Psalm 53
21 2Ki 14; Psalm 54
22 2Ki 15; Psalm 55
23 2Ki 16; Psalm 56
24 2Ki 17; Psalm 57
25 2Ki 18; Psalm 58
26 2Ki 19; Psalm 59
27 2Ki 20; Psalm 60
28 2Ki 21; Psalm 61
29 2Ki 22; Psalm 62
30 2Ki 23; Psalm 63

December

1 2Ki 24; Psalm 64
2 2Ki 25; Psalm 65
3 Catch Up; Psalm 66
4 1 Chr 1; Psalm 67
5 1 Chr 2; Psalm 68
6 1 Chr 3; Psalm 69
7 1 Chr 4; Psalm 70
8 1 Chr 5; Psalm 71
9 1 Chr 6; Psalm 72
10 1 Chr 7; Psalm 73
11 1 Chr 8; Psalm 74
12 1 Chr 9; Psalm 75
13 1 Chr 10; Psalm 76
14 1 Chr 11; Psalm 77
15 1 Chr 12; Psalm 78
16 1 Chr 13; Psalm 79
17 1 Chr 14; Psalm 80
18 1 Chr 15; Psalm 81
19 1 Chr 16; Psalm 82
20 1 Chr 17; Psalm 83
21 1 Chr 18; Psalm 84
22 1 Chr 19; Psalm 85
23 1 Chr 20; Psalm 86
24 1 Chr 21; Psalm 87
25 1 Chr 22; Psalm 88

26 1 Chr 23; Psalm 89
27 1 Chr 24; Psalm 90
28 1 Chr 25; Psalm 91
29 1 Chr 26; Psalm 92
30 1 Chr 27; Psalm 93
31 1 Chr 28-29; Ps. 94

Year 2

January
1 Catch Up; Psalm 95
2 2 Chr. 1; Psalm 96
3 2 Chr. 2; Psalm 97
4 2 Chr. 3; Psalm 98
5 2 Chr. 4; Psalm 99
6 2 Chr. 5; Psalm 100
7 2 Chr. 6; Psalm 101
8 2 Chr. 7; Psalm 102
9 2 Chr. 8; Psalm 103
10 2 Chr. 9; Psalm 104
11 2 Chr. 10; Psalm 105
12 2 Chr. 11; Psalm 106
13 2 Chr. 12; Psalm 107
14 2 Chr. 13; Psalm 108
15 2 Chr. 14; Psalm 109
16 2 Chr. 15; Psalm 110
17 2 Chr. 16; Psalm 111
18 2 Chr. 17; Psalm 112
19 2 Chr. 18; Psalm 113
20 2 Chr. 19; Psalm 114
21 2 Chr. 20; Psalm 115
22 2 Chr. 21; Psalm 116-17
23 2 Chr. 22; Psalm 118
24 2 Chr. 23; Ps. 119:1-40
25 2 Chr. 24; Ps. 119:41-88
26 2 Chr. 25; Ps 119:89-144
27 2 Chr. 26; Ps 119:145-170
28 2 Chr. 27; Psalm 120
29 2 Chr. 28; Psalm 121
30 2 Chr. 29; Psalm 122
31 2 Chr. 30; Psalm 123

February
1 2 Chr. 31; Psalm 124
2 2 Chr. 32; Psalm 125
3 2 Chr. 33; Psalm 126
4 2 Chr. 34; Psalm 127
5 2 Chr. 35; Psalm 128
6 2 Chr. 36; Psalm 129
7 Catch Up; Psalm 130
8 Ezra 1; Psalm 131
9 Ezra 2; Psalm 132
10 Ezra 3; Psalm 133
11 Ezra 4; Psalm 134
12 Ezra 5; Psalm 135
13 Ezra 6; Psalm 136
14 Ezra 7; Psalm 137
15 Ezra 8; Psalm 138
16 Ezra 9; Psalm 139
17 Ezra 10; Psalm 140
18 Neh. 1; Psalm 141
19 Neh. 2; Psalm 142
20 Neh. 3; Psalm 143
21 Neh. 4; Psalm 144
22 Neh. 5; Psalm 145
23 Neh. 6; Psalm 146
24 Neh. 7; Psalm 147
25 Neh. 8; Psalm 148
26 Neh. 9; Psalm 149
27 Neh. 10; Psalm 150
28 Neh. 11; Catch Up

March
1 Neh. 12; Prov. 1
2 Neh. 13; Prov. 2
3 Esther 1; Prov. 3
4 Esther 2; Prov. 4
5 Esther 3; Prov. 5
6 Esther 4; Prov. 6
7 Esther 5; Prov. 7
8 Esther 6; Prov. 8
9 Esther 7; Prov. 9
10 Esther 8; Prov. 10
11 Esther 9; Prov. 11
12 Esther 10; Prov. 12
13 Catch Up; Prov. 13
14 Job 1; Prov. 14
15 Job 2; Prov. 15
16 Job 3; Prov. 16
17 Job 4; Prov. 17
18 Job 5; Prov. 18
19 Job 6; Prov. 19
20 Job 7; Prov. 20
21 Job 8; Prov. 21
22 Job 9; Prov. 22
23 Job 10; Prov. 23
24 Job 11; Prov. 24

25 Job 12; Prov. 25
26 Job 13; Prov. 26
27 Job 14; Prov. 27
28 Job 15; Prov. 28
29 Job 16; Prov. 29
30 Job 17; Prov. 30
31 Job 18; Prov. 31

April

1 Job 19; Eccl. 1
2 Job 20; Eccl. 2
3 Job 21; Eccl. 3
4 Job 22; Eccl. 4
5 Job 23; Eccl. 5
6 Job 24; Eccl. 6
7 Job 25; Eccl. 7
8 Job 26; Eccl. 8
9 Job 27; Eccl. 9
10 Job 28; Eccl. 10
11 Job 29; Eccl. 11
12 Job 30; Eccl. 12
13 Job 31; Matt. 1
14 Job 32; Matt. 2
15 Job 33; Matt. 3
16 Job 34; Matt. 4
17 Job 35; Matt. 5
18 Job 36; Matt. 6
19 Job 37; Matt. 7
20 Job 38; Matt. 8
21 Job 39; Matt. 9
22 Job 40; Matt. 10
23 Job 41; Matt. 11
24 Job 42; Matt. 12
25 Catch Up; Matt. 13
26 Song 1; Matt. 14
27 Song 2; Matt. 15
28 Song 3; Matt. 16
29 Song 4; Matt. 17
30 Song 5; Matt. 18

May

1 Song 6; Matt. 19

2 Song 7; Matt. 20
3 Song 8; Matt. 21
4 Isaiah 1; Matt. 22
5 Isaiah 2; Matt. 23
6 Isaiah 3; Matt. 24
7 Isaiah 4; Matt. 25
8 Isaiah 5; Matt. 26
9 Isaiah 6; Matt. 27
10 Isaiah 7; Matt. 28
11 Isaiah 8; Catch Up
12 Isaiah 9; Mark 1
13 Isaiah 10; Mark 2
14 Isaiah 11; Mark 3
15 Isaiah 12; Mark 4
16 Isaiah 13; Mark 5
17 Isaiah 14; Mark 6
18 Isaiah 15; Mark 7
19 Isaiah 16; Mark 8
20 Isaiah 17; Mark 9
21 Isaiah 18; Mark 10
22 Isaiah 19; Mark 11
23 Isaiah 20; Mark 12
24 Isaiah 21; Mark 13
25 Isaiah 22; Mark 14
26 Isaiah 23; Mark 15
27 Isaiah 24; Mark 16
28 Isaiah 25; Luke 1
29 Isaiah 26; Luke 2
30 Isaiah 27; Luke 3
Isaiah 28; Luke 4

June

1 Isaiah 29; Luke 5
2 Isaiah 30; Luke 6
3 Isaiah 31; Luke 7
4 Isaiah 32; Luke 8
5 Isaiah 33; Luke 9
6 Isaiah 34; Luke 10
7 Isaiah 35; Luke 11
8 Isaiah 36; Luke 12
9 Isaiah 37; Luke 13
10 Isaiah 38; Luke 14

11 Isaiah 39; Luke 15
12 Isaiah 40; Luke 16
13 Isaiah 41; Luke 17
14 Isaiah 42; Luke 18
15 Isaiah 43; Luke 19
16 Isaiah 44; Luke 20
17 Isaiah 45; Luke 21
18 Isaiah 46; Luke 22
19 Isaiah 47; Luke 23
20 Isaiah 48; Luke 24
21 Isaiah 49; Catch Up
22 Isaiah 50; John 1
23 Isaiah 51; John 2
24 Isaiah 52; John 3
25 Isaiah 53; John 4
26 Isaiah 54; John 5
27 Isaiah 55; John 6
28 Isaiah 56; John 7
29 Isaiah 57; John 8
30 Isaiah 58; John 9

July
1 Isaiah 59; John 10
2 Isaiah 60; John 11
3 Isaiah 61; John 12
4 Isaiah 62; John 13
5 Isaiah 63; John 14
6 Isaiah 64; John 15
7 Isaiah 65; John 16
8 Isaiah 66; John 17
9 Catch Up; John 18
10 Jer. 1-2; John 19
11 Jer. 3; John 20
12 Jer. 4; John 21
13 Jer. 5; Catch Up
14 Jer. 6; Acts 1
15 Jer. 7; Acts 2
16 Jer. 8; Acts 3
17 Jer. 9; Acts 4
18 Jer. 10; Acts 5
19 Jer. 11; Acts 6
20 Jer. 12; Acts 7
21 Jer. 13; Acts 8

22 Jer. 14; Acts 9
23 Jer. 15; Acts 10
24 Jer. 16; Acts 11
25 Jer. 17; Acts 12
26 Jer. 18; Acts 13
27 Jer. 19; Acts 14
28 Jer. 20-21; Acts 15
29 Jer. 22; Acts 16
30 Jer. 23; Acts 17
31 Jer. 24; Acts 18

August
1 Jer. 25; Acts 19
2 Jer. 26; Acts 20
3 Jer. 27; Acts 21
4 Jer. 28; Acts 22
5 Jer. 29; Acts 23
6 Jer. 30; Acts 24
7 Jer. 31; Acts 25
8 Jer. 32; Acts 26
9 Jer. 33; Acts 27
10 Jer. 34; Acts 28
11 Jer. 35; Catch Up
12 Jer. 36; Romans 1
13 Jer. 37; Romans 2
14 Jer. 38; Romans 3
15 Jer. 39; Romans 4
16 Jer. 40; Romans 5
17 Jer. 41; Romans 6
18 Jer. 42-43; Rom. 7
19 Jer. 44; Romans 8
20 Jer. 45; Romans 9
21 Jer. 46; Rom. 10
22 Jer. 47; Rom. 11
23 Jer. 48; Rom. 12
24 Jer. 49; Rom. 13
25 Jer. 50; Rom. 14
26 Jer. 51; Rom. 15
27 Jer. 52; Rom. 16
28 Catch Up; 1 Cor. 1
29 Lam. 1; 1 Cor. 2
30 Lam. 2; 1 Cor. 3

31 Lam. 3; 1 Cor. 4

September
1 Lam. 4; 1 Cor. 5
2 Lam. 5; 1 Cor. 6
3 Ezek. 1; 1 Cor. 7
4 Ezek. 2; 1 Cor. 8
5 Ezek. 3; 1 Cor. 9
6 Ezek. 4; 1 Cor. 10
7 Ezek. 5; 1 Cor. 11
8 Ezek. 6; 1 Cor. 12
9 Ezek. 7; 1 Cor. 13
10 Ezek. 8; 1 Cor. 14
11 Ezek. 9; 1 Cor. 15
12 Ezek. 10; 1 Cor. 16
13 Ezek. 11; Catch Up
14 Ezek. 12; 2 Cor. 1
15 Ezek. 13; 2 Cor. 2
16 Ezek. 14; 2 Cor. 3
17 Ezek. 15; 2 Cor. 4
18 Ezek. 16; 2 Cor. 5
19 Ezek. 17; 2 Cor. 6
20 Ezek. 18; 2 Cor. 7
21 Ezek. 19; 2 Cor. 8
22 Ezek. 20; 2 Cor. 9
23 Ezek. 21; 2 Cor. 10
24 Ezek. 22; 2 Cor. 11
25 Ezek. 23; 2 Cor. 12
26 Ezek. 24; 2 Cor. 13
27 Ezek. 25; Gal. 1
28 Ezek. 26; Gal. 2
29 Ezek. 27; Gal. 3
30 Ezek. 28; Gal. 4

October
1 Ezek. 29; Gal. 5
2 Ezek. 30; Gal. 6
3 Ezek. 31; Eph. 1
4 Ezek. 32; Eph. 2
5 Ezek. 33; Eph. 3
6 Ezek. 34; Eph. 4
7 Ezek. 35; Eph. 5
8 Ezek. 36; Eph. 6
9 Ezek. 37; Phil. 1
10 Ezek. 38; Phil. 2
11 Ezek. 39; Phil. 3
12 Ezek. 40; Phil. 4
13 Ezek. 41; Col. 1
14 Ezek. 42; Col. 2
15 Ezek. 43; Col. 3
16 Ezek. 44; Col. 4
17 Ezek. 45; 1 Thess. 1
18 Ezek. 46; 1 Thess. 2
19 Ezek. 47; 1 Thess. 3
20 Ezek. 48; 1 Thess. 4
21 Catch Up; 1 Thess. 5
22 Daniel 1; Catch Up
23 Daniel 2; 2 Thess. 1
24 Daniel 3; 2 Thess. 2
25 Daniel 4; 2 Thess. 3
26 Daniel 5; 1 Tim. 1
27 Daniel 6; 1 Tim. 2-3
28 Daniel 7; 1 Tim. 4
29 Daniel 8; 1 Tim. 5
30 Daniel 9; 1 Tim. 6
31 Daniel 10; 2 Tim. 1

November
1 Daniel 11; 2 Tim. 2
2 Daniel 12; 2 Tim. 3
3 Hosea 1; 2 Tim. 4
4 Hosea 2; Titus 1
5 Hosea 3-4; Titus 2
6 Hosea 5; Titus 3
7 Hosea 6; Philemon 1
8 Hosea 7; Hebrews 1
9 Hosea 8; Hebrews 2
10 Hosea 9; Hebrews 3
11 Hosea 10; Hebrews 4
12 Hosea 11; Hebrews 5
13 Hosea 12; Hebrews 6
14 Hosea 13; Hebrews 7
15 Hosea 14; Hebrews 8
16 Joel 1; Hebrews 9

17 Joel 2; Hebrews 10
18 Joel 3; Hebrews 11
19 Amos 1; Hebrews 12
20 Amos 2; Hebrews 13
21 Amos 3; Catch Up
22 Amos 4; James 1
23 Amos 5; James 2
24 Amos 6; James 3
25 Amos 7; James 4
26 Amos 8; James 5
27 Amos 9; 1 Peter 1
28 Catch Up; 1 Peter 2
29 Obadiah 1; 1 Peter 3
30 Jonah 1-2; 1 Peter 4

December
1 Jonah 3-4; 1 Peter 5
2 Micah 1-2; 2 Peter 1
3 Micah 3-4; 2 Peter 2
4 Micah 5; 2 Peter 3
5 Micah 6; 1 John 1
6 Micah 7; 1 John 2
7 Nahum 1-2; 1 John 3
8 Nahum 3; 1 John 4
9 Catch Up; 1 John 5
10 Hab. 1; 2 & 3 John
11 Hab. 2; Jude
12 Hab. 3; Rev. 1
13 Zeph. 1; Rev. 2
14 Zeph. 2; Rev. 3
15 Zeph. 3; Rev. 4-5
16 Haggai 1-2; Rev. 6
17 Zech. 1-2; Rev. 7
18 Zech. 3-4; Rev. 8-9
19 Zech. 5-6; Rev. 10
20 Zech. 7; Rev. 11
21 Zech. 8; Rev. 12
22 Zech. 9; Rev. 13
23 Zech. 10; Rev. 14
24 Zech. 11; Rev. 15
25 Zech. 12; Rev. 16
26 Zech. 13; Rev. 17

27 Zech. 14; Rev. 18
28 Mal 1; Rev. 19
29 Mal 2; Rev. 20
30 Mal 3; Rev. 21
31 Mal 4; Rev. 22

XIII. Daily Prayer Sessions

Daily Morning Session 1

For Spouses with Child(ren)

* *If you have not already prayed* **Waking Gratitude (1)**, *do so now.*

For Confession

Loving and merciful God, be gracious to me and hear my prayer *(Ps. 4:1)*. **I acknowledge my sins and iniquities and do not hide them** *(Ps. 32:5)*. **I confess that I have sinned against You in thought, word, and deed, by what I have done, and by what I have left undone** *(BOCP)*. **[State sins] Father, forgive me of my sins, and cleanse me from all my unrighteousness** *(1 Jn. 1:9)*. **Wash me thoroughly and I shall be whiter than snow** *(Ps. 51:7)*, **through the blood of Your Son** *(Re. 7:14)*. **(Amen)**

For My Time in God's Word

God of all truth, Your Word is lamp to my feet and a light to my path *(Ps. 119:105)*. **It is breathed out by You and profitable for my learning, correction, and training in righteousness** *(2 Ti. 3:16)*. **Teach me, that I may walk in Your truth** *(Ps. 86:11)*. **Teach me to do Your will, for You are my God** *(Ps. 143:10)*. **Give me knowledge, understanding, discretion, and wisdom** *(Pr. 2:6; 8:12)*. **And bless me as I store up Your Word in my heart, that I might not sin against you** *(Ps. 119:11)*. **(Amen)**

Bible Reading

Go to Section ***XII***, find by date, and read your daily Bible passages.

Devotions

Go to Section ***XIV***, find by date, and read your daily devotions. Or substitute with the devotional of your choice.

Praises

Go to Section **VI**, find by date, and read your daily Praises.

For My Morning

God Most High, Possessor of Heaven and Earth *(Ge. 14:22)*, **this morning, my prayer comes before You** *(Ps. 88:13)*. **You have said, "Seek my face." So, my heart says to You, "Your face, LORD, do I seek** *(Ps. 27:8)*.**" That I may know You** *(Ex. 33:13)*, **and keep Your Word** *(Ps. 119:101)*. **That I may serve You this day with gladness** *(Ps. 100:2)*. **For You are God, You made me, and I am Yours** *(Ps. 100:3)*. **In You, I live, move, and have my being** *(Ac. 17:28)*. **And through Your Son, Jesus, I have obtained Salvation** *(He. 2:3)*; **which is guarded by Your power and through my faith** *(1 Pe. 1:5)*. **I give thanks to Your holy Name** *(Ps. 106:47)*, **for Your love for me never ceases, and Your mercies are new**

every morning *(La. 3:23)*. **Guide me** *(Ps. 73:24)*, that I may do Your will *(Mt. 26:42)*. **Provide for me** *(1 Ti. 6:17)*, that I may live for You. **Protect me** *(Ps. 59:1)*, that I may dwell safely *(Pr. 1:33)*. Grant to me escape from every temptation and trouble; or else strengthen me to bear it *(1 Co. 10:13)*. And now, fill me with Your Holy Spirit *(Lk. 11:13)*, to make me useful to You, and ready for every good work *(2 Ti. 2:21)*, that I may be witness of You in the world *(Ac. 1:8)*, and bring glory to Your name upon the earth *(Mt. 5:16)*. **(Amen)**

From a Husband   *Prayed by only the husband*
God my Father, from Whom every family on earth is named *(Ep. 3:15)*, I have found favor with You, for You have given me a wife *(Ge. 2:22; Pr. 18:22)*. Today, I will work to provide for her *(1 Ti. 5:8)*. I will fight to protect her *(1 Co. 13:7)*. I will honor her *(1 Pe. 3:7)*. I will be loyal to her *(He. 13:4)*. I will be the head of our home *(1 Co. 11:3)*, and gently lead her in Your ways *(1 Pe. 3:2)*. I will make time for her. I will listen to her. I will render the affection that is due her *(1 Co. 7:3)*. And I will endeavor to love her selflessly and sacrificially, even as You have loved Your church *(Ep. 5:25)*. **(Amen)**

For My Wife/Marriage   *Prayed by only the husband*
Heavenly Father, thank You for the wife You have given me *(Ge. 2:22)*. May she be like a tree planted by streams of water and may all that she does prosper in Your sight *(Ps. 1:3)*. May she fear You, Lord *(Pr. 31:30)*, walking in the way of righteousness with firm footing *(Pr. 8:20; Ps. 17:5)*. May she be clothed with strength and dignity and laugh without fear of the future. May her work inside and outside the home be industrious and blessed. *(Pr. 31:11-31)*. Grace our marriage with health, that her prayers be not hindered *(1 Pe. 3:7)*, guiding her in the way of wisdom and leading her along straight paths *(Pr. 4:11)*, and fill her with the knowledge of Your will in all spiritual wisdom and understanding, so that she may walk in a manner worthy of You, fully pleasing to You, bearing fruit in every good work and increasing in all godly knowledge *(Cl. 1:9,10)*. **(Amen)**

From a Wife   *Prayed by only the Wife*
God my Father, from Whom every family on earth is named *(Ep. 3:15)*, You have answered my longing and have brought me to a husband, giving me to him as his wife *(Ge. 2:22)*. Today, I will stay by his side, and support and help him *(Ge. 2:18)*. I will honor him. I will be loyal to him *(He. 13:4)*. I will respect him. I will endeavor to be patient, as he leads our home *(1 Pe. 3:2)*, and will submit to him whenever necessary, as to You, Lord *(Ep. 5:22)*. I will make time for Him. I will listen to him. I will render the affection that is due him *(1 Co. 7:3)*. I will love him *(Tt. 2:4)* and be loved by him *(Ep. 5:25)*. **(Amen)**

For My Husband/Marriage   *Prayed by only the Wife*

Heavenly Father, thank You for giving me as wife to my husband. May he be like a tree planted by streams of water and may all that he does prosper in Your sight *(Ps. 1:3)*. Strengthen him to be watchful, to stand firm in the faith, to act like a man, and to be strong *(1 Co. 16:13)*. Grace our marriage with health, that his prayers be not hindered *(1 Pe. 3:7)*, guiding him in the way of wisdom and leading him along straight paths *(Pr. 4:11)*. Lord, let Your favor rest upon him and establish the work of his hands *(Ps. 90:17)*, and fill him with the knowledge of Your will in all spiritual wisdom and understanding, so that he may walk in a manner worthy of You, fully pleasing to You, bearing fruit in every good work and increasing in all godly knowledge *(Cl. 1:9,10)*. (**Amen**)

For My Child*(ren)*

God my Father, I have been given reward and heritage from You through my child*(ren)* *(Ps. 127:3)*. *[State names]* I pray that they may grow in wisdom and stature, in Your favor, and in the favor of mankind *(Lk. 2:52)*. Make them blameless and innocent, Your children without blemish in the midst of this cooked and perverted generation *(Ph. 2:15)*. Show them that Your ways give more life than the ways of the world, and that following You is better than chasing after selfish goals *(BOCP)*. Guard their heart*(s)* and mind*(s)* from every evil way and influence *(Ph. 4:7; Pr. 8:13)*, and set their thoughts on what is true, honorable, just, pure, lovely, commendable, and excellent in Your sight *(Ph. 4:8)*. (**Amen**)

From a Child   *Prayed by only the child(ren)*

God my Father, from Whom every family on earth is named *(Ep. 3:15)*, thank You for giving me Godly parents *(Ep. 6:2)*. I will obey them, even as I obey You *(Ep. 6:1)*. (**Amen**)

For My Household

Master and Lord, as for me and my house, we will serve You *(Jn. 24:15)*. We will seek Your kingdom first *(Jn. 24:15; Mt. 6:33)*. That which we need, you will provide according to Your good will *(Mt. 6:33; Mt. 6:8)*. That which we have, you have graciously given *(Ja. 1:17)*, and our household rejoices in You *(Dt. 14:26)*. Be gracious to protect and prosper all things pertaining to us: our physical health, our spiritual health, our home, our land, our possessions, our provisions, and our finances. Grant us grace that we may honor You with all of our thriving, and as we remember the account we must one day give, may we be faithful stewards of our bounty *(BOCP)*. (**Amen**)

For Their Household(s)

Master and Lord, I ask of You for my friends *(and/or, family)* and their household(s), that they may serve You *(Js. 24:15)*, and seek Your kingdom first *(Jn. 24:15; Mt. 6:33)*. *[State names]* That which they need, You will provide according to Your good will *(Mt. 6:33; Mt. 6:8)*. That which they have, You have graciously given *(Ja. 1:17)*, and may their household rejoice in You *(Dt. 14:26)*. Be gracious to protect and prosper all things pertaining to them: their physical health, their spiritual health, their home, their land, their possessions, their provisions, and their finances. Grant them grace that they may honor You with all of their thriving, remembering the account they must one day give, may they be faithful stewards of their bounty *(BOCP)*. (Amen)

For My Local Church

God and Father, You have arranged each member in our local body as You have chosen *(1 Co. 12:18)* and we give thanks to You for all of them *(1 Th. 1:2)*. Grant that we may continue steadfastly in sound doctrine, and in prayer, and in fellowship, and in the breaking of bread *(Tt. 2:1; Ac. 2:42)*; united in the same mind and judgment *(1 Co. 1:10)*, continuing stable and steadfast in the faith, not shifting from the hope of the Gospel *(Cl. 1:23)*. Lord, cause our love to abound more and more, with knowledge and all discernment *(Ph.1:9,10)* and let us bear one another's burdens *(Ga. 6:2)* and encourage and edify one another *(1 Th. 5:11)*, seeking to spur one another on toward love and good deeds *(He. 10:24)*; that we may be a city set on a hill, whose light cannot be hidden *(Mt. 5:14-16)*, declaring Your glory and Your marvelous works to those outside *(Ps. 96:3)*, making disciples and baptizing them in the name of the Father and of the Son and of the Holy Spirit *(Mt. 28:19)*, teaching them to observe all that You have commanded. (Amen)

For My Local Church Workers/Spouses

Lord, we thank You that You give pastors after your own heart *(Je. 3:15)*, and evangelists, and teachers, along with those gifted for service and activities by the Spirit *(1 Co. 12:4-11)*, to equip us for the work of ministry and build up our local church body *(Ep. 4:11,12)*. We pray for them and the spouses that assist and support them, that they may be steadfast, immovable, always abounding in Your work, never growing weary of doing good, knowing that their labor is not in vain, and that in due season they will reap, if they do not give up *(1 Co. 15:58; Ga. 6:9)*. Lord, we ask that You strengthen them with all power, according to Your glorious might, for all endurance and patience with joy *(Cl. 1:11)*, granting them wisdom and understanding as they present themselves to You as workers without shame *(2 Ti. 2:15)*. (Amen)

* If today is a church day, pray **70. For Our Upcoming Meeting/Service**.

For those Sick/Unwell
Heavenly Father, have mercy on my friend*(s) (and/or, family) (Ps. 6:2)*. *[State names]* for they are afflicted and in pain *(Ps. 69:29)*. They cry out to You *(Je. 17:14)*, for the restoration of their health and the healing of their wounds *(Je. 30:17)*. Strengthen them during the days of their illness and help them to learn from it *(Is. 41:10; Ps. 119:71)*. May my prayer be a prayer of faith, and may You mercifully hasten to save them from this sickness and graciously hasten to raise them up *(Ps. 70:5; Ja. 5:15)*. (**Amen**)

For Their Salvation
Blessed be the God of Salvation *(Ps. 68:20)*, Who desires all people to be saved and come to the knowledge of the truth. *[State names]* My heart's desire and prayer for them is that they may be saved *(Ro. 10:1)*. Lord Jesus, stand at their door and knock, that perhaps they may bid you entry *(Re. 3:20)*. And, if it be Your will, open the door to me, that I may share the Word, and declare the mystery of Christ to them *(Cl. 4:3)*. (**Amen**)

For Our Country/Government
Almighty God, Who has given us this good land for our heritage, we humbly ask Your help, that we may always prove ourselves a people mindful of Your favor and glad to do Your will. Bless our land with honorable industry, sound learning, and pure manners. Save us from violence, discord, and confusion, from pride and arrogance, and from every evil way. Defend our liberties, and form into one united people, the multitudes brought here out of many kindreds and tongues. Endue with the spirit of wisdom, those to whom—in Your Name—we entrust the authority of government, that there may be justice and peace at home. And that, through obedience to Your Law, we may show forth Your praise among the nations of the earth. In the time of prosperity, fill our hearts with thankfulness. And in the day of trouble, suffer not our trust in You to fail *(BOCP)*. (**Amen**)

For Israel/Jerusalem
God of Abraham, Isaac, and Jacob, Your blessing be upon Your people Israel, the Holy Land, and the Holy City of Jerusalem. Protect them from their enemies, and let Your peace reign among them. And grant it, Lord, that the Jewish nation come to know the Salvation that is their Messiah, Jesus. (**Amen**)

For My Forgiveness of Others

Loving and merciful Father of all, Your Son commanded us to love even our enemies *(BOCP)*. *[State names]* You have loved me, so I will love them. You have been merciful to me, so I will be merciful to them *(Lk. 6:36)*. You have forgiven me, so I will forgive them *(Ep. 4:32)*. You have reconciled me, so I will minister reconciliation to them *(2 Co. 5:18)*, bearing with them *(Cl. 3:13)*, in kindness and tenderheartedness *(Ep. 4:32)*. Let me not repay evil for evil *(1 Th. 5:15)*. Bless me to be a peacemaker *(Mt. 5:9)*. And in Your good time, enable us to stand reconciled before You (BOCP). *(*Amen)

For My Basic Needs
Gracious Lord, who gives good gifts to those who ask of you *(Mt. 7:11)*, and who opens his hand to satisfy the desire of every living thing *(Ps. 145:16)*. you know my needs before I ask *(Mt. 6:8)*, yet desire my petitions *(Mt. 7:7; Ja. 4:2)*: Provide the things that are necessary: my food, my drink, my clothing; a dry and safe place to dwell, that is cool in the summer and warm in the winter *(Siddur)*. Give me not poverty, lest I steal and profane Your Name. Give me not riches, lest I be full and deny You *(Pr. 30:7-9)*. *[State additional needs]* I will trust that, according to Your promise, You will supply all my needs *(Mt. 6:33; Ph. 4:19)*. (**Amen**)

For My Leisure
O God, in the course of this busy life, give us times of refreshment and peace. And grant that we may so use our leisure and hobby, to rebuild our bodies and renew our minds, that our hearts may be ever more aware of the goodness of the life that You have given to us *(BOCP)*. (**Amen**)

Collects from the Book of Common Prayer
Go to Section **VII**, if it's a Holiday, or Section **VIII**, if it's a regular day, find by Day of the Month, and pray the daily Collect.

Prayers of Choice
Browse through the extensive list of over 250 Prayers in Sections **I-XI** of this book and pray according to want or need.

Benediction
Go to Section **X** or **XI**, and select a benediction to close out your morning prayer time. And may the Lord hear your prayers and bless your day, Amen.

Daily Morning Session 2

For Spouses without Child(ren)

* *If you have not already prayed* **Waking Gratitude (1)**, *do so now.*

For Confession

Loving and merciful God, be gracious to me and hear my prayer *(Ps. 4:1)*. I acknowledge my sins and iniquities and do not hide them *(Ps. 32:5)*. I confess that I have sinned against You in thought, word, and deed, by what I have done, and by what I have left undone *(BOCP)*. [State sins] Father, forgive me of my sins, and cleanse me from all my unrighteousness *(1 Jn. 1:9)*. Wash me thoroughly and I shall be whiter than snow *(Ps. 51:7)*, through the blood of Your Son *(Re. 7:14)*. (Amen)

For My Time in God's Word

God of all truth, Your Word is lamp to my feet and a light to my path *(Ps. 119:105)*. It is breathed out by You and profitable for my learning, correction, and training in righteousness *(2 Ti. 3:16)*. Teach me, that I may walk in Your truth *(Ps. 86:11)*. Teach me to do Your will, for You are my God *(Ps. 143:10)*. Give me knowledge, understanding, discretion, and wisdom *(Pr. 2:6; 8:12)*. And bless me as I store up Your Word in my heart, that I might not sin against you *(Ps. 119:11)*. (Amen)

Bible Reading

Go to Section *XII*, find by date, and read your daily Bible passages.

Devotions

Go to Section *XIV*, find by date, and read your daily devotions. Or substitute with the devotional of your choice.

Praises

Go to Section **VI**, find by date, and read your daily Praises.

For My Morning

God Most High, Possessor of Heaven and Earth *(Ge. 14:22)*, this morning, my prayer comes before You *(Ps. 88:13)*. You have said, "Seek my face." So, my heart says to You, "Your face, LORD, do I seek *(Ps. 27:8)*." That I may know You *(Ex. 33:13)*, and keep Your Word *(Ps. 119:101)*. That I may serve You this day with gladness *(Ps. 100:2)*. For You are God, You made me, and I am Yours *(Ps. 100:3)*. In You, I live, move, and have my being *(Ac. 17:28)*. And through Your Son, Jesus, I have obtained Salvation *(He. 2:3)*; which is guarded by Your power and

through my faith *(1 Pe. 1:5)*. I give thanks to Your holy Name *(Ps. 106:47)*, for Your love for me never ceases, and Your mercies are new every morning *(La. 3:23)*. Guide me *(Ps. 73:24)*, that I may do Your will *(Mt. 26:42)*. Provide for me *(1 Ti. 6:17)*, that I may live for You. Protect me *(Ps. 59:1)*, that I may dwell safely *(Pr. 1:33)*. Grant to me escape from every temptation and trouble; or else strengthen me to bear it *(1 Co. 10:13)*. And now, fill me with Your Holy Spirit *(Lk. 11:13)*, to make me useful to You, and ready for every good work *(2 Ti. 2:21)*, that I may be witness of You in the world *(Ac. 1:8)*, and bring glory to Your name upon the earth *(Mt. 5:16)*. (Amen)

From a Husband   *Prayed by only the husband*
God my Father, from Whom every family on earth is named *(Ep. 3:15)*, I have found favor with You, for You have given me a wife *(Ge. 2:22; Pr. 18:22)*. Today, I will work to provide for her *(1 Ti. 5:8)*. I will fight to protect her *(1 Co. 13:7)*. I will honor her *(1 Pe. 3:7)*. I will be loyal to her *(He. 13:4)*. I will be the head of our home *(1 Co. 11:3)*, and gently lead her in Your ways *(1 Pe. 3:2)*. I will make time for her. I will listen to her. I will render the affection that is due her *(1 Co. 7:3)*. And I will endeavor to love her selflessly and sacrificially, even as You have loved Your church *(Ep. 5:25)*. (Amen)

For My Wife/Marriage   *Prayed by only the husband*
Heavenly Father, thank You for the wife You have given me *(Ge. 2:22)*. May she be like a tree planted by streams of water and may all that she does prosper in Your sight *(Ps. 1:3)*. May she fear You, Lord *(Pr. 31:30)*, walking in the way of righteousness with firm footing *(Pr. 8:20; Ps. 17:5)*. May she be clothed with strength and dignity and laugh without fear of the future. May her work inside and outside the home be industrious and blessed. *(Pr. 31:11-31)*. Grace our marriage with health, that her prayers be not hindered *(1 Pe. 3:7)*, guiding her in the way of wisdom and leading her along straight paths *(Pr. 4:11)*, and fill her with the knowledge of Your will in all spiritual wisdom and understanding, so that she may walk in a manner worthy of You, fully pleasing to You, bearing fruit in every good work and increasing in all godly knowledge *(Cl. 1:9,10)*. (Amen)

From a Wife   *Prayed by only the Wife*
God my Father, from Whom every family on earth is named *(Ep. 3:15)*, You have answered my longing and have brought me to a husband, giving me to him as his wife *(Ge. 2:22)*. Today, I will stay by his side, and support and help him *(Ge. 2:18)*. I will honor him. I will be loyal to him *(He. 13:4)*. I will respect him. I will endeavor to be patient, as he leads our home *(1 Pe. 3:2)*, and will submit to him whenever necessary, as to You, Lord *(Ep. 5:22)*. I will make time for Him. I will listen to him. I will

render the affection that is due him *(1 Co. 7:3)*. I will love him *(Tt. 2:4)* and be loved by him *(Ep. 5:25)*. **(Amen)**

For My Husband/Marriage   *Prayed by only the Wife*
Heavenly Father, thank You for giving me as wife to my husband. May he be like a tree planted by streams of water and may all that he does prosper in Your sight *(Ps. 1:3)*. Strengthen him to be watchful, to stand firm in the faith, to act like a man, and to be strong *(1 Co. 16:13)*. Grace our marriage with health, that his prayers be not hindered *(1 Pe. 3:7)*, guiding him in the way of wisdom and leading him along straight paths *(Pr. 4:11)*. Lord, let Your favor rest upon him and establish the work of his hands *(Ps. 90:17)*, and fill him with the knowledge of Your will in all spiritual wisdom and understanding, so that he may walk in a manner worthy of You, fully pleasing to You, bearing fruit in every good work and increasing in all godly knowledge *(Cl. 1:9,10)*. **(Amen)**

For My Household
Master and Lord, as for me and my house, we will serve You *(Jn. 24:15)*. We will seek Your kingdom first *(Jn. 24:15; Mt. 6:33)*. That which we need, you will provide according to Your good will *(Mt. 6:33; Mt. 6:8)*. That which we have, you have graciously given *(Ja. 1:17)*, and our household rejoices in You *(Dt. 14:26)*. Be gracious to protect and prosper all things pertaining to us: our physical health, our spiritual health, our home, our land, our possessions, our provisions, and our finances. Grant us grace that we may honor You with all of our thriving, and as we remember the account we must one day give, may we be faithful stewards of our bounty *(BOCP)*. **(Amen)**

For Their Household(s)
Master and Lord, I ask of You for my friends *(and/or, family)* and their household(s), that they may serve You *(Js. 24:15)*, and seek Your kingdom first *(Jn. 24:15; Mt. 6:33)*. *[State names]* That which they need, You will provide according to Your good will *(Mt. 6:33; Mt. 6:8)*. That which they have, You have graciously given *(Ja. 1:17)*, and may their household rejoice in You *(Dt. 14:26)*. Be gracious to protect and prosper all things pertaining to them: their physical health, their spiritual health, their home, their land, their possessions, their provisions, and their finances. Grant them grace that they may honor You with all of their thriving, remembering the account they must one day give, may they be faithful stewards of their bounty *(BOCP)*. **(Amen)**

For My Local Church
God and Father, You have arranged each member in our local body as You have chosen *(1 Co. 12:18)* and we give thanks to You for all of them

(1 Th. 1:2). Grant that we may continue steadfastly in sound doctrine, and in prayer, and in fellowship, and in the breaking of bread *(Tt. 2:1; Ac. 2:42)*; united in the same mind and judgment *(1 Co. 1:10)*, continuing stable and steadfast in the faith, not shifting from the hope of the Gospel *(Cl. 1:23)*. Lord, cause our love to abound more and more, with knowledge and all discernment *(Ph.1:9,10)* and let us bear one another's burdens *(Ga. 6:2)* and encourage and edify one another *(1 Th. 5:11)*, seeking to spur one another on toward love and good deeds *(He. 10:24)*; that we may be a city set on a hill, whose light cannot be hidden *(Mt. 5:14-16)*, declaring Your glory and Your marvelous works to those outside *(Ps. 96:3)*, making disciples and baptizing them in the name of the Father and of the Son and of the Holy Spirit *(Mt. 28:19)*, teaching them to observe all that You have commanded. (Amen)

For My Local Church Workers/Spouses

Lord, we thank You that You give pastors after your own heart *(Je. 3:15)*, and evangelists, and teachers, along with those gifted for service and activities by the Spirit *(1 Co. 12:4-11)*, to equip us for the work of ministry and build up our local church body *(Ep. 4:11,12)*. We pray for them and the spouses that assist and support them, that they may be steadfast, immovable, always abounding in Your work, never growing weary of doing good, knowing that their labor is not in vain, and that in due season they will reap, if they do not give up *(1 Co. 15:58; Ga. 6:9)*. Lord, we ask that You strengthen them with all power, according to Your glorious might, for all endurance and patience with joy *(Cl. 1:11)*, granting them wisdom and understanding as they present themselves to You as workers without shame *(2 Ti. 2:15)*. (Amen)

* If today is a church day, pray **70. For Our Upcoming Meeting/Service**.

For those Sick/Unwell

Heavenly Father, have mercy on my friend(s) (and/or, family) *(Ps. 6:2)*. *[State names]* for they are afflicted and in pain *(Ps. 69:29)*. They cry out to You *(Je. 17:14)*, for the restoration of their health and the healing of their wounds *(Je. 30:17)*. Strengthen them during the days of their illness and help them to learn from it *(Is. 41:10; Ps. 119:71)*. May my prayer be a prayer of faith, and may You mercifully hasten to save them from this sickness and graciously hasten to raise them up *(Ps. 70:5; Ja. 5:15)*. (Amen)

For Their Salvation

Blessed be the God of Salvation *(Ps. 68:20)*, Who desires all people to be saved and come to the knowledge of the truth. *[State names]* My heart's desire and prayer for them is that they may be saved *(Ro. 10:1)*.

Lord Jesus, stand at their door and knock, that perhaps they may bid you entry *(Re. 3:20)*. And, if it be Your will, open the door to me, that I may share the Word, and declare the mystery of Christ to them *(Cl. 4:3)*. (Amen)

For Our Country/Government

Almighty God, Who has given us this good land for our heritage, we humbly ask Your help, that we may always prove ourselves a people mindful of Your favor and glad to do Your will. Bless our land with honorable industry, sound learning, and pure manners. Save us from violence, discord, and confusion, from pride and arrogance, and from every evil way. Defend our liberties, and form into one united people, the multitudes brought here out of many kindreds and tongues. Endue with the spirit of wisdom, those to whom—in Your Name—we entrust the authority of government, that there may be justice and peace at home. And that, through obedience to Your Law, we may show forth Your praise among the nations of the earth. In the time of prosperity, fill our hearts with thankfulness. And in the day of trouble, suffer not our trust in You to fail *(BOCP)*. (Amen)

For Israel/Jerusalem

God of Abraham, Isaac, and Jacob, Your blessing be upon Your people Israel, the Holy Land, and the Holy City of Jerusalem. Protect them from their enemies, and let Your peace reign among them. And grant it, Lord, that the Jewish nation come to know the Salvation that is their Messiah, Jesus. (Amen)

For My Forgiveness of Others

Loving and merciful Father of all, Your Son commanded us to love even our enemies *(BOCP)*. *[State names]* You have loved me, so I will love them. You have been merciful to me, so I will be merciful to them *(Lk. 6:36)*. You have forgiven me, so I will forgive them *(Ep. 4:32)*. You have reconciled me, so I will minister reconciliation to them *(2 Co. 5:18)*, bearing with them *(Cl. 3:13)*, in kindness and tenderheartedness *(Ep. 4:32)*. Let me not repay evil for evil *(1 Th. 5:15)*. Bless me to be a peacemaker *(Mt. 5:9)*. And in Your good time, enable us to stand reconciled before You (BOCP). *(*Amen)

For My Basic Needs

Gracious Lord, who gives good gifts to those who ask of you *(Mt. 7:11)*, and who opens his hand to satisfy the desire of every living thing *(Ps. 145:16)*. you know my needs before I ask *(Mt. 6:8)*, yet desire my petitions *(Mt. 7:7; Ja. 4:2)*: Provide the things that are necessary: my food, my drink, my clothing; a dry and safe place to dwell, that is cool in the summer and warm in the winter *(Siddur)*. **Give me not poverty, lest I steal and profane Your Name. Give me not riches, lest I be full and deny You** *(Pr. 30:7-9)*. *[State additional needs]* **I will trust that, according to Your promise, You will supply all my needs** *(Mt. 6:33; Ph. 4:19)*. **(Amen)**

For My Leisure
O God, in the course of this busy life, give us times of refreshment and peace. And grant that we may so use our leisure and hobby, to rebuild our bodies and renew our minds, that our hearts may be ever more aware of the goodness of the life that You have given to us *(BOCP)*. **(Amen)**

Collects from the Book of Common Prayer
Go to Section **VII**, if it's a Holiday, or Section **VIII**, if it's a regular day, find by Day of the Month, and pray the daily Collect.

Prayers of Choice
Browse through the extensive list of over 250 Prayers in Sections **I-XI** of this book and pray according to want or need.

Free-From-Form Prayer
Pray from the heart whatever the Holy Spirit brings to Your attention.

Benediction
Go to Section **X** or **XI**, and select a benediction to close out your morning prayer time. And may the Lord hear your prayers and bless your day, Amen.

Daily Morning Session 3

For Single People with Child(ren)

---

* *If you have not already prayed* **Waking Gratitude (1)**, *do so now.*

For Confession
Loving and merciful God, be gracious to me and hear my prayer *(Ps. 4:1)*. I acknowledge my sins and iniquities and do not hide them *(Ps. 32:5)*. I confess that I have sinned against You in thought, word, and deed, by what I have done, and by what I have left undone *(BOCP)*. [State sins] Father, forgive me of my sins, and cleanse me from all my unrighteousness *(1 Jn. 1:9)*. Wash me thoroughly and I shall be whiter than snow *(Ps. 51:7)*, through the blood of Your Son *(Re. 7:14)*. (Amen)

For My Time in God's Word
God of all truth, Your Word is lamp to my feet and a light to my path *(Ps. 119:105)*. It is breathed out by You and profitable for my learning, correction, and training in righteousness *(2 Ti. 3:16)*. Teach me, that I may walk in Your truth *(Ps. 86:11)*. Teach me to do Your will, for You are my God *(Ps. 143:10)*. Give me knowledge, understanding, discretion, and wisdom *(Pr. 2:6; 8:12)*. And bless me as I store up Your Word in my heart, that I might not sin against you *(Ps. 119:11)*. (Amen)

Bible Reading
Go to Section ***XII***, find by date, and read your daily Bible passages.

Devotions
Go to Section ***XIV***, find by date, and read your daily devotions. Or substitute with the devotional of your choice.

Praises
Go to Section **VI**, find by date, and read your daily Praises.

For My Morning
God Most High, Possessor of Heaven and Earth *(Ge. 14:22)*, this morning, my prayer comes before You *(Ps. 88:13)*. You have said, "Seek my face." So, my heart says to You, "Your face, LORD, do I seek *(Ps. 27:8)*." That I may know You *(Ex. 33:13)*, and keep Your Word *(Ps. 119:101)*. That I may serve You this day with gladness *(Ps. 100:2)*. For You are God, You made me, and I am Yours *(Ps. 100:3)*. In You, I live, move, and have my being *(Ac. 17:28)*. And through Your Son, Jesus, I have obtained Salvation *(He. 2:3)*; which is guarded by Your power and

through my faith *(1 Pe. 1:5)*. I give thanks to Your holy Name *(Ps. 106:47)*, for Your love for me never ceases, and Your mercies are new every morning *(La. 3:23)*. Guide me *(Ps. 73:24)*, that I may do Your will *(Mt. 26:42)*. Provide for me *(1 Ti. 6:17)*, that I may live for You. Protect me *(Ps. 59:1)*, that I may dwell safely *(Pr. 1:33)*. Grant to me escape from every temptation and trouble; or else strengthen me to bear it *(1 Co. 10:13)*. And now, fill me with Your Holy Spirit *(Lk. 11:13)*, to make me useful to You, and ready for every good work *(2 Ti. 2:21)*, that I may be witness of You in the world *(Ac. 1:8)*, and bring glory to Your name upon the earth *(Mt. 5:16)*. **(Amen)**

For My Child*(ren)*
God my Father, I have been given reward and heritage from You through my child*(ren) (Ps. 127:3)*. *[State names]* I pray that they may grow in wisdom and stature, in Your favor, and in the favor of mankind *(Lk. 2:52)*. Make them blameless and innocent, Your children without blemish in the midst of this cooked and perverted generation *(Ph. 2:15)*. Show them that Your ways give more life than the ways of the world, and that following You is better than chasing after selfish goals *(BOCP)*. Guard their heart*(s)* and mind*(s)* from every evil way and influence *(Ph. 4:7; Pr. 8:13)*, and set their thoughts on what is true, honorable, just, pure, lovely, commendable, and excellent in Your sight *(Ph. 4:8)*. **(Amen)**

From a Child   *Prayed by only the child(ren)*
God my Father, from Whom every family on earth is named *(Ep. 3:15)*, thank You for giving me Godly parents *(Ep. 6:2)*. I will obey them, even as I obey You *(Ep. 6:1)*. **(Amen)**

For My Household
Master and Lord, as for me and my house, we will serve You *(Jn. 24:15)*. We will seek Your kingdom first *(Jn. 24:15; Mt. 6:33)*. That which we need, you will provide according to Your good will *(Mt. 6:33; Mt. 6:8)*. That which we have, you have graciously given *(Ja. 1:17)*, and our household rejoices in You *(Dt. 14:26)*. Be gracious to protect and prosper all things pertaining to us: our physical health, our spiritual health, our home, our land, our possessions, our provisions, and our finances. Grant us grace that we may honor You with all of our thriving, and as we remember the account we must one day give, may we be faithful stewards of our bounty *(BOCP)*. **(Amen)**

For Their Household*(s)*
Master and Lord, I ask of You for my friends *(and/or, family)* and their household*(s)*, that they may serve You *(Js. 24:15)*, and seek Your

kingdom first *(Jn. 24:15; Mt. 6:33)*. [State names] That which they need, You will provide according to Your good will *(Mt. 6:33; Mt. 6:8)*. That which they have, You have graciously given *(Ja. 1:17)*, and may their household rejoice in You *(Dt. 14:26)*. Be gracious to protect and prosper all things pertaining to them: their physical health, their spiritual health, their home, their land, their possessions, their provisions, and their finances. Grant them grace that they may honor You with all of their thriving, remembering the account they must one day give, may they be faithful stewards of their bounty *(BOCP)*. (Amen)

For My Local Church

God and Father, You have arranged each member in our local body as You have chosen *(1 Co. 12:18)* and we give thanks to You for all of them *(1 Th. 1:2)*. Grant that we may continue steadfastly in sound doctrine, and in prayer, and in fellowship, and in the breaking of bread *(Tt. 2:1; Ac. 2:42)*; united in the same mind and judgment *(1 Co. 1:10)*, continuing stable and steadfast in the faith, not shifting from the hope of the Gospel *(Cl. 1:23)*. Lord, cause our love to abound more and more, with knowledge and all discernment *(Ph.1:9,10)* and let us bear one another's burdens *(Ga. 6:2)* and encourage and edify one another *(1 Th. 5:11)*, seeking to spur one another on toward love and good deeds *(He. 10:24)*; that we may be a city set on a hill, whose light cannot be hidden *(Mt. 5:14-16)*, declaring Your glory and Your marvelous works to those outside *(Ps. 96:3)*, making disciples and baptizing them in the name of the Father and of the Son and of the Holy Spirit *(Mt. 28:19)*, teaching them to observe all that You have commanded. (Amen)

For My Local Church Workers/Spouses

Lord, we thank You that You give pastors after your own heart *(Je. 3:15)*, and evangelists, and teachers, along with those gifted for service and activities by the Spirit *(1 Co. 12:4-11)*, to equip us for the work of ministry and build up our local church body *(Ep. 4:11,12)*. We pray for them and the spouses that assist and support them, that they may be steadfast, immovable, always abounding in Your work, never growing weary of doing good, knowing that their labor is not in vain, and that in due season they will reap, if they do not give up *(1 Co. 15:58; Ga. 6:9)*. Lord, we ask that You strengthen them with all power, according to Your glorious might, for all endurance and patience with joy *(Cl. 1:11)*, granting them wisdom and understanding as they present themselves to You as workers without shame *(2 Ti. 2:15)*. (Amen)

* If today is a church day, pray **70. For Our Upcoming Meeting/Service**.

For those Sick/Unwell

Heavenly Father, have mercy on my friend*(s) (and/or, family) (Ps. 6:2)*. *[State names]* for they are afflicted and in pain *(Ps. 69:29)*. They cry out to You *(Je. 17:14)*, for the restoration of their health and the healing of their wounds *(Je. 30:17)*. Strengthen them during the days of their illness and help them to learn from it *(Is. 41:10; Ps. 119:71)*. May my prayer be a prayer of faith, and may You mercifully hasten to save them from this sickness and graciously hasten to raise them up *(Ps. 70:5; Ja. 5:15)*. (**Amen**)

For Their Salvation

Blessed be the God of Salvation *(Ps. 68:20)*, Who desires all people to be saved and come to the knowledge of the truth. *[State names]* My heart's desire and prayer for them is that they may be saved *(Ro. 10:1)*. Lord Jesus, stand at their door and knock, that perhaps they may bid you entry *(Re. 3:20)*. And, if it be Your will, open the door to me, that I may share the Word, and declare the mystery of Christ to them *(Cl. 4:3)*. (**Amen**)

For Our Country/Government

Almighty God, Who has given us this good land for our heritage, we humbly ask Your help, that we may always prove ourselves a people mindful of Your favor and glad to do Your will. Bless our land with honorable industry, sound learning, and pure manners. Save us from violence, discord, and confusion, from pride and arrogance, and from every evil way. Defend our liberties, and form into one united people, the multitudes brought here out of many kindreds and tongues. Endue with the spirit of wisdom, those to whom—in Your Name—we entrust the authority of government, that there may be justice and peace at home. And that, through obedience to Your Law, we may show forth Your praise among the nations of the earth. In the time of prosperity, fill our hearts with thankfulness. And in the day of trouble, suffer not our trust in You to fail *(BOCP)*. (**Amen**)

For Israel/Jerusalem

God of Abraham, Isaac, and Jacob, Your blessing be upon Your people Israel, the Holy Land, and the Holy City of Jerusalem. Protect them from their enemies, and let Your peace reign among them. And grant it, Lord, that the Jewish nation come to know the Salvation that is their Messiah, Jesus. (**Amen**)

For My Forgiveness of Others

Loving and merciful Father of all, Your Son commanded us to love even our enemies *(BOCP)*. *[State names]* You have loved me, so I will love them. You have been merciful to me, so I will be merciful to them *(Lk.*

6:36). You have forgiven me, so I will forgive them *(Ep. 4:32).* You have reconciled me, so I will minister reconciliation to them *(2 Co. 5:18),* bearing with them *(Cl. 3:13),* in kindness and tenderheartedness *(Ep. 4:32).* Let me not repay evil for evil *(1 Th. 5:15).* Bless me to be a peacemaker *(Mt. 5:9).* And in Your good time, enable us to stand reconciled before You (BOCP). *(*Amen)

For My Personal Holiness
Holy Lord God Almighty, You chose me before the foundation of the world, that I should be holy and blameless before You *(Ep. 1:4).* You foreknew me and predestined me to be conformed to the image of Your Son *(Ro. 8:29),* as an obedient child, not being conformed to my previous passions *(1 Pe. 1:14),* but that I might be holy in all my conduct, because You are holy *(1 Pe. 1:15,16).* For without holiness, no one will see You *(He. 12:14).* Grant it today, that I be crucified with Christ, that Christ might live in me *(Ga. 2:20),* and strengthen me by Your grace to flee lusts and pursue righteousness, along with those who call on You from a pure heart *(2 Ti. 2:22).* (Amen)

For My Witness
God our Savior, let me be a light for You, that the world may see my good works and give You glory. *(Mt. 5:14, 16).* Send me out as Your ambassador, as though You were making Your appeal to others through me, that I may implore them on behalf of Your Son to be reconciled to You *(2 Co. 5:20).* Fill me with Your Spirit, so that I may boldly proclaim this mystery *(Ep. 6:19).* Let me not be ashamed of the gospel, for in it is the power of Your salvation *(Ro. 1:16).* Lord, Help me to always be prepared to make a defense to anyone who asks for a reason for the hope that is in me *(1 Pe. 3:15).* May my life be above reproach *(Cl. 1:22),* and may my speech always be gracious, seasoned with salt, so that I may know how to answer each person *(Cl. 4:6).* (Amen)

For My Spiritual Maturation
Holy Father, I seek the growth that comes from Your grace and from the knowledge of Your Son *(2 Pe. 3:18),* that I would not be childish, tossed and carried by waves and winds of misdirections, but that I may grow up in Christ in every way *(Ep. 4:14-15).* Teach me to put away childish things and pursue godly things in righteousness *(1 Co. 13:11; 1 Ti. 6:11).* Conform me to the image of Jesus *(Ro. 8:29),* and guide me to walk in a manner that is worthy of You and fully pleasing to You, bearing fruit in every good work *(Cl. 1:9,10).* (Amen)

For God's Will/Guidance for Me

Sovereign Lord, You alone know the plans You have for my future *(Je. 29:11)*. Grant me help to trust in You with all my heart, not leaning on my own understanding, but submitting all my ways to You, that You might make my path clear to me *(Pr. 3:5,6)*. *[State specific will/guidance needed]* Lord, if in anything, I seem to lack the knowledge of Your will for me, may I be ever mindful of what You have already shown me—that which is good, and that which is required of me—to act justly, to love mercy, and to walk humbly with You *(Mi.6:8)*. Now may, You, God, equip me to do Your will, and work in me what is Pleasing to You. *(He. 13:20,21)*. **(Amen)**

For My Basic Needs
Gracious Lord, who gives good gifts to those who ask of you *(Mt. 7:11)*, and who opens his hand to satisfy the desire of every living thing *(Ps. 145:16)*. you know my needs before I ask *(Mt. 6:8)*, yet desire my petitions *(Mt. 7:7; Ja. 4:2)*: **Provide the things that are necessary: my food, my drink, my clothing; a dry and safe place to dwell, that is cool in the summer and warm in the winter** *(Siddur)*. Give me not poverty, lest I steal and profane Your Name. Give me not riches, lest I be full and deny You *(Pr. 30:7-9)*. *[State additional needs]* I will trust that, according to Your promise, You will supply all my needs *(Mt. 6:33; Ph. 4:19)*. **(Amen)**

For My Leisure
O God, in the course of this busy life, give us times of refreshment and peace. And grant that we may so use our leisure and hobby, to rebuild our bodies and renew our minds, that our hearts may be ever more aware of the goodness of the life that You have given to us *(BOCP)*. **(Amen)**

Collects from the Book of Common Prayer
Go to Section **VII**, if it's a Holiday, or Section **VIII**, if it's a regular day, find by Day of the Month, and pray the daily Collect.

Prayers of Choice
Browse through the extensive list of over 250 Prayers in Sections **I-XI** of this book and pray according to want or need.

Benediction
Go to Section **X** or **XI**, and select a benediction to close out your prayer time. And may the Lord hear your prayers and bless your day, Amen.

Daily Morning Session 4
For Single People without Child(ren)

---

* *If you have not already prayed* **Waking Gratitude (1)**, *do so now.*

For Confession
Loving and merciful God, be gracious to me and hear my prayer *(Ps. 4:1)*. I acknowledge my sins and iniquities and do not hide them *(Ps. 32:5)*. I confess that I have sinned against You in thought, word, and deed, by what I have done, and by what I have left undone *(BOCP)*. [State sins] Father, forgive me of my sins, and cleanse me from all my unrighteousness *(1 Jn. 1:9)*. Wash me thoroughly and I shall be whiter than snow *(Ps. 51:7)*, through the blood of Your Son *(Re. 7:14)*. (Amen)

For My Time in God's Word
God of all truth, Your Word is lamp to my feet and a light to my path *(Ps. 119:105)*. It is breathed out by You and profitable for my learning, correction, and training in righteousness *(2 Ti. 3:16)*. Teach me, that I may walk in Your truth *(Ps. 86:11)*. Teach me to do Your will, for You are my God *(Ps. 143:10)*. Give me knowledge, understanding, discretion, and wisdom *(Pr. 2:6; 8:12)*. And bless me as I store up Your Word in my heart, that I might not sin against you *(Ps. 119:11)*. (Amen)

Bible Reading
Go to Section ***XII***, find by date, and read your daily Bible passages.

Devotions
Go to Section ***XIV***, find by date, and read your daily devotions. Or substitute with the devotional of your choice.

Praises
Go to Section **VI**, find by date, and read your daily Praises.

For My Morning
God Most High, Possessor of Heaven and Earth *(Ge. 14:22)*, this morning, my prayer comes before You *(Ps. 88:13)*. You have said, "Seek my face." So, my heart says to You, "Your face, LORD, do I seek *(Ps. 27:8)*." That I may know You *(Ex. 33:13)*, and keep Your Word *(Ps. 119:101)*. That I may serve You this day with gladness *(Ps. 100:2)*. For You are God, You made me, and I am Yours *(Ps. 100:3)*. In You, I live, move, and have my being *(Ac. 17:28)*. And through Your Son, Jesus, I have obtained Salvation *(He. 2:3)*; which is guarded by Your power and

through my faith *(1 Pe. 1:5)*. I give thanks to Your holy Name *(Ps. 106:47)*, for Your love for me never ceases, and Your mercies are new every morning *(La. 3:23)*. Guide me *(Ps. 73:24)*, that I may do Your will *(Mt. 26:42)*. Provide for me *(1 Ti. 6:17)*, that I may live for You. Protect me *(Ps. 59:1)*, that I may dwell safely *(Pr. 1:33)*. Grant to me escape from every temptation and trouble; or else strengthen me to bear it *(1 Co. 10:13)*. And now, fill me with Your Holy Spirit *(Lk. 11:13)*, to make me useful to You, and ready for every good work *(2 Ti. 2:21)*, that I may be witness of You in the world *(Ac. 1:8)*, and bring glory to Your name upon the earth *(Mt. 5:16)*. (Amen)

For My Household

Master and Lord, I will serve You *(Jn. 24:15)*. I will seek Your kingdom first *(Jn. 24:15; Mt. 6:33)*. That which I need, you will provide according to Your good will *(Mt. 6:33; Mt. 6:8)*. That which I have, you have graciously given *(Ja. 1:17)*, and I rejoice in You *(Dt. 14:26)*. Be gracious to protect and prosper all things pertaining to me: my physical health, my spiritual health, my home, my land, my possessions, my provisions, and my finances. Grant me grace that I may honor You with all of my thriving, and as I remember the account we must one day give, may I be a faithful steward of our bounty *(BOCP)*. (Amen)

For Their Household(s)

Master and Lord, I ask of You for my friends *(and/or, family)* and their household(s), that they may serve You *(Js. 24:15)*, and seek Your kingdom first *(Jn. 24:15; Mt. 6:33)*. *[State names]* That which they need, You will provide according to Your good will *(Mt. 6:33; Mt. 6:8)*. That which they have, You have graciously given *(Ja. 1:17)*, and may their household rejoice in You *(Dt. 14:26)*. Be gracious to protect and prosper all things pertaining to them: their physical health, their spiritual health, their home, their land, their possessions, their provisions, and their finances. Grant them grace that they may honor You with all of their thriving, remembering the account they must one day give, may they be faithful stewards of their bounty *(BOCP)*. (Amen)

For My Local Church

God and Father, You have arranged each member in our local body as You have chosen *(1 Co. 12:18)* and we give thanks to You for all of them *(1 Th. 1:2)*. Grant that we may continue steadfastly in sound doctrine, and in prayer, and in fellowship, and in the breaking of bread *(Tt. 2:1; Ac. 2:42)*; united in the same mind and judgment *(1 Co. 1:10)*, continuing stable and steadfast in the faith, not shifting from the hope of the Gospel *(Cl. 1:23)*. Lord, cause our love to abound more and more, with knowledge and all discernment *(Ph.1:9,10)* and let us bear one another's burdens *(Ga. 6:2)* and encourage and edify one another

(1 Th. 5:11), seeking to spur one another on toward love and good deeds *(He. 10:24)*; that we may be a city set on a hill, whose light cannot be hidden *(Mt. 5:14-16)*, declaring Your glory and Your marvelous works to those outside *(Ps. 96:3)*, making disciples and baptizing them in the name of the Father and of the Son and of the Holy Spirit *(Mt. 28:19)*, teaching them to observe all that You have commanded. **(Amen)**

For My Local Church Workers/Spouses

Lord, we thank You that You give pastors after your own heart *(Je. 3:15)*, and evangelists, and teachers, along with those gifted for service and activities by the Spirit *(1 Co. 12:4-11)*, to equip us for the work of ministry and build up our local church body *(Ep. 4:11,12)*. We pray for them and the spouses that assist and support them, that they may be steadfast, immovable, always abounding in Your work, never growing weary of doing good, knowing that their labor is not in vain, and that in due season they will reap, if they do not give up *(1 Co. 15:58; Ga. 6:9)*. Lord, we ask that You strengthen them with all power, according to Your glorious might, for all endurance and patience with joy *(Cl. 1:11)*, granting them wisdom and understanding as they present themselves to You as workers without shame *(2 Ti. 2:15)*. **(Amen)**

* If today is a church day, pray **70. For Our Upcoming Meeting/Service**.

For those Sick/Unwell

Heavenly Father, have mercy on my friend(s) (and/or, family) *(Ps. 6:2)*. *[State names]* for they are afflicted and in pain *(Ps. 69:29)*. They cry out to You *(Je. 17:14)*, for the restoration of their health and the healing of their wounds *(Je. 30:17)*. Strengthen them during the days of their illness and help them to learn from it *(Is. 41:10; Ps. 119:71)*. May my prayer be a prayer of faith, and may You mercifully hasten to save them from this sickness and graciously hasten to raise them up *(Ps. 70:5; Ja. 5:15)*. **(Amen)**

For Their Salvation

Blessed be the God of Salvation *(Ps. 68:20)*, Who desires all people to be saved and come to the knowledge of the truth. *[State names]* My heart's desire and prayer for them is that they may be saved *(Ro. 10:1)*. Lord Jesus, stand at their door and knock, that perhaps they may bid you entry *(Re. 3:20)*. And, if it be Your will, open the door to me, that I may share the Word, and declare the mystery of Christ to them *(Cl. 4:3)*. **(Amen)**

For Our Country/Government

Almighty God, Who has given us this good land for our heritage, we humbly ask Your help, that we may always prove ourselves a people mindful of Your favor and glad to do Your will. Bless our land with honorable industry, sound learning, and pure manners. Save us from violence, discord, and confusion, from pride and arrogance, and from every evil way. Defend our liberties, and form into one united people, the multitudes brought here out of many kindreds and tongues. Endue with the spirit of wisdom, those to whom—in Your Name—we entrust the authority of government, that there may be justice and peace at home. And that, through obedience to Your Law, we may show forth Your praise among the nations of the earth. In the time of prosperity, fill our hearts with thankfulness. And in the day of trouble, suffer not our trust in You to fail *(BOCP)*. (Amen)

For Israel/Jerusalem
God of Abraham, Isaac, and Jacob, Your blessing be upon Your people Israel, the Holy Land, and the Holy City of Jerusalem. Protect them from their enemies, and let Your peace reign among them. And grant it, Lord, that the Jewish nation come to know the Salvation that is their Messiah, Jesus. (Amen)

For My Forgiveness of Others
Loving and merciful Father of all, Your Son commanded us to love even our enemies *(BOCP)*. *[State names]* You have loved me, so I will love them. You have been merciful to me, so I will be merciful to them *(Lk. 6:36)*. You have forgiven me, so I will forgive them *(Ep. 4:32)*. You have reconciled me, so I will minister reconciliation to them *(2 Co. 5:18)*, bearing with them *(Cl. 3:13)*, in kindness and tenderheartedness *(Ep. 4:32)*. Let me not repay evil for evil *(1 Th. 5:15)*. Bless me to be a peacemaker *(Mt. 5:9)*. And in Your good time, enable us to stand reconciled before You (BOCP). *(*Amen)

For My Personal Holiness
Holy Lord God Almighty, You chose me before the foundation of the world, that I should be holy and blameless before You *(Ep. 1:4)*. You foreknew me and predestined me to be conformed to the image of Your Son *(Ro. 8:29)*, as an obedient child, not being conformed to my previous passions *(1 Pe. 1:14)*, but that I might be holy in all my conduct, because You are holy *(1 Pe. 1:15,16)*. For without holiness, no one will see You *(He. 12:14)*. Grant it today, that I be crucified with Christ, that Christ might live in me *(Ga. 2:20)*, and strengthen me by Your grace to flee lusts and pursue righteousness, along with those who call on You from a pure heart *(2 Ti. 2:22)*. (Amen)

For My Increased Faith

All-knowing and all-powerful God, I ask for increased faith that comes through hearing your Word *(Ro. 10:17)*. As I learn of you, may I believe and trust in You more deeply, knowing that faith as small as a mustard seed can move mountains *(Mt. 17:20)*. Let me be fully convinced that You are able to do far more abundantly than all that I ask or think *(Ep. 3:20)*. Increase my faith that I may live by it, walking confidently in your promises and trusting in your provision *(2 Co. 5:7; He. 11:1)*. And as I believe, Lord, help my unbelief *(Mt. 9:24)*, with growing faith that is rooted in the knowledge of Your grace and truth *(Cl. 2:7; Jn. 1:17)*. (Amen)

For My Spiritual Strength

Mighty God, strengthen me with all power for Christian endurance, according to Your glorious might *(Cl. 1:11)*. You know my frame, that I am dust *(Ps. 103:14)*, for my flesh is weak, but my spirit is willing. Draw me to watch with You *(Mk. 14:38)*, and teach me to wait upon You, that my strength might be renewed *(Is. 40:31)*. Where I am weak—and will be weak—let your strength be made perfect in me *(2 Co. 12:9)*, that I may say that I am strong *(Jl. 3:10)*, and do all things through Christ as He strengthens me *(Ph. 4:13)*. (Amen)

For My Spiritual Maturation

Holy Father, I seek the growth that comes from Your grace and from the knowledge of Your Son *(2 Pe. 3:18)*, that I would not be childish, tossed and carried by waves and winds of misdirections, but that I may grow up in Christ in every way *(Ep. 4:14-15)*. Teach me to put away childish things and pursue godly things in righteousness *(1 Co. 13:11; 1 Ti. 6:11)*. Conform me to the image of Jesus *(Ro. 8:29)*, and guide me to walk in a manner that is worthy of You and fully pleasing to You, bearing fruit in every good work *(Cl. 1:9,10)*. (Amen)

For My Witness

God our Savior, let me be a light for You, that the world may see my good works and give You glory. *(Mt. 5:14, 16)*. Send me out as Your ambassador, as though You were making Your appeal to others through me, that I may implore them on behalf of Your Son to be reconciled to You *(2 Co. 5:20)*. Fill me with Your Spirit, so that I may boldly proclaim this mystery *(Ep. 6:19)*. Let me not be ashamed of the gospel, for in it is the power of Your salvation *(Ro. 1:16)*. Lord, Help me to always be prepared to make a defense to anyone who asks for a reason for the hope that is in me *(1 Pe. 3:15)*. May my life be above reproach *(Cl. 1:22)*, and may my speech always be gracious, seasoned with salt, so that I may know how to answer each person *(Cl. 4:6)*. (Amen)

For My Basic Needs
Gracious Lord, who gives good gifts to those who ask of you *(Mt. 7:11)*, and who opens his hand to satisfy the desire of every living thing *(Ps. 145:16)*. you know my needs before I ask *(Mt. 6:8)*, yet desire my petitions *(Mt. 7:7; Ja. 4:2)*: Provide the things that are necessary: my food, my drink, my clothing; a dry and safe place to dwell, that is cool in the summer and warm in the winter *(Siddur)*. Give me not poverty, lest I steal and profane Your Name. Give me not riches, lest I be full and deny You *(Pr. 30:7-9)*. *[State additional needs]* I will trust that, according to Your promise, You will supply all my needs *(Mt. 6:33; Ph. 4:19)*. (Amen)

For My Leisure
O God, in the course of this busy life, give us times of refreshment and peace. And grant that we may so use our leisure and hobby, to rebuild our bodies and renew our minds, that our hearts may be ever more aware of the goodness of the life that You have given to us *(BOCP)*. (Amen)

Collects from the Book of Common Prayer
Go to Section **VII**, if it's a Holiday, or Section **VIII**, if it's a regular day, find by Day of the Month, and pray the daily Collect.

Prayers of Choice
Browse through the extensive list of over 250 Prayers in Sections **I-XI** of this book and pray according to want or need.

Free-From-Form Prayer
Pray from the heart whatever the Holy Spirit brings to Your attention.

Benediction
Go to Section **X** or **XI**, and select a benediction to close out your prayer time. And may the Lord hear your prayers and bless your day, Amen.

Daily Afternoon Session
For Individual or Family

The Lord's Prayer
Our Father in heaven, Hallowed be Your name. Your kingdom come. Your will be done On earth as *it is* in heaven. Give us this day our daily bread. And forgive us our debts, As we forgive our debtors. And do not lead us into temptation, But deliver us from the evil one. For Yours is the kingdom and the power and the glory forever. Amen *(Mt. 6:9-13-NKJV)*.

For My Gratitude/Thankfulness
I will give thanks to You, Lord, with all my heart, and will recount all Your wonderful deeds *(Ps. 9:1)*. My heart leaps for joy, and with my song I give thanks to You *(Ps. 28:7)*. For every good and perfect gift is from You, the Father of Lights from above *(Ja. 1:17)*. *[State any special gratitude]* Lord, You are good and Your love endures forever; and Your faithfulness extends to all generations *(Ps. 100:4,5)*. May the fruit of my lips always give thanks to Your Name *(He. 13:15)*. And may my ultimate expression of gratitude be the offering up of my body as a living sacrifice that is holy and pleasing to You *(Ro. 12:1)*. **(Amen)**

For My Personal Holiness
Holy Lord God Almighty, You chose me before the foundation of the world, that I should be holy and blameless before You *(Ep. 1:4)*. You foreknew me and predestined me to be conformed to the image of Your Son *(Ro. 8:29)*, as an obedient child, not being conformed to my previous passions *(1 Pe. 1:14)*, but that I might be holy in all my conduct, because You are holy *(1 Pe. 1:15,16)*. For without holiness, no one will see You *(He. 12:14)*. Grant it today, that I be crucified with Christ, that Christ might live in me *(Ga. 2:20)*, and strengthen me by Your grace to flee lusts and pursue righteousness, along with those who call on You from a pure heart *(2 Ti. 2:22)*. **(Amen)**

For My Spiritual Strength
Mighty God, strengthen me with all power for Christian endurance, according to Your glorious might *(Cl. 1:11)*. You know my frame, that I am dust *(Ps. 103:14)*, for my flesh is weak, but my spirit is willing. Draw me to watch with You *(Mk. 14:38)*, and teach me to wait upon You, that my strength might be renewed *(Is. 40:31)*. Where I am weak—and will be weak—let your strength be made perfect in me *(2 Co. 12:9)*, that I may say that I am strong *(Jl. 3:10)*, and do all things through Christ as He strengthens me *(Ph. 4:13)*. **(Amen)**

For My Choices/Decisions
Eternal God, Who declares the end from the beginning *(Is. 46:10)*, order all my steps *(Ps. 37:23)* and establish my plans *(Pr. 16:3)*. Life on earth is but a vapor that appears for a little while and then vanishes away *(Ja. 4:14)*, so teach me to number my days *(Ps. 90:12)*, and to trust in You, involving You in all my ways, instead of leaning on my own understanding. Make my paths straight *(Pr. 3:5,6)*, so that I walk—not unwisely—but wisely, making the best use of my time in this present evil world *(Ep. 5:15,16)*. **(Amen)**

Prayers of Choice
Browse through the extensive list of over 250 Prayers in Sections **I-XI** of this book and pray according to want or need.

Free-From-Form Prayer
Pray from the heart whatever the Holy Spirit brings to Your attention.

For My Afternoon
O Lord, support me the rest of this day, until the shadows lengthen, and the evening comes, and the busy world is hushed, and the fever of this day is over, and our work is done. Then, in Your mercy, grant me a safe time of dwelling, and a holy rest, and peace at the last *(BOCP)*. **(In Jesus Name, Amen)**

Daily Evening/Bedtime Session
For Individual or Family

For Confession
Loving and merciful God, be gracious to me and hear my prayer *(Ps. 4:1)*. I acknowledge my sins and iniquities and do not hide them *(Ps. 32:5)*. I confess that I have sinned against You in thought, word, and deed, by what I have done, and by what I have left undone *(BOCP)*. [State sins] Father, forgive me of my sins, and cleanse me from all my unrighteousness *(1 Jn. 1:9)*. Wash me thoroughly and I shall be whiter than snow *(Ps. 51:7)*, through the blood of Your Son *(Re. 7:14)*. **(Amen)**

Scriptures of Choice
Spend about 5-15 minutes reading the scriptures of Your choice.

Praises
Go to Section **VI**, find by date, and pray your daily Praises again.

Collects from the Book of Common Prayer
Go to Section **VII**, if it's a Holiday, or Section **VIII**, if it's a regular day, find by Holiday or Day of the Month, and pray the daily Collect again.

Prayers of Choice
Browse through the extensive list of over 250 Prayers in Sections **I-XI** of this book and pray according to want or need.

Free-From-Form Prayer
Pray from the heart whatever the Holy Spirit brings to Your attention.

For My Evening
Let my prayer be set forth in Your sight as the incense, and let the lifting up of my hands be an evening sacrifice *(Ps. 141:2)*. Morning and evening, I bring my life as a consecration offering to You *(2 Ch. 31:3)*. For the day is yours, O God, and also the night. You have established the sun and the moon *(BOCP; Ps. 74:15,16)*. **(Amen)**

For Bedtime
Lord Almighty, grant me a perfect day's end, and a peaceful night *(Ps. 74:15,16)*, that I may lie down in peace, and at once fall asleep. For only You, Lord, make me dwell in safety, and give Your beloved rest *(Ps. 127:2)*. Be my light in the darkness and defend me from all the perils of this night. Visit this place and drive far from it all snares of the enemy.

Give Your holy angels charge over me to preserve me and guard my dreams. For into Your hands, I commend my spirit. Let Your blessing be upon me always; as waking, so sleeping *(BOCP, Compline)*. (In the Name of Jesus, Amen)

IV. Devotions

My Utmost For His Highest

By Oswald Chambers

January 1
LET US KEEP TO THE POINT

"My eager desire and hope being that I may never feel ashamed, but that now as ever I may do honour to Christ in my own person by fearless courage." Philippians 1:20 (MOFFATT)

My Utmost for His Highest. "My eager desire and hope being that I may never feel ashamed." We shall all feel very much ashamed if we do not yield to Jesus on the point He has asked us to yield to Him. Paul says - "My determination is to be my utmost for His Highest." To get there is a question of will, not of debate nor of reasoning, but a surrender of will, an absolute and irrevocable surrender on that point. An overweening consideration for ourselves is the thing that keeps us from that decision, though we put it that we are considering others. When we consider what it will cost others if we obey the call of Jesus, we tell God He does not know what our obedience will mean. Keep to the point; He does know. Shut out every other consideration and keep yourself before God for this one thing only - My Utmost for His Highest. I am determined to be absolutely and entirely for Him and for Him alone.My Undeterredness for His Holiness. "Whether that means life or death, no matter!" (v.21.) Paul is determined that nothing shall deter him from doing exactly what God wants. God's order has to work up to a crisis in our lives because we will not heed the gentler way. He brings us to the place where He asks us to be our utmost for Him, and we begin to debate; then He produces a providential crisis where we have to decide - for or against, and from that point the "Great Divide" begins. If the crisis has come to you on any line, surrender your will to Him absolutely and irrevocably.

January 2
WILL YOU GO OUT WITHOUT KNOWING?

"He went out, not knowing whither he went." Hebrews 11:8

Have you been "out" in this way? If so, there is no logical statement possible when anyone asks you what you are doing. One of the difficulties in Christian work is this question - "What do you expect to do?" You do not know what you are going to do; the only thing you know is that God knows what He is doing. Continually revise your attitude towards God and see if it is a going out of everything, trusting in God entirely. It is this attitude that keeps you in perpetual wonder - you do not know what God is going to do next. Each morning you wake it is to be a "going out," building in confidence on God. "Take no thought for your life, . . . nor yet for your body" -take no thought for the things for which you did take thought before you "went out." Have you been asking God what He is going to do? He will never tell you. God does not tell you what He is going to do; He reveals to you Who He is. Do you believe in a miracle-working God, and will you go out in surrender to Him until you are not surprised an atom at anything He does? Suppose God is the God you know Him to be when you are nearest to Him - what an impertinence worry is! Let the attitude of the life be a continual "going out" in dependence upon God, and your life will have an ineffable charm about it which is a satisfaction to Jesus. You have to learn to go out of convictions, out of creeds, out of experiences, until so far as your faith is concerned, there is nothing between yourself and God

---

January 3
CLOUDS AND DARKNESS

"Clouds and darkness are round about Him." Psalm 97:2

A man who has not been born of the Spirit of God will tell you that the teachings of Jesus are simple. But when you are baptized with the Holy Ghost, you find "clouds and darkness are round about Him." When we come into close contact with the teachings of Jesus Christ we have our first insight into this aspect of things. The only possibility of understanding the teaching of Jesus is by the light of the Spirit of God on the inside. If we have never had the experience of taking our commonplace religious shoes off our commonplace religious feet, and getting rid of all the undue familiarity with which we approach God, it is questionable whether we have ever stood in His presence. The people who are flippant and familiar are those who have never yet been introduced to Jesus Christ. After the amazing delight and liberty of realizing what Jesus Christ does, comes the impenetrable darkness of realizing Who He is. Jesus said: "The words that I speak unto you," not the words I have spoken, "they are spirit, and they are life." The Bible has been so many words to us - clouds and darkness - then all of a sudden the words become spirit and life because Jesus re-speaks them to us in a particular condition. That is the way God speaks to us, not by visions and dreams, but by words. When a man gets to God it is by the most simple way of words.

January 4
WHY CANNOT I FOLLOW THEE NOW?

"Peter said unto Him, Lord, why cannot I follow Thee now?" John 13:37

There are times when you cannot understand why you cannot do what you want to do. When God brings the blank space, see that you do not fill it in, but wait. The blank space may come in order to teach you what sanctification means, or it may come after sanctification to teach you what service means. Never run before God's guidance. If there is the slightest doubt, then He is not guiding. Whenever there is doubt - don't. In the beginning you may see clearly what God's will is - the severance of a friendship, the breaking off of a business relationship, something you feel distinctly before God is His will for you to do, never do it on the impulse of that feeling. If you do, you will end in making difficulties that will take years of time to put right. Wait for God's time to bring it round and He will do it without any heartbreak or disappointment. When it is a question of the providential will of God, wait for God to move. Peter did not wait on God, he forecast in his mind where the test would come, and the test came where he did not expect it. "I will lay down my life for Thy sake." Peter's declaration was honest but ignorant. "Jesus answered him ...The cock shall not crow, till thou hast denied Me thrice." This was said with a deeper knowledge of Peter than Peter had of himself. He could not follow Jesus because he did not know himself, of what he was capable. Natural devotion may be all very well to attract us to Jesus, to make us feel His fascination, but it will never make us disciples. Natural devotion will always deny Jesus somewhere or other.

January 5
THE AFTERWARDS OF THE LIFE OF POWER

Whither I go, thou canst not follow Me now; but thou shalt follow Me afterwards." John 13:36

"And when He had spoken this, He saith unto him, Follow Me." Three years before, Jesus had said - "Follow Me," and Peter had followed easily, the fascination of Jesus was upon him, he did not need the Holy Spirit to help him to do it. Then he came to the place where he denied Jesus, and his heart broke. Then he received the Holy Spirit, and now Jesus says again - "Follow Me." There is no figure in front now saving the Lord Jesus Christ. The first "Follow Me" had nothing mystical in it, it was an external following; now it is a following in internal martyrdom (cf. John 21:18). Between these times Peter had denied Jesus with oaths and curses, he had come to the end of himself and all his self-sufficiency, there was not one strand of himself he would ever rely upon again, and in his destitution he was in a fit condition to receive an impartation from the risen Lord. "He breathed on them, and saith unto them, Receive ye the Holy Ghost." No matter what changes God has wrought in you, never rely upon them, build only on a Person, the Lord Jesus Christ, and on the Spirit He gives. All our vows and resolutions end in denial because we have no power to carry them out. When we have come to the end of ourselves, not in imagination but really, we are able to receive the Holy Spirit. "Receive ye the Holy Ghost" - the idea is that of invasion. There is only one lodestar in the life now, the Lord Jesus Christ.

January 6
WORSHIP

"And he pitched his tent having Bethel on the west and Ai on the east: and there he builded an altar." Genesis 12:8

Worship is giving God the best that He has given you. Be careful what you do with the best you have. Whenever you get a blessing from God, give it back to Him as a love gift. Take time to meditate before God and offer the blessing back to Him in a deliberate act of worship. If you hoard a thing for yourself, it will turn into spiritual dry rot, as the manna did when it was hoarded. God will never let you hold a spiritual thing for yourself, it has to be given back to Him that He may make it a blessing to others. Bethel is the symbol of communion with God; Ai is the symbol of the world. Abraham pitched his tent between the two. The measure of the worth of our public activity for God is the private profound communion we have with Him. Rush is wrong every time, there is always plenty of time to worship God. Quiet days with God may be a snare. We have to pitch our tents where we shall always have quiet times with God, however noisy our times with the world may be. There are not three stages in spiritual life - worship, waiting and work. Some of us go in jumps like spiritual frogs, we jump from worship to waiting, and from waiting to work. God's idea is that the three should go together. They were always together in the life of Our Lord. He was unhasting and unresting. It is a discipline, we cannot get into it all at once.

January 7
INTIMATE WITH JESUS

"Have I been so long with you, and yet hast thou not known Me?" John 14:9

These words are not spoken as a rebuke, nor even with surprise; Jesus is leading Philip on. The last One with whom we get intimate is Jesus.

Before Pentecost the disciples knew Jesus as the One Who gave them power to conquer demons and to bring about a revival (see Luke 10:18-20). It was a wonderful intimacy, but there was a much closer intimacy to come - "I have called you friends." Friendship is rare on earth. It means identity in thought and heart and spirit. The whole discipline of life is to enable us to enter into this closest relationship with Jesus Christ. We receive His blessings and know His word, but do we know Him? Jesus said, "It is expedient for you that I go away" - in that relationship, so that He might lead them on. It is a joy to Jesus when a disciple takes time to step more intimately with Him. Fruit bearing is always mentioned as the manifestation of an intimate union with Jesus Christ (John 15:1-4). When once we get intimate with Jesus we are never lonely, we never need sympathy, we can pour out all the time without being pathetic. The saint who is intimate with Jesus will never leave impressions of himself, but only the impression that Jesus is having unhindered way, because the last abyss of his nature has been satisfied by Jesus. The only impression left by such a life is that of the strong calm sanity that Our Lord gives to those who are intimate with Him.

January 8
DOES MY SACRIFICE LIVE?

"And Abraham built an altar . . and bound Isaac his son." Genesis 22:9

This incident is a picture of the blunder we make in thinking that the final thing God wants of us is the sacrifice of death. What God wants is the sacrifice through death which enables us to do what Jesus did, viz., sacrifice our lives. Not - I am willing to go to death with Thee, but - I am willing to be identified with Thy death so that I may sacrifice my life to God. We seem to think that God wants us to give up things! God purified Abraham from this blunder, and the same discipline goes on in our lives. God nowhere tells us to give up things for the sake of giving them up. He tells us to give them up for the sake of the only thing worth having - viz., life with Himself. It is a question of loosening the bands that hinder the life, and immediately those bands are loosened by identification with the death of Jesus, we enter into a relationship with God whereby we can sacrifice our lives to Him. It is of no value to God to give Him your life for death. He wants you to be a "living sacrifice," to let Him have all your powers that have been saved and sanctified through Jesus. This is the thing that is acceptable to God.

January 9
INTERCESSORY INTROSPECTION

"And I pray God your whole spirit and soul and body be preserved blameless." 1 Thess 5:23

"Your whole spirit. . ." The great mystical work of the Holy Spirit is in the dim regions of our personality which we cannot get at. Read the 139th Psalm; the Psalmist implies - "Thou art the God of the early mornings, the God of the late at nights, the God of the mountain peaks, and the God of the sea; but, my God, my soul has further horizons than the early mornings, deeper darkness than the nights of earth, higher peaks than any mountain peaks, greater depths than any sea in nature - Thou Who art the God of all these, be my God. I cannot reach to the heights or to the depths; there are motives I cannot trace, dreams I cannot get at - my God, search me out." Do we believe that God can garrison the imagination far beyond where we can go? "The blood of Jesus Christ cleanseth us from all sin" - if that means in conscious experience only, may God have mercy on us. The man who has been made obtuse by sin will say he is not conscious of sin. Cleansing from sin is to the very heights and depths of our spirit if we will keep in the light as God is in the light, and the very Spirit that fed the life of Jesus Christ will feed the life of our spirits. It is only when we are garrisoned by God with the stupendous sanctity of the Holy Spirit, that spirit, soul and body are preserved in unspotted integrity, undeserving of censure in God's sight, until Jesus comes. We do not allow our minds to dwell as they should on these great massive truths of God.

January 10
THE OPENED SIGHT

"To open their eyes . . . that they may receive . . ." Acts 26:18

This verse is the grandest condensation of the propaganda of a disciple of Jesus Christ in the whole of the New Testament. The first sovereign work of grace is summed up in the word - "that they may receive remission of sins." When a man fails in personal Christian experience, it is nearly always because he has never received anything. The only sign that a man is saved is that he has received something from Jesus Christ. Our part as workers for God is to open men's eyes that they may turn themselves from darkness to light; but that is not salvation, that is conversion - the effort of a roused human being. I do not think it is too sweeping to say that the majority of nominal Christians are of this order; their eyes are opened, but they have received nothing. Conversion is not regeneration. This is one of the neglected factors in our preaching today. When a man is born again, he knows that it is because he has received something as a gift from Almighty God and not because of his own decision. People register their vows, and sign their pledges, and determine to go through, but none of this is salvation. Salvation means that we are brought to the place where we are able to receive something from God on the authority of Jesus Christ, viz., remission of sins. Then there follows the second mighty work of grace - "an inheritance among them which are sanctified." In sanctification the regenerated soul deliberately gives up his right to himself to Jesus Christ, and identifies himself entirely with God's interest in other men.

January 11
WHAT MY OBEDIENCE TO GOD COSTS OTHER PEOPLE

"They laid hold upon one Simon . . . and on him they laid the cross." Luke 23:26

If we obey God it is going to cost other people more than it costs us, and that is where the sting comes in. If we are in love with our Lord, obedience does not cost us anything, it is a delight, but it costs those who do not love Him a good deal. If we obey God it will mean that other people's plans are upset, and they will gibe us with it - "You call this Christianity?" We can prevent the suffering; but if we are going to obey God, we must not prevent it, we must let the cost be paid. Our human pride entrenches itself on this point, and we say - I will never accept anything from anyone. We shall have to, or disobey God. We have no right to expect to be in any other relation than our Lord Himself was in (see Luke 8:2-3). Stagnation in spiritual life comes when we say we will bear the whole thing ourselves. We cannot. We are so involved in the universal purposes of God that immediately we obey God, others are affected. Are we going to remain loyal in our obedience to God and go through the humiliation of refusing to be independent, or are we going to take the other line and say - I will not cost other people suffering? We can disobey God if we choose, and it will bring immediate relief to the situation, but we shall be a grief to our Lord. Whereas if we obey God, He will look after those who have been pressed into the consequences of our obedience. We have simply to obey and to leave all consequences with Him. Beware of the inclination to dictate to God as to what you will allow to happen if you obey Him.

January 12
HAVE YOU EVER BEEN ALONE WITH GOD?

"When they were alone, He expounded all things to His disciples." Mark 4:34

Our Solitude with Him. Jesus does not take us alone and expound things to us all the time; He expounds things to us as we can understand them. Other lives are parables. God is making us spell out our own souls. It is slow work, so slow that it takes God all time and eternity to make a man and woman after His own purpose. The only way we can be of use to God is to let Him take us through the crooks and crannies of our own characters. It is astounding how ignorant we are about ourselves! We do not know envy when we see it, or laziness, or pride. Jesus reveals to us all that this body has been harbouring before His grace began to work. How many of us have learned to look in with courage? We have to get rid of the idea that we understand ourselves, it is the last conceit to go. The only One Who understands us is God. The greatest curse in spiritual life is conceit. If we have ever had a glimpse of what we are like in the sight of God, we shall never say - "Oh, I am so unworthy," because we shall know we are, beyond the possibility of stating it. As long as we are not quite sure that we are unworthy, God will keep narrowing us in until He gets us alone. Wherever there is any element of pride or of conceit, Jesus cannot expound a thing. He will take us through the disappointment of a wounded pride of intellect, through disappointment of heart. He will reveal inordinate affection - things over which we never thought He would have to get us alone. We listen to many things in classes, but they are not an exposition to us yet. They will be when God gets us alone over them.

January 13
HAVE YOU EVER BEEN ALONE WITH GOD?

"When He was alone the twelve . . . asked of Him . . ." Mark 4:10

His Solitude with Us. When God gets us alone by affliction, heartbreak, or temptation, by disappointment, sickness, or by thwarted affection, by a broken friendship, or by a new friendship -when He gets us absolutely alone, and we are dumbfounded, and cannot ask one question, then He begins to expound. Watch Jesus Christ's training of the twelve. It was the disciples, not the crowd outside, who were perplexed. They constantly asked Him questions, and He constantly expounded things to them; but they only understood after they had received the Holy Spirit (see John 14:26). If you are going on with God, the only thing that is clear to you, and the only thing God intends to be clear, is the way He deals with your own soul. Your brother's sorrows and perplexities are an absolute confusion to you. We imagine we understand where the other person is, until God gives us a dose of the plague of our own hearts. There are whole tracts of stubbornness and ignorance to be revealed by the Holy Spirit in each one of us, and it can only be done when Jesus gets us alone. Are we alone with Him now, or are we taken up with little fussy notions, fussy comradeships in God's service, fussy ideas about our bodies? Jesus can expound nothing until we get through all the noisy questions of the head and are alone with Him.

January 14
CALLED OF GOD

"Whom shall I send, and who will go for us? Then said I, Here am I; send me." Isaiah 6:8

God did not address the call to Isaiah; Isaiah overheard God saying, "Who will go for us?" The call of God is not for the special few, it is for everyone. Whether or not I hear God's call depends upon the state of my ears; and what I hear depends upon my disposition. "Many are called but few are chosen," that is, few prove themselves the chosen ones. The chosen ones are those who have come into a relationship with God through Jesus Christ whereby their disposition has been altered and their ears unstopped, and they hear the still small voice questioning all the time, "Who will go for us?" It is not a question of God singling out a man and saying, "Now, you go." God did not lay a strong compulsion on Isaiah; Isaiah was in the presence of God and he overheard the call, and realized that there was nothing else for him but to say, in conscious freedom, "Here am I, send me." Get out of your mind the idea of expecting God to come with compulsions and pleadings. When our Lord called His disciples there was no irresistible compulsion from outside. The quiet passionate insistence of His "Follow Me" was spoken to men with every power wide awake. If we let the Spirit of God bring us face to face with God, we too shall hear something akin to what Isaiah heard, the still small voice of God; and in perfect freedom will say, "Here am I; send me."

January 15
DO YOU WALK IN WHITE?

"Buried with Him . . . that . . . even so we also should walk in newness of life." Romans 6:4

No one enters into the experience of entire sanctification without going through a "white funeral" - the burial of the old life. If there has never been this crisis of death, sanctification is nothing more than a vision. There must be a "white funeral," - a death that has only one resurrection - a resurrection into the life of Jesus Christ. Nothing can upset such a life, it is one with God for one purpose, to be a witness to Him. Have you come to your last days really? You have come to them often in sentiment, but have you come to them really? You cannot go to your funeral in excitement, or die in excitement. Death means you stop being. Do you agree with God that you stop being the striving, earnest kind of Christian you have been? We skirt the cemetery and all the time refuse to go to death. It is not striving to go to death, it is dying - "baptized into His death." Have you had your "white funeral," or are you sacredly playing the fool with your soul? Is there a place in your life marked as the last day, a place to which the memory goes back with a chastened and extraordinarily grateful remembrance - "Yes, it was then, at that 'white funeral,' that I made an agreement with God." "This is the will of God, even your sanctification." When you realize what the will of God is, you will enter into sanctification as naturally as can be. Are you willing to go through that "white funeral" now? Do you agree with Him that this is your last day on earth? The moment of agreement depends upon you.

January 16
THE VOICE OF THE NATURE OF GOD

"I heard the voice of the Lord saying, Whom shall I send?" Isaiah 6:8

When we speak of the call of God, we are apt to forget the most important feature, viz., the nature of the One Who calls. There is the call of the sea, the call of the mountains, the call of the great ice barriers, but these calls are only heard by the few. The call is the expression of the nature from which it comes, and we can only record the call if the same nature is in us. The call of God is the expression of God's nature, not of our nature. There are strands of the call of God providentially at work for us which we recognize and no one else does. It is the threading of God's voice to us in some particular matter, and it is no use consulting anyone else about it. We have to keep that profound relationship between our souls and God. The call of God is not the echo of my nature; my affinities and personal temperament are not considered. As long as I consider my personal temperament and think about what I am fitted for, I shall never hear the call of God. But when I am brought into relationship with God, I am in the condition Isaiah was in. Isaiah's soul was so attuned to God by the tremendous crisis he had gone through that he recorded the call of God to his amazed soul. The majority of us have no ear for anything but ourselves, we cannot hear a thing God says.

To be brought into the zone of the call of God is to be profoundly altered.

January 17
THE VOCATION OF THE NATURAL LIFE

"But when it pleased God . . . to reveal His Son in me . . ." Galatians 1:15-16

The call of God is not a call to any particular service; my interpretation of it may be because contact with the nature of God has made me realize what I would like to do for Him. The call of God is essentially expressive of His nature; service is the outcome of what is fitted to my nature. The vocation of the natural life is stated by the apostle Paul - "When it pleased God to reveal His Son in me that I might preach Him" (i.e., sacramentally express) "among the Gentiles." Service is the overflow of superabounding devotion; but, profoundly speaking, there is no call to that, it is my own little actual bit and is the echo of my identification with the nature of God. Service is the natural part of my life. God gets me into a relationship with Himself whereby I understand His call, then I do things out of sheer love for Him on my own account. To serve God is the deliberate love-gift of a nature that has heard the call of God.

Service is expressive of that which is fitted to my nature: God's call is expressive of His nature; consequently when I receive His nature and hear His call, the voice of the Divine nature sounds in both and the two work together. The Son of God reveals Himself in me, and I serve Him in the ordinary ways of life out of devotion to Him.

January 18
IT IS THE LORD!

"Thomas answered and said unto Him, My Lord and my God." John 20:28

"Give Me to drink." How many of us are set upon Jesus Christ slaking our thirst when we ought to be satisfying Him? We should be pouring out now, spending to the last limit, not drawing on Him to satisfy us. "Ye shall be witnesses unto Me" - that means a life of unsullied, uncompromising and unbribed devotion to the Lord Jesus, a satisfaction to Him wherever He places us. Beware of anything that competes with loyalty to Jesus Christ. The greatest competitor of devotion to Jesus is service for Him. It is easier to serve than to be drunk to the dregs. The one aim of the call of God is the satisfaction of God, not a call to do something for Him. We are not sent to battle for God, but to be used by God in His battlings. Are we being more devoted to service than to Jesus Christ?

January 19
VISION AND DARKNESS

"An horror of great darkness fell upon him." Genesis 15:12

Whenever God gives a vision to a saint, He puts him, as it were, in the shadow of His hand, and the saint's duty is to be still and listen. There is a darkness which comes from excess of light, and then is the time to listen. Genesis 16 is an illustration of listening to good advice when it is dark instead of waiting for God to send the light. When God gives a vision and darkness follows, wait. God will make you in accordance with the vision He has given if you will wait His time. Never try and help God fulfil His word. Abraham went through thirteen years of silence, but in those years all self-sufficiency was destroyed; there was no possibility left of relying on common-sense ways. Those years of silence were a time of discipline, not of displeasure. Never pump up joy and confidence, but stay upon God (cf. Isaiah 50:10,11). Have I any confidence in the flesh? Or have I got beyond all confidence in myself and in men and women of God; in books and prayers and ecstasies; and is my confidence placed now in God Himself, not in His blessings? "I am the Almighty God" - ElShaddai, the Father-Mother God. The one thing for which we are all being disciplined is to know that God is real. As soon as God becomes real, other people become shadows. Nothing that other saints do or say can ever perturb the one who is built on God.

January 20
ARE YOU FRESH FOR EVERYTHING?

"Except a man be born again, he cannot see the kingdom of God." John 3:3

Sometimes we are fresh for a prayer meeting but not fresh for cleaning boots! Being born again of the Spirit is an unmistakable work of God, as mysterious as the wind, as surprising as God Himself. We do not know where it begins, it is hidden away in the depths of our personal life. Being born again from above is a perennial, perpetual and eternal beginning; a freshness all the time in thinking and in talking and in living, the continual surprise of the life of God. Staleness is an indication of something out of joint with God - "I must do this thing or it will never be done." That is the first sign of staleness. Are we freshly born this minute or are we stale, raking in our minds for something to do? Freshness does not come from obedience but from the Holy Spirit; obedience keeps us in the light as God is in the light. Guard jealously your relationship to God. Jesus prayed "that they may be one, even as we are one" - nothing between. Keep all the life perennially open to Jesus Christ, don't pretend with Him. Are you drawing your life from any other source than God Himself? If you are depending upon anything but Him, you will never know when He is gone. Being born of the Spirit means much more than we generally take it to mean. It gives us a new vision and keeps us absolutely fresh for everything by the perennial supply of the life of God.

January 21
RECALL WHAT GOD REMEMBERS

"I remember . . . the kindness of thy youth." Jeremiah 2:2

Am I as spontaneously kind to God as I used to be, or am I only expecting God to be kind to me? Am I full of the little things that cheer His heart over me, or am I whimpering because things are going hardly with me? There is no joy in the soul that has forgotten what God prizes. It is a great thing to think that Jesus Christ has need of me - "Give Me to drink." How much kindness have I shown Him this past week? Have I been kind to His reputation in my life? God is saying to His people - You are not in love with Me now, but I remember the time when you were - "I remember . . . the love of thine espousals." Am I as full of the extravagance of love to Jesus Christ as I was in the beginning, when I went out of my way to prove my devotion to Him? Does He find me recalling the time when I did not care for anything but Himself? Am I there now, or have I become wise over loving Him? Am I so in love with Him that I take no account of where I go? or am I watching for the respect due to me; weighing how much service I ought to give? If, as I recall what God remembers about me, I find He is not what He used to be to me, let it produce shame and humiliation, because that shame will bring the godly sorrow that works repentance.

January 22
WHAT AM I LOOKING AT?

"Look unto Me, and be ye saved." Isaiah 45:22

Do we expect God to come to us with His blessings and save us? He says - Look unto Me, and be saved. The great difficulty spiritually is to concentrate on God, and it is His blessings that make it difficult. Troubles nearly always make us look to God; His blessings are apt to make us look elsewhere. The teaching of the Sermon on the Mount is, in effect - Narrow all your interests until the attitude of mind and heart and body is concentration on Jesus Christ. "Look unto Me." Many of us have a mental conception of what a Christian should be, and the lives of the saints become a hindrance to our concentration on God. There is no salvation in this way, it is not simple enough. "Look unto Me" and - not "you will be saved," but "you are saved."

The very thing we look for, we shall find if we will concentrate on Him. We get preoccupied and sulky with God, while all the time He is saying - "Look up and be saved." The difficulties and trials - the casting about in our minds as to what we shall do this summer, or tomorrow, all vanish when we look to God. Rouse yourself up and look to God. Build your hope on Him. No matter if there are a hundred and one things that press, resolutely exclude them all and look to Him. "Look unto Me," and salvation is, the moment you look.

January 23
TRANSFORMED BY INSIGHT

We all, with open face, beholding as in a glass the glory of the Lord, are changed into the same image." 2 Corinthians 3:18

The outstanding characteristic of a Christian is this unveiled frankness before God so that the life becomes a mirror for other lives. By being filled with the Spirit we are transformed, and by beholding we become mirrors. You always know when a man has been beholding the glory of the Lord, you feel in your inner spirit that he is the mirror of the Lord's own character. Beware of anything which would sully that mirror in you; it is nearly always a good thing, the good that is not the best. The golden rule for your life and mine is this concentrated keeping of the life open towards God. Let everything else - work, clothes, food, everything on earth - go by the board, saving that one thing. The rush of other things always tends to obscure this concentration on God. We have to maintain ourselves in the place of beholding, keeping the life absolutely spiritual all through. Let other things come and go as they may, let other people criticize as they will, but never allow anything to obscure the life that is hid with Christ in God. Never be hurried out of the relationship of abiding in Him. It is the one thing that is apt to fluctuate but it ought not to. The severest discipline of a Christian's life is to learn how to keep "beholding as in a glass the glory of the Lord."

January 24
THE OVERMASTERING DIRECTION

"I have appeared unto thee for this purpose." Acts 26:16

The vision Paul had on the road to Damascus was no passing emotion, but a vision that had very clear and emphatic directions for him, and he says, "I was not disobedient to the heavenly vision." Our Lord said, in effect, to Paul - Your whole life is to be overmastered by Me; you are to have no end, no aim, and no purpose but Mine. "I have chosen him." When we are born again we all have visions, if we are spiritual at all, of what Jesus wants us to be, and the great thing is to learn not to be disobedient to the vision, not to say that it cannot be attained. It is not sufficient to know that God has redeemed the world, and to know that the Holy Spirit can make all that Jesus did effectual in me; I must have the basis of a personal relationship to Him. Paul was not given a message or a doctrine to proclaim, he was brought into a vivid, personal, overmastering relationship to Jesus Christ. Verse 16 is immensely commanding - "to make thee a minister and a witness." There is nothing there apart from the personal relationship. Paul was devoted to a Person not to a cause. He was absolutely Jesus Christ's, he saw nothing else, he lived for nothing else. "For I determined not to know anything among you, save Jesus Christ, and Him crucified."

January 25
LEAVE ROOM FOR GOD

But when it pleased God. . ." Galatians 1:15

As workers for God we have to learn to make room for God - to give God "elbow room." We calculate and estimate, and say that this and that will happen, and we forget to make room for God to come in as He chooses. Would we be surprised if God came into our meeting or into our preaching in a way we had never looked for Him to come? Do not look for God to come in any particular way, but look for Him. That is the way to make room for Him. Expect Him to come, but do not expect Him only in a certain way. However much we may know God, the great lesson to learn is that at any minute He may break in. We are apt to over look this element of surprise, yet God never works in any other way. All of a sudden God meets the life - "When it was the good pleasure of God. . ." Keep your life so constant in its contact with God that His surprising power may break out on the right hand and on the left. Always be in a state of expectancy, and see that you leave room for God to come in as He likes.

January 26
LOOK AGAIN AND CONSECRATE

"If God so clothe the grass of the field . . . shall He not much more clothe you?" Matthew 6:30

A simple statement of Jesus is always a puzzle to us if we are not simple. How are we going to be simple with the simplicity of Jesus? By receiving His Spirit, recognizing and relying on Him, obeying Him as He brings the word of God, and life will become amazingly simple. "Consider," says Jesus, "how much more your Father Who clothes the grass of the field will clothe you, if you keep your relationship right with Him." Every time we have gone back in spiritual communion it has been because we have impertinently known better than Jesus Christ. We have allowed the cares of the world to come in, and have forgotten the "much more" of our Heavenly Father. "Behold the fowls of the air" - their main aim is to obey the principle of life that is in them and God looks after them. Jesus says that if you are rightly related to Him and obey His Spirit that is in you, God will look after your 'feathers.' "Consider the lilies of the field" - they grow where they are put. Many of us refuse to grow where we are put, consequently we take root nowhere. Jesus says that if we obey the life God has given us, He will look after all the other things. Has Jesus Christ told us a lie? If we are not experiencing the "much more," it is because we are not obeying the life God has given us, we are taken up with confusing considerations. How much time have we taken up worrying God with questions when we should have been absolutely free to concentrate on His work? Consecration means the continual separating of myself to one particular thing. We cannot consecrate once and for all. Am I continually separating myself to consider God every day of my life?

January 27
LOOK AGAIN AND THINK

"Take no thought for your life." Matthew 6:25

A warning which needs to be reiterated is that the cares of this world, the deceitfulness of riches, and the lust of other things entering in, will choke all that God puts in. We are never free from the recurring tides of this encroachment. If it does not come on the line of clothes and food, it will come on the line of money or lack of money; of friends or lack of friends; or on the line of difficult circumstances. It is one steady encroachment all the time, and unless we allow the Spirit of God to raise up the standard against it, these things will come in like a flood. "Take no thought for your life." "Be careful about one thing only," says our Lord - "your relationship to Me." Common sense shouts loud and says - "That is absurd, I must consider how I am going to live, I must consider what I am going to eat and drink." Jesus says you must not. Beware of allowing the thought that this statement is made by One Who does not understand our particular circumstances. Jesus Christ knows our circumstances better than we do, and He says we must not think about these things so as to make them the one concern of our life. Whenever there is competition, be sure that you put your relationship to God first. "Sufficient unto the day is the evil thereof." How much evil has begun to threaten you to-day? What kind of mean little imps have been looking in and saying - Now what are you going to do next month - this summer? "Be anxious for nothing," Jesus says. Look again and think. Keep your mind on the "much more" of your heavenly Father.

January 28
BUT IT IS HARDLY CREDIBLE THAT ONE COULD SO PERSECUTE JESUS!

"Saul, Saul, why persecutest thou Me?" Acts 26:14

Am I set on my own way for God? We are never free from this snare until we are brought into the experience of the baptism of the Holy Ghost and fire. Obstinacy and self-will will always stab Jesus Christ. It may hurt no one else, but it wounds His Spirit. Whenever we are obstinate and self-willed and set upon our own ambitions, we are hurting Jesus. Every time we stand on our rights and insist that this is what we intend to do, we are persecuting Jesus. Whenever we stand on our dignity we systematically vex and grieve His Spirit; and when the knowledge comes home that it is Jesus Whom we have been persecuting all the time, it is the most crushing revelation there could be. Is the word of God tremendously keen to me as I hand it on to you, or does my life give the lie to the things I profess to teach? I may teach sanctification and yet exhibit the spirit of Satan, the spirit that persecutes Jesus Christ. The Spirit of Jesus is conscious of one thing only - a perfect oneness with the Father, and He says, "Learn of Me, for I am meek and lowly in heart." All I do ought to be founded on a perfect oneness with Him, not on a self-willed determination to be godly. This will mean that I can be easily put upon, easily over-reached, easily ignored; but if I submit to it for His sake, I prevent Jesus Christ being persecuted.

January 29
BUT IT IS HARDLY CREDIBLE THAT ONE COULD BE SO POSITIVELY IGNORANT!

"Who art Thou, Lord?" Acts 26:15

"The Lord spake thus to me with a strong hand." There is no escape when Our Lord speaks, He always comes with an arrestment of the understanding. Has the voice of God come to you directly? If it has, you cannot mistake the intimate insistence with which it has spoken to you in the language you know best, not through your ears, but through your circumstances. God has to destroy our determined confidence in our own convictions. "I know this is what I should do" - and suddenly the voice of God speaks in a way that overwhelms us by revealing the depths of our ignorance. We have shown our ignorance of Him in the very way we determined to serve Him. We serve Jesus in a spirit that is not His, we hurt Him by our advocacy for Him, we push His claims in the spirit of the devil. Our words sound all right, but our spirit is that of an enemy. "He rebuked them, and said, Ye know not what manner of spirit ye are of." The spirit of our Lord in an advocate of His is described in 1 Corinthians 13. Have I been persecuting Jesus by a zealous determination to serve Him in my own way? If I feel I have done my duty and yet have hurt Him in doing it, I may be sure it was not my duty, because it has not fostered the meek and quiet spirit, but the spirit of self-satisfaction. We imagine that whatever is unpleasant is our duty! Is that anything like the spirit of our Lord - "I delight to do Thy will, O My God."

January 30
THE DILEMMA OF OBEDIENCE

"And Samuel feared to shew Eli the vision." 1 Samuel 3:15

God never speaks to us in startling ways, but in ways that are easy to misunderstand, and we say, "I wonder if that is God's voice?" Isaiah said that the Lord spake to him "with a strong hand," that is, by the pressure of circumstances. Nothing touches our lives but it is God Himself speaking. Do we discern His hand or only mere occurrence? Get into the habit of saying, "Speak, Lord," and life will become a romance. Every time circumstances press, say, "Speak, Lord"; make time to listen. Chastening is more than a means of discipline, it is meant to get me to the place of saying, "Speak, Lord." Recall the time when God did speak to you. Have you forgotten what He said? Was it Luke 11:13, or was it 1 Thess. 5:23? As we listen, our ear gets acute, and, like Jesus, we shall hear God all the time. Shall I tell my "Eli" what God has shown to me? That is where the dilemma of obedience comes in. We disobey God by becoming amateur providences - I must shield "Eli," the best people we know. God did not tell Samuel to tell Eli; he had to decide that for himself. God's call to you may hurt your "Eli;" but if you try to prevent the suffering in another life, it will prove an obstruction between your soul and God. It is at your own peril that you prevent the cutting off of the right hand or the plucking out of the eye. Never ask the advice of another about anything God makes you decide before Him. If you ask advice, you will nearly always side with Satan. "Immediately I conferred not with flesh and blood."

January 31
DO YOU SEE YOUR CALLING?

"Separated unto the Gospel." Romans 1:1

Our calling is not primarily to be holy men and women, but to be proclaimers of the Gospel of God. The one thing that is all important is that the Gospel of God should be realized as the abiding Reality. Reality is not human goodness, nor holiness, nor heaven, nor hell; but Redemption; and the need to perceive this is the most vital need of the Christian worker to-day. As workers we have to get used to the revelation that Redemption is the only Reality. Personal holiness is an effect, not a cause, and if we place our faith in human goodness, in the effect of Redemption, we shall go under when the test comes. Paul did not say he separated himself, but - "when it pleased God who separated me. . ." Paul had not a hypersensitive interest in his own character. As long as our eyes are upon our own personal whiteness we shall never get near the reality of Redemption. Workers break down because their desire is for their own whiteness, and not for God. "Don't ask me to come into contact with the rugged reality of Redemption on behalf of the filth of human life as it is; what I want is anything God can do for me to make me more desirable in my own eyes." To talk in that way is a sign that the reality of the Gospel of God has not begun to touch me; there is no reckless abandon to God. God cannot deliver me while my interest is merely in my own character. Paul is unconscious of himself, he is recklessly abandoned, separated by God for one purpose - to proclaim the Gospel of God (cf. Rom. 9:3.)

February 1

THE CALL OF GOD

"For Christ sent me not to baptize, but to preach the gospel." 1 Corinthians 1:17

Paul states here that the call of God is to preach the gospel; but remember what Paul means by "the gospel," viz., the reality of Redemption in our Lord Jesus Christ. We are apt to make sanctification the end-all of our preaching. Paul alludes to personal experience by way of illustration, never as the end of the matter. We are nowhere commissioned to preach salvation or sanctification; we are commissioned to lift up Jesus Christ (John 12:32). It is a travesty to say that Jesus Christ travailed in Redemption to make me a saint. Jesus Christ travailed in Redemption to redeem the whole world, and place it unimpaired and rehabilitated before the throne of God. The fact that Redemption can be experienced by us is an illustration of the power of the reality of Redemption, but that is not the end of Redemption. If God were human, how sick to the heart and weary He would be of the constant requests we make for our salvation, for our sanctification. We tax His energies from morning till night for things for ourselves - something for me to be delivered from! When we touch the bedrock of the reality of the Gospel of God, we shall never bother God any further with little personal plaints. The one passion of Paul's life was to proclaim the Gospel of God. He welcomed heart-breaks, disillusionments, tribulation, for one reason only, because these things kept him in unmoved devotion to the Gospel of God.

February 2
THE CONSTRAINT OF THE CALL
Woe is unto me, if I preach not the gospel!" 1 Corinthians 9:16

Beware of stopping your ears to the call of God. Everyone who is saved is called to testify to the fact; but that is not the call to preach, it is merely an illustration in preaching. Paul is referring to the pangs produced in him by the constraint to preach the Gospel. Never apply what Paul says in this connection to souls coming in contact with God for salvation. There is nothing easier than getting saved because it is God's sovereign work - Come unto Me and I will save you. Our Lord never lays down the conditions of discipleship as the conditions of salvation. We are condemned to salvation through the Cross of Jesus Christ. Discipleship has an option with it - "IF any man. . . " Paul's words have to do with being made a servant of Jesus Christ, and our permission is never asked as to what we will do or where we will go. God makes us broken bread and poured-out wine to please Himself. To be "separated unto the gospel" means to hear the call of God; and when a man begins to overhear that call, then begins agony that is worthy of the name. Every ambition is nipped in the bud, every desire of life quenched, every outlook completely extinguished and blotted out, saving one thing only - "separated unto the gospel." Woe be to the soul who tries to put his foot in any other direction when once that call has come to him. This College exists for you, and you - to see whether God has a man or woman here who cares about proclaiming His Gospel; to see whether God grips you. And beware of competitors when God does grip you.

February 3
THE RECOGNIZED BAN OF RELATIONSHIP

"We are made as the filth of the world." 1 Corinthians 4:9-13

These words are not an exaggeration. The reason they are not true of us who call ourselves ministers of the gospel is not that Paul forgot the exact truth in using them, but that we have too many discreet affinities to allow ourselves to be made refuse. "Filling up that which is behind of the afflictions of Christ" is not an evidence of sanctification, but of being "separated unto the gospel." "Think it not strange concerning the fiery trial which is to try you," says Peter. If we do think it strange concerning the things we meet with, it is because we are craven-hearted. We have discreet affinities that keep us out of the mire - I won't stoop, I won't bend. You do not need to, you can be saved by the skin of your teeth if you like; you can refuse to let God count you as one separated unto the gospel. Or you may say - "I do not care if I am treated as the offscouring of the earth as long as the Gospel is proclaimed." A servant of Jesus Christ is one who is willing to go to martyrdom for the reality of the gospel of God. When a merely moral man or woman comes in contact with baseness and immorality and treachery, the recoil is so desperately offensive to human goodness that the heart shuts up in despair. The marvel of the Redemptive Reality of God is that the worst and the vilest can never get to the bottom of His love. Paul did not say that God separated him to show what a wonderful man He could make of him, but "to reveal His Son in me."

February 4
THE OVERMASTERING MAJESTY OF PERSONAL POWER

"For the love of Christ constraineth us." 2 Corinthians 5:14

Paul says he is overruled, overmastered, held as in a vice, by the love of Christ. Very few of us know what it means to be held in a grip by the love of God; we are held by the constraint of our experience only. The one thing that held Paul, until there was nothing else on his horizon, was the love of God. "The love of Christ constraineth us" - when you hear that note in a man or woman, you can never mistake it. You know that the Spirit of God is getting unhindered way in that life. When we are born again of the Spirit of God, the note of testimony is on what God has done for us, and rightly so. But the baptism of the Holy Ghost obliterates that for ever, and we begin to realize what Jesus meant when He said - "Ye shall be witnesses unto Me." Not witnesses to what Jesus can do - that is an elementary witness but "witnesses unto Me." We will take everything that happens as happening to Him, whether it be praise or blame, persecution or commendation. No one can stand like that for Jesus Christ who is not constrained by the majesty of His personal power. It is the only thing that matters, and the strange thing is that it is the last thing realized by the Christian worker. Paul says he is gripped by the love of God, that is why he acts as he does. Men may call him mad or sober, but he does not care; there is only one thing he is living for, and that is to persuade men of the judgment seat of God, and of the love of Christ. This abandon to the love of Christ is the one thing that bears fruit in the life, and it will always leave the impression of the holiness and of the power of God, never of our personal holiness.

February 5
ARE YOU READY TO BE OFFERED?

"Yea, and if I be offered upon the sacrifice and service of your faith, I joy and rejoice with you all." Philippians 2:17

Are you willing to be offered for the work of the faithful - to pour out your life blood as a libation on the sacrifice of the faith of others? Or do you say - "I am not going to be offered up just yet, I do not want God to choose my work. I want to choose the scenery of my own sacrifice; I want to have the right kind of people watching and saying, 'Well done.' It is one thing to go on the lonely way with dignified heroism, but quite another thing if the line mapped out for you by God means being a door-mat under other people's feet. Suppose God wants to teach you to say, "I know how to be abased" - are you ready to be offered up like that? Are you ready to be not so much as a drop in a bucket - to be so hopelessly insignificant that you are never thought of again in connection with the life you served? Are you willing to spend and be spent; not seeking to be ministered unto, but to minister? Some saints cannot do menial work and remain saints because it is beneath their dignity.

February 6
ARE YOU READY TO BE OFFERED?

"I am already being poured out as a drink offering." 2 Timothy 4:6 (R. V. Marg.)

"I am ready to be offered." It is a transaction of will, not of sentiment. Tell God you are ready to be offered; then let the consequences be what they may, there is no strand of complaint now, no matter what God chooses. God puts you through the crisis in private, no one person can help an other. Externally the life may be the same; the difference is in will. Go through the crisis in will, then when it comes externally there will be no thought of the cost. If you do not transact in will with God along this line, you will end in awakening sympathy for yourself. "Bind the sacrifice with cords, even unto the horns of the altar." The altar means fire - burning and purification and insulation for one purpose only, the destruction of every affinity that God has not started and of every attachment that is not an attachment in God. You do not destroy it, God does; you bind the sacrifice to the horns of the altar; and see that you do not give way to self-pity when the fire begins. After this way of fire, there is nothing that oppresses or depresses. When the crisis arises, you realize that things cannot touch you as they used to do. What is your way of fire? Tell God you are ready to be offered, and God will prove Himself to be all you ever dreamed He would be.

February 7
THE DISCIPLINE OF DEJECTION

"But we trusted . . . and beside all this, to-day is the third day . . ." Luke 24:21

Every fact that the disciples stated was right; but the inferences they drew from those facts were wrong. Anything that savours of dejection spiritually is always wrong. If depression and oppression visit me, I am to blame; God is not, nor is anyone else. Dejection springs from one of two sources - I have either satisfied a lust or I have not. Lust means - I must have it at once. Spiritual lust makes me demand an answer from God, instead of seeking God Who gives the answer. What have I been trusting God would do? And to-day - the immediate present - is the third day, and He has not done it; therefore I imagine I am justified in being dejected and in blaming God. Whenever the insistence is on the point that God answers prayer, we are off the track. The meaning of prayer is that we get hold of God, not of the answer. It is impossible to be well physically and to be dejected. Dejection is a sign of sickness, and the same thing is true spiritually. Dejection spiritually is wrong, and we are always to blame for it. We look for visions from heaven, for earthquakes and thunders of God's power (the fact that we are dejected proves that we do), and we never dream that all the time God is in the commonplace things and people around us. If we will do the duty that lies nearest, we shall see Him. One of the most amazing revelations of God comes when we learn that it is in the commonplace things that the Deity of Jesus Christ is realized.

February 8
SANCTIFICATION

"And the very God of peace sanctify you wholly." 1 Thessalonians 5:23-24

When we pray to be sanctified, are we prepared to face the standard of these verses? We take the term sanctification much too lightly. Are we prepared for what sanctification will cost? It will cost an intense narrowing of all our interests on earth, and an immense broadening of all our interests in God. Sanctification means intense concentration on God's point of view. It means every power of body, soul and spirit chained and kept for God's purpose only. Are we prepared for God to do in us all that He separated us for? And then after His work is done in us, are we prepared to separate ourselves to God even as Jesus did? "For their sakes I sanctify Myself." The reason some of us have not entered into the experience of sanctification is that we have not realized the meaning of sanctification from God's standpoint. Sanctification means being made one with Jesus so that the disposition that ruled Him will rule us. Are we prepared for what that will cost? It will cost everything that is not of God in us. Are we prepared to be caught up into the swing of this prayer of the apostle Paul's? Are we prepared to say - "Lord, make me as holy as You can make a sinner saved by grace"? Jesus has prayed that we might be one with Him as He is one with the Father. The one and only characteristic of the Holy Ghost in a man is a strong family likeness to Jesus Christ, and freedom from everything that is unlike Him. Are we prepared to set ourselves apart for the Holy Spirit's ministrations in us?

February 9

ARE YOU EXHAUSTED SPIRITUALLY?

"The everlasting God . . . fainteth not, neither is weary." Isaiah 40:28

Exhaustion means that the vital forces are worn right out. Spiritual exhaustion never comes through sin but only through service, and whether or not you are exhausted will depend upon where you get your supplies. Jesus said to Peter - "Feed My sheep," but He gave him nothing to feed them with. The process of being made broken bread and poured out wine means that you have to be the nourishment for other souls until they learn to feed on God. They must drain you to the dregs. Be careful that you get your supply, or before long you will be utterly exhausted. Before other souls learn to draw on the life of the Lord Jesus direct, they have to draw on it through you; you have to be literally "sucked," until they learn to take their nourishment from God. We owe it to God to be our best for His lambs and His sheep as well as for Himself. Has the way in which you have been serving God betrayed you into exhaustion? If so, then rally your affections. Where did you start the service from? From your own sympathy or from the basis of the Redemption of Jesus Christ? Continually go back to the foundation of your affections and recollect where the source of power is. You have no right to say - "O Lord, I am so exhausted." He saved and sanctified you in order to exhaust you. Be exhausted for God, but remember that your supply comes from Him. "All my fresh springs shall be in Thee."

February 10
IS YOUR IMAGINATION OF GOD STARVED?

"Lift up your eyes on high, and behold who hath created these things." Isaiah 40:26

The people of God in Isaiah's day had starved their imagination by looking on the face of idols, and Isaiah made them look up at the heavens, that is, he made them begin to use their imagination aright. Nature to a saint is sacramental. If we are children of God, we have a tremendous treasure in Nature. In every wind that blows, in every night and day of the year, in every sign of the sky, in every blossoming and in every withering of the earth, there is a real coming of God to us if we will simply use our starved imagination to realize it. The test of spiritual concentration is bringing the imagination into captivity. Is your imagination looking on the face of an idol? Is the idol yourself? Your work? Your conception of what a worker should be? Your experience of salvation and sanctification? Then your imagination of God is starved, and when you are up against difficulties you have no power, you can only endure in darkness. If your imagination is starved, do not look back to your own experience; it is God Whom you need. Go right out of yourself, away from the face of your idols, away from everything that has been starving your imagination. Rouse yourself, take the gibe that Isaiah gave the people, and deliberately turn your imagination to God. One of the reasons of stultification in prayer is that there is no imagination, no power of putting ourselves deliberately before God. We have to learn how to be broken bread and poured out wine on the line of intercession more than on the line of personal contact. Imagination is the power God gives a saint to posit himself out of himself into relationships he never was in.

February 11
IS YOUR HOPE IN GOD FAINT AND DYING?

"Thou wilt keep him in perfect peace whose imagination is stayed on Thee." Isaiah 26:3 (R. V. marg.)

Is your imagination stayed on God or is it starved? The starvation of the imagination is one of the most fruitful sources of exhaustion and sapping in a worker's life. If you have never used your imagination to put yourself before God, begin to do it now. It is no use waiting for God to come; you must put your imagination away from the face of idols and look unto Him and be saved. Imagination is the greatest gift God has given us and it ought to be devoted entirely to Him. If you have been bringing every thought into captivity to the obedience of Christ, it will be one of the greatest assets to faith when the time of trial comes, because your faith and the Spirit of God will work together. Learn to associate ideas worthy of God with all that happens in Nature - the sunrises and the sunsets, the sun and the stars, the changing seasons, and your imagination will never be at the mercy of your impulses, but will always be at the service of God. "We have sinned with our fathers; . . . and have forgotten" - then put a stiletto in the place where you have gone to sleep. "God is not talking to me just now," but He ought to be. Remember Whose you are and Whom you serve. Provoke yourself by recollection, and your affection for God will increase tenfold; your imagination will not be starved any longer, but will be quick and enthusiastic, and your hope will be inexpressibly bright.

February 12
MUST I LISTEN?

"And they said unto Moses, Speak thou with us and we will hear: but let not God speak with us, lest we die." Exodus 20:19

We do not consciously disobey God, we simply do not heed Him. God has given us His commands; there they are, but we do not pay any attention to them, not because of wilful disobedience but because we do not love and respect Him. "If ye love Me, ye will keep My commandments." When once we realize that we have been "disrespecting" God all the time, we are covered with shame and humiliation because we have not heeded Him. "Speak thou with us . . . but let not God speak with us." We show how little we love God by preferring to listen to His servants only. We like to listen to personal testimonies, but we do not desire that God Himself should speak to us. Why are we so terrified lest God should speak to us? Because we know that if God does speak, either the thing must be done or we must tell God we will not obey Him. If it is only the servant's voice we hear, we feel it is not imperative, we can say, "Well, that is simply your own idea, though I don't deny it is probably God's truth." Am I putting God in the humiliating position of having treated me as a child of His whilst all the time I have been ignoring Him? When I do hear Him, the humiliation I have put on Him comes back on me - "Lord, why was I so dull and so obstinate?" This is always the result when once we do hear God. The real delight of hearing Him is tempered with shame in having been so long in hearing Him.

February 13
THE DEVOTION OF HEARING

"Speak; for Thy servant heareth." 1 Samuel 3:10

Because I have listened definitely to one thing from God, it does not follow that I will listen to everything He says. The way in which I show God that I neither love nor respect Him is by the obtuseness of my heart and mind towards what He says. If I love my friend, I intuitively detect what he wants, and Jesus says, "Ye are My friends." Have I disobeyed some command of my Lord's this week? If I had realized that it was a command of Jesus, I would not consciously have disobeyed it; but most of us show such disrespect to God that we do not even hear what He says, He might never have spoken. The destiny of my spiritual life is such identification with Jesus Christ that I always hear God, and I know that God always hears me (John 11:41). If I am united with Jesus Christ, I hear God, by the devotion of hearing all the time. A lily, or a tree, or a servant of God, may convey God's message to me. What hinders me from hearing is that I am taken up with other things. It is not that I will not hear God, but I am not devoted in the right place. I am devoted to things, to service, to convictions, and God may say what He likes but I do not hear Him. The child attitude is always, "Speak, Lord, for Thy servant heareth." If I have not cultivated this devotion of hearing, I can only hear God's voice at certain times; at other times I am taken up with things - things which I say I must do, and I become deaf to Him, I am not living the life of a child. Have I heard God's voice to-day?

February 14
THE DISCIPLINE OF HEEDING

"What I tell you in darkness, that speak ye in light: and what ye hear in the ear, that preach ye upon the housetops." Matthew 10:27

At times God puts us through the discipline of darkness to teach us to heed Him. Song birds are taught to sing in the dark, and we are put into the shadow of God's hand until we learn to hear Him. "What I tell you in darkness" - watch where God puts you into darkness, and when you are there keep your mouth shut. Are you in the dark just now in your circumstances, or in your life with God? Then remain quiet. If you open your mouth in the dark, you will talk in the wrong mood: darkness is the time to listen. Don't talk to other people about it; don't read books to find out the reason of the darkness, but listen and heed. If you talk to other people, you cannot hear what God is saying. When you are in the dark, listen, and God will give you a very precious message for someone else when you get into the light. After every time of darkness there comes a mixture of delight and humiliation (if there is delight only, I question whether we have heard God at all), delight in hearing God speak, but chiefly humiliation - What a long time I was in hearing that! How slow I have been in understanding that! And yet God has been saying it all these days and weeks. Now He gives you the gift of humiliation which brings the softness of heart that will always listen to God now.

February 15
AM I MY BROTHER'S KEEPER?

"None of us liveth to himself." Romans 14:7.

Has it ever dawned on you that you are responsible for other souls spiritually before God? For instance, if I allow any private deflection from God in my life, everyone about me suffers. We "sit together in heavenly places." "Whether one member suffer, all the members suffer with it."

When once you allow physical selfishness, mental slovenliness, moral obtuseness, spiritual density, everyone belonging to your crowd will suffer. "But," you say, "who is sufficient for these things if you erect a standard like that?" "Our sufficiency is of God," and of Him alone. "Ye shall be My witnesses." How many of us are willing to spend every ounce of nervous energy, of mental, moral and spiritual energy we have for Jesus Christ? That is the meaning of a witness in God's sense of the word. It takes time, be patient with yourself. God has left us on the earth - what for? To be saved and sanctified? No, to be at it for Him. Am I willing to be broken bread and poured out wine for Him? To be spoilt for this age, for this life, to be spoilt from every standpoint but one - saving as I can disciple men and women to the Lord Jesus Christ. My life as a worker is the way I say "thank you" to God for His unspeakable salvation. Remember it is quite possible for any one of us to be flung out as reprobate silver - ". . . lest that by any means when I have preached to others, I myself should be a castaway."

February 16
THE INSPIRATION OF SPIRITUAL INITIATIVE

"Arise from the dead." Ephesians 5:14

All initiative is not inspired. A man may say to you - "Buck up, take your disinclination by the throat, throw it overboard, and walk out into the thing!" That is ordinary human initiative. But when the Spirit of God comes in and says, in effect, "Buck up," we find that the initiative is inspired. We all have any number of visions and ideals when we are young, but sooner or later we find that we have no power to make them real. We cannot do the things we long to do, and we are apt to settle down to the visions and ideals as dead, and God has to come and say - "Arise from the dead." When the inspiration of God does come, it comes with such miraculous power that we are able to arise from the dead and do the impossible thing. The remarkable thing about spiritual initiative is that the life comes after we do the "bucking up." God does not give us overcoming life; He gives us life as we overcome. When the inspiration of God comes, and He says - "Arise from the dead," we have to get up; God does not lift us up. Our Lord said to the man with the withered hand - "Stretch forth thy hand," and as soon as the man did so, his hand was healed, but he had to take the initiative. If we will do the overcoming, we shall find we are inspired of God because He gives life immediately.

February 17

THE INITIATIVE AGAINST DEPRESSION

"Arise and eat." 1 Kings 19:5

The angel did not give Elijah a vision, or explain the Scriptures to him, or do anything remarkable; he told Elijah to do the most ordinary thing, viz., to get up and eat. If we were never depressed we should not be alive; it is the nature of a crystal never to be depressed. A human being is capable of depression, otherwise there would be no capacity for exaltation. There are things that are calculated to depress, things that are of the nature of death; and in taking an estimate of yourself, always take into account the capacity for depression. When the Spirit of God comes He does not give us visions, He tells us to do the most ordinary things conceivable. Depression is apt to turn us away from the ordinary commonplace things of God's creation, but whenever God comes, the inspiration is to do the most natural simple thing - the things we would never have imagined God was in, and as we do them we find He is there. The inspiration which comes to us in this way is an initiative against depression; we have to do the next thing and do it in the inspiration of God. If we do a thing in order to overcome depression, we deepen the depression; but if the Spirit of God makes us feel intuitively that we must do the thing, and we do it, the depression is gone. Immediately we arise and obey, we enter on a higher plane of life.

February 18
THE INITIATIVE AGAINST DESPAIR
"Rise, let us be going." Matthew 26:46

The disciples went to sleep when they should have kept awake, and when they realized what they had done it produced despair. The sense of the irreparable is apt to make us despair, and we say - "It is all up now, it is no use trying any more." If we imagine that this kind of despair is exceptional, we are mistaken, it is a very ordinary human experience. Whenever we realize that we have not done that which we had a magnificent opportunity of doing, then we are apt to sink into despair; and Jesus Christ comes and says - "Sleep on now, that opportunity is lost for ever, you cannot alter it, but arise and go to the next thing." Let the past sleep, but let it sleep on the bosom of Christ, and go out into the irresistible future with Him. There are experiences like this in each of our lives. We are in despair, the despair that comes from actualities, and we cannot lift ourselves out of it. The disciples in this instance had done a downright unforgivable thing; they had gone to sleep instead of watching with Jesus, but He came with a spiritual initiative against their despair and said - "Arise and do the next thing." If we are inspired of

God, what is the next thing? To trust Him absolutely and to pray on the ground of His Redemption. Never let the sense of failure corrupt your new action.

February 19
THE INITIATIVE AGAINST DRUDGERY

"Arise, shine." Isaiah 60:1

We have to take the first step as though there were no God. It is no use to wait for God to help us, He will not; but immediately we arise we find He is there. Whenever God inspires, the initiative is a moral one. We must do the thing and not lie like a log. If we will arise and shine, drudgery becomes divinely transfigured. Drudgery is one of the finest touchstones of character there is. Drudgery is work that is very far removed from anything to do with the ideal - the utterly mean grubby things; and when we come in contact with them we know instantly whether or not we are spiritually real. Read John 13. We see there the Incarnate God doing the most desperate piece of drudgery, washing fishermen's feet, and He says - "If I then, your Lord and Master, have washed your feet, ye also ought to wash one another's feet." It requires the inspiration of God to go through drudgery with the light of God upon it. Some people do a certain thing and the way in which they do it hallows that thing for ever afterwards. It may be the most commonplace thing, but after we have seen them do it, it becomes different. When the Lord does a thing through us, He always transfigures it. Our Lord took on Him our human flesh and transfigured it, and it has become for every saint the temple of the Holy Ghost.

February 20
THE INITIATIVE AGAINST DREAMING

"Arise, let us go hence." John 14:31

Dreaming about a thing in order to do it properly is right; but dreaming about it when we should be doing it is wrong. After Our Lord had said those wonderful things to His disciples, we might have expected that He would tell them to go away and meditate over them all; but Our Lord never allowed "mooning." When we are getting into contact with God in order to find out what He wants, dreaming is right; but when we are inclined to spend our time in dreaming over what we have been told to do, it is a bad thing and God's blessing is never on it. God's initiative is always in the nature of a stab against this kind of dreaming, the stab that bids us "neither sit nor stand but go." If we are quietly waiting before God and He has said - "Come ye yourselves apart," then that is meditation before God in order to get at the line He wants; but always beware of giving over to mere dreaming when once God has spoken. Leave Him to be the source of all your dreams and joys and delights, and go out and obey what He has said. If you are in love, you do not sit down and dream about the one you love all the time, you go and do something for him; and that is what Jesus Christ expects us to do. Dreaming after God has spoken is an indication that we do not trust Him.

February 21
HAVE YOU EVER BEEN CARRIED AWAY FOR HIM?

"She hath wrought a good work on Me." Mark 14:6

If human love does not carry a man beyond himself, it is not love. If love is always discreet, always wise, always sensible and calculating, never carried beyond itself, it is not love at all. It may be affection, it may be warmth of feeling, but it has not the true nature of love in it. Have I ever been carried away to do something for God not because it was my duty, nor because it was useful, nor because there was anything in it at all beyond the fact that I love Him? Have I ever realized that I can bring to God things which are of value to Him, or am I mooning round the magnitude of His Redemption whilst there are any number of things I might be doing? Not Divine, colossal things which could be recorded as marvellous, but ordinary, simple human things which will give evidence to God that I am abandoned to Him? Have I ever produced in the heart of the Lord Jesus what Mary of Bethany produced? There are times when it seems as if God watches to see if we will give Him the abandoned tokens of how genuinely we do love Him. Abandon to God is of more value than personal holiness. Personal holiness focuses the eye on our own whiteness; we are greatly concerned about the way we walk and talk and look, fearful lest we offend Him. Perfect love casts out all that when once we are abandoned to God. We have to get rid of this notion - "Am I of any use?" and make up our minds that we are not, and we may be near the truth. It is never a question of being of use, but of being of value to God Himself. When we are abandoned to God, He works through us all the time.

February 22
THE DISCIPLINE OF SPIRITUAL TENACITY

"Be still, and know that I am God." Psalm 46:10

Tenacity is more than endurance, it is endurance combined with the absolute certainty that what we are looking for is going to transpire. Tenacity is more than hanging on, which may be but the weakness of being too afraid to fall off. Tenacity is the supreme effort of a man refusing to believe that his hero is going to be conquered. The greatest fear a man has is not that he will be damned, but that Jesus Christ will be worsted, that the things He stood for - love and justice and forgiveness and kindness among men - will not win out in the end; the things He stands for look like will-o'-the-wisps. Then comes the call to spiritual tenacity, not to hang on and do nothing, but to work deliberately on the certainty that God is not going to be worsted. If our hopes are being disappointed just now, it means that they are being purified. There is nothing noble the human mind has ever hoped for or dreamed of that will not be fulfilled. One of the greatest strains in life is the strain of waiting for God. "Because thou hast kept the word of my patience." Remain spiritually tenacious.

February 23
THE DETERMINATION TO SERVE

The Son of Man came not to be ministered unto, but to minister."
Matthew 20:28

Paul's idea of service is the same as Our Lord's: "I am among you as He that serveth;" "ourselves your servants for Jesus' sake." We have the idea that a man called to the ministry is called to be a different kind of being from other men. According to Jesus Christ, he is called to be the "door-mat" of other men; their spiritual leader, but never their superior. "I know how to be abased," says Paul. This is Paul's idea of service - "I will spend myself to the last ebb for you; you may give me praise or give me blame, it will make no difference." So long as there is a human being who does not know Jesus Christ, I am his debtor to serve him until he does. The mainspring of Paul's service is not love for men, but love for Jesus Christ. If we are devoted to the cause of humanity, we shall soon be crushed and broken-hearted, for we shall often meet with more ingratitude from men than we would from a dog; but if our motive is love to God, no ingratitude can hinder us from serving our fellow men. Paul's realization of how Jesus Christ had dealt with him is the secret of his determination to serve others. "I was before a perjurer, a blasphemer, an injurious person" - no matter how men may treat me, they will never treat me with the spite and hatred with which I treated Jesus Christ. When we realize that Jesus Christ has served us to the end of our meanness, our selfishness, and sin, nothing that we meet with from others can exhaust our determination to serve men for His sake.

February 24
THE DELIGHT OF SACRIFICE

"I will very gladly spend and be spent for you;" 2 Corinthians 12:15

When the Spirit of God has shed abroad the love of God in our hearts, we begin deliberately to identify ourselves with Jesus Christ's interests in other people, and Jesus Christ is interested in every kind of man there is. We have no right in Christian work to be guided by our affinities; this is one of the biggest tests of our relationship to Jesus Christ. The delight of sacrifice is that I lay down my life for my Friend, not fling it away, but deliberately lay my life out for Him and His interests in other people, not for a cause. Paul spent himself for one purpose only - that he might win men to Jesus Christ. Paul attracted to Jesus all the time, never to himself. "I am made all things to all men, that I might by all means save some." When a man says he must develop a holy life alone with God, he is of no more use to his fellow men: he puts himself on a pedestal, away from the common run of men. Paul became a sacramental personality; wherever he went, Jesus Christ helped Himself to his life. Many of us are after our own ends, and Jesus Christ cannot help Himself to our lives. If we are abandoned to Jesus, we have no ends of our own to serve. Paul said he knew how to be a "door-mat" without resenting it, because the mainspring of his life was devotion to Jesus. We are apt to be devoted, not to Jesus Christ, but to the things which emancipate us spiritually. That was not Paul's motive. "I could wish my self were accursed from Christ for my brethren" - wild, extravagant - is it? When a man is in love it is not an exaggeration to talk in that way, and Paul is in love with Jesus Christ.

February 25
THE DESTITUTION OF SERVICE

"Though the more abundantly I love you, the less I be loved." 2 Corinthians 12:15

Natural love expects some return, but Paul says - I do not care whether you love me or not, I am willing to destitute myself completely, not merely for your sakes, but that I may get you to God. "For ye know the grace of our Lord Jesus Christ, that, though He was rich, yet for your sakes He became poor." Paul's idea of service is exactly along that line - I do not care with what extravagance I spend myself, and I will do it gladly. It was a joyful thing to Paul. The ecclesiastical idea of a servant of God is not Jesus Christ's idea. His idea is that we serve Him by being the servants of other men. Jesus Christ out-socialists the socialists. He says that in His Kingdom he that is greatest shall be the servant of all. The real test of the saint is not preaching the gospel, but washing disciples' feet, that is, doing the things that do not count in the actual estimate of men but count everything in the estimate of God. Paul delighted to spend himself out for God's interests in other people, and he did not care what it cost. We come in with our economical notions - "Suppose God wants me to go there - what about the salary? What about the climate? How shall I be looked after? A man must consider these things." All that is an indication that we are serving God with a reserve. The apostle Paul had no reserve. Paul focuses Jesus Christ's idea of a New Testament saint in his life, viz.: not one who proclaims the Gospel merely, but one who becomes broken bread and poured out wine in the hands of Jesus Christ for other lives.

February 26
INFERIOR MISGIVINGS ABOUT JESUS

Sir, Thou hast nothing to draw with." John 4:11

"I am impressed with the wonder of what God says, but He cannot expect me really to live it out in the details of my life!" When it comes to facing Jesus Christ on His own merits, our attitude is one of pious superiority - Your ideals are high and they impress us, but in touch with actual things, it cannot be done. Each of us thinks about Jesus in this way in some particular. These misgivings about Jesus start from the amused questions put to us when we talk of our transactions with God - Where are you going to get your money from? How are you going to be looked after? Or they start from ourselves when we tell Jesus that our case is a bit too hard for Him. It is all very well to say "Trust in the Lord," but a man must live, and Jesus has nothing to draw with - nothing whereby to give us these things. Beware of the pious fraud in you which says - I have no misgivings about Jesus, only about myself. None of us ever had misgivings about ourselves; we know exactly what we cannot do, but we do have misgivings about Jesus. We are rather hurt at the idea that He can do what we cannot. My misgivings arise from the fact that I ransack my own person to find out how He will be able to do it. My questions spring from the depths of my own inferiority. If I detect these misgivings in myself, let me bring them to the light and confess them - "Lord, I have had misgivings about Thee, I have not believed in

Thy wits apart from my own; I have not believed in Thine almighty power apart from my finite understanding of it."

February 27
IMPOVERISHED MINISTRY OF JESUS

"From whence then hast Thou that living water?" John 4:11

"The well is deep" - and a great deal deeper than the Samaritan woman knew! Think of the depths of human nature, of human life, think of the depths of the "wells" in you. Have you been impoverishing the ministry of Jesus so that He can not do anything? Suppose there is a well of fathomless trouble inside your heart, and Jesus comes and says - "Let not your heart be troubled"; and you shrug your shoulders and say, "But, Lord, the well is deep; You cannot draw up quietness and comfort out of it." No, He will bring them down from above. Jesus does not bring anything up from the wells of human nature. We limit the Holy One of Israel by remembering what we have allowed Him to do for us in the past, and by saying, "Of course I cannot expect God to do this thing." The thing that taxes almightiness is the very thing which we as disciples of Jesus ought to believe He will do. We impoverish His ministry the moment we forget He is Almighty; the impoverishment is in us, not in Him. We will come to Jesus as Comforter or as Sympathizer, but we will not come to Him as Almighty. The reason some of us are such poor specimens of Christianity is because we have no Almighty Christ. We have Christian attributes and experiences, but there is no abandonment to Jesus Christ. When we get into difficult circumstances, we impoverish His ministry by saying - "Of course He cannot do any thing," and we struggle down to the deeps and try to get the water for ourselves. Beware of the satisfaction of sinking back and saying - "It can't be done"; you know it can be done if you look to Jesus. The well of your incompleteness is deep, but make the effort and look away to Him.

February 28
DO YE NOW BELIEVE?

"By this we believe . . . Jesus answered, Do ye now believe?" John 16:30-31

Now we believe. Jesus says - Do you? The time is coming when you will leave Me alone. Many a Christian worker has left Jesus Christ alone and gone into work from a sense of duty, or from a sense of need arising out of his own particular discernment. The reason for this is the absence of the resurrection life of Jesus. The soul has got out of intimate contact with God by leaning to its own religious understanding. There is no sin in it, and no punishment attached to it; but when the soul realizes how he has hindered his understanding of Jesus Christ, and produced for himself perplexities and sorrows and difficulties, it is with shame and contrition he has to come back. We need to rely on the resurrection life of Jesus much deeper down than we do, to get into the habit of steadily referring everything back to Him; instead of this we make our common - sense decisions and ask God to bless them. He cannot, it is not in His domain, it is severed from reality. If we do a thing from a sense of duty, we are putting up a standard in competition with Jesus Christ. We become a "superior person," and say - "Now in this matter I must do this and that." We have put our sense of duty on the throne instead of the resurrection life of Jesus. We are not told to walk in the light of conscience or of a sense of duty, but to walk in the light as God is in the light. When we do anything from a sense of duty, we can back it up by argument; when we do anything in obedience to the Lord, there is no argument possible; that is why a saint can be easily ridiculed.

February 29
WHAT DO YOU WANT THE LORD TO DO FOR YOU?

Lord, that I may receive my sight." Luke 18:41

What is the thing that not only disturbs you but makes you a disturbance? It is always some thing you cannot deal with yourself. "They rebuked him that he should hold his peace . . . but he cried so much the more." Persist in the disturbance until you get face to face with the Lord Himself; do not deify common sense. When Jesus asks us what we want Him to do for us in regard to the incredible thing with which we are faced, remember that He does not work in common-sense ways, but in supernatural ways. Watch how we limit the Lord by remembering what we have allowed Him to do for us in the past: I always failed there, and I always shall; consequently we do not ask for what we want. "It is ridiculous to ask God to do this." If it is an impossibility, it is the thing we have to ask. If it is not an impossible thing, it is not a real disturbance. God will do the absolutely impossible. This man received his sight. The most impossible thing to you is that you should be so identified with the Lord that there is nothing of the old life left. He will do it if you ask Him. But you have to come to the place where you believe Him to be Almighty. Faith is not in what Jesus says but in Himself; if we only look at what He says we shall never believe. When once we see Jesus, He does the impossible thing as naturally as breathing. Our agony comes through the wilful stupidity of our own

160

heart. We won't believe, we won't cut the shore line, we prefer to worry on.

March 1
THE UNDEVIATING QUESTION

"Lovest thou Me?" John 21:17

Peter declares nothing now (cf. Matthew 26:33-35). Natural individuality professes and declares; the love of the personality is only discovered by the hurt of the question of Jesus Christ. Peter loved Jesus in the way in which any natural man loves a good man. That is temperamental love; it may go deep into the individuality, but it does not touch the centre of the person. True love never professes anything. Jesus said - "Whosoever shall confess Me before men," i.e., confess his love not merely by his words, but by everything he does. Unless we get hurt right out of every deception about ourselves, the word of God is not having its way with us. The word of God hurts as no sin can ever hurt, because sin blunts feeling. The question of the Lord intensifies feeling, until to be hurt by Jesus is the most exquisite hurt conceivable. It hurts not only in the natural way but in the profound personal way. The word of the Lord pierces even to the dividing asunder of soul and spirit, there is no deception left. There is no possibility of being sentimental with the Lord's question; you cannot say nice things when the Lord speaks directly to you, the hurt is too terrific. It is such a hurt that it stings every other concern out of account. There never can be any mistake about the hurt of the Lord's word when it comes to His child; but the point of the hurt is the great point of revelation.

March 2
HAVE YOU FELT THE HURT OF THE LORD?

"Jesus said unto him the third time, Lovest thou Me?" John 21:17

Have you felt the hurt of the Lord to the uncovered quick, the place where the real sensitiveness of your life is lodged? The devil never hurts there, neither sin nor human affection hurts there, nothing goes through to that place but the word of God. "Peter was grieved because Jesus said unto him the third time. . . ." He was awakening to the fact that in the real true centre of his personal life he was devoted to Jesus, and he began to see what the patient questioning meant. There was not the slightest strand of delusion left in Peter's mind, he never could be deluded again. There was no room for passionate utterance, no room for exhilaration or sentiment. It was a revelation to him to realize how much he did love the Lord, and with amazement he said – "Lord, Thou knowest all things." Peter began to see how much he did love Jesus; but he did not say – "Look at this or that to confirm it." Peter was beginning to discover to himself how much he did love the Lord, that there was no one in heaven above or upon earth beneath beside Jesus Christ; but he did not know it until the probing, hurting questions of the Lord came. The Lord's questions always reveal me to myself. The patient directness and skill of Jesus Christ with Peter! Our Lord never asks questions until the right time. Rarely, but probably once, He will get us into a corner where He will hurt us with His undeviating questions, and we will realize that we do love Him far more deeply than any profession can ever show.

March 3
THE UNRELIEVED QUEST

"Feed My sheep." John 21:17

This is love in the making. The love of God is un-made, it is God's nature. When we receive the Holy Spirit He unites us with God so that His love is manifested in us. When the soul is united to God by the indwelling Holy Spirit, that is not the end; the end is that we may be one with the Father as Jesus was. What kind of oneness had Jesus Christ with the Father? Such a oneness that the Father sent Him down here to be spent for us, and He says – "As the Father hath sent Me, even so send I you." Peter realizes now with the revelation of the Lord's hurting question that he does love Him; then comes the point – "Spend it out." Don't testify how much you love Me, don't profess about the marvellous revelation you have had, but – "Feed My sheep." And Jesus has some extraordinarily funny sheep, some bedraggled, dirty sheep, some awkward, butting sheep, some sheep that have gone astray! It is impossible to weary God's love, and it is impossible to weary that love in me if it springs from the one centre. The love of God pays no attention to the distinctions made by natural individuality. If I love my Lord I have no business to be guided by natural temperament; I have to feed His sheep. There is no relief and no release from this commission. Beware of counterfeiting the love of God by working along the line of natural human sympathy, because that will end in blaspheming the love of God.

March 4
COULD THIS BE TRUE OF ME?

"But none of these things move me, neither count I my life dear unto myself." Acts 20:24

It is easier to serve God without a vision, easier to work for God without a call, because then you are not bothered by what God requires; common sense is your guide, veneered over with Christian sentiment. You will be more prosperous and successful, more leisure-hearted, if you never realize the call of God. But if once you receive a commission from Jesus Christ, the memory of what God wants will always come like a goad; you will no longer be able to work for Him on the common-sense basis. What do I really count dear? If I have not been gripped by Jesus Christ, I will count service dear, time given to God dear, my life dear unto myself. Paul says he counted his life dear only in order that he might fulfil the ministry he had received; he refused to use his energy for any other thing. Acts 20:24 states Paul's almost sublime annoyance at being asked to consider himself; he was absolutely indifferent to any consideration other than that of fulfilling the ministry he had received. Practical work may be a competitor against abandonment to God, because practical work is based on this argument - Remember how 'useful you are here, or - Think how much value you would be in that particular type of work." That attitude does not put Jesus Christ as the Guide as to where we should go, but our judgment as to where we are of most use. Never consider whether you are of use; but ever consider that you are not your own but His.

March 5
IS HE REALLY LORD?

". . . so that I might finish my course with joy, and the ministry, which I have received of the Lord Jesus." Acts 20:24

Joy means the perfect fulfilment of that for which I was created and regenerated, not the successful doing of a thing. The joy Our Lord had lay in doing what the Father sent Him to do, and He says - "As My Father hath sent Me, even so am I sending you." Have I received a ministry from the Lord? If so, I have to be loyal to it, to count my life precious only for the fulfilling of that ministry. Think of the satisfaction it will be to hear Jesus say - "Well done, good and faithful servant"; to know that you have done what He sent you to do. We have all to find our niche in life, and spiritually we find it when we receive our ministry from the Lord. In order to do this we must have companied with Jesus; we must know Him as more than a personal Saviour. "I will show him how great things he must suffer for My sake." "Lovest thou Me?" Then - "Feed My sheep." There is no choice of service, only absolute loyalty to Our Lord's commission; loyalty to what you discern when you are in closest contact with God. If you have received a ministry from the Lord Jesus, you will know that the need is never the call: the need is the opportunity. The call is loyalty to the ministry you received when you were in real touch with Him. This does not imply that there is a campaign of service marked out for you, but it does mean that you will have to ignore the demands for service along other lines.

March 6
AMID A CROWD OF PALTRY THINGS

". . . in much patience, in afflictions, in necessities, in distresses." 2 Corinthians 6:4

It takes Almighty grace to take the next step when there is no vision and no spectator - the next step in devotion, the next step in your study, in your reading, in your kitchen; the next step in your duty, when there is no vision from God, no enthusiasm and no spectator. It takes far more of the grace of God, far more conscious drawing upon God to take that step, than it does to preach the Gospel. Every Christian has to partake of what was the essence of the Incarnation, he must bring the thing down into flesh and blood actualities and work it out through the finger tips. We flag when there is no vision, no uplift, but just the common round, the trivial task. The thing that tells in the long run for God and for men is the steady persevering work in the unseen, and the only way to keep the life uncrushed is to live looking to God. Ask God to keep the eyes of your spirit open to the Risen Christ, and it will be impossible for drudgery to damp you. Continually get away from pettiness and paltriness of mind and thought out into the thirteenth chapter of St. John's Gospel.

March 7
UNDAUNTED RADIANCE

"Nay, in all these things, we are more than conquerors through Him that loved us." Romans 8:37

Paul is speaking of the things that might seem likely to separate or wedge in between the saint and the love of God; but the remarkable thing is that nothing can wedge in between the love of God and the saint. These things can and do come in between the devotional exercises of the soul and God and separate individual life from God; but none of them is able to wedge in between the love of God and the soul of the saint. The bedrock of our Christian faith is the unmerited, fathomless marvel of the love of God exhibited on the Cross of Calvary, a love we never can and never shall merit. Paul says this is the reason we are more than conquerors in all these things, super-victors, with a joy we would not have but for the very things which look as if they are going to overwhelm us. The surf that distresses the ordinary swimmer produces in the surfrider the super-joy of going clean through it. Apply that to our own circumstances, these very things - tribulation, distress, persecution, produce in us the super-joy; they are not things to fight. We are more than conquerors through Him in all these things, not in spite of them, but in the midst of them. The saint never knows the joy of the Lord in spite of tribulation, but because of it - "I am exceeding joyful in all our tribulation," says Paul. Undaunted radiance is not built on anything passing, but on the love of God that nothing can alter. The experiences of life, terrible or monotonous, are impotent to touch the love of God, which is in Christ Jesus our Lord.

March 8
THE RELINQUISHED LIFE

"I am crucified with Christ." Galatians 2:20

No one is ever united with Jesus Christ until he is willing to relinquish not sin only, but his whole way of looking at things. To be born from above of the Spirit of God means that we must let go before we lay hold, and in the first stages it is the relinquishing of all pretence. What Our Lord wants us to present to Him is not goodness, nor honesty, nor endeavour, but real solid sin; that is all He can take from us. And what does He give in exchange for our sin? Real solid righteousness. But we must relinquish all pretence of being any thing, all claim of being worthy of God's consideration. Then the Spirit of God will show us what further there is to relinquish. There will have to be the relinquishing of my claim to my right to myself in every phase. Am I willing to relinquish my hold on all I possess, my hold on my affections, and on everything, and to be identified with the death of Jesus Christ? There is always a sharp painful disillusionment to go through before we do relinquish. When a man really sees himself as the Lord sees him, it is not the abominable sins of the flesh that shock him, but the awful nature of the pride of his own heart against Jesus Christ. When he sees himself in the light of the Lord, the shame and the horror and the desperate conviction come home. If you are up against the question of relinquishing, go through the crisis, relinquish all, and God will make you fit for all that He requires of you.

March 9
THE TIME OF RELAPSE

"Will ye also go away?" John 6:67

A penetrating question. Our Lord's words come home most when He talks in the most simple way. We know Who Jesus is, but in spite of that He says - "Will ye also go away?" We have to maintain a venturing attitude toward Him all the time. "From that time many of His disciples went back, and walked no more with Him." They went back from walking with Jesus, not into sin, but they relapsed. Many to-day are spending and being spent in work for Jesus Christ, but they do not walk with Him. The one thing God keeps us to steadily is that we may be one with Jesus Christ. After sanctification the discipline of our spiritual life is along this line. If God gives a clear and emphatic realization to your soul of what He wants, do not try to keep yourself in that relationship by any particular method, but live a natural life of absolute dependence on Jesus Christ. Never try to live the life with God on any other line than God's line, and that line is absolute devotion to Him. The certainty that I do not know - that is the secret of going with Jesus. Peter only saw in Jesus Someone to minister salvation to him and to the world. Our Lord wants us to be yoke-fellows with Him. v. 70. Jesus answers the great lack in Peter. We cannot answer for others.

March 10
HAVE A MESSAGE AND BE ONE

"Preach the word." 2 Timothy 4:2

We are not saved to be "channels only," but to be sons and daughters of God. We are not turned into spiritual mediums, but into spiritual messengers; the message must be part of ourselves. The Son of God was His own message, His words were spirit and life; and as His disciples our lives must be the sacrament of our message. The natural heart will do any amount of serving, but it takes the heart broken by conviction of sin, and baptized by the Holy Ghost, and crumpled into the purpose of God before the life becomes the sacrament of its message. There is a difference between giving a testimony and preaching. A preacher is one who has realized the call of God and is determined to use his every power to proclaim God's truth. God takes us out of our own ideas for our lives and we are "batter'd to shape and use," as the disciples were after Pentecost. Pentecost did not teach the disciples any thing; it made them the incarnation of what they preached - "Ye shall be witnesses unto Me." Let God have perfect liberty when you speak. Before God's message can liberate other souls, the liberation must be real in you. Gather your material, and set it alight when you speak.

March 11
VISION

"I was not disobedient unto the heavenly vision." Acts 26:19

If we lose the vision, we alone are responsible, and the way we lose the vision is by spiritual leakage. If we do not run our belief about God into practical issues, it is all up with the vision God has given. The only way to be obedient to the heavenly vision is to give our utmost for God's highest, and this can only be done by continually and resolutely recalling the vision. The test is the sixty seconds of every minute, and the sixty minutes of every hour, not our times of prayer and devotional meetings. "Though it tarry, wait for it." We cannot attain to a vision, we must live in the inspiration of it until it accomplishes itself. We get so practical that we forget the vision. At the beginning we saw it but did not wait for it; we rushed off into practical work, and when the vision was fulfilled, we did not see it. Waiting for the vision that tarries is the test of our loyalty to God. It is at the peril of our soul's welfare that we get caught up in practical work and miss the fulfilment of the vision. Watch God's cyclones. The only way God sows His saints is by His whirlwind. Are you going to prove an empty pod? It will depend on whether or not you are actually living in the light of what you have seen. Let God fling you out, and do not go until He does. If you select your own spot, you will prove an empty pod. If God sows you, you will bring forth fruit. It is essential to practise the walk of the feet in the light of the vision.

March 12
ABANDONMENT

"Then Peter began to say unto Him, Lo, we have left all, and have followed Thee. . . ." Mark 10:28

Our Lord replies in effect, that abandonment is for Himself, and not for what the disciples themselves will get from it. Beware of an abandonment which has the commercial spirit in it - "I am going to give myself to God because I want to be delivered from sin, because I want to be made holy." All that is the result of being right with God, but that spirit is not of the essential nature of Christianity. Abandonment is not for anything at all. We have got so commercialized that we only go to God for something from Him, and not for Himself. It is like saying, "No, Lord, I don't want Thee, I want myself; but I want myself clean and filled with the Holy Ghost; I want to be put in Thy show room and be able to say - 'This is what God has done for me.'" If we only give up something to God because we want more back, there is nothing of the Holy Spirit in our abandonment; it is miserable commercial self-interest. That we gain heaven, that we are delivered from sin, that we are made useful to God - these things never enter as considerations into real abandonment, which is a personal sovereign preference for Jesus Christ Himself. When we come up against the barriers of natural relationship, where is Jesus Christ? Most of us desert Him - "Yes, Lord, I did hear Thy call; but my mother is in the road, my wife, my self-interest, and I can go no further." "Then," Jesus says, "you cannot be My disciple." The test of abandonment is always over the neck of natural devotion. Go over it, and God's own abandonment will embrace all those you had to hurt in abandoning. Beware of stopping short of abandonment to God. Most of us know abandonment in vision only.

March 13
THE ABANDONMENT OF GOD

"God so loved the world that He gave. . ." John 3:16

Salvation is not merely deliverance from sin, nor the experience of personal holiness; the salvation of God is deliverance out of self entirely into union with Himself. My experimental knowledge of salvation will be along the line of deliverance from sin and of personal holiness; but salvation means that the Spirit of God has brought me into touch with God's personality, and I am thrilled with something infinitely greater than myself, I am caught up into the abandonment of God. To say that we are called to preach holiness or sanctification, is to get into a side eddy. We are called to proclaim Jesus Christ. The fact that He saves from sin and makes us holy is part of the effect of the wonderful abandonment of God. Abandonment never produces the consciousness of its own effort, because the whole life is taken up with the One to Whom we abandon. Beware of talking about abandonment if you know nothing about it, and you will never know anything about it until you have realized that John 3:16 means that God gave Himself absolutely. In our abandonment we give ourselves over to God just as God gave Himself for us, without any calculation. The consequence of abandonment never enters into our outlook because our life is taken up with Him.

March 14
OBEDIENCE

"His servants ye are to whom ye obey." Romans 6:16

The first thing to do in examining the power that dominates me is to take hold of the unwelcome fact that I am responsible for being thus dominated. If I am a slave to myself, I am to blame because at a point away back I yielded to myself. Likewise, if I obey God I do so because I have yielded myself to Him. Yield in childhood to selfishness, and you will find it the most enchaining tyranny on earth. There is no power in the human soul of itself to break the bondage of a disposition formed by yielding. Yield for one second to anything in the nature of lust (remember what lust is: "I must have it at once," whether it be the lust of the flesh or the lust of the mind) - once yield and though you may hate yourself for having yielded, you are a bondslave to that thing. There is no release in human power at all but only in the Redemption. You must yield yourself in utter humiliation to the only One Who can break the dominating power viz., the Lord Jesus Christ - "He hath anointed me . . . to preach deliverance to all captives." You find this out in the most ridiculously small ways - "Oh, I can give that habit up when I like." You cannot, you will find that the habit absolutely dominates you because you yielded to it willingly. It is easy to sing - "He will break every fetter" and at the same time be living a life of obvious slavery to yourself. Yielding to Jesus will break every form of slavery in any human life.

March 15
THE DISCIPLINE OF DISMAY

"And as they followed, they were afraid." Mark 10:32

At the beginning we were sure we knew all about Jesus Christ, it was a delight to sell all and to fling ourselves out in a hardihood of love; but now we are not quite so sure. Jesus is on in front and He looks strange: "Jesus went before them and they were amazed." There is an aspect of Jesus that chills the heart of a disciple to the core and makes the whole spiritual life gasp for breath. This strange Being with His face "set like a flint" and His striding determination, strikes terror into me. He is no longer Counsellor and Comrade, He is taken up with a point of view I know nothing about, and I am amazed at Him. At first I was confident that I understood Him, but now I am not so sure. I begin to realize there is a distance between Jesus Christ and me; I can no longer be familiar with Him. He is ahead of me and He never turns round; I have no idea where He is going, and the goal has become strangely far off. Jesus Christ had to fathom every sin and every sorrow man could experience, and that is what makes Him seem strange. When we see Him in this aspect we do not know Him, we do not recognize one feature of His life, and we do not know how to begin to follow Him. He is on in front, a

Leader Who is very strange, and we have no comradeship with Him. The discipline of dismay is essential in the life of discipleship. The danger is to get back to a little fire of our own and kindle enthusiasm at it (cf. Isaiah 1:10-11). When the darkness of dismay comes, endure until it is over, because out of it will come that following of Jesus which is an unspeakable joy.

March 16
THE MASTER ASSIZES

"For we must all appear before the judgment seat of Christ." 2 Corinthians 5:10

Paul says that we must all, preacher and people alike, "appear before the judgment seat of Christ." If you learn to live in the white light of Christ here and now, judgment finally will cause you to delight in the work of God in you. Keep yourself steadily faced by the judgment seat of Christ; walk now in the light of the holiest you know. A wrong temper of mind about another soul will end in the spirit of the devil, no matter how saintly you are. One carnal judgment, and the end of it is hell in you. Drag it to the light at once and say - "My God, I have been guilty there." If you don't, hardness will come all through. The penalty of sin is confirmation in sin. It is not only God who punishes for sin; sin confirms itself in the sinner and gives back full pay. No struggling nor praying will enable you to stop doing some things, and the penalty of sin is that gradually you get used to it and do not know that it is sin. No power save the incoming of the Holy Ghost can alter the inherent consequences of sin. "But if we walk in the light as He is in the light." Walking in the light means for many of us walking according to our standard for another person. The deadliest Pharisaism to-day is not hypocrisy, but unconscious unreality.

March 17
THE WORKER'S RULING PASSION

"Wherefore we labour that . . we may be accepted of Him." 2 Corinthians 5:9 "

Wherefore we labour . . . ." It is arduous work to keep the master ambition in front. It means holding one's self to the high ideal year in and year out, not being ambitious to win souls or to establish churches or to have revivals, but being ambitious only to be "accepted of Him." It is not lack of spiritual experience that leads to failure, but lack of labouring to keep the ideal right. Once a week at least take stock before God and see whether you are keeping your life up to the standard He wishes. Paul is like a musician who does not heed the approval of the audience if he can catch the look of approval from his Master. Any ambition which is in the tiniest degree away from this central one of being "approved unto God" may end in our being castaways. Learn to discern where the ambition leads, and you will see why it is so necessary to live facing the Lord Jesus Christ. Paul says - "Lest my body should make me take another line, I am constantly watching so that I may bring it into subjection and keep it under." (1 Cor. 9:27.) I have to learn to relate everything to the master ambition, and to maintain it without any cessation. My worth to God in public is what I am in private. Is my master ambition to please Him and be acceptable to Him, or is it something less, no matter how noble?

March 18
SHALL I ROUSE MYSELF UP TO THIS?

"Perfecting holiness in the fear of God." 2 Corinthians 7:1

"Having therefore these promises." I claim the fulfilment of God's promises, and rightly, but that is only the human side; the Divine side is that through the promises I recognize God's claim on me. For instance, am I realizing that my body is the temple of the Holy Ghost, or have I a habit of body that plainly will not bear the light of God on it? By sanctification the Son of God is formed in me, then I have to transform my natural life into a spiritual life by obedience to Him. God educates us down to the scruple. When He begins to check, do not confer with flesh and blood, cleanse yourself at once. Keep yourself cleansed in your daily walk. I have to cleanse myself from all filthiness of the flesh and spirit until both are in accord with the nature of God. Is the mind of my spirit in perfect agreement with the life of the Son of God in me, or am I insubordinate in intellect? Am I forming the mind of Christ, Who never spoke from His right to Himself, but maintained an inner watchfulness whereby He continually submitted His spirit to His Father? I have the responsibility of keeping my spirit in agreement with His Spirit, and by degrees Jesus lifts me up to where He lived - in perfect consecration to His Father's will, paying no attention to any other thing. Am I perfecting this type of holiness in the fear of God? Is God getting His way with me, and are other people beginning to see God in my life more and more? Be serious with God and leave the rest gaily alone. Put God first literally.

March 19

THE WAY OF ABRAHAM IN FAITH

He went out, not knowing whither he went." Hebrews 11:8

In the Old Testament, personal relationship with God showed itself in separation, and this is symbolized in the life of Abraham by his separation from his country and from his kith and kin. To day the separation is more of a mental and moral separation from the way that those who are dearest to us look at things, that is, if they have not a personal relationship with God. Jesus Christ emphasized this (see Luke 14:26). Faith never knows where it is being led, but it loves and knows the One Who is leading. It is a life of Faith, not of intellect and reason, but a life of knowing Who makes us "go." The root of faith is the knowledge of a Person, and one of the biggest snares is the idea that God is sure to lead us to success. The final stage in the life of faith is attainment of character. There are many passing transfigurations of character; when we pray we feel the blessing of God enwrapping us and for the time being we are changed, then we get back to the ordinary days and ways and the glory vanishes. The life of faith is not a life of mounting up with wings, but a life of walking and not fainting. It is not a question of sanctification; but of something infinitely further on than sanctification, of faith that has been tried and proved and has stood the test. Abraham is not a type of sanctification, but a type of the life of faith, a tried faith built on a real God. "Abraham believed God."

March 20
FRIENDSHIP WITH GOD

"Shall I hide from Abraham that thing which I do?" Genesis 18:17

Its Delights. This chapter brings out the delight of real friendship with God as compared with occasional feelings of His presence in prayer. To be so much in contact with God that you never need to ask Him to show you His will, is to be nearing the final stage of your discipline in the life of faith. When you are rightly related to God, it is a life of freedom and liberty and delight, you are God's will, and all your common-sense decisions are His will for you unless He checks. You decide things in perfect delightful friendship with God, knowing that if your decisions are wrong He will always check; when He checks, stop at once. Its Difficulties. Why did Abraham stop praying when he did? He was not intimate enough yet to go boldly on until God granted his desire, there was something yet to be desired in his relationship to God. Whenever we stop short in prayer and say - "Well, I don't know; perhaps it is not God's will," there is still another stage to go. We are not so intimately acquainted with God as Jesus was, and as He wants us to be - "That they may be one even as we are one." Think of the last thing you prayed about - were you devoted to your desire or to God? Determined to get some gift of the Spirit or to get at God? "Your Heavenly Father knoweth what things ye have need of before ye ask Him." The point of asking is that you may get to know God better. "Delight thyself also in the Lord; and He shall give thee the desires of thine heart." Keep praying in order to get a perfect understanding of God Himself.

March 21
INTEREST OR IDENTIFICATION?

"I have been crucified with Christ." Galatians 2:20

The imperative need spiritually is to sign the death warrant of the disposition of sin, to turn all emotional impressions and intellectual beliefs into a moral verdict against the disposition of sin, viz., my claim to my right to myself. Paul says - "I have been crucified with Christ"; he does not say - "I have determined to imitate Jesus Christ," or, "I will endeavour to follow Him" - but - "I have been identified with Him in His death." When I come to such a moral decision and act upon it, then all that Christ wrought for me on the Cross is wrought in me. The free committal of myself to God gives the Holy Spirit the chance to impart to me the holiness of Jesus Christ. ". . . nevertheless I live. . . ." The individuality remains, but the mainspring, the ruling disposition, is radically altered. The same human body remains, but the old satanic right to myself is destroyed. "And the life which I now live in the flesh . . . ," not the life which I long to live and pray to live, but the life I now live in my mortal flesh, the life which men can see, "I live by the faith of the Son of God." This faith is not Paul's faith in Jesus Christ, but the faith that the Son of God has imparted to him - "the faith of the Son of God." It is no longer faith in faith, but faith which has overleapt all conscious bounds, the identical faith of the Son of God.

March 22
THE BURNING HEART

"Did not our heart burn within us?" Luke 24:32

We need to learn this secret of the burning heart. Suddenly Jesus appears to us, the fires are kindled, we have wonderful visions, then we have to learn to keep the secret of the burning heart that will go through anything. It is the dull, bald, dreary, commonplace day, with commonplace duties and people, that kills the burning heart unless we have learned the secret of abiding in Jesus. Much of our distress as Christians comes not because of sin, but because we are ignorant of the laws of our own nature. For instance, the only test as to whether we ought to allow an emotion to have its way is to see what the outcome of the emotion will be. Push it to its logical conclusion, and if the outcome is something God would condemn, allow it no more way. But if it be an emotion kindled by the Spirit of God and you do not let that emotion have its right issue in your life, it will react on a lower level. That is the way sentimentalists are made. The higher the emotion is, the deeper the degradation will be, if it is not worked out on its proper level. If the Spirit of God has stirred you, make as many things inevitable as possible, let the consequences be what they will. We cannot stay on the mount of transfiguration, but we must obey the light we received there; we must act it out. When God gives a vision, transact business on that line, no matter what it costs. "We cannot kindle when we will The fire which in the heart resides, The spirit bloweth and is still, In mystery our soul abides; But tasks in hours of insight will'd Can be through hours of gloom fulfill'd."

March 23
AM I CARNALLY MINDED?

Whereas there is among you jealousy and strife, are ye not carnal?" 1 Corinthians 3:3

No natural man knows anything about carnality. The flesh lusting against the Spirit that came in at regeneration, and the Spirit lusting against the flesh, produces carnality. "Walk in the Spirit," says Paul, "and ye shall not fulfil the lusts of the flesh"; and carnality will disappear. Are you contentious, easily troubled about trifles? "Oh, but no one who is a Christian ever is!" Paul says they are, he connects these things with carnality. Is there a truth in the Bible that instantly awakens petulance in you? That is a proof that you are yet carnal. If sanctification is being worked out, there is no trace of that spirit left. If the Spirit of God detects anything in you that is wrong, He does not ask you to put it right; He asks you to accept the light, and He will put it right. A child of the light confesses instantly and stands bared before God; a child of the darkness says - "Oh, I can explain that away." When once the light breaks and the conviction of wrong comes, be a child of the light, and confess, and God will deal with what is wrong; if you vindicate yourself, you prove yourself to be a child of the darkness. What is the proof that carnality has gone? Never deceive yourself; when carnality is gone it is the most real thing imaginable. God will see that you have any number of opportunities to prove to yourself the marvel of His grace. The practical test is the only proof. "Why," you say, "if this had happened before, there would have been the spirit of resentment!" You will never cease to be the most amazed person on earth at what God has done for you on the inside.

March 24
DECREASING INTO HIS PURPOSE

"He must increase, but I must decrease." John 3:30

If you become a necessity to a soul, you are out of God's order. As a worker, your great responsibility is to be a friend of the Bridegroom. When once you see a soul in sight of the claims of Jesus Christ, you know that your influence has been in the right direction, and instead of putting out a hand to prevent the throes, pray that they grow ten times stronger until there is no power on earth or in hell that can hold that soul away from Jesus Christ. Over and over again, we become amateur providences, we come in and prevent God; and say - "This and that must not be." Instead of proving friends of the Bridegroom, we put our sympathy in the way, and the soul will one day say - "That one was a thief, he stole my affections from Jesus, and I lost my vision of Him." Beware of rejoicing with a soul in the wrong thing, but see that you do rejoice in the right thing. "The friend of the Bridegroom . . . rejoiceth greatly because of the Bridegroom's voice: this my joy therefore is fulfilled. He must increase, but I must decrease." This is spoken with joy and not with sadness - at last they are to see the Bridegroom! And John says this is his joy. It is the absolute effacement of the worker, he is never thought of again. Watch for all you are worth until you hear the Bridegroom's voice in the life of another. Never mind what havoc it brings, what upsets, what crumblings of health, rejoice with divine hilarity when once His voice is heard. You may often see Jesus Christ wreck a life before He saves it. (Cf. Matt. 10:34.)

March 25
THE MOST DELICATE MISSION ON EARTH

"The friend of the Bridegroom." John 3:29

Goodness and purity ought never to attract attention to themselves, they ought simply to be magnets to draw to Jesus Christ. If my holiness is not drawing towards Him, it is not holiness of the right order, but an influence that will awaken inordinate affection and lead souls away into side-eddies. A beautiful saint may be a hindrance if he does not present Jesus Christ but only what Christ has done for him. He will leave the impression - "What a fine character that man is!" That is not being a true friend of the Bridegroom; I am increasing all the time, He is not. In order to maintain this friendship and loyalty to the Bridegroom, we have to be more careful of our moral and vital relationship to Him than of any other thing, even of obedience. Sometimes there is nothing to obey, the only thing to do is to maintain a vital connection with Jesus Christ, to see that nothing interferes with that. Only occasionally do we have to obey. When a crisis arises we have to find out what God's will is, but the greater part of the life is not conscious obedience but the maintenance of this relationship - the friend of the Bridegroom. Christian work may be a means of evading the soul's concentration on Jesus Christ. Instead of being friends of the Bridegroom, we may become amateur providences, and may work against Him whilst we use His weapons.

March 26
VISION BY PERSONAL PURITY

"Blessed are the pure in heart; for they shall see God." Matthew 5:8

Purity is not innocence, it is much more. Purity is the outcome of sustained spiritual sympathy with God. We have to grow in purity. The life with God may be right and the inner purity remain unsullied, and yet every now and again the bloom on the outside may be sullied. God does not shield us from this possibility, because in this way we realize the necessity of maintaining the vision by personal purity. If the spiritual bloom of our life with God is getting impaired in the tiniest degree, we must leave off everything and get it put right. Remember that vision depends on character - the pure in heart see God. God makes us pure by His sovereign grace, but we have something to look after, this bodily life by which we come in contact with other people and with other points of view, it is these that are apt to sully. Not only must the inner sanctuary be kept right with God, but the outer courts as well are to be brought into perfect accord with the purity God gives us by His grace. The spiritual understanding is blurred immediately the outer court is sullied. If we are going to retain personal contact with the Lord Jesus Christ, it will mean there are some things we must scorn to do or to think, some legitimate things we must scorn to touch. A practical way of keeping personal purity unsullied in relation to other people is to say to yourself - That man, that woman, perfect in Christ Jesus! That friend, that relative, perfect in Christ Jesus!

March 27
VISION BY PERSONAL CHARACTER

"Come up hither, and I will shew thee things." Revelation 4:1

An elevated mood can only come out of an elevated habit of personal character. If in the externals of your life you live up to the highest you know, God will continually say - "Friend, go up higher." The golden rule in temptation is - Go higher. When you get higher up, you face other temptations and characteristics. Satan uses the strategy of elevation in temptation, and God does the same, but the effect is different. When the devil puts you into an elevated place, he makes you screw your idea of holiness beyond what flesh and blood could ever bear, it is a spiritual acrobatic performance, you are just poised and dare not move; but when God elevates you by His grace into the heavenly places, instead of finding a pinnacle to cling to, you find a great table-land where it is easy to move. Compare this week in your spiritual history with the same week last year and see how God has called you up higher. We have all been brought to see from a higher standpoint. Never let God give you one point of truth which you do not instantly live up to. Always work it out, keep in the light of it. Growth in grace is measured not by the fact that you have not gone back, but that you have an insight into where you are spiritually; you have heard God say "Come up higher," not to you personally, but to the insight of your character. "Shall I hide from Abraham that thing which I do?" God has to hide from us what He does until by personal character we get to the place where He can reveal it.

March 28
ISN'T THERE SOME MISUNDERSTANDING?

"Let us go into Judea. His disciples say unto Him . . . Goest Thou thither again?" John 11:7-8

I may not understand what Jesus Christ says, but it is dangerous to say that therefore He was mistaken in what He said. It is never right to think that my obedience to a word of God will bring dishonour to Jesus. The only thing that will bring dishonour is not obeying Him. To put my view of His honour in place of what He is plainly impelling me to do is never right, although it may arise from a real desire to prevent Him being put to open shame. I know when the proposition comes from God because of its quiet persistence: When I have to weigh the pros and cons, and doubt and debate come in, I am bringing in an element that is not of God, and I come to the conclusion that the suggestion was not a right one. Many of us are loyal to our notions of Jesus Christ, but how many of us are loyal to Him? Loyalty to Jesus means I have to step out where I do not see anything (cf. Matt. 14:29); loyalty to my notions means that I clear the ground first by my intelligence. Faith is not intelligent understanding, faith is deliberate commitment to a Person where I see no way. Are you debating whether to take a step in faith in Jesus or to wait until you can see how to do the thing yourself? Obey Him with glad reckless joy. When He says something and you begin to debate, it is because you have a conception of His honour which is not His honour. Are you loyal to Jesus or loyal to your notion of Him? Are you loyal to what He says, or are you trying to compromise with conceptions which never came from Him? "Whatsoever He saith unto you, do it."

March 29
OUR LORD'S SURPRISE VISITS

"Be ye therefore ready also." Luke 12:40

The great need for the Christian worker is to be ready to face Jesus Christ at any and every turn. This is not easy, no matter what our experience is. The battle is not against sin or difficulties or circumstances, but against being so absorbed in work that we are not ready to face Jesus Christ at every turn. That is the one great need, not the facing our belief, or our creed, the question whether we are of any use, but to face Him. Jesus rarely comes where we expect Him; He appears where we least expect Him, and always in the most illogical connections. The only way a worker can keep true to God is by being ready for the Lord's surprise visits. It is not service that matters, but intense spiritual reality, expecting Jesus Christ at every turn. This will give our life the attitude of child-wonder which He wants it to have. If we are going to be ready for Jesus Christ, we have to stop being religious (that is, using religion as a higher kind of culture) and be spiritually real. If you are "looking off unto Jesus," avoiding the call of the religious age you live in, and setting your heart on what He wants, on thinking on His line - you will be called unpractical and dreamy; but when He appears in the burden and the heat of the day, you will be the only one who is ready. Trust no one, not even the finest saint who ever walked this earth, ignore him, if he hinders your sight of Jesus Christ.

March 30
HOLINESS V. HARDNESS Towards GOD

"And He . . . wondered that there was no intercessor." Isaiah 59:16

The reason many of us leave off praying and become hard towards God is because we have only a sentimental interest in prayer. It sounds right to say that we pray; we read books on prayer which tell us that prayer is beneficial, that our minds are quieted and our souls uplifted when we pray; but Isaiah implies that God is amazed at such thoughts of prayer. Worship and intercession must go together, the one is impossible without the other. Intercession means that we rouse ourselves up to get the mind of Christ about the one for whom we pray. Too often instead of worshipping God, we construct statements as to how prayer works. Are we worshipping or are we in dispute with God - "I don't see how You are going to do it." This is a sure sign that we are not worshipping. When we lose sight of God we become hard and dogmatic. We hurl our own petitions at God's throne and dictate to Him as to what we wish Him to do. We do not worship God, nor do we seek to form the mind of Christ. If we are hard towards God, we will become hard towards other people. Are we so worshipping God that we rouse ourselves up to lay hold on Him so that we may be brought into contact with His mind about the ones for whom we pray? Are we living in a holy relationship to God, or are we hard and dogmatic? "But there is no one interceding properly" - then be that one yourself, be the one who worships God and who lives in holy relationship to Him. Get into the real work of intercession, and remember it is a work, a work that taxes every power; but a work which has no snare. Preaching the gospel has a snare; intercessory prayer has none.

March 31
HEEDFULNESS V. HYPOCRISY IN OURSELVES

"If any man see his brother sin a sin which is not unto death, he shall ask, and He shall give him Life for them that sin not unto death." 1 John 5:16

If we are not heedful of the way the Spirit of God works in us, we will become spiritual hypocrites. We see where other folks are failing, and we turn our discernment into the gibe of criticism instead of into intercession on their behalf. The revelation is made to us not through the acuteness of our minds, but by the direct penetration of the Spirit of God, and if we are not heedful of the source of the revelation, we will become criticizing centres and forget that God says - ". . . he shall ask, and He shall give him life for them that sin not unto death." Take care lest you play the hypocrite by spending all your time trying to get others right before you worship God yourself. One of the subtlest burdens God ever puts on us as saints is this burden of discernment concerning other souls. He reveals things in order that we may take the burden of these souls before Him and form the mind of Christ about them, and as we intercede on His line, God says He will give us "life for them that sin not unto death." It is not that we bring God into touch with our minds, but that we rouse ourselves until God is able to convey His mind to us about the one for whom we intercede. Is Jesus Christ seeing of the travail of His soul in us? He cannot unless we are so identified with Himself that we are roused up to get His view about the people for whom we pray. May we learn to intercede so whole-heartedly that Jesus Christ will be abundantly satisfied with us as intercessors.

April 1
HEARTINESS V. HEARTLESSNESS TOWARDS OTHERS

"It is Christ . . . who also maketh intercession for us." "The Spirit . . . maketh intercession for the saints." Romans 8:34, 27

Do we need any more argument than this to become intercessors - that Christ "ever liveth to make intercession;" that the Holy Spirit "maketh intercession for the saints"? Are we living in such a vital relationship to our fellow men that we do the work of intercession as the Spirit-taught children of God? Begin with the circumstances we are in - our homes, our business, our country, the present crisis as it touches us and others - are these things crushing us? Are they badgering us out of the presence of God and leaving us no time for worship? Then let us call a halt, and get into such living relationship with God that our relationship to others may be maintained on the line of intercession whereby God works His marvels. Beware of outstripping God by your very longing to do His will. We run ahead of Him in a thousand and one activities, consequently we get so burdened with persons and with difficulties that we do not worship God, we do not intercede. If once the burden and the pressure come upon us and we are not in the worshipping attitude, it will produce not only hardness toward God but despair in our own souls. God continually introduces us to people for whom we have no affinity, and unless we are worshipping God, the most natural thing to do is to treat them heartlessly, to give them a text like the jab of a spear, or leave them with a rapped-out counsel of God and go. A heartless Christian must be a terrible grief to Our Lord. Are we in the direct line of the intercession of our Lord and of the Holy Spirit?

April 2
THE GLORY THAT EXCELS

"The Lord . . . hath sent me that thou mightest receive thy sight." Acts 9:17

When Paul received his sight, he received spiritually an insight into the Person of Jesus Christ, and the whole of his subsequent life and preaching was nothing but Jesus Christ - "I determined not to know anything among you, save Jesus Christ, and Him crucified." No attraction was ever allowed to hold the mind and soul of Paul save the face of Jesus Christ. We have to learn to maintain an unimpaired state of character up to the last notch revealed in the vision of Jesus Christ. The abiding characteristic of a spiritual man is the interpretation of the Lord Jesus Christ to himself, and the interpretation to others of the purposes of God. The one concentrated passion of the life is Jesus Christ. Whenever you meet this note in a man, you feel he is a man after God's own heart. Never allow anything to deflect you from insight into Jesus Christ. It is the test of whether you are spiritual or not. To be unspiritual means that other things have a growing fascination for you. "Since mine eyes have looked on Jesus, I've lost sight of all beside, So enchained my spirit's vision, Gazing on the Crucified."

April 3
IF THOU HADST KNOWN!

"If thou hadst known . . . in this thy day, the things which belong unto thy peace! but now they are hid from thine eyes." Luke 19:42

Jesus had entered into Jerusalem in triumph, the city was stirred to its foundations; but a strange god was there, the pride of Pharisaism; it was religious and upright, but a "whited sepulchre." What is it that blinds me in this "my day"? Have I a strange god - not a disgusting monster, but a disposition that rules me? More than once God has brought me face to face with the strange god and I thought I should have to yield, but I did not do it. I got through the crisis by the skin of my teeth and I find myself in the possession of the strange god still; I am blind to the things which belong to my peace. It is an appalling thing that we can be in the place where the Spirit of God should be getting at us unhinderedly, and yet increase our condemnation in God's sight. "If thou hadst known" - God goes direct to the heart, with the tears of Jesus behind. These words imply culpable responsibility; God holds us responsible for what we do not see. "Now they are hid from thine eyes" - because the disposition has never been yielded. The unfathomable sadness of the "might have been!" God never opens doors that have been closed. He opens other doors, but He reminds us that there are doors which we have shut, doors which need never have been shut, imaginations which need never have been sullied. Never be afraid when God brings back the past. Let memory have its way. It is a minister of God with its rebuke and chastisement and sorrow. God will turn the "might have been" into a wonderful culture for the future.

April 4
THOSE BORDERS OF DISTRUST

"Behold, the hour cometh . . . that ye shall be scattered." John 16:32

Jesus is not rebuking the disciples, their faith was real, but it was disturbed; it was not at work in actual things. The disciples were scattered to their own interests, alive to interests that never were in Jesus Christ. After we have been perfectly related to God in sanctification, our faith has to be worked out in actualities. We shall be scattered, not into work, but into inner desolations and made to know what internal death to God's blessings means. Are we prepared for this? It is not that we choose it, but that God engineers our circumstances so that we are brought there. Until we have been through that experience, our faith is bolstered up by feelings and by blessings. When once we get there, no matter where God places us or what the inner desolations are, we can praise God that all is well. That is faith being worked out in actualities. ". . . and shall leave Me alone." Have we left Jesus alone by the scattering of His providence? Because we do not see God in our circumstances? Darkness comes by the sovereignty of God. Are we prepared to let God do as He likes with us - prepared to be separated from conscious blessings? Until Jesus Christ is Lord, we all have ends of our own to serve; our faith is real, but it is not permanent yet. God is never in a hurry; if we wait, we shall see that God is pointing out that we have not been interested in Himself but only in His blessings. The sense of God's blessing is elemental. "Be of good cheer, I have overcome the world." Spiritual grit is what we need.

April 5
HIS AGONY AND OUR FELLOWSHIP

"Then cometh Jesus with them unto a place called Gethsemane, and saith unto the disciples, tarry ye here, and watch with Me." Matthew 26:36, 38

We can never fathom the agony in Gethsemane, but at least we need not misunderstand it. It is the agony of God and Man in one, face to face with sin. We know nothing about Gethsemane in personal experience.

Gethsemane and Calvary stand for something unique; they are the gateway into Life for us. It was not the death on the cross that Jesus feared in Gethsemane; He stated most emphatically that He came on purpose to die. In Gethsemane He feared lest He might not get through as Son of Man. He would get through as Son of God - Satan could not touch Him there; but Satan's onslaught was that He would get through as an isolated Figure only; and that would mean that He could be no Saviour. Read the record of the agony in the light of the temptation: "Then the devil leaveth Him for a season." In Gethsemane Satan came back and was again overthrown. Satan's final onslaught against our Lord as Son of Man is in Gethsemane. The agony in Gethsemane is the agony of the Son of God in fulfilling His destiny as the Saviour of the world. The veil is drawn aside to reveal all it cost Him to make it possible for us to become sons of God. His agony is the basis of the simplicity of our salvation. The Cross of Christ is a triumph for the Son of Man. It was not only a sign that Our Lord had triumphed, but that He had triumphed to save the human race. Every human being can get through into the presence of God now because of what the Son of Man went through.

April 6
THE COLLISION OF GOD AND SIN

"Who His own self bare our sins in His own body on the tree." 1 Peter 2:24

The Cross of Jesus is the revelation of God's judgment on sin. Never tolerate the idea of martyrdom about the Cross of Jesus Christ. The Cross was a superb triumph in which the foundations of hell were shaken. There is nothing more certain in Time or Eternity than what Jesus Christ did on the Cross: He switched the whole of the human race back into a right relationship with God. He made Redemption the basis of human life, that is, He made a way for every son of man to get into communion with God. The Cross did not happen to Jesus: He came on purpose for it. He is "the Lamb slain from the foundation of the world." The whole meaning of the Incarnation is the Cross. Beware of separating God manifest in the flesh from the Son becoming sin. The Incarnation was for the purpose of Redemption. God became incarnate for the purpose of putting away sin; not for the purpose of Self-realization. The Cross is the centre of Time and of Eternity, the answer to the enigmas of both. The Cross is not the cross of a man but the Cross of God, and the Cross of God can never be realized in human experience. The Cross is the exhibition of the nature of God, the gateway whereby any individual of the human race can enter into union with God. When we get to the Cross, we do not go through it; we abide in the life to which the Cross is the gateway. The centre of salvation is the Cross of Jesus, and the reason it is so easy to obtain salvation is because it cost God so much. The Cross is the point where God and sinful man merge with a crash and the way to life is opened - but the crash is on the heart of God.

April 7
WHY ARE WE NOT TOLD PLAINLY?

"He charged them that they should tell no man what things they had seen, till the Son of man were risen from the dead." Mark 9:9 Say nothing until the Son of man is risen in you - until the life of the risen Christ so dominates you that you understand what the historic Christ taught. When you get to the right state on the inside, the word which Jesus has spoken is so plain that you are amazed you did not see it before. You could not understand it before, you were not in the place in disposition where it could be borne. Our Lord does not hide these things; they are unbearable until we get into a fit condition of spiritual life. "I have yet many things to say unto you, but ye cannot bear them now." There must be communion with His risen life before a particular word can be borne by us. Do we know anything about the impartation of the risen life of Jesus? The evidence that we do is that His word is becoming interpretable to us. God cannot reveal anything to us if we have not His Spirit. An obstinate outlook will effectually hinder God from revealing anything to us. If we have made up our minds about a doctrine, the light of God will come no more to us on that line, we cannot get it. This obtuse stage will end immediately [when] His resurrection life has its way with us. "Tell no man . . " - so many do tell what they saw on the mount of transfiguration. They have had the vision and they testify to it, but the life does not tally with it, the Son of man is not yet risen in them. I wonder when He is going to be formed in you and in me?

April 8
HIS RESURRECTION DESTINY

Ought not Christ to have suffered these things, and to enter into His glory?" Luke 24:26

Our Lord's Cross is the gateway into His life: His Resurrection means that He has power now to convey His life to me. When I am born again from above, I receive from the Risen Lord His very life. Our Lord's Resurrection destiny is to bring "many sons unto glory." The fulfilling of His destiny gives Him the right to make us sons and daughters of God. We are never in the relationship to God that the Son of God is in; but we are brought by the Son into the relation of sonship. When Our Lord rose from the dead, He rose to an absolutely new life, to a life He did not live before He was incarnate. He rose to a life that had never been before; and His resurrection means for us that we are raised to His risen life, not to our old life. One day we shall have a body like unto His glorious body, but we can know now the efficacy of His resurrection and walk in newness of life. "I would know Him in the power of His resurrection." "As Thou hast given Him power over all flesh, that He should give eternal life to as many as Thou hast given Him." "Holy Spirit" is the experimental name for Eternal Life working in human beings here and now. The Holy Spirit is the Deity in proceeding power Who applies the Atonement to our experience. Thank God it is gloriously and majestically true that the Holy Ghost can work in us the very nature of Jesus if we will obey Him.

April 9
HAVE I SEEN HIM?

After that He appeared in another form unto two of them." Mark 16:12

Being saved and seeing Jesus are not the same thing. Many are partakers of God's grace who have never seen Jesus. When once you have seen Jesus, you can never be the same, other things do not appeal as they used to do. Always distinguish between what you see Jesus to be, and what He has done for you. If you only know what He has done for you, you have not a big enough God; but if you have had a vision of Jesus as He is, experiences can come and go, you will endure "as seeing Him Who is invisible." The man blind from his birth did not know Who Jesus was until He appeared and revealed Himself to him. Jesus appears to those for whom He has done something; but we cannot dictate when He will come. Suddenly at any turn He may come. "Now I see Him!" Jesus must appear to your friend as well as to you, no one can see Jesus with your eyes. Severance takes place where one and not the other has seen Jesus. You cannot bring your friend unless God brings him. Have you seen Jesus? Then you will want others to see Him too. "And they went and told it unto the residue, neither believed they them." You must tell, although they do not believe. "O could I tell, ye surely would believe it! O could I only say what I have seen! How should I tell or how can ye receive it, How, till He bringeth you where I have been?"

April 10
MORAL DECISION ABOUT SIN

"Knowing this, that our old man is crucified with Him, that the body of sin might be destroyed, that henceforth we should not serve sin." Romans 6:6

Co-Crucifixion. Have I made this decision about sin - that it must be killed right out in me? It takes a long time to come to a moral decision about sin, but it is the great moment in my life when I do decide that just as Jesus Christ died for the sin of the world, so sin must die out in me, not be curbed or suppressed or counteracted, but crucified. No one can bring anyone else to this decision. We may be earnestly convinced, and religiously convinced, but what we need to do is to come to the decision which Paul forces here. Haul yourself up, take a time alone with God, make the moral decision and say - "Lord, identify me with Thy death until I know that sin is dead in me." Make the moral decision that sin in you must be put to death. It was not a divine anticipation on the part of Paul, but a very radical and definite experience. Am I prepared to let the Spirit of God search me until I know what the disposition of sin is - the thing that lusts against the Spirit of God in me? Then if so, will I agree with God's verdict on that disposition of sin - that it should be identified with the death of Jesus? I cannot reckon myself "dead indeed unto sin" unless I have been through this radical issue of will before God. Have I entered into the glorious privilege of being crucified with Christ until all that is left is the life of Christ in my flesh and blood? "I am crucified with Christ; nevertheless I live; yet not I, but Christ liveth in me."

April 11
MORAL DIVINITY

"For if we have been planted together in the likeness of His death, we shall be also in the likeness of His resurrection." Romans 6:5 Co-Resurrection. The proof that I have been through crucifixion with Jesus is that I have a decided likeness to Him. The incoming of the Spirit of Jesus into me readjusts my personal life to God. The resurrection of Jesus has given Him authority to impart the life of God to me, and my experimental life must be constructed on the basis of His life. I can have the resurrection life of Jesus now, and it will show itself in holiness. The idea all through the apostle Paul's writings is that after the moral decision to be identified with Jesus in His death has been made, the resurrection life of Jesus invades every bit of my human nature. It takes omnipotence to live the life of the Son of God in mortal flesh. The Holy Spirit cannot be located as a Guest in a house, He invades everything. When once I decide that my "old man" (i.e., the heredity of sin) should be identified with the death of Jesus, then the Holy Spirit invades me. He takes charge of everything, my part is to walk in the light and to obey all that He reveals. When I have made the moral decision about sin, it is easy to reckon actually that I am dead unto sin, because I find the life of Jesus there all the time. Just as there is only one stamp of humanity, so there is only one stamp of holiness, the holiness of Jesus, and it is His holiness that is gifted to me. God puts the holiness of His Son into me, and I belong to a new order spiritually.

April 12
MORAL DOMINION

"Death hath no more dominion over Him . . . in that He liveth, He liveth unto God. Likewise reckon ye also yourselves to be dead indeed unto sin, but alive unto God." Romans 6:9-11

Co-Eternal Life. Eternal life was the life which Jesus Christ exhibited on the human plane, and it is the same life, not a copy of it, which is manifested in our mortal flesh when we are born of God. Eternal life is not a gift from God, eternal life is the gift of God. The energy and the power which was manifested in Jesus will be manifested in us by the sheer sovereign grace of God when once we have made the moral decision about sin. "Ye shall receive the power of the Holy Ghost" - not power as a gift from the Holy Ghost; the power is the Holy Ghost, not something which He imparts. The life that was in Jesus is made ours by means of His Cross when once we make the decision to be identified with Him. If it is difficult to get right with God, it is because we will not decide definitely about sin. Immediately we do decide, the full life of God comes in. Jesus came to give us endless supplies of life: "that ye might be filled with all the fulness of God." Eternal Life has nothing to do with Time, it is the life which Jesus lived when He was down here. The only source of Life is the Lord Jesus Christ. The weakest saint can experience the power of the Deity of the Son of God if once he is willing to "let go." Any strand of our own energy will blur the life of Jesus. We have to keep letting go, and slowly and surely the great full life of God will invade us in every part, and men will take knowledge of us that we have been with Jesus.

April 13
WHAT TO DO UNDER THE CONDITIONS

"Cast thy burden upon the Lord." Psalm 55:22

We must distinguish between the burden-bearing that is right and the burden-bearing that is wrong. We ought never to bear the burden of sin or of doubt, but there are burdens placed on us by God which He does not intend to lift off, He wants us to roll them back on Him. "Cast that He hath given thee upon the Lord." (R.V. marg.) If we undertake work for God and get out of touch with Him, the sense of responsibility will be overwhelmingly crushing; but if we roll back on God that which He has put upon us, He takes away the sense of responsibility by bringing in the realization of Himself. Many workers have gone out with high courage and fine impulses, but with no intimate fellowship with Jesus Christ, and before long they are crushed. They do not know what to do with the burden, it produces weariness, and people say - "What an embittered end to such a beginning!" "Roll thy burden upon the Lord" - you have been bearing it all; deliberately put one end on the shoulders of God. "The government shall be upon His shoulder." Commit to God "that He hath given thee"; not fling it off, but put it over on to Him and yourself with it, and the burden is lightened by the sense of companionship. Never disassociate yourself from the burden.

April 14
INSPIRED INVINCIBILITY

"Take My yoke upon you, and learn of Me." Matthew 11:29

"Whom the Lord loveth, He chasteneth." How petty our complaining is! Our Lord begins to bring us into the place where we can have communion with Him, and we groan and say - "O Lord, let me be like other people!" Jesus is asking us to take one end of the yoke - "My yoke is easy, get alongside Me and we will pull together." Are you identified with the Lord Jesus like that? If so, you will thank God for the pressure of His hand. "To them that have no might He increaseth strength." God comes and takes us out of our sentimentality, and our complaining turns into a pæan of praise. The only way to know the strength of God is to take the yoke of Jesus upon us and learn of Him. "The joy of the Lord is your strength." Where do the saints get their joy from? If we did not know some saints, we would say - "Oh, he, or she, has nothing to bear." Lift the veil. The fact that the peace and the light and the joy of God are there is proof that the burden is there too. The burden God places squeezes the grapes and out comes the wine; most of us see the wine only. No power on earth or in hell can conquer the Spirit of God in a human spirit, it is an inner unconquerableness. If you have the whine in you, kick it out ruthlessly. It is a positive crime to be weak in God's strength.

April 15
THE RELAPSE OF CONCENTRATION

"But the high places were not taken away out of Israel; nevertheless the heart of Asa was perfect all his days." 2 Chronicles 15:17

Asa was incomplete in his external obedience, he was right in the main but not entirely right. Beware of the thing of which you say - "Oh, that does not matter much." The fact that it does not matter much to you may mean that it matters a very great deal to God. Nothing is a light matter with a child of God. How much longer are some of us going to keep God trying to teach us one thing? He never loses patience. You say - "I know I am right with God", but still the "high places" remain, there is something over which you have not obeyed. Are you protesting that your heart is right with God, and yet is there something in your life about which He has caused you to doubt? Whenever there is doubt, quit immediately, no matter what it is. Nothing is a mere detail. Are there some things in connection with your bodily life, your intellectual life, upon which you are not concentrating at all? You are all right in the main but you are slipshod; there is a relapse on the line of concentration. You no more need a holiday from spiritual concentration than your heart needs a holiday from beating. You cannot have a moral holiday and remain moral, nor can you have a spiritual holiday and remain spiritual. God wants you to be entirely His, and this means that you have to watch to keep yourself fit. It takes a tremendous amount of time. Some of us expect to "clear the numberless ascensions" in about two minutes.

April 16
CAN YOU COME DOWN?

"While ye have light, believe in the light." John 12:36

We all have moments when we feel better than our best, and we say - "I feel fit for anything; if only I could be like this always!" We are not meant to be. Those moments are moments of insight which we have to live up to when we do not feel like it. Many of us are no good for this workaday world when there is no high hour. We must bring our commonplace life up to the standard revealed in the high hour. Never allow a feeling which was stirred in you in the high hour to evaporate. Don't put your mental feet on the mantelpiece and say - "What a marvellous state of mind to be in!" Act immediately, do something, if only because you would rather not do it. If in a prayer meeting God has shown you something to do, don't say - "I'll do it"; do it! Take yourself by the scruff of the neck and shake off your incarnate laziness. Laziness is always seen in cravings for the high hour; we talk about working up to a time on the mount. We have to learn to live in the grey day according to what we saw on the mount. Don't cave in because you have been baffled once, get at it again. Burn your bridges behind you, and stand committed to God by your own act. Never revise your decisions, but see that you make your decisions in the light of the high hour.

April 17
NECK OR NOTHING

"Now when Simon Peter heard that it was the Lord, he girt his fisher's coat unto him . . . and did cast himself into the sea." John 21:7

Have you ever had a crisis in which you deliberately and emphatically and recklessly abandoned everything? It is a crisis of will. You may come up to it many times externally, but it amounts to nothing. The real deep crisis of abandonment is reached internally, not externally. The giving up of external things may be an indication of being in total bondage. Have you deliberately committed your will to Jesus Christ? It is a transaction of will, not of emotion; the emotion is simply the gilt-edge of the transaction. If you allow emotion first, you will never make the transaction. Do not ask God what the transaction is to be, but make it in regard to the thing you do see, either in the shallow or the profound place. If you have heard Jesus Christ's voice on the billows, let your convictions go to the winds, let your consistency go to the winds, but maintain your relationship to Him.

April 18
READINESS

"God called unto him and he said, Here am I" Exodus 3:4

When God speaks, many of us are like men in a fog, we give no answer. Moses' reply revealed that he was somewhere. Readiness means a right relationship to God and a knowledge of where we are at present. We are so busy telling God where we would like to go. The man or woman who is ready for God and His work is the one who carries off the prize when the summons comes. We wait with the idea of some great opportunity, something sensational, and when it comes we are quick to cry - "Here am I." Whenever Jesus Christ is in the ascendant, we are there, but we are not ready for an obscure duty. Readiness for God means that we are ready to do the tiniest little thing or the great big thing, it makes no difference. We have no choice in what we want to do, whatever God's programme may be we are there, ready. When any duty presents itself we hear God's voice as Our Lord heard His Father's voice, and we are ready for it with all the alertness of our love for Him. Jesus Christ expects to do with us as His Father did with Him. He can put us where He likes, in pleasant duties or in mean duties, because the union is that of the Father and Himself. "That they may be one, even as We are one." Be ready for the sudden surprise visits of God. A ready person never needs to get ready. Think of the time we waste trying to get ready when God has called! The burning bush is a symbol of everything that surrounds the ready soul, it is ablaze with the presence of God.

April 19
IS IT NOT IN THE LEAST LIKELY?

"For Joab had turned after Adonijah, though he turned not after Absalom." 1 Kings 2:28

Joab stood the big test, he remained absolutely loyal and true to David and did not turn after the fascinating and ambitious Absalom, but yet towards the end of his life he turned after the craven Adonijah. Always remain alert to the fact that where one man has gone back is exactly where any one may go back (see 1 Cor. 10:13). You have gone through the big crisis, now be alert over the least things; take into calculation the "retired sphere of the leasts." We are apt to say - "It is not in the least likely that having been through the supreme crisis, I shall turn now to the things of the world." Do not forecast where the temptation will come, it is the least likely thing that is the peril. In the aftermath of a great spiritual transaction the "retired sphere of the leasts" begins to tell; it is not dominant, but remember it is there, and if you are not warned, it will trip you up. You have remained true to God under great and intense trials, now beware of the undercurrent. Do not be morbidly introspective, looking forward with dread, but keep alert; keep your memory bright before God. Unguarded strength is double weakness because that is where the "retired sphere of the leasts" saps. The Bible characters fell on their strong points, never on their weak ones. "Kept by the power of God" - that is the only safety.

April 20
CAN A SAINT SLANDER GOD?

"For all the promises of God in Him are yea, and in Him Amen." 2 Corinthians 1:20

Jesus told the parable of the talents recorded in Matthew 25 as a warning that it is possible for us to misjudge our capacity. This parable has not to do with natural gifts, but with the Pentecostal gift of the Holy Ghost. We must not measure our spiritual capacity by education or by intellect; our capacity in spiritual things is measured by the promises of God. If we get less than God wants us to have, before long we will slander Him as the servant slandered his master: "You expect more than You give me power to do; You demand too much of me, I cannot stand true to You where I am placed." When it is a question of God's Almighty Spirit, never say "I can't." Never let the limitation of natural ability come in. If we have received the Holy Spirit, God expects the work of the Holy Spirit to be manifested in us. The servant justified himself in everything he did and condemned his lord on every point - "Your demand is out of all proportion to what you give." Have we been slandering God by daring to worry when He has said: "Seek ye first the Kingdom of God, and His righteousness; and all these things shall be added unto you"? Worrying means exactly what this servant implied - "I know You mean to leave me in the lurch." The person who is lazy naturally is always captious - "I haven't had a decent chance," and the one who is lazy spiritually is captious with God. Lazy people always strike out on an independent line. Never forget that our capacity in spiritual matters is measured by the promises of God. Is God able to fulfil His promises? Our answer depends on whether we have received the Holy Spirit.

April 21
NOW DON'T HURT THE LORD!

"Have I been so long time with you, and yet hast thou not known Me, Philip?" John 14:9

Our Lord must be repeatedly astounded at us - astounded at how un-simple we are. It is opinions of our own which make us stupid, when we are simple we are never stupid, we discern all the time. Philip expected the revelation of a tremendous mystery, but not in the One Whom he knew. The mystery of God is not in what is going to be, it is now; we look for it presently, in some cataclysmic event. We have no reluctance in obeying Jesus, but it is probable that we are hurting Him by the questions we ask. "Lord, show us the Father." His answer comes straight back - "There He is, always here or nowhere." We look for God to manifest Himself to His children: God only manifests Himself in His children. Other people see the manifestation, the child of God does not.

We want to be conscious of God; we cannot be conscious of our consciousness and remain sane. If we are asking God to give us experiences, or if conscious experience is in the road, we hurt the Lord. The very questions we ask hurt Jesus because they are not the questions of a child. "Let not your heart be troubled" - then am I hurting Jesus by allowing my heart to be troubled? If I believe the character of Jesus, am I living up to my belief? Am I allowing anything to perturb my heart, any morbid questions to come in? I have to get to the implicit relationship that takes everything as it comes from Him. God never guides presently, but always now. Realize that the Lord is here now, and the emancipation is immediate.

April 22
THE LIGHT THAT FAILS

"We all with open face beholding . . . the glory of the Lord." 2 Corinthians 3:18

A servant of God must stand so much alone that he never knows he is alone. In the first phases of Christian life disheartenments come, people who used to be lights flicker out, and those who used to stand with us pass away. We have to get so used to it that we never know we are standing alone. "All men forsook me . . notwithstanding the Lord stood with me" (2 Tim. 4:16-17). We must build our faith, not on the fading light, but on the light that never fails. When "big" men go we are sad, until we see that they are meant to go, the one thing that remains is looking in the face of God for ourselves. Allow nothing to keep you from looking God sternly in the face about yourself and about your doctrine, and every time you preach see that you look God in the face about things first, then the glory will remain all through. A Christian worker is one who perpetually looks in the face of God and then goes forth to talk to people. The characteristic of the ministry of Christ is that of unconscious glory that abides. "Moses wist not that the skin of his face shone while he talked with Him." We are never called on to parade our doubts or to express the hidden ecstasies of our life with God. The secret of the worker's life is that he keeps in tune with God all the time.

April 23
THE WORSHIP OF THE WORK

"Labourers together with God." 1 Corinthians 3:9

Beware of any work for God which enables you to evade concentration on Him. A great many Christian workers worship their work. The one concern of a worker should be concentration on God, and this will mean that all the other margins of life, mental, moral and spiritual, are free with the freedom of a child, a worshipping child, not a wayward child. A worker without this solemn dominant note of concentration on God is apt to get his work on his neck; there is no margin of body, mind or spirit free, consequently he becomes spent out and crushed. There is no freedom, no delight in life; nerves, mind and heart are so crushingly burdened that God's blessing cannot rest. But the other side is just as true - when once the concentration is on God, all the margins of life are free and under the dominance of God alone. There is no responsibility on you for the work; the only responsibility you have is to keep in living constant touch with God, and to see that you allow nothing to hinder your co-operation with Him. The freedom after sanctification is the freedom of a child, the things that used to keep the life pinned down are gone. But be careful to remember that you are freed for one thing only - to be absolutely devoted to your co-Worker. We have no right to judge where we should be put, or to have preconceived notions as to what God is fitting us for. God engineers everything; wherever He puts us our one great aim is to pour out a whole-hearted devotion to Him in that particular work. "Whatsoever thy hand findeth to do, do it with thy might."

April 24
THE WARNING AGAINST WANTONING

"Notwithstanding in this rejoice not, that the spirits are subject unto you." Luke 10:20

As Christian workers, worldliness is not our snare, sin is not our snare, but spiritual wantoning is, viz.: taking the pattern and print of the religious age we live in, making eyes at spiritual success. Never court anything other than the approval of God, go "without the camp, bearing His reproach." Jesus told the disciples not to rejoice in successful service, and yet this seems to be the one thing in which most of us do rejoice. We have the commercial view - so many souls saved and sanctified, thank God, now it is all right. Our work begins where God's grace has laid the foundation; we are not to save souls, but to disciple them. Salvation and sanctification are the work of God's sovereign grace; our work as His disciples is to disciple lives until they are wholly yielded to God. One life wholly devoted to God is of more value to God than one hundred lives simply awakened by His Spirit. As workers for God we must reproduce our own kind spiritually, and that will be God's witness to us as workers. God brings us to a standard of life by His grace, and we are responsible for reproducing that standard in others. Unless the worker lives a life hidden with Christ in God, he is apt to become an irritating dictator instead of an indwelling disciple. Many of us are dictators, we dictate to people and to meetings. Jesus never dictates to us in that way. Whenever Our Lord talked about discipleship, He always prefaced it with an "IF," never with an emphatic assertion - "You must." Discipleship carries an option with it.

April 25
INSTANT IN SEASON

Be instant in season, out of season." 2 Timothy 4:2

Many of us suffer from the morbid tendency to be instant "out of season." The season does not refer to time, but to us - 'Be instant in season, out of season," whether we feel like it or not. If we do only what we feel inclined to do, some of us would do nothing for ever and ever. There are unemployables in the spiritual domain, spiritually decrepit people, who refuse to do anything unless they are supernaturally inspired. The proof that we are rightly related to God is that we do our best whether we feel inspired or not. One of the great snares of the Christian worker is to make a fetish of his rare moments. When the Spirit of God gives you a time of inspiration and insight, you say - "Now I will always be like this for God." No, you will not, God will take care you are not. Those times are the gift of God entirely. You cannot give them to yourself when you choose. If you say you will only be at your best, you become an intolerable drag on God; you will never do anything unless God keeps you consciously inspired. If you make a god of your best moments, you will find that God will fade out of your life and never come back until you do the duty that lies nearest, and have learned not to make a fetish of your rare moments.

April 26
THE SUPREME CLIMB

"Take now thy son . . and offer him there for a burnt-offering upon one of the mountains which I will tell thee of." Genesis 22:2

Character determines how a man interprets God's will (cf. Psalm 18:25-26). Abraham interpreted God's command to mean that he had to kill his son, and he could only leave this tradition behind by the pain of a tremendous ordeal. God could purify his faith in no other way. If we obey what God says according to our sincere belief, God will break us from those traditions that misrepresent Him. There are many such beliefs to be got rid of, e.g., that God removes a child because the mother loves him too much - a devil's lie! and a travesty of the true nature of God. If the devil can hinder us from taking the supreme climb and getting rid of wrong traditions about God, he will do so; but if we keep true to God, God will take us through an ordeal which will bring us out into a better knowledge of Himself. The great point of Abraham's faith in God was that he was prepared to do anything for God. He was there to obey God, no matter to what belief he went contrary. Abraham was not a devotee of his convictions, or he would have slain Isaac and said that the voice of the angel was the voice of the devil. That is the attitude of a fanatic. If you will remain true to God, God will lead you straight through every barrier into the inner chamber of the knowledge of Himself; but there is always this point of giving up convictions and traditional beliefs. Don't ask God to test you. Never declare as Peter did - "I will do anything, I will go to death with Thee." Abraham did not make any such declaration, he remained true to God, and God purified his faith.

April 27
WHAT DO YOU WANT?

"Seekest thou great things for thyself?" Jeremiah 45:5

Are you seeking great things for yourself? Not seeking to be a great one, but seeking great things from God for yourself. God wants you in a closer relationship to Himself than receiving His gifts, He wants you to get to know Him. A great thing is accidental, it comes and goes. God never gives us anything accidental. There is nothing easier than getting into a right relationship with God except when it is not God Whom you want but only what He gives. If you have only come the length of asking God for things, you have never come to the first strand of abandonment, you have become a Christian from a standpoint of your own. "I did ask God for the Holy Spirit, but He did not give me the rest and the peace I expected." Instantly God puts His finger on the reason - you are not seeking the Lord at all, you are seeking something for yourself. Jesus says - "Ask, and it shall be given you." Ask God for what you want, and you cannot ask if you are not asking for a right thing. When you draw near to God, you cease from asking for things. "Your Father knoweth what things ye have need of, before ye ask Him." Then why ask? That you may get to know Him. Are you seeking great things for yourself? "O Lord, baptize me with the Holy Ghost." If God does not, it is because you are not abandoned enough to Him, there is something you will not do. Are you prepared to ask yourself what it is you want from God and why you want it? God always ignores the present perfection for the ultimate perfection. He is not concerned about making you blessed and happy just now; He is working out His ultimate perfection all the time - "that they may be one even as We are."

April 28
WHAT YOU WILL GET

"Thy life will I give thee for a prey in all places whither thou goest." Jeremiah 45:5

This is the unshakable secret of the Lord to those who trust Him - "I will give thee thy life." What more does a man want than his life? It is the essential thing. "Thy life for a prey" means that wherever you may go, even if it is into hell, you will come out with your life, nothing can harm it. So many of us are caught up in the shows of things, not in the way of property and possessions, but of blessings. All these have to go; but there is something grander that never can go - the life that is "hid with Christ in God." Are you prepared to let God take you into union with Himself, and pay no more attention to what you call the great things? Are you prepared to abandon entirely and let go? The test of abandonment is in refusing to say - "Well, what about this?" Beware of suppositions. Immediately you allow - What about this? - it means you have not abandoned, you do not really trust God. Immediately you do abandon, you think no more about what God is going to do. Abandon means to refuse yourself the luxury of asking any questions. If you abandon entirely to God, He says at once, "Thy life will I give thee for a prey." The reason people are tired of life is because God has not given them anything, they have not got their life as a prey. The way to get out of that state is to abandon to God. When you do get through to abandonment to God, you will be the most surprised and delighted creature on earth; God has got you absolutely and has given you your life. If you are not there, it is either because of disobedience or a refusal to be simple enough.

April 29
THE GRACIOUSNESS OF UNCERTAINTY

"It doth not yet appear what we shall be." 1 John 3:2

Naturally, we are inclined to be so mathematical and calculating that we look upon uncertainty as a bad thing. We imagine that we have to reach some end, but that is not the nature of spiritual life. The nature of spiritual life is that we are certain in our uncertainty, consequently we do not make our nests anywhere. Common sense says - "Well, supposing I were in that condition . . ." We cannot suppose ourselves in any condition we have never been in. Certainty is the mark of the common-sense life: gracious uncertainty is the mark of the spiritual life. To be certain of God means that we are uncertain in all our ways, we do not know what a day may bring forth. This is generally said with a sigh of sadness, it should be rather an expression of breathless expectation. We are uncertain of the next step, but we are certain of God. Immediately we abandon to God, and do the duty that lies nearest, He packs our life with surprises all the time. When we become advocates of a creed, something dies; we do not believe God, we only believe our belief about Him. Jesus said, "Except ye become as little children." Spiritual life is the life of a child. We are not uncertain of God, but uncertain of what He is going to do next. If we are only certain in our beliefs, we get dignified and severe and have the ban of finality about our views; but when we are rightly related to God, life is full of spontaneous, joyful uncertainty and expectancy. "Believe also in Me," said Jesus, not - "Believe certain things about Me." Leave the whole thing to Him, it is gloriously uncertain how He will come in, but He will come. Remain loyal to Him.

April 30
THE SPONTANEITY OF LOVE

"Love suffereth long, and is kind . . ." 1 Corinthians 13:4-8

Love is not premeditated, it is spontaneous, i.e., it bursts up in extraordinary ways. There is nothing of mathematical certainty in Paul's category of love. We cannot say - "Now I am going to think no evil; I am going to believe all things." The characteristic of love is spontaneity. We do not set the statements of Jesus in front of us as a standard; but when His Spirit is having His way with us, we live according to His standard with out knowing it, and on looking back we are amazed at the disinterestedness of a particular emotion, which is the evidence that the spontaneity of real love was there. In everything to do with the life of God in us, its nature is only discerned when it is past. The springs of love are in God, not in us. It is absurd to look for the love of God in our hearts naturally, it is only there when it has been shed abroad in our hearts by the Holy Spirit. If we try to prove to God how much we love Him, it is a sure sign that we do not love Him. The evidence of our love for Him is the absolute spontaneity of our love, it comes naturally. In looking back we cannot tell why we did certain things, we did them according to the spontaneous nature of His love in us. The life of God manifests itself in this spontaneous way because the springs of love are in the Holy Ghost. (Romans 5:5.)

May 1
INSIGHT NOT EMOTION

"I have to lead my life in faith, without seeing Him." 2 Corinthians 5:7 (MOFFATT)

For a time we are conscious of God's attentions, then, when God begins to use us in His enterprises, we take on a pathetic look and talk of the trials and the difficulties, and all the time God is trying to make us do our duty as obscure people. None of us would be obscure spiritually if we could help it. Can we do our duty when God has shut up heaven? Some of us always want to be illuminated saints with golden haloes and the flush of inspiration, and to have the saints of God dealing with us all the time. A gilt-edged saint is no good, he is abnormal, unfit for daily life, and altogether unlike God. We are here as men and women, not as half-fledged angels, to do the work of the world, and to do it with an infinitely greater power to stand the turmoil because we have been born from above. If we try to re-introduce the rare moments of inspiration, it is a sign that it is not God we want. We are making a fetish of the moments when God did come and speak, and insisting that He must do it again; whereas what God wants us to do is to "walk by faith." How many of us have laid ourselves by, as it were, and said - "I cannot do any more until God appears to me." He never will, and without any inspiration, without any sudden touch of God, we will have to get up. Then comes the surprise - "Why, He was there all the time, and I never knew it!" Never live for the rare moments, they are surprises. God will give us touches of inspiration when He sees we are not in danger of being led away by them. We must never make our moments of inspiration our standard; our standard is our duty.

May 2
THE PASSION OF PATIENCE

"Though it tarry, wait for it." Habakkuk 2:3

Patience is not indifference; patience conveys the idea of an immensely strong rock withstanding all onslaughts. The vision of God is the source of patience, because it imparts a moral inspiration. Moses endured, not because he had an ideal of right and duty, but because he had a vision of God. He "endured, as seeing Him Who is invisible." A man with the vision of God is not devoted to a cause or to any particular issue; he is devoted to God Himself. You always know when the vision is of God because of the inspiration that comes with it; things come with largeness and tonic to the life because everything is energized by God. If God gives you a time spiritually, as He gave His Son actually, of temptation in the wilderness, with no word from Himself at all, endure, and the power to endure is there because you see God. "Though it tarry, wait for it." The proof that we have the vision is that we are reaching out for more than we have grasped. It is a bad thing to be satisfied spiritually. "What shall I render unto the Lord?" said the Psalmist. "I will take the cup of salvation." We are apt to look for satisfaction in ourselves - "Now I have got the thing; now I am entirely sanctified; now I can endure." Instantly we are on the road to ruin. Our reach must exceed our grasp. "Not as though I had already attained, either were already perfect." If we have only what we have experienced, we have nothing; if we have the inspiration of the vision of God, we have more than we can experience. Beware of the danger of relaxation spiritually.

May 3
VITAL INTERCESSION

"Praying always with all prayer and supplication in the Spirit." Ephesians 6:18

As we go on in intercession we may find that our obedience to God is going to cost other people more than we thought. The danger then is to begin to intercede in sympathy with those whom God was gradually lifting to a totally different sphere in answer to our prayers. Whenever we step back from identification with God's interest in others into sympathy with them, the vital connection with God has gone, we have put our sympathy, our consideration for them in the way, and this is a deliberate rebuke to God. It is impossible to intercede vitally unless we are perfectly sure of God, and the greatest dissipator of our relationship to God is personal sympathy and personal prejudice. Identification is the key to intercession, and whenever we stop being identified with God, it is by sympathy, not by sin. It is not likely that sin will interfere with our relationship to God, but sympathy will, sympathy with ourselves or with others which makes us say - "I will not allow that thing to happen." Instantly we are out of vital connection with God. Intercession leaves you neither time nor inclination to pray for your own "sad sweet self." The thought of yourself is not kept out, because it is not there to keep out; you are completely and entirely identified with God's interests in other lives. Discernment is God's call to intercession, never to fault finding.

May 4
VICARIOUS INTERCESSION

"Having therefore, brethren, boldness to enter into the holiest by the blood of Jesus." Hebrews 10:19

Beware of imagining that intercession means bringing our personal sympathies into the presence of God and demanding that He does what we ask. Our approach to God is due entirely to the vicarious identification of our Lord with sin. We have "boldness to enter into the holiest by the blood of Jesus." Spiritual stubbornness is the most effectual hindrance to intercession, because it is based on sympathy with that in ourselves and in others that we do not think needs atoning for. We have the notion that there are certain right and virtuous things in us which do not need to be based on the Atonement, and just in the domain of "stodge" that is produced by this idea we cannot intercede. We do not identify ourselves with God's interests in others, we get petulant with God; we are always ready with our own ideas, and intercession becomes the glorification of our own natural sympathies. We have to realize that the identification of Jesus with sin means the radical alteration of all our sympathies. Vicarious intercession means that we deliberately substitute God's interests in others for our natural sympathy with them. Am I stubborn or substituted? Petted or perfect in my relationship to God? Sulky or spiritual? Determined to have my own way or determined to be identified with Him?

May 5
JUDGMENT ON THE ABYSS OF LOVE

For the time is come that judgment must begin at the house of God." 1 Peter 4:17

The Christian worker must never forget that salvation is God's thought, not man's; therefore it is an unfathomable abyss. Salvation is the great thought of God, not an experience. Experience is only a gateway by which salvation comes into our conscious life. Never preach the experience; preach the great thought of God behind. When we preach we are not proclaiming how man can be saved from hell and be made moral and pure; we are conveying good news about God. In the teachings of Jesus Christ the element of judgment is always brought out, it is the sign of God's love. Never sympathize with a soul who finds it difficult to get to God, God is not to blame. It is not for us to find out the reason why it is difficult, but so to present the truth of God that the Spirit of God will show what is wrong. The great sterling test in preaching is that it brings everyone to judgment. The Spirit of God locates each one to himself. If Jesus ever gave us a command He could not enable us to fulfil, He would be a liar; and if we make our inability a barrier to obedience, it means we are telling God there is something He has not taken into account. Every element of self-reliance must be slain by the power of God. Complete weakness and dependence will always be the occasion for the Spirit of God to manifest His power.

May 6
LIBERTY ON THE ABYSS OF THE GOSPEL

"Stand fast therefore in the liberty wherewith Christ hath made us free." Galatians 5:1

A spiritually minded man will never come to you with the demand - "Believe this and that;" but with the demand that you square your life with the standards of Jesus. We are not asked to believe the Bible, but to believe the One Whom the Bible reveals (cf. John 5:39-40). We are called to present liberty of conscience, not liberty of view. If we are free with the liberty of Christ, others will be brought into that same liberty - the liberty of realizing the dominance of Jesus Christ. Always keep your life measured by the standards of Jesus. Bow your neck to His yoke alone, and to no other yoke whatever; and be careful to see that you never bind a yoke on others that is not placed by Jesus Christ. It takes God a long time to get us out of the way of thinking that unless everyone sees as we do, they must be wrong. That is never God's view. There is only one liberty, the liberty of Jesus at work in our conscience enabling us to do what is right. Don't get impatient, remember how God dealt with you - with patience and with gentleness; but never water down the truth of God. Let it have its way and never apologize for it. Jesus said, "Go and make disciples," not "make converts to your opinions."

May 7
BUILDING FOR ETERNITY

"For which of you, intending to build a tower, sitteth not down first, and counteth the cost, whether he have sufficient to finish it?" Luke 14:28

Our Lord refers not to a cost we have to count, but to a cost which He has counted. The cost was those thirty years in Nazareth, those three years of popularity, scandal and hatred, the deep unfathomable agony in

Gethsemane, and the onslaught at Calvary - the pivot upon which the whole of Time and Eternity turns. Jesus Christ has counted the cost. Men are not going to laugh at Him at last and say - "This man began to build, and was not able to finish." The conditions of discipleship laid down by Our Lord in vv. 26, 27 and 33 mean that the men and women He is going to use in His mighty building enterprises are those in whom He has done everything. "If any man come to Me, and hate not . . . he cannot be My disciple." Our Lord implies that the only men and women He will use in His building enterprises are those who love Him personally, passionately and devotedly beyond any of the closest ties on earth. The conditions are stern, but they are glorious. All that we build is going to be inspected by God. Is God going to detect in His searching fire that we have built on the foundation of Jesus some enterprise of our own? These are days of tremendous enterprises, days when we are trying to work for God, and therein is the snare. Profoundly speaking, we can never work for God. Jesus takes us over for His enterprises, His building schemes entirely, and no soul has any right to claim where he shall be put.

May 8
THE PATIENCE OF FAITH

"Because thou hast kept the word of My patience." Revelation 3:10

Patience is more than endurance. A saint's life is in the hands of God like a bow and arrow in the hands of an archer. God is aiming at something the saint cannot see, and He stretches and strains, and every now and again the saint says - "I cannot stand any more." God does not heed, He goes on stretching till His purpose is in sight, then He lets fly. Trust yourself in God's hands. For what have you need of patience just now? Maintain your relationship to Jesus Christ by the patience of faith. "Though He slay me, yet will I wait for Him." Faith is not a pathetic sentiment, but robust vigorous confidence built on the fact that God is holy love. You cannot see Him just now, you cannot understand what He is doing, but you know Him. Shipwreck occurs where there is not that mental poise which comes from being established on the eternal truth that God is holy love. Faith is the heroic effort of your life, you fling yourself in reckless confidence on God. God has ventured all in Jesus Christ to save us, now He wants us to venture our all in abandoned confidence in Him. There are spots where that faith has not worked in us as yet, places untouched by the life of God. There were none of those spots in Jesus Christ's life, and there are to be none in ours. "This is life eternal, that they might know Thee." The real meaning of eternal life is a life that can face anything it has to face without wavering. If we take this view, life becomes one great romance, a glorious opportunity for seeing marvellous things all the time. God is disciplining us to get us into this central place of power.

May 9
GRASP WITHOUT REACH

"Where there is no vision, the people cast off restraint." Proverbs 29:18 (R.V.)

There is a difference between an ideal and a vision. An ideal has no moral inspiration; a vision has. The people who give themselves over to ideals rarely do anything. A man's conception of Deity may be used to justify his deliberate neglect of his duty. Jonah argued that because God was a God of justice and of mercy, therefore everything would be all right. I may have a right conception of God, and that may be the very reason why I do not do my duty. But wherever there is vision, there is also a life of rectitude because the vision imparts moral incentive. Ideals may lull to ruin. Take stock of yourself spiritually and see whether you have ideals only or if you have vision. "Ah, but a man's reach should exceed his grasp, Or what's a heaven for?" "Where there is no vision. . . ." When once we lose sight of God, we begin to be reckless, we cast off certain restraints, we cast off praying, we cast off the vision of God in little things, and begin to act on our own initiative. If we are eating what we have out of our own hand, doing things on our own initiative without expecting God to come in, we are on the downward path, we have lost the vision. Is our attitude to-day an attitude that springs from our vision of God? Are we expecting God to do greater things than He has ever done? Is there a freshness and vigour in our spiritual out look?

May 10
TAKE THE INITIATIVE

"Add to your faith virtue. . ." ("Furnish your faith with resolution.") (MOFFATT.) 2 Peter 1:5

"Add" means there is something we have to do. We are in danger of forgetting that we cannot do what God does, and that God will not do what we can do. We cannot save ourselves nor sanctify ourselves, God does that; but God will not give us good habits, He will not give us character, He will not make us walk aright. We have to do all that ourselves, we have to work out the salvation God has worked in. "Add" means to get into the habit of doing things, and in the initial stages it is difficult. To take the initiative is to make a beginning, to instruct yourself in the way you have to go. Beware of the tendency of asking the way when you know it perfectly well. Take the initiative, stop hesitating, and take the first step. Be resolute when God speaks, act in faith immediately on what He says, and never revise your decisions. If you hesitate when God tells you to do a thing, you endanger your standing in grace. Take the initiative, take it yourself, take the step with your will now, make it impossible to go back. Burn your bridges behind you - "I will write that letter"; "I will pay that debt." Make the thing inevitable. We have to get into the habit of hearkening to God about everything, to form the habit of finding out what God says. If when a crisis comes, we instinctively turn to God, we know that the habit has been formed. We have to take the initiative where we are, not where we are not.

May 11
YOU WON'T REACH IT ON TIPTOE

"Add to your brotherliness . . . love." 2 Peter 1:7

Love is indefinite to most of us, we do not know what we mean when we talk about love. Love is the sovereign preference of one person for another, and spiritually Jesus demands that that preference be for Himself (cf. Luke 14:26). When the love of God is shed abroad in our hearts by the Holy Ghost, Jesus Christ is easily first; then we must practise the working out of these things mentioned by Peter. The first thing God does is to knock pretence and the pious pose right out of me. The Holy Spirit reveals that God loved me not because I was lovable, but because it was His nature to do so. Now, He says to me, show the same love to others - "Love as I have loved you." "I will bring any number of people about you whom you cannot respect, and you must exhibit My love to them as I have exhibited it to you." You won't reach it on tiptoe. Some of us have tried to, but we were soon tired. "The Lord suffereth long. . . ." Let me look within and see His dealings with me. The knowledge that God has loved me to the uttermost, to the end of all my sin and meanness and selfishness and wrong, will send me forth into the world to love in the same way. God's love to me is inexhaustible, and I must love others from the bedrock of God's love to me. Growth in grace stops the moment I get huffed. I get huffed because I have a peculiar person to live with. Just think how disagreeable I have been to God! Am I prepared to be so identified with the Lord Jesus that His life and His sweetness are being poured out all the time? Neither natural love nor Divine love will remain unless it is cultivated. Love is spontaneous, but it has to be maintained by discipline.

May 12
MAKE a HABIT of HAVING no HABITS

"For if these things are yours and abound, they make you to be not idle nor unfruitful." 2 Peter 1:8 (R.V.)

When we begin to form a habit we are conscious of it. There are times when we are conscious of becoming virtuous and patient and godly, but it is only a stage; if we stop there we shall get the strut of the spiritual prig. The right thing to do with habits is to lose them in the life of the Lord, until every habit is so practised that there is no conscious habit at all. Our spiritual life continually resolves into introspection because there are some qualities we have not added as yet. Ultimately the relationship is to be a completely simple one. Your god may be your little Christian habit, the habit of prayer at stated times, or the habit of Bible reading. Watch how your Father will upset those times if you begin to worship your habit instead of what the habit symbolizes - I can't do that just now, I am praying; it is my hour with God. No, it is your hour with your habit. There is a quality that is lacking in you. Recognize the defect and then look for the opportunity of exercising yourself along the line of the quality to be added. Love means that there is no habit visible, you have come to the place where the habit is lost, and by practice you do the thing unconsciously. If you are consciously holy, there are certain things you imagine you cannot do, certain relationships in which you are far from simple; that means there is something to be added. The only supernatural life is the life the Lord Jesus lived, and He was at home with God anywhere. Is there anywhere where you are not at home with God? Let God press through in that particular circumstance until you gain Him, and life becomes the simple life of a child.

May 13
The HABIT of a GOOD CONSCIENCE

"A conscience void of offence toward God, and toward men." Acts 24:16

God's commands are given to the life of His Son in us, consequently to the human nature in which His Son has been formed, His commands are difficult, but immediately we obey they become divinely easy. Conscience is that faculty in me which attaches itself to the highest that I know, and tells me what the highest I know demands that I do. It is the eye of the soul which looks out either towards God or towards what it regards as the highest, and therefore conscience records differently in different people. If I am in the habit of steadily facing myself with God, my conscience will always introduce God's perfect law and indicate what

I should do. The point is, will I obey? I have to make an effort to keep my conscience so sensitive that I walk without offence. I should be living in such perfect sympathy with God's Son, that in every circumstance the spirit of my mind is renewed, and I "make out" at once "what is that good, and acceptable, and perfect, will of God." God always educates us down to the scruple. Is my ear so keen to hear the tiniest whisper of the Spirit that I know what I should do? "Grieve not the Holy Spirit." He does not come with a voice like thunder; His voice is so gentle that it is easy to ignore it. The one thing that keeps the conscience sensitive to Him is the continual habit of being open to God on the inside. When there is any debate, quit. "Why shouldn't I do this?" You are on the wrong track. There is no debate possible when conscience speaks. At your peril, you allow one thing to obscure your inner communion with God. Drop it, whatever it is, and see that you keep your inner vision clear.

May 14
THE HABIT OF ENJOYING THE DISAGREEABLE

"That life also of Jesus might be made manifest in our mortal flesh." 2 Corinthians 4:10

We have to form habits to express what God's grace has done in us. It is not a question of being saved from hell, but of being saved in order to manifest the life of the Son of God in our mortal flesh, and it is the disagreeable things which make us exhibit whether or not we are manifesting His life. Do I manifest the essential sweetness of the Son of God, or the essential irritation of "myself" apart from Him? The only thing that will enable me to enjoy the disagreeable is the keen enthusiasm of letting the life of the Son of God manifest itself in me. No matter how disagreeable a thing may be, say - "Lord, I am delighted to obey Thee in this matter," and instantly the Son of God will press to the front, and there will be manifested in my human life that which glorifies Jesus. There must be no debate. The moment you obey the light, the Son of God presses through you in that particular; but if you debate you grieve the Spirit of God. You must keep yourself fit to let the life of the Son of God be manifested, and you cannot keep yourself fit if you give way to self-pity. Our circumstances are the means of manifesting how wonderfully perfect and extraordinarily pure the Son of God is. The thing that ought to make the heart beat is a new way of manifesting the Son of God. It is one thing to choose the disagreeable, and another thing to go into the disagreeable by God's engineering. If God puts you there, He is amply sufficient. Keep your soul fit to manifest the life of the Son of God. Never live on memories; let the word of God be always living and active in you.

May 15
The HABIT of RISING to the OCCASION

"That ye may know what is the hope of His calling . . ." Ephesians 1:18

Remember what you are saved for - that the Son of God might be manifested in your mortal flesh. Bend the whole energy of your powers to realize your election as a child of God; rise to the occasion every time. You cannot do anything for your salvation, but you must do something to manifest it, you must work out what God has worked in. Are you working it out with your tongue, and your brain and your nerves? If you are still the same miserable crosspatch, set on your own way, then it is a lie to say that God has saved and sanctified you. God is the Master Engineer, He allows the difficulties to come in order to see if you can vault over them properly - "By my God have I leaped over a wall." God will never shield you from any of the requirements of a son or daughter of His. Peter says - "Think it not strange concerning the fiery trial which is to try you." Rise to the occasion; do the thing. It does not matter how it hurts as long as it gives God the chance to manifest Himself in your mortal flesh. May God not find the whine in us any more, but may He find us full of spiritual pluck and athleticism, ready to face anything He brings. We have to exercise ourselves in order that the Son of God may be manifested in our mortal flesh. God never has museums. The only aim of the life is that the Son of God may be manifested, and all dictation to God vanishes. Our Lord never dictated to His Father, and we are not here to dictate to God; we are here to submit to His will so that He may work through us what He wants. When we realize this, He will make us broken bread and poured out wine to feed and nourish others.

May 16
THE HABIT OF WEALTH

"Partakers of the divine nature." 2 Peter 1:4

We are made partakers of the Divine nature through the promises; then we have to "manipulate" the Divine nature in our human nature by habits, and the first habit to form is the habit of realizing the provision God has made. "Oh, I can't afford it," we say - one of the worst lies is tucked up in that phrase. It is ungovernably bad taste to talk about money in the natural domain, and so it is spiritually, and yet we talk as if our Heavenly Father had cut us off with a shilling! We think it a sign of real modesty to say at the end of a day - "Oh, well, I have just got through, but it has been a severe tussle." And all the Almighty God is ours in the Lord Jesus! And He will tax the last grain of sand and the remotest star to bless us if we will obey Him. What does it matter if external circumstances are hard? Why should they not be! If we give way to self-pity and indulge in the luxury of misery, we banish God's riches from our own lives and hinder others from entering into His provision. No sin is worse than the sin of selfpity, because it obliterates God and puts self-interest upon the throne. It opens our mouths to spit out murmurings and our lives become craving spiritual sponges, there is nothing lovely or generous about them. When God is beginning to be satisfied with us He will impoverish everything in the nature of fictitious wealth, until we learn that all our fresh springs are in Him. If the majesty and grace and power of God are not being manifested in us (not to our consciousness), God holds us responsible. "God is able to make all grace abound," then learn to lavish the grace of God on others. Be stamped with God's nature, and His blessing will come through you all the time.

May 17
HIS ASCENSION AND OUR UNION

And it came to pass, while He blessed them, He was parted from them, and carried up into heaven." Luke 24:51

We have no corresponding experience to the events in Our Lord's life after the Transfiguration. From then onwards Our Lord's life' was altogether vicarious. Up to the time of the Transfiguration He had exhibited the normal perfect life of a man; from the Transfiguration onwards - Gethsemane, the Cross, the Resurrection - everything is unfamiliar to us. His Cross is the door by which every member of the human race can enter into the life of God; by His Resurrection He has the right to give eternal life to any man, and by His Ascension Our Lord enters heaven and keeps the door open for humanity. On the Mount of Ascension the Transfiguration is completed. If Jesus had gone to heaven from the Mount of Transfiguration, He would have gone alone; He would have been nothing more to us than a glorious Figure. But He turned His back on the glory, and came down from the Mount to identify Himself with fallen humanity. The Ascension is the consummation of the Transfiguration. Our Lord does now go back into His primal glory; but He does not go back simply as Son of God; He goes back to God as Son of Man as well as Son of God. There is now freedom of access for anyone straight to the very throne of God by the Ascension of the Son of Man. As Son of Man Jesus Christ deliberately limited omnipotence, omnipresence and omniscience in Himself. Now they are His in absolute full power. As Son of Man Jesus Christ has all power at the throne of

God. He is King of kings and Lord of lords from the day of His Ascension until now.

May 18
CAREFUL UNREASONABLENESS

"Behold the fowls of the air." . . . "Consider the lilies of the field." Matthew 6:26, 28

Consider the lilies of the field, how they grow, they simply are! Think of the sea, the air, the sun, the stars and the moon - all these are, and what a ministration they exert. So often we mar God's designed influence through us by our self-conscious effort to be consistent and useful. Jesus says that there is only one way to develop spiritually, and that is by concentration on God. "Do not bother about being of use to others; believe on Me" - pay attention to the Source, and out of you will flow rivers of living water. We cannot get at the springs of our natural life by common sense, and Jesus is teaching that growth in spiritual life does not depend on our watching it, but on concentration on our Father in heaven. Our heavenly Father knows the circumstances we are in, and if we keep concentrated on Him we will grow spiritually as the lilies. The people who influence us most are not those who buttonhole us and talk to us, but those who live their lives like the stars in heaven and the lilies in the field, perfectly simply and unaffectedly. Those are the lives that mould us. If you want to be of use to God, get rightly related to Jesus Christ and He will make you of use unconsciously every minute you live.

May 19
"OUT OF THE WRECK I RISE" "

Who shall separate us from the love of Christ?" Romans 8:35

God does not keep a man immune from trouble; He says - "I will be with him in trouble." It does not matter what actual troubles in the most extreme form get hold of a man's life, not one of them can separate him from his relationship to God. We are "more than conquerors in all these things." Paul is not talking of imaginary things, but of things that are desperately actual; and he says we are super-victors in the midst of them, not by our ingenuity, or by our courage, or by anything other than the fact that not one of them affects our relationship to God in Jesus Christ. Rightly or wrongly, we are where we are, exactly in the condition we are in. I am sorry for the Christian who has not something in his circumstances he wishes was not there. "Shall tribulation . . . ?"

Tribulation is never a noble thing; but let tribulation be what it may - exhausting, galling, fatiguing, it is not able to separate us from the love of God. Never let cares or tribulations separate you from the fact that God loves you. "Shall anguish . . . ?" - can God's love hold when everything says that His love is a lie, and that there is no such thing as justice? "Shall famine . . . ?" - can we not only believe in the love of God but be more than conquerors, even while we are being starved? Either Jesus Christ is a deceiver and Paul is deluded, or some extraordinary thing happens to a man who holds on to the love of God when the odds are all against God's character. Logic is silenced in the face of every one of these things. Only one thing can account for it - the love of God in Christ Jesus. "Out of the wreck I rise" every time.

May 20
THE REALM OF THE REAL

"In your patience possess ye your souls." Luke 21:19

When a man is born again, there is not the same robustness in his thinking or reasoning for a time as formerly. We have to make an expression of the new life, to form the mind of Christ. "Acquire your soul with patience." Many of us prefer to stay at the threshold of the Christian life instead of going on to construct a soul in accordance with the new life God has put within. We fail because we are ignorant of the way we are made, we put things down to the devil instead of our own undisciplined natures. Think what we can be when we are roused! There are certain things we must not pray about - moods, for instance. Moods never go by praying, moods go by kicking. A mood nearly always has its seat in the physical condition, not in the moral. It is a continual effort not to listen to the moods which arise from a physical condition, never submit to them for a second. We have to take ourselves by the scruff of the neck and shake ourselves, and we will find that we can do what we said we could not. The curse with most of us is that we won't. The Christian life is one of incarnate spiritual pluck.

May 21
DIVINE REASONINGS OF FAITH

"But seek ye first the kingdom of God, and His righteousness; and all these things shall be added unto you." Matthew 6:33

Immediately we look at these words of Jesus, we find them the most revolutionary statement human ears ever listened to. "Seek ye first the kingdom of God." We argue in exactly the opposite way, even the most spiritually-minded of us - "But I must live; I must make so much money; I must be clothed; I must be fed." The great concern of our lives is not the kingdom of God, but how we are to fit ourselves to live. Jesus reverses the order: Get rightly related to God first, maintain that as the great care of your life, and never put the concern of your care on the other things. "Take no thought for your life. . . ." Our Lord points out the utter unreasonableness from His standpoint of being so anxious over the means of living. Jesus is not saying that the man who takes thought for nothing is blessed - that man is a fool. Jesus taught that a disciple has to make his relationship to God the dominating concentration of his life, and to be carefully careless about every thing else in comparison to that. Jesus is saying - "Don't make the ruling factor of your life what you shall eat and what you shall drink, but be concentrated absolutely on God." Some people are careless over what they eat and drink, and they suffer for it; they are careless about what they wear, and they look as they have no business to look; they are careless about their earthly affairs, and God holds them responsible. Jesus is saying that the great care of the life is to put the relationship to God first, and everything else second. It is one of the severest disciplines of the Christian life to allow the Holy Spirit to bring us into harmony with the teaching of Jesus in these verses.

May 22
NOW THIS EXPLAINS IT

"That they all may be one; as thou, Father, art in me, and I in thee, that they also may be one in us." John 17:21

If you are going through a solitary way, read John 17, it will explain exactly why you are where you are - Jesus has prayed that you may be one with the Father as He is. Are you helping God to answer that prayer, or have you some other end for your life? Since you became a disciple you cannot be as independent as you used to be. The purpose of God is not to answer our prayers, but by our prayers we come to discern the mind of God, and this is revealed in John 17. There is one prayer God must answer, and that is the prayer of Jesus - "that they may be one, even as We are One." Are we as close to Jesus Christ as that? God is not concerned about our plans; He does not say - Do you want to go through this bereavement; this upset? He allows these things for His own purpose. The things we are going through are either making us sweeter, better, nobler men and women; or they are making us more captious and fault-finding, more insistent upon our own way. The things that happen either make us fiends, or they make us saints; it depends entirely upon the relationship we are in to God. If we say - "Thy will be done," we get the consolation of John 17, the consolation of knowing that our Father is working according to His own wisdom. When we understand what God is after we will not get mean and cynical. Jesus has prayed nothing less for us than absolute oneness with Himself as He was one with the Father. Some of us are far off it, and yet God will not leave us alone until we are one with Him, because Jesus has prayed that we may be.

May 23
CAREFUL INFIDELITY

"Take no thought for your life, what ye shall eat, or what ye shall drink; nor yet for your body what ye shall put on." Matthew 6:25

Jesus sums up common-sense carefulness in a disciple as infidelity. If we have received the Spirit of God, He will press through and say - Now where does God come in in this relationship, in this mapped out holiday, in these new books? He always presses the point until we learn to make Him our first consideration. Whenever we put other things first, there is confusion. "Take no thought . . ." don't take the pressure of forethought upon yourself. It is not only wrong to worry, it is infidelity, because worrying means that we do not think that God can look after the practical details of our lives, and it is never any thing else that worries us. Have you ever noticed what Jesus said would choke the word He puts in? The devil? No, the cares of this world. It is the little worries always. I will not trust where I cannot see, that is where infidelity begins. The only cure for infidelity is obedience to the Spirit. The great word of Jesus to His disciples is abandon.

May 24
THE DELIGHT OF DESPAIR

"And when I saw Him, I fell at His feet as dead." Revelation 1:17

It may be that like the apostle John you know Jesus Christ intimately, when suddenly He appears with no familiar characteristic at all, and the only thing you can do is to fall at His feet as dead. There are times when God cannot reveal Himself in any other way than in His majesty, and it is the awfulness of the vision which brings you to the delight of despair; if you are ever to be raised up, it must be by the hand of God. "He laid His right hand upon me." In the midst of the awfulness, a touch comes, and you know it is the right hand of Jesus Christ. The right hand not of restraint nor of correction nor of chastisement, but the right hand of the Everlasting Father. Whenever His hand is laid upon you, it is ineffable peace and comfort, the sense that "underneath are the everlasting arms," full of sustaining and comfort and strength. When once His touch comes, nothing at all can cast you into fear again. In the midst of all His ascended glory the Lord Jesus comes to speak to an insignificant disciple, and to say - "Fear not." His tenderness is ineffably sweet. Do I know Him like that? Watch some of the things that strike despair. There is despair in which there is no delight, no horizon, no hope of anything brighter; but the delight of despair comes when I know that "in me (that is, in my flesh) dwelleth no good thing." I delight to know that there is that in me which must fall prostrate before God when He manifests Himself, and if I am ever to be raised up it must be by the hand of God. God can do nothing for me until I get to the limit of the possible.

May 25
THE TEST OF SELF-INTEREST

"If thou wilt take the left hand, then I will go to the right; or if thou depart to the right hand, then I will go to the left." Genesis 13:9

As soon as you begin to live the life of faith in God, fascinating and luxurious prospects will open up before you, and these things are yours by right; but if you are living the life of faith you will exercise your right to waive your rights, and let God choose for you. God sometimes allows you to get into a place of testing where your own welfare would be the right and proper thing to consider if you were not living a life of faith; but if you are, you will joyfully waive your right and leave God to choose for you. This is the discipline by means of which the natural is transformed into the spiritual by obedience to the voice of God. Whenever right is made the guidance in the life, it will blunt the spiritual insight. The great enemy of the life of faith in God is not sin, but the good which is not good enough. The good is always the enemy of the best. It would seem the wisest thing in the world for Abraham to choose, it was his right, and the people around would consider him a fool for not choosing. Many of us do not go on spiritually because we prefer to choose what is right instead of relying on God to choose for us. We have to learn to walk according to the standard which has its eye on God. "Walk before Me."

May 26
THINK AS JESUS TAUGHT

"Pray without ceasing." 1 Thessalonians 5:17

We think rightly or wrongly about prayer according to the conception we have in our minds of prayer. If we think of prayer as the breath in our lungs and the blood from our hearts, we think rightly. The blood flows ceaselessly, and breathing continues ceaselessly; we are not conscious of it, but it is always going on. We are not always conscious of Jesus keeping us in perfect joint with God, but if we are obeying Him, He always is. Prayer is not an exercise, it is the life. Beware of anything that stops ejaculatory prayer. "Pray without ceasing," keep the childlike habit of ejaculatory prayer in your heart to God all the time. Jesus never mentioned unanswered prayer, He had the boundless certainty that prayer is always answered. Have we by the Spirit the unspeakable certainty that Jesus had about prayer, or do we think of the times when God does not seem to have answered prayer? "Every one that asketh receiveth." We say - "But . . . , but . . ." God answers prayer in the best way, not sometimes, but every time, although the immediate manifestation of the answer in the domain in which we want it may not always follow. Do we expect God to answer prayer? The danger with us is that we want to water down the things that Jesus says and make them mean something in accordance with common sense; if it were only common sense, it was not worth while for Him to say it. The things Jesus says about prayer are supernatural revelations.

May 27
THE LIFE THAT LIVES

"Tarry ye in the city of Jerusalem, until ye be endued with power from on high." Luke 24:49

The disciples had to tarry until the day of Pentecost not for their own preparation only; they had to wait until the Lord was glorified historically. As soon as He was glorified, what happened? "Therefore being by the right hand of God exalted, and having received of the Father the promise of the Holy Ghost, He hath shed forth this, which ye now see and hear." The parenthesis in John 7:39 ("For the Holy Ghost was not yet given; because that Jesus was not yet glorified") does not apply to us; the Holy Ghost has been given, the Lord is glorified; the waiting depends not on God's providence, but on our fitness. The Holy Spirit's influence and power were at work before Pentecost, but He was not here. Immediately Our Lord was glorified in Ascension, the Holy Spirit came into this world, and He has been here ever since. We have to receive the revelation that He is here. The reception of the Holy Spirit is the maintained attitude of a believer. When we receive the Holy Spirit, we receive quickening life from the ascended Lord. It is not the baptism of the Holy Ghost which changes men, but the power of the ascended Christ coming into men's lives by the Holy Ghost that changes them. We too often divorce what the New Testament never divorces. The baptism of the Holy Ghost is not an experience apart from Jesus Christ: it is the evidence of the ascended Christ. The baptism of the Holy Ghost does not make you think of Time or Eternity, it is one amazing glorious NOW. "This is life eternal that they might know Thee." Begin to know Him now, and finish never.

May 28
UNQUESTIONED REVELATION

"And in that day ye shall ask Me nothing." John 16:23

When is "that day"? When the Ascended Lord makes you one with the Father. In that day you will be one with the Father as Jesus is, and "in that day," Jesus says, "ye shall ask Me nothing." Until the resurrection life of Jesus is manifested in you, you want to ask this and that; then after a while you find all questions gone, you do not seem to have any left to ask. You have come to the place of entire reliance on the resurrection life of Jesus which brings you into perfect contact with the purpose of God. Are you living that life now? If not, why shouldn't you? There may be any number of things dark to your understanding, but they do not come in between your heart and God. "And in that day ye shall ask Me no question" - you do not need to, you are so certain that God will bring things out in accordance with His will. John 14:1 has become the real state of your heart, and there are no more questions to be asked. If anything is a mystery to you and it is coming in between you and God, never look for the explanation in your intellect, look for it in your disposition, it is that which is wrong. When once your disposition is willing to submit to the life of Jesus, the understanding will be perfectly clear, and you will get to the place where there is no distance between the Father and His child because the Lord has made you one, and "in that day ye shall ask Me no question."

May 29
UNDISTURBED RELATIONSHIP

"At that day ye shall ask in My name . . ." "The Father Himself loveth you." John 16:26, 27

"At that day ye shall ask in My name," i.e., in My nature. Not - "You shall use My name as a magic word," but - "You will be so intimate with Me that you will be one with Me." "That day" is not a day hereafter, but a day meant for here and now. "The Father Himself loveth you" - the union is so complete and absolute. Our Lord does not mean that life will be free from external perplexities, but that just as He knew the Father's heart and mind, so by the baptism of the Holy Ghost He can lift us into the heavenly places where He can reveal the counsels of God to us. "Whatsoever ye shall ask the Father in My name. . . ." "That day" is a day of undisturbed relationship between God and the saint. Just as Jesus stood unsullied in the presence of His Father, so by the mighty efficacy of the baptism of the Holy Ghost, we can be lifted into that relationship - "that they may be one, even as We are One." "He will give it you." Jesus says that God will recognize our prayers. What a challenge! By the Resurrection and Ascension power of Jesus, by the sent-down Holy Ghost, we can be lifted into such a relationship with the Father that we are at one with the perfect sovereign will of God by our free choice even as Jesus was. In that wonderful position, placed there by Jesus Christ, we can pray to God in His name, in His nature, which is gifted to us by the Holy Ghost, and Jesus says - "What soever ye shall ask the Father in My name, He will give it you." - The sovereign character of Jesus Christ is tested by His own statements.

May 30
"YES - BUT . . . !"

"Lord, I will follow Thee; but . . ." Luke 9:61

Supposing God tells you to do something which is an enormous test to your common sense, what are you going to do? Hang back? If you get into the habit of doing a thing in the physical domain, you will do it every time until you break the habit determinedly; and the same is true spiritually. Again and again you will get up to what Jesus Christ wants, and every time you will turn back when it comes to the point, until you abandon resolutely. "Yes, but - supposing I do obey God in this matter, what about . . . ?" "Yes, I will obey God if He will let me use my common sense, but don't ask me to take a step in the dark." Jesus Christ demands of the man who trusts Him the same reckless sporting spirit that the natural man exhibits. If a man is going to do anything worth while, there are times when he has to risk everything on his leap, and in the spiritual domain Jesus Christ demands that you risk everything you hold by common sense and leap into what He says, and immediately you do, you find that what He says fits on as solidly as common sense. At the bar of common sense Jesus Christ's statements may seem mad; but bring them to the bar of faith, and you begin to find with awestruck spirit that they are the words of God. Trust entirely in God, and when He brings you to the venture, see that you take it. We act like pagans in a crisis, only one out of a crowd is daring enough to bank his faith in the character of God.

May 31
GOD FIRST Put God First in Trust.

"Jesus did not commit Himself unto them . . . for He knew what was in man." John 2:24-25

Our Lord trusted no man; yet He was never suspicious, never bitter, never in despair about any man, because He put God first in trust; He trusted absolutely in what God's grace could do for any man. If I put my trust in human beings first, I will end in despairing of everyone; I will become bitter, because I have insisted on man being what no man ever can be - absolutely right. Never trust anything but the grace of God in yourself or in anyone else. Put God's Needs First. "Lo, I come to do Thy will, O God." Hebrews 10:9 A man's obedience is to what he sees to be a need; Our Lord's obedience was to the will of His Father. The cry to-day is - "We must get some work to do; the heathen are dying without God; we must go and tell them of Him." We have to see first of all that God's needs in us personally are being met. "Tarry ye until. . . ." The purpose of this College is to get us rightly related to the needs of God. When God's needs in us have been met, then He will open the way for us to realize His needs elsewhere. Put God's Trust First. "And whoso receiveth one such little child in my name receiveth Me." Matthew 18:5 God's trust is that He gives me Himself as a babe. God expects my personal life to be a "Bethlehem." Am I allowing my natural life to be slowly transfigured by the indwelling life of the Son of God? God's ultimate purpose is that His Son might be manifested in my mortal flesh.

June 1
THE STAGGERING QUESTION

"Son of man, can these bones live?" Ezekiel 37:3

Can that sinner be turned into a saint? Can that twisted life be put right? There is only one answer: "O Lord, Thou knowest, I don't." Never trample in with religious common sense and say - "Oh, yes, with a little more Bible reading and devotion and prayer, I see how it can be done." It is much easier to do something than to trust in God; we mistake panic for inspiration. That is why there are so few fellow workers with God and so many workers for Him. We would far rather work for God than believe in Him. Am I quite sure that God will do what I cannot do? I despair of men in the degree in which I have never realized that God has done anything for me. Is my experience such a wonderful realization of God's power and might that I can never despair of anyone I see? Have I had any spiritual work done in me at all? The degree of panic is the degree of the lack of personal spiritual experience. "Behold, O my people, I will open your graves." When God wants to show you what human nature is like apart from Himself, He has to show it you in yourself. If the Spirit of God has given you a vision of what you are apart from the grace of God (and He only does it when His Spirit is at work), you know there is no criminal who is half so bad in actuality as you know yourself to be in possibility. My "grave" has been opened by God and "I know that in me (that is, in my flesh) dwelleth no good thing." God's Spirit continually reveals what human nature is like apart from His grace.

June 2
WHAT ARE YOU HAUNTED BY?

What man is he that feareth the Lord?" Psalm 25:12

What are you haunted by? You will say - By nothing, but we are all haunted by something, generally by ourselves, or, if we are Christians, by our experience. The Psalmist says we are to be haunted by God. The abiding consciousness of the life is to be God, not thinking about Him. The whole of our life inside and out is to be absolutely haunted by the presence of God. A child's consciousness is so mother-haunted that although the child is not consciously thinking of its mother, yet when calamity arises, the relationship that abides is that of the mother. So we are to live and move and have our being in God, to look at everything in relation to God, because the abiding consciousness of God pushes itself to the front all the time. If we are haunted by God, nothing else can get in, no cares, no tribulation, no anxieties. We see now why Our Lord so emphasized the sin of worry. How can we dare be so utterly unbelieving when God is round about us? To be haunted by God is to have an effective barricade against all the onslaughts of the enemy. "His soul shall dwell at ease." In tribulation, misunderstanding, slander, in the midst of all these things, if our life is hid with Christ in God, He will keep us at ease. We rob ourselves of the marvellous revelation of this abiding companionship of God. "God is our Refuge" - nothing can come through that shelter.

June 3

THE SECRET OF THE LORD

"The secret (friendship R.V.) of the Lord is with them that fear Him." Psalm 25:14

What is the sign of a friend? That he tells you secret Sorrows? No, that he tells you secret joys. Many will confide to you their secret sorrows, but the last mark of intimacy is to confide secret joys. Have we ever let God tell us any of His joys, or are we telling God our secrets so continually that we leave no room for Him to talk to us? At the beginning of our Christian life we are full of requests to God, then we find that God wants to get us into relationship with Himself, to get us in touch with His purposes. Are we so wedded to Jesus Christ's idea of prayer - "Thy will be done" - that we catch the secrets of God? The things that make God dear to us are not so much His great big blessings as the tiny things, because they show His amazing intimacy with us; He knows every detail of our individual lives. ". . . him shall He teach in the way that He shall choose." At first we want the consciousness of being guided by God, then as we go on we live so much in the consciousness of God that we do not need to ask what His will is, because the thought of choosing any other will never occur to us. If we are saved and sanctified God guides us by our ordinary choices, and if we are going to choose what He does not want, He will check, and we must heed. Whenever there is doubt, Stop at once. Never reason it out and say - "I wonder why I shouldn't?" God instructs us in what we choose, that is, He guides our common sense, and we no longer hinder His Spirit by continually saying - "Now, Lord, what is Thy will?"

June 4
THE NEVER-FAILING GOD

For He hath said, I will never leave thee, nor forsake thee." Hebrews 13:5

What line does my thought take? Does it turn to what God says or to what I fear? Am I learning to say not what God says, but to say something after I have heard what He says? "He hath said, I will never leave thee, nor forsake thee. So that we may boldly say, The Lord is my helper, and I will not fear what man shall do unto me." "I will in no wise fail thee" - not for all my sin and selfishness and stubbornness and waywardness. Have I really let God say to me that He will never fail me? If I have listened to this say-so of God's, then let me listen again. "Neither will I in any wise forsake thee." Sometimes it is not difficulty that makes me think God will forsake me, but drudgery. There is no Hill Difficulty to climb, no vision given, nothing wonderful or beautiful, just the commonplace day in and day out - can I hear God's say-so in these things? We have the idea that God is going to do some exceptional thing, that He is preparing and fitting us for some extraordinary thing by and bye, but as we go on in grace we find that God is glorifying Himself here and now, in the present minute. If we have God's sayso behind us, the most amazing strength comes, and we learn to sing in the ordinary days and ways.

June 5
GOD'S SAY-SO

"He hath said . . . so that we may boldly say . . ." Hebrews 13:5-6

My say-so is to be built on God's say-so. God says - "I will never leave thee," then I can with good courage say - "The Lord is my helper, I will not fear - " I will not be haunted by apprehension. This does not mean that I will not be tempted to fear, but I will remember God's say-so. I will be full of courage, like a child "bucking himself up" to reach the standard his father wants. Faith in many a one falters when the apprehensions come, they forget the meaning of God's sayso, forget to take a deep breath spiritually. The only way to get the dread taken out of us is to listen to God's say-so. What are you dreading? You are not a coward about it, you are going to face it, but there is a feeling of dread. When there is nothing and no one to help you, say - "But the Lord is my Helper, this second, in my present outlook." Are you learning to say things after listening to God, or are you saying things and trying to make God's word fit in? Get hold of the Father's say-so, and then say with good courage - "I will not fear." It does not matter what evil or wrong may be in the way, He has said - "I will never leave thee." Frailty is another thing that gets in between God's say-so and ours. When we realize how feeble we are in facing difficulties, the difficulties become like giants, we become like grasshoppers, and God becomes a nonentity. Remember God's say-so - "I will in no wise fail you." Have we learned to sing after hearing God's keynote? Are we always possessed with the courage to say - "The Lord is my helper," or are we succumbing?

June 6
WORK OUT WHAT GOD WORKS IN

"Work out your own salvation." Philippians 2:12-13

Your will agrees with God, but in your flesh there is a disposition which renders you powerless to do what you know you ought to do. When the

Lord is presented to the conscience, the first thing conscience does is to rouse the will, and the will always agrees with God. You say - "But I do not know whether my will is in agreement with God." Look to Jesus and you will find that your will and your conscience are in agreement with Him every time. The thing in you which makes you say "I shan't" is something less profound than your will; it is perversity, or obstinacy, and they are never in agreement with God. The profound thing in man is his will, not sin. Will is the essential element in God's creation of man: sin is a perverse disposition which entered into man. In a regenerated man the source of will is almighty. "For it is God which worketh in you both to will and to do of His good pleasure." You have to work out with concentration and care what God works in; not work your own salvation, but work it out, while you base resolutely in unshaken faith on the complete and perfect Redemption of the Lord. As you do this, you do not bring an opposed will to God's will, God's will is your will, and your natural choices are along the line of God's will, and the life is as natural as breathing. God is the source of your will, therefore you are able to work out His will. Obstinacy is an unintelligent 'wadge' that refuses to be enlightened; the only thing is for it to be blown up with dynamite, and the dynamite is obedience to the Holy Spirit. Do I believe that Almighty God is the source of my will? God not only expects me to do His will, but He is in me to do it.

June 7
DON'T SLACK OFF

"Whatsoever ye shalt ask in My name, that will I do." John 14:13

Am I fulfilling this ministry of the interior? There is no snare or any danger of infatuation or pride in intercession, it is a hidden ministry that brings forth fruit whereby the Father is glorified. Am I allowing my spiritual life to be frittered away, or am I bringing it all to one centre - the Atonement of my Lord? Is Jesus Christ more and more dominating every interest in my life? If the one central point, the great exerting influence in my life is the Atonement of the Lord, then every phase of my life will bear fruit for Him. I must take time to realize what is the central point of power. Do I give one minute out of sixty to concentrate upon it? "If ye abide in Me" - continue to act and think and work from that centre - "ye shall ask what ye will, and it shall be done unto you." Am I abiding? Am I taking time to abide? What is the greatest factor of power in my life? Is it work, service, sacrifice for others, or trying to work for God? The thing that ought to exert the greatest power in my life is the Atonement of the Lord. It is not the thing we spend the most time on that moulds us most; the greatest element is the thing that exerts most power. We must determine to be limited and concentrate our affinities. "Whatsoever ye shall ask in My name, that will I do." The disciple who abides in Jesus is the will of God, and his apparently free choices are God's fore-ordained decrees. Mysterious? Logically contradictory and absurd? Yes, but a glorious truth to a saint.

June 8
WHAT NEXT?

"If ye know these things, happy are ye if ye do them." John 13:17

If you do not cut the moorings, God will have to break them by a storm and send you out. Launch all on God, go out on the great swelling tide of His purpose, and you will get your eyes open. If you believe in Jesus, you are not to spend all your time in the smooth waters just inside the harbour bar, full of delight, but always moored; you have to get out through the harbour bar into the great deeps of God and begin to know for yourself, begin to have spiritual discernment. When you know you should do a thing, and do it, immediately you know more. Revise where you have become stodgy spiritually, and you will find it goes back to a point where there was something you knew you should do, but you did not do it because there seemed no immediate call to, and now you have no perception, no discernment; at a time of crisis you are spiritually distracted instead of spiritually self-possessed. It is a dangerous thing to refuse to go on knowing. The counterfeit of obedience is a state of mind in which you work up occasions to sacrifice yourself; ardour is mistaken for discernment. It is easier to sacrifice yourself than to fulfil your spiritual destiny, which is stated in Romans 12:1-2. It is a great deal better to fulfil the purpose of God in your life by discerning His will than to perform great acts of self-sacrifice. "To obey is better than sacrifice." Beware of harking back to what you were once when God wants you to be something you have never been. "If any man will do . . . he shall know."

June 9
THE NEXT BEST THING TO DO

"For every one that asketh receiveth." Luke 11:10

There is nothing more difficult than to ask. We will long and desire and crave and suffer, but not until we are at the extreme limit will we ask. A sense of unreality makes us ask. Have you ever asked out of the depths of moral poverty? "If any of you lack wisdom, let him ask of God . . . but be sure that you do lack wisdom. You cannot bring yourself up against

Reality when you like. The next best thing to do if you are not spiritually real, is to ask God for the Holy Spirit on the word of Jesus Christ (see Luke 11:13). The Holy Spirit is the One Who makes real in you all that Jesus did for you. "For every one that asketh receiveth." This does not mean you will not get if you do not ask (cf. Matt. 5:45), but until you get to the point of asking you won't receive from God. To receive means you have come into the relationship of a child of God, and now you perceive with intelligent and moral appreciation and spiritual understanding that these things come from God. "If any of you lack wisdom . . ." If you realize you are lacking, it is because you have come in contact with spiritual reality; do not put your reasonable blinkers on again. People say - Preach us the simple gospel: don't tell us we have to be holy, because that produces a sense of abject poverty, and it is not nice to feel abjectly poor. "Ask" means beg. Some people are poor enough to be interested in their poverty, and some of us are like that spiritually. We will never receive if we ask with an end in view; if we ask, not out of our poverty but out of our lust. A pauper does not ask from any other reason than the abject panging condition of his poverty, he is not ashamed to beg. - Blessed are the paupers in spirit.

June 10
THE NEXT BEST THING TO DO

"Seek, and ye shall find." Luke 11:9

"Ye ask, and receive not, because ye ask amiss." If you ask for things from life instead of from God, you ask amiss, i.e., you ask from a desire for self-realization. The more you realize yourself the less will you seek God. "Seek, and ye shall find." Get to work, narrow your interests to this one. Have you ever sought God with your whole heart, or have you only given a languid cry to Him after a twinge of moral neuralgia? Seek, concentrate, and you will find. "Ho, every one that thirsteth, come ye to the waters." Are you thirsty, or smugly indifferent - so satisfied with your experience that you want nothing more of God? Experience is a gateway, not an end. Beware of building your faith on experience, the metallic note will come in at once, the censorious note. You can never give another person that which you have found, but you can make him homesick for what you have. "Knock, and it shall be opened unto you." "Draw nigh to God." Knock - the door is closed, and you suffer from palpitation as you knock. "Cleanse your hands" - knock a bit louder, you begin to find you are dirty. "Purify your heart" - this is more personal still, you are desperately in earnest now - you will do anything. "Be afflicted" - have you ever been afflicted before God at the state of your inner life? There is no strand of self-pity left, but a heartbreaking affliction of amazement to find you are the kind of person that you are. "Humble yourself" - it is a humbling business to knock at God's door - you have to knock with the crucified thief. "To him that knocketh, it shall be opened."

June 11
GETTING THERE

"Come unto Me." Matthew 11:28

Do I want to get there? I can now. The questions that matter in life are remarkably few, and they are all answered by the words - "Come unto Me." Not - Do this, or don't do that; but - "Come unto Me." If I will come to Jesus my actual life will be brought into accordance with my real desires; I will actually cease from sin, and actually find the song of the Lord begin. Have you ever come to Jesus? Watch the stubbornness of your heart, you will do anything rather than the one simple childlike thing - "Come unto Me." If you want the actual experience of ceasing from sin, you must come to Jesus. Jesus Christ makes Himself the touchstone. Watch how He used the word "Come." At the most unexpected moments there is the whisper of the Lord - "Come unto Me," and you are drawn immediately. Personal contact with Jesus alters everything. Be stupid enough to come and commit yourself to what He says. The attitude of coming is that the will resolutely lets go of everything and deliberately commits all to Him. ". . . and I will give you rest," i.e., I will stay you. Not - I will put you to bed and hold your hand and sing you to sleep; but - I will get you out of bed, out of the languor and exhaustion, out of the state of being half dead while you are alive; I will imbue you with the spirit of life, and you will be stayed by the perfection of vital activity. We get pathetic and talk about "suffering the will of the Lord!" Where is the majestic vitality and might of the Son of God about that?

June 12
GETTING THERE
"Master, where dwellest Thou? . . Come and see." "Come with Me." John 1:39

"They abode with Him that day." That is about all some of us ever do, then we wake up to actualities, self-interest arises and the abiding is passed. There is no condition of life in which we cannot abide in Jesus. "Thou art Simon, thou shalt be called Cephas." God writes the new name on those places only in our lives where He has erased the pride and self-sufficiency and self-interest. Some of us have the new name in spots only, like spiritual measles. In sections we look all right. When we have our best spiritual mood on, you would think we were very high-toned saints; but don't look at us when we are not in that mood. The disciple is one who has the new name written all over him; self-interest and pride and self-sufficiency have been completely erased. Pride is the deification of self, and this to-day in some of us is not of the order of the Pharisee, but of the publican. To say "Oh, I'm no saint," is acceptable to human pride, but it is unconscious blasphemy against God. It literally means that you defy God to make you a saint, "I am much too weak and hopeless, I am outside the reach of the Atonement." Humility before men may be unconscious blasphemy before God. Why are you not a saint? It is either that you do not want to be a saint, or that you do not believe God can make you one. It would be all right, you say, if God saved you and took you straight to heaven. That is just what He will do! "We will come unto him, and make our abode with him." Make no conditions, let Jesus be everything, and He will take you home with Him not only for a day, but for ever.

June 13
GETTING THERE

"Come ye after Me." Mark 1:17

One of the greatest hindrances in coming to Jesus is the excuse of temperament. We make our temperament and our natural affinities barriers to coming to Jesus. The first thing we realize when we come to Jesus is that He pays no attention whatever to our natural affinities. We have the notion that we can consecrate our gifts to God. You cannot consecrate what is not yours; there is only one thing you can consecrate to God, and that is your right to yourself (Romans 12:1). If you will give God your right to yourself, He will make a holy experiment out of you. God's experiments always succeed. The one mark of a saint is the moral originality which springs from abandonment to Jesus Christ. In the life of a saint there is this amazing wellspring of original life all the time; the Spirit of God is a well of water springing up, perennially fresh. The saint realizes that it is God Who engineers circumstances, consequently there is no whine, but a reckless abandon to Jesus. Never make a principle out of your experience; let God be as original with other people as He is with you. If you abandon to Jesus, and come when He says "Come," He will continue to say "Come" through you; you will go out into life reproducing the echo of Christ's "Come." That is the result in every soul who has abandoned and come to Jesus. Have I come to Jesus? Will I come now?

June 14
GET A MOVE ON

Abide in Me." John 15:4

The Spirit of Jesus is put into me by the Atonement, then I have to construct with patience the way of thinking that is exactly in accordance with my Lord. God will not make me think like Jesus, I have to do it myself; I have to bring every thought into captivity to the obedience of Christ. "Abide in Me" - in intellectual matters, in money matters, in every one of the matters that make human life what it is. It is not a handbox life. Am I preventing God from doing things in my circumstances because I say it will hinder my communion with Him? That is an impertinence. It does not matter what my circumstances are, I can be as sure of abiding in Jesus in them as in a prayer meeting. I have not to change and arrange my circumstances myself. With Our Lord the inner abiding was unsullied; He was at home with God wherever His body was placed. He never chose His own circumstances, but was meek towards His Father's dispensations for Him. Think of the amazing leisure of Our Lord's life! We keep God at excitement point, there is none of the serenity of the life hid with Christ in God about us. Think of the things that take you out of abiding in Christ - Yes, Lord, just a minute, I have got this to do; Yes, I will abide when once this is finished; when this week is over, it will be all right, I will abide then. Get a move on; begin to abide now. In the initial stages it is a continual effort until it becomes so much the law of life that you abide in Him unconsciously. Determine to abide in Jesus wherever you are placed.

June 15
GET A MOVE ON

"And beside this . . . add . ." 2 Peter 1:5

You have inherited the Divine nature, says Peter (v.4), now screw your attention down and form habits, give diligence, concentrate. "Add" means all that character means. No man is born either naturally or supernaturally with character, he has to make character. Nor are we born with habits; we have to form habits on the basis of the new life God has put into us. We are not meant to be illuminated versions, but the common stuff of ordinary life exhibiting the marvel of the grace of God. Drudgery is the touchstone of character. The great hindrance in spiritual life is that we will look for big things to do. "Jesus took a towel .

. . and began to wash the disciples' feet." There are times when there is no illumination and no thrill, but just the daily round, the common task. Routine is God's way of saving us between our times of inspiration. Do not expect God always to give you His thrilling minutes, but learn to live in the domain of drudgery by the power of God. It is the "adding" that is difficult. We say we do not expect God to carry us to heaven on flowery beds of ease, and yet we act as if we did! The tiniest detail in which I obey has all the omnipotent power of the grace of God behind it. If I do my duty, not for duty's sake, but because I believe God is engineering my circumstances, then at the very point of my obedience the whole superb grace of God is mine through the Atonement.

June 16
WHAT DO YOU MAKE OF THIS?

"Greater love hath no man than this, that a man lay down his life for his friend." . . . "I have called you friends." John 15:13, 15

Jesus does not ask me to die for Him, but to lay down my life for Him. Peter said - "I will lay down my life for Thy sake" and he meant it; his sense of the heroic was magnificent. It would be a bad thing to be incapable of making such a declaration as Peter made; the sense of our duty is only realized by our sense of the heroic. Has the Lord ever asked you - "Wilt thou lay down thy life for My sake?" It is far easier to die than to lay down the life day in and day out with the sense of the high calling. We are not made for brilliant moments, but we have to walk in the light of them in ordinary ways. There was only one brilliant moment in the life of Jesus, and that was on the Mount of Transfiguration; then He emptied Himself the second time of His glory, and came down into the demon-possessed valley. For thirty-three years Jesus laid out His life to do the will of His Father, and, John says, "we ought to lay down our lives for the brethren." It is contrary to human nature to do it. If I am a friend of Jesus, I have deliberately and carefully to lay down my life for Him. It is difficult, and thank God it is difficult. Salvation is easy because it cost God so much, but the manifestation of it in my life is difficult. God saves a man and endues him with the Holy Spirit, and then says in effect - "Now work it out, be loyal to Me, whilst the nature of things round about you would make you disloyal." "I have called you friends." Stand loyal to your Friend, and remember that His honour is at stake in your bodily life.

June 17
THE UNCRITICAL TEMPER

"Judge not, that ye be not judged." Matthew 7:1

Jesus says regarding judging - Don't. The average Christian is the most penetratingly critical individual. Criticism is a part of the ordinary faculty of man; but in the spiritual domain nothing is accomplished by criticism. The effect of criticism is a dividing up of the powers of the one criticized; the Holy Ghost is the only One in the true position to criticize, He alone is able to show what is wrong without hurting and wounding. It is impossible to enter into communion with God when you are in a critical temper; it makes you hard and vindictive and cruel, and leaves you with the flattering unction that you are a superior person. Jesus says, as a disciple cultivate the uncritical temper. It is not done once and for all. Beware of anything that puts you in the superior person's place. There is no getting away from the penetration of Jesus. If I see the mote in your eye, it means I have a beam in my own. Every wrong thing that I see in you, God locates in me. Every time I judge, I condemn myself (see Romans 2:17-20). Stop having a measuring rod for other people. There is always one fact more in every man's case about which we know nothing. The first thing God does is to give us a spiritual spring-cleaning; there is no possibility of pride left in a man after that. I have never met the man I could despair of after discerning what lies in me apart from the grace of God.

June 18
DON'T THINK NOW, TAKE THE ROAD

"And Peter . . . walked on the water to go to Jesus. But when he saw the wind boisterous, he was afraid." Matthew 14:29-30

The wind was actually boisterous, the waves were actually high, but Peter did not see them at first. He did not reckon with them, he simply recognized his Lord and stepped out in recognition of Him, and walked on the water. Then he began to reckon with the actual things, and down he went instantly. Why could not our Lord have enabled him to walk at the bottom of the waves as well as on the top of them? Neither could be done saving by recognition of the Lord Jesus. We step right out on God over some things, then self-consideration enters in and down we go. If you are recognizing your Lord, you have no business with where He engineers your circumstances. The actual things are, but immediately you look at them you are overwhelmed, you cannot recognize Jesus, and the rebuke comes: "Wherefore didst thou doubt?" Let actual circumstances be what they may, keep recognizing Jesus, maintain complete reliance on Him. If you debate for a second when God has spoken, it is all up. Never begin to say – "Well, I wonder if He did speak?" Be reckless immediately, fling it all out on Him. You do not know when His voice will come, but whenever the realization of God comes in the faintest way imaginable, recklessly abandon. It is only by abandon that you recognize Him. You will only realize His voice more clearly by recklessness.

June 19
SERVICE OF PASSIONATE DEVOTION

"Lovest thou Me? . . . Feed My sheep." John 21:16

Jesus did not say – Make converts to your way of thinking, but look after My sheep, see that they get nourished in the knowledge of Me. We count as service what we do in the way of Christian work; Jesus Christ calls service what we are to Him, not what we do for Him. Discipleship is based on devotion to Jesus Christ, not on adherence to a belief or a creed. "If any man come to Me and hate not . . . , he cannot be My disciple." There is no argument and no compulsion, but simply – If you would be My disciple, you must be devoted to Me. A man touched by the Spirit of God suddenly says – "Now I see Who Jesus is," and that is the source of devotion. To-day we have substituted credal belief for personal belief, and that is why so many are devoted to causes and so few devoted to Jesus Christ. People do not want to be devoted to Jesus, but only to the cause He started. Jesus Christ is a source of deep offence to the educated mind of to-day that does not want Him in any other way than as a Comrade. Our Lord's first obedience was to the will of His Father, not to the needs of men; the saving of men was the natural outcome of His obedience to the Father. If I am devoted to the cause of humanity only, I will soon be exhausted and come to the place where my love will falter; but if I love Jesus Christ personally and passionately, I can serve humanity though men treat me as a door-mat. The secret of a disciple's life is devotion to Jesus Christ, and the characteristic of the life is its unobtrusiveness. It is like a corn of wheat, which falls into the ground and dies, but presently it will spring up and alter the whole landscape (John 12:24).

June 20
HAVE YOU COME TO "WHEN" YET?

"And the Lord turned the captivity of Job when he prayed for his friends." Job 42:10

The plaintive, self-centred, morbid kind of prayer, a dead-set that I want to be right, is never found in the New Testament. The fact that I am trying to be right with God is a sign that I am rebelling against the Atonement. "Lord, I will purify my heart if You will answer my prayer; I will walk rightly if You will help me." I cannot make myself right with God, I cannot make my life perfect; I can only be right with God if I accept the Atonement of the Lord Jesus Christ as an absolute gift. Am I humble enough to accept it? I have to resign every kind of claim and cease from every effort, and leave myself entirely alone in His hands, and then begin to pour out in the priestly work of intercession. There is much prayer that arises from real disbelief in the Atonement. Jesus is not beginning to save us, He has saved us, the thing is done, and it is an insult to ask Him to do it. If you are not getting the hundredfold more, not getting insight into God's word, then start praying for your friends, enter into the ministry of the interior. "The Lord turned the captivity of Job when he prayed for his friends." The real business of your life as a saved soul is intercessory prayer. Wherever God puts you in circumstances, pray immediately, pray that His Atonement may be realized in other lives as it has been in yours. Pray for your friends now; pray for those with whom you come in contact now.

June 21
THE MINISTRY OF THE INTERIOR

"But ye are . . . a royal priesthood." 1 Peter 2:9

By what right do we become "a royal priesthood"? By the right of the Atonement. Are we prepared to leave ourselves resolutely alone and to launch out into the priestly work of prayer? The continual grubbing on the inside to see whether we are what we ought to be generates a self-centred, morbid type of Christianity, not the robust, simple life of the child of God. Until we get into a right relationship to God, it is a case of hanging on by the skin of our teeth, and we say - What a wonderful victory I have got. There is nothing indicative of the miracle of Redemption in that. Launch out in reckless belief that the Redemption is complete, and then bother no more about yourself, but begin to do as Jesus Christ said - pray for the friend who comes to you at midnight, pray for the saints, pray for all men. Pray on the realization that you are only perfect in Christ Jesus, not on this plea - "O Lord, I have done my best, please hear me." How long is it going to take God to free us from the morbid habit of thinking about ourselves? We must get sick unto death of ourselves, until there is no longer any surprise at anything God can tell us about ourselves. We cannot touch the depths of meanness in ourselves. There is only one place where we are right, and that is in

Christ Jesus. When we are there, then we have to pour out for all we are worth in this ministry of the interior.

June 22
THE UNDEVIATING TEST

"For with what judgment ye judge, ye shall be judged; and with what measure ye mete, it shall be measured to you again." Matthew 7:2

This statement is not a haphazard guess, it is an eternal law of God. Whatever judgment you give, it is measured to you again. There is a difference between retaliation and retribution. Jesus says that the basis of life is retribution - "with what measure ye mete, it shall be measured to you again." If you have been shrewd in finding out the defects in others, remember that will be exactly the measure given to you. Life serves back in the coin you pay. This law works from God's throne downwards (cf. Psalm 18:25-26). Romans 2 applies it in a still more definite way, and says that the one who criticizes another is guilty of the very same thing. God looks not only at the act, He looks at the possibility. We do not believe the statements of the Bible to begin with. For instance, do we believe this statement, that the things we criticize in others we are guilty of ourselves? The reason we see hypocrisy and fraud and unreality in others is because they are all in our own hearts. The great characteristic of a saint is humility - Yes, all those things and other evils would have been manifested in me but for the grace of God, therefore I have no right to judge. Jesus says - "Judge not, that ye be not judged" if you do judge, it will be measured to you exactly as you have judged. Who of us would dare to stand before God and say - "My God, judge me as I have judged my fellow men?" We have judged our fellow men as sinners; if God should judge us like that we would be in hell. God judges us through the marvellous Atonement of Jesus Christ.

June 23
ACQUAINTANCE WITH GRIEF

"A Man of sorrows and acquainted with grief." Isaiah 53:3

We are not acquainted with grief in the way in which Our Lord was acquainted with it; we endure it, we get through it, but we do not become intimate with it. At the beginning of life we do not reconcile ourselves to the fact of sin. We take a rational view of life and say that a man by controlling his instincts, and by educating himself, can produce a life which will slowly evolve into the life of God. But as we go on, we find the presence of something which we have not taken into consideration, viz., sin, and it upsets all our calculations. Sin has made the basis of things wild and not rational. We have to recognize that sin is a fact, not a defect; sin is red-handed mutiny against God. Either God or sin must die in my life. The New Testament brings us right down to this one issue. If sin rules in me, God's life in me will be killed; if God rules in me, sin in me will be killed. There is no possible ultimate but that. The climax of sin is that it crucified Jesus Christ, and what was true in the history of God on earth will be true in your history and in mine. In our mental outlook we have to reconcile ourselves to the fact of sin as the only explanation as to why Jesus Christ came, and as the explanation of the grief and sorrow in life.

June 24
RECONCILING ONE'S SELF TO THE FACT OF SIN

This is your hour, and the power of darkness." Luke 22:53

It is not being reconciled to the fact of sin that produces all the disasters in life. You may talk about the nobility of human nature, but there is something in human nature which will laugh in the face of every ideal you have. If you refuse to agree with the fact that there is vice and self-seeking, something downright spiteful and wrong in human beings, instead of reconciling yourself to it, when it strikes your life, you will compromise with it and say it is of no use to battle against it. Have you made allowance for this hour and the power of darkness, or do you take a recognition of yourself that misses out sin? In your bodily relationships and friendships do you reconcile yourself to the fact of sin? If not, you will be caught round the next corner and you will compromise with it. If you reconcile yourself to the fact of sin, you will realize the danger at once - Yes, I see what that would mean. The recognition of sin does not destroy the basis of friendship; it establishes a mutual regard for the fact that the basis of life is tragic. Always beware of an estimate of life which does not recognize the fact that there is sin. Jesus Christ never trusted human nature, yet He was never cynical, never suspicious, because He trusted absolutely in what He could do for human nature. The pure man or woman, not the innocent, is the safeguarded man or woman. You are never safe with an innocent man or woman. Men and women have no business to be innocent; God demands that they be pure and virtuous. Innocence is the characteristic of a child; it is a blameworthy thing for a man or woman not to be reconciled to the fact of sin.

June 25

RECEIVING ONE'S SELF IN THE FIRES OF SORROW

"What shall I say? Father, save me, from this hour? But for this cause came I unto this hour. Father, glorify Thy name." John 12:27- 29 (R.V.)

My attitude as a saint to sorrow and difficulty is not to ask that they may be prevented, but to ask that I may preserve the self God created me to be through every fire of sorrow. Our Lord received Himself in the fire of sorrow, He was saved not from the hour, but out of the hour. We say that there ought to be no sorrow, but there is sorrow, and we have to receive ourselves in its fires. If we try and evade sorrow, refuse to lay our account with it, we are foolish. Sorrow is one of the biggest facts in life; it is no use saying sorrow ought not to be. Sin and sorrow and suffering are, and it is not for us to say that God has made a mistake in allowing them. Sorrow burns up a great amount of shallowness, but it does not always make a man better. Suffering either gives me my self or it destroys my self. You cannot receive your self in success, you lose your head; you cannot receive your self in monotony, you grouse. The way to find yourself is in the fires of sorrow. Why it should be so is another matter, but that it is so is true in the Scriptures and in human experience. You always know the man who has been through the fires of sorrow and received himself, you are certain you can go to him in trouble and find that he has ample leisure for you. If a man has not been through the fires of sorrow, he is apt to be contemptuous, he has no time for you. If you receive yourself in the fires of sorrow, God will make you nourishment for other people.

June 26
ALWAYS NOW

"We . . . beseech you that ye receive not the grace of God in vain." 2 Corinthians 6:1

The grace you had yesterday will not do for to-day. Grace is the overflowing favour of God; you can always reckon it is there to draw upon. "In much patience, in afflictions, in necessities, in distresses" - that is where the test for patience comes. Are you failing the grace of God there? Are you saying - Oh, well, I won't count this time? It is not a question of praying and asking God to help you; it is taking the grace of God now. We make prayer the preparation for work, it is never that in the Bible. Prayer is the exercise of drawing on the grace of God. Don't say - I will endure this until I can get away and pray. Pray now; draw on the grace of God in the moment of need. Prayer is the most practical thing, it is not the reflex action of devotion. Prayer is the last thing in which we learn to draw on God's grace. "In stripes, in imprisonments, in tumults, in labours" - in all these things manifest a drawing upon the grace of God that will make you a marvel to yourself and to others. Draw now, not presently. The one word in the spiritual vocabulary is Now. Let circumstances bring you where they will, keep drawing on the grace of God in every conceivable condition you may be in. One of the greatest proofs that you are drawing on the grace of God is that you can be humiliated without manifesting the slightest trace of anything but His grace. "Having nothing . . ." Never reserve anything. Pour out the best you have, and always be poor. Never be diplomatic and careful about the treasure God gives. This is poverty triumphant.

June 27
THE OVERSHADOWING PERSONAL DELIVERANCE

"I am with thee to deliver thee, saith the Lord." Jeremiah 1:8

God promised Jeremiah that He would deliver him personally - "Thy life will I give unto thee for a prey." That is all God promises His children. Wherever God sends us, He will guard our lives. Our personal property and possessions are a matter of indifference, we have to sit loosely to all those things; if we do not, there will be panic and heartbreak and distress. That is the inwardness of the overshadowing of personal deliverance. The Sermon on the Mount indicates that when we are on Jesus Christ's errands, there is no time to stand up for ourselves. Jesus says, in effect, Do not be bothered with whether you are being justly dealt with or not. To look for justice is a sign of deflection from devotion to Him. Never look for justice in this world, but never cease to give it. If we look for justice, we will begin to grouse and to indulge in the discontent of self-pity - Why should I be treated like this? If we are devoted to Jesus Christ we have nothing to do with what we meet, whether it is just or unjust. Jesus says - Go steadily on with what I have told you to do and I will guard your life. If you try to guard it yourself, you remove yourself from My deliverance. The most devout among us become atheistic in this connection; we do not believe God, we enthrone common sense and tack the name of God on to it. We do lean to our own understanding, instead of trusting God with all our hearts.

June 28
APPREHENDED BY GOD

"If that I may apprehend that for which also I am apprehended." Philippians 3:12

Never choose to be a worker; but when once God has put His call on you, woe be to you if you turn to the right hand or to the left. We are not here to work for God because we have chosen to do so, but because God has apprehended us. There is never any thought of - "Oh, well, I am not fitted for this." What you are to preach is determined by God, not by your own natural inclinations. Keep your soul steadfastly related to God, and remember that you are called not to bear testimony only, but to preach the gospel. Every Christian must testify, but when it comes to the call to preach, there must be the agonizing grip of God's hand on you, your life is in the grip of God for that one thing. How many of us are held like that? Never water down the word of God, preach it in its undiluted sternness; there must be unflinching loyalty to the word of God; but when you come to personal dealing with your fellow men, remember who you are - not a special being made up in heaven, but a sinner saved by grace. "I count not myself to have apprehended: but this one thing I do . . ."

June 29
DIRECTION OF DISCIPLINE

"And if thy right hand offend thee, cut it off and cast it from thee: for it is profitable for thee that one of thy members should perish, and not that thy whole body should be cast into hell." Matthew 5:30

Jesus did not say that everyone must cut off the right hand, but - If your right hand offends you in your walk with Me, cut it off. There are many things that are perfectly legitimate, but if you are going to concentrate on God you cannot do them. Your right hand is one of the best things you have, but, says Jesus, if it hinders you in following His precepts, cut it off. This line of discipline is the sternest one that ever struck mankind. When God alters a man by regeneration, the characteristic of the life to begin with is that it is maimed. There are a hundred and one things you dare not do, things that to you and in the eyes of the world that knows you are as your right hand and your eye, and the unspiritual person says - Whatever is wrong in that? How absurd you are! There never has been a saint yet who did not have to live a maimed life to start with. But it is better to enter into life maimed and lovely in God's sight than to be lovely in man's sight and lame in God's. In the beginning Jesus Christ by His Spirit has to check you from doing a great many things that may be perfectly right for everyone else but not right for you. See that you do not use your limitations to criticize someone else. It is a maimed life to begin with, but in v.48 Jesus gives the picture of a perfectly full-orbed life - "Ye shall be perfect, as your heavenly Father is perfect."

June 30
DO IT NOW

"Agree with thine adversary quickly." Matthew 5:25

Jesus Christ is laying down this principle - Do what you know you must do, now, and do it quickly; if you do not, the inevitable process will begin to work and you will have to pay to the last farthing in pain and agony and distress. God's laws are unalterable; there is no escape from them. The teaching of Jesus goes straight to the way we are made up. To see that my adversary gives me my rights is natural; but Jesus says that it is a matter of eternal and imperative importance to me that I pay my adversary what I owe him. From our Lord's standpoint it does not matter whether I am defrauded or not; what does matter is that I do not defraud. Am I insisting on my rights, or am I paying what I owe from Jesus Christ's standpoint? Do the thing quickly, bring yourself to judgment now. In moral and spiritual matters, you must do it at once; if you do not, the inexorable process will begin to work. God is determined to have His child as pure and clean and white as driven snow, and as long as there is disobedience in any point of His teaching, He will prevent none of the working of His spirit. Our insistence in proving that we are right is nearly always an indication that there has been some point of disobedience. No wonder the Spirit so strongly urges to keep steadfastly in the light! "Agree with thine adversary quickly." Have you suddenly turned a corner in any relationship and found that you had anger in your heart? Confess it quickly, quickly put it right before God, be reconciled to that one - do it now.

July 1
THE INEVITABLE PENALTY

"Verily I say unto thee, Thou shalt by no means come out thence, till thou have paid the uttermost farthing." Matthew 5:26

There is no heaven with a little corner of hell in it. God is determined to make you pure and holy and right; He will not allow you to escape for one moment from the scrutiny of the Holy Spirit. He urged you to come to judgment right away when He convicted you, but you did not; the inevitable process began to work and now you are in prison, and you will only get out when you have paid the uttermost farthing. "Is this a God of mercy, and of love?" you say. Seen from God's side, it is a glorious ministry of love. God is going to bring you out pure and spotless and undefiled; but He wants you to recognize the disposition you were showing - the disposition of your right to yourself. The moment you are willing that God should alter your disposition, His recreating forces will begin to work. The moment you realize God's purpose, which is to get you rightly related to Himself and then to your fellow men, He will tax the last limit of the universe to help you take the right road. Decide it now - "Yes, Lord, I will write that letter to-night"; "I will be reconciled to that man now." These messages of Jesus Christ are for the will and the conscience, not for the head. If you dispute the Sermon on the Mount with your head, you will blunt the appeal to your heart. "I wonder why I don't go on with God?" Are you paying your debts from God's standpoint? Do now what you will have to do some day. Every moral call has an "ought" behind it.

July 2
THE CONDITIONS OF DISCIPLESHIP

"If any man come to Me, and hate not . . . he cannot be My disciple." Luke 14:26, also 27, 33

If the closest relationships of life clash with the claims of Jesus Christ, He says it must be instant obedience to Himself. Discipleship means personal, passionate devotion to a Person, Our Lord Jesus Christ. There is a difference between devotion to a Person and devotion to principles or to a cause. Our Lord never proclaimed a cause; He proclaimed personal devotion to Himself. To be a disciple is to be a devoted love-slave of the Lord Jesus. Many of us who call ourselves Christians are not devoted to Jesus Christ. No man on earth has this passionate love to the Lord Jesus unless the Holy Ghost has imparted it to him. We may admire Him, we may respect Him and reverence Him, but we cannot love Him. The only Lover of the Lord Jesus is the Holy Ghost, and He sheds abroad the very love of God in our hearts. Whenever the Holy Ghost sees a chance of glorifying Jesus, He will take your heart, your nerves, your whole personality, and simply make you blaze and glow with devotion to Jesus Christ. The Christian life is stamped by 'moral spontaneous originality,' consequently the disciple is open to the same charge that Jesus Christ was, viz., that of inconsistency. But Jesus Christ was always consistent to God, and the Christian must be consistent to the life of the Son of God in him, not consistent to hard and fast creeds. Men pour them selves into creeds, and God has to blast them out of their prejudices before they can become devoted to Jesus Christ.

July 3

THE CONCENTRATION OF PERSONAL SIN

"Woe is me! for I am undone; because I am a man of unclean lips." Isaiah 6:5 When I get into the presence of God, I do not realize that I am a sinner in an indefinite sense; I realize the concentration of sin in a particular feature of my life. A man will say easily - 'Oh, yes, I know I am a sinner'; but when he gets into the presence of God he cannot get off with that statement. The conviction is concentrated on - I am this, or that, or the other. This is always the sign that a man or woman is in the presence of God. There is never any vague sense of sin, but the concentration of sin in some personal particular. God begins by convicting us of the one thing fixed on in the mind that is prompted by His Spirit, if we will yield to His conviction on that point, He will lead us down to the great disposition of sin underneath. That is the way God always deals with us when we are consciously in His presence. This experience of the concentration of sin is true in the greatest and the least of saints as well as in the greatest and the least of sinners. When a man is on the first rung of the ladder of experience, he may say - I do not know where I have gone wrong; but the Spirit of God will point out some particular definite thing. The effect of the vision of the holiness of the Lord on Isaiah was to bring home to him that he was a man of unclean lips. "And he laid it upon my mouth, and said Lo, this hath touched thy lips; and thine iniquity is taken away, and thy sin purged." The cleansing fire had to be applied where the sin had been concentrated.

July 4
ONE OF GOD'S GREAT DON'TS

"Fret not thyself, it tendeth only to evil doing." Psalm 37:8 (R.V.)

Fretting means getting out at elbows mentally or spiritually. It is one thing to say "Fret not," but a very different thing to have such a disposition that you find yourself able not to fret. It sounds so easy to talk about "resting in the Lord" and "waiting patiently for Him" until the nest is upset - until we live, as so many are doing, in tumult and anguish, is it possible then to rest in the Lord? If this "don't" does not work there, it will work nowhere. This "don't" must work in days of perplexity as well as in days of peace, or it never will work. And if it will not work in your particular case, it will not work in anyone else's case. Resting in the Lord does not depend on external circumstances at all, but on your relationship to God Himself. Fussing always ends in sin. We imagine that a little anxiety and worry are an indication of how really wise we are; it is much more an indication of how really wicked we are. Fretting springs from a determination to get our own way. Our Lord never worried and

He was never anxious, because He was not "out" to realize His own ideas; He was "out" to realize God's ideas. Fretting is wicked if you are a child of God. Have you been bolstering up that stupid soul of yours with the idea that your circumstances are too much for God? Put all "supposing" on one side and dwell in the shadow of the Almighty. Deliberately tell God that you will not fret about that thing. All our fret and worry is caused by calculating without God.

July 5
DON'T CALCULATE WITHOUT GOD

"Commit thy way unto the Lord; trust also in Him; and He shall bring it to pass." Psalm 37:5

Don't calculate without God. God seems to have a delightful way of upsetting the things we have calculated on without taking Him into account. We get into circumstances which were not chosen by God, and suddenly we find we have been calculating without God; He has not entered in as a living factor. The one thing that keeps us from the possibility of worrying is bringing God in as the greatest factor in all our calculations. In our religion it is customary to put God first, but we are apt to think it is an impertinence to put Him first in the practical issues of our lives. If we imagine we have to put on our Sunday moods before we come near to God, we will never come near Him. We must come as we are. Don't calculate with the evil in view. Does God really mean us to take no account of the evil? "Love . . . taketh no account of the evil." Love is not ignorant of the existence of the evil, but it does not take it in as a calculating factor. Apart from God, we do reckon with evil; we calculate with it in view and work all our reasonings from that standpoint. Don't calculate with the rainy day in view. You cannot lay up for a rainy day if you are trusting Jesus Christ. Jesus said - "Let not your heart be troubled." God will not keep your heart from being troubled. It is a command - "Let not . . ." Haul yourself up a hundred and one times a day in order to do it, until you get into the habit of putting God first and calculating with Him in view.

July 6
VISION AND REALITY

"And the parched ground shall become a pool." Isaiah 35:7

We always have visions, before a thing is made real. When we realize that although the vision is real, it is not real in us, then is the time that

Satan comes in with his temptations, and we are apt to say it is no use to go on. Instead of the vision becoming real, there has come the valley of humiliation. "Life is not as idle ore, But iron dug from central gloom, And batter'd by the shocks of doom To shape and use." God gives us the vision, then He takes us down to the valley to batter us into the shape of the vision, and it is in the valley that so many of us faint and give way. Every vision will be made real if we will have patience. Think of the enormous leisure of God! He is never in a hurry. We are always in such a frantic hurry. In the light of the glory of the vision we go forth to do things, but the vision is not real in us yet; and God has to take us into the valley, and put us through fires and floods to batter us into shape, until we get to the place where He can trust us with the veritable reality. Ever since we had the vision God has been at work, getting us into the shape of the ideal, and over and over again we escape from His hand and try to batter ourselves into our own shape. The vision is not a castle in the air, but a vision of what God wants you to be. Let Him put you on His wheel and whirl you as He likes, and as sure as God is God and you are you, you will turn out exactly in accordance with the vision. Don't lose heart in the process. If you have ever had the vision of God, you may try as you like to be satisfied on a lower level, but God will never let you.

July 7
ALL NOBLE THINGS ARE DIFFICULT

"Enter ye in at the strait gate . . because strait is the gate, and narrow is the way. . ." Matthew 7:13-14

If we are going to live as disciples of Jesus, we have to remember that all noble things are difficult. The Christian life is gloriously difficult, but the difficulty of it does not make us faint and cave in, it rouses us up to overcome. Do we so appreciate the marvellous salvation of Jesus Christ that we are our utmost for His highest? God saves men by His sovereign grace through the Atonement of Jesus; He works in us to will and to do of His good pleasure; but we have to work out that salvation in practical living. If once we start on the basis of His Redemption to do what He commands, we find that we can do it. If we fail, it is because we have not practised. The crisis will reveal whether we have been practising or not. If we obey the Spirit of God and practise in our physical life what God has put in us by His Spirit, then when the crisis comes, we shall find that our own nature as well as the grace of God will stand by us. Thank God He does give us difficult things to do! His salvation is a glad thing, but it is also a heroic, holy thing. It tests us for all we are worth. Jesus is bringing many "sons" unto glory, and God will not shield us from the requirements of a son. God's grace turns out men and women with a strong family likeness to Jesus Christ, not milk sops. It takes a tremendous amount of discipline to live the noble life of a disciple of Jesus in actual things. It is always necessary to make an effort to be noble.

July 8
THE WILL TO LOYALTY

Choose you this day whom ye will serve." Joshua 24:15

Will is the whole man active. I cannot give up my will, I must exercise it. I must will to obey, and I must will to receive God's Spirit. When God gives a vision of truth it is never a question of what He will do, but of what we will do. The Lord has been putting before us all some big propositions, and the best thing to do is to remember what you did when you were touched by God before - the time when you were saved, or first saw Jesus, or realized some truth. It was easy then to yield allegiance to God; recall those moments now as the Spirit of God brings before you some new proposition. "Choose you this day whom ye will serve." It is a deliberate calculation, not something into which you drift easily; and everything else is in abeyance until you decide. The proposition is between you and God; do not confer with flesh and blood about it. With every new proposition other people get more and more "out of it," that is where the strain comes. God allows the opinion of His saints to matter to you, and yet you are brought more and more out of the certainty that others understand the step you are taking. You have no business to find out where God is leading, the only thing God will explain to you is Himself. Profess to Him - 'I will be loyal.' Immediately you choose to be loyal to Jesus Christ, you are a witness against yourself. Don't consult other Christians, but profess before Him - I will serve Thee. Will to be loyal - and give other people credit for being loyal too.

July 9
THE GREAT PROBING

"Ye cannot serve the Lord." Joshua 24:19

Have you the slightest reliance on anything other than God? Is there a remnant of reliance left on any natural virtue, any set of circumstances? Are you relying on yourself in any particular in this new proposition which God has put before you? That is what the probing means. It is quite true to say - "I cannot live a holy life," but you can decide to let Jesus Christ make you holy. "Ye cannot serve the Lord God"; but you can put yourself in the place where God's almighty power will come through you. Are you sufficiently right with God to expect Him to manifest His wonderful life in you? "Nay, but we will serve the Lord." It is not an impulse, but a deliberate commitment. You say - But God can never have called me to this, I am too unworthy, it can't mean me. It does mean you, and the weaker and feebler you are, the better. The one who has something to trust in is the last one to come anywhere near saying - "I will serve the Lord." We say - "If I really could believe!" The point is - If I really will believe. No wonder Jesus Christ lays such emphasis on the sin of unbelief. "And He did not many mighty works there because of their unbelief." If we really believed that God meant what He said - what should we be like! Dare I really let God be to me all that He says He will be?

July 10
THE SPIRITUAL SLUGGARD

"Let us consider one another to provoke unto love and to good works; not forsaking the assembling of ourselves together." Hebrews 10:24-25

We are all capable of being spiritual sluggards; we do not want to mix with the rough and tumble of life as it is, our one object is to secure retirement. The note struck in Hebrews 10 is that of provoking one another and of keeping together - both of which require initiative, the initiative of Christ-realization, not of self-realization. To live a remote, retired, secluded life is the antipodes of spirituality as Jesus Christ taught it. The test of our spirituality comes when we come up against injustice and meanness and ingratitude and turmoil, all of which have the tendency to make us spiritual sluggards. We want to use prayer and Bible reading for the purpose of retirement. We utilize God for the sake of getting peace and joy, that is, we do not want to realize Jesus Christ, but only our enjoyment of Him. This is the first step in the wrong direction. All these things are effects and we try to make them causes. "I think it meet," said Peter, ". . . to stir you up by putting you in remembrance." It is a most disturbing thing to be smitten in the ribs by some provoker of God, by someone who is full of spiritual activity. Active work and spiritual activity are not the same thing. Active work may be the counterfeit of spiritual activity. The danger of spiritual sluggishness is that we do not wish to be stirred up, all we want to hear about is spiritual retirement. Jesus Christ never encourages the idea of retirement - "Go tell My brethren . ."

July 11

THE SPIRITUAL SAINT

That I may know Him." Philippians 3:10

The initiative of the saint is not towards self-realization, but towards knowing Jesus Christ. The spiritual saint never believes circumstances to be haphazard, or thinks of his life as secular and sacred; he sees everything he is dumped down in as the means of securing the knowledge of Jesus Christ. There is a reckless abandonment about him. The Holy Spirit is determined that we shall realize Jesus Christ in every domain of life, and He will bring us back to the same point again and again until we do. Self-realization leads to the enthronement of work; whereas the saint enthrones Jesus Christ in his work. Whether it be eating or drinking or washing disciples feet, whatever it is, we have to take the initiative of realizing Jesus Christ in it. Every phase of our actual life has its counterpart in the life of Jesus. Our Lord realized His relationship to the Father even in the most menial work. "Jesus knowing . . . that He was come from God, and went to God . . . took a towel . . . and began to wash the disciples' feet." The aim of the spiritual saint is "that I may know Him." Do I know Him where I am to-day? If not, I am failing Him. I am here not to realize myself, but to know Jesus. In Christian work the initiative is too often the realization that something has to be done and I must do it. That is never the attitude of the spiritual saint, his aim is to secure the realization of Jesus Christ in every set of circumstances he is in.

July 12
THE SPIRITUAL SOCIETY

"Till we all come . . unto the measure of the stature of the fulness of Christ." Ephesians 4:13

Rehabilitation means the putting back of the whole human race into the relationship God designed it to be in, and this is what Jesus Christ did in Redemption. The Church ceases to be a spiritual society when it is on the look-out for the development of its own organization. The rehabilitation of the human race on Jesus Christ's plan means the realization of Jesus Christ in corporate life as well as in individual life. Jesus Christ sent apostles and teachers for this purpose - that the corporate Personality might be realized. We are not here to develop a spiritual life of our own, or to enjoy spiritual retirement; we are here so to realize Jesus Christ that the Body of Christ may be built up. Am I building up the Body of Christ, or am I looking for my own personal development only? The essential thing is my personal relationship to

Jesus Christ - "That I may know Him." To fulfil God's design means entire abandonment to Him. Whenever I want things for myself, the relationship is distorted. It will be a big humiliation to realize that I have not been concerned about realizing Jesus Christ, but only about realizing what He has done for me. "My goal is God Himself, not joy nor peace, Nor even blessing, but Himself, my God." Am I measuring my life by this standard or by anything less?

July 13
THE PRICE OF VISION

In the year that King Uzziah died, I saw also the Lord." Isaiah 6:1

Our soul's history with God is frequently the history of the "passing of the hero." Over and over again God has to remove our friends in order to bring Himself in their place, and that is where we faint and fail and get discouraged. Take it personally: In the year that the one who stood to me for all that God was, died - I gave up everything? I became ill? I got disheartened? or - I saw the Lord? My vision of God depends upon the state of my character. Character determines revelation. Before I can say "I saw also the Lord," there must be something corresponding to God in my character. Until I am born again and begin to see the Kingdom of God, I see along the line of my prejudices only; I need the surgical operation of external events and an internal purification. It must be God first, God second, and God third, until the life is faced steadily with God and no one else is of any account whatever. "In all the world there is none but thee, my God, there is none but thee." Keep paying the price. Let God see that you are willing to live up to the vision.

July 14
THE ACCOUNT WITH PERSECUTION

But I say unto you, That ye resist not evil; but whosoever shall smite thee on thy right cheek, turn to him the other also." Matthew 5:39, etc

These verses reveal the humiliation of being a Christian. Naturally, if a man does not hit back, it is because he is a coward; but spiritually if a man does not hit back, it is a manifestation of the Son of God in him. When you are insulted, you must not only not resent it, but make it an occasion to exhibit the Son of God. You cannot imitate the disposition of Jesus; it is either there or it is not. To the saint personal insult becomes the occasion of revealing the incredible sweetness of the Lord Jesus. The teaching of the Sermon on the Mount is not - Do your duty, but - Do what is not your duty. It is not your duty to go the second mile, to turn the other cheek, but Jesus says if we are His disciples we shall always do these things. There will be no spirit of - "Oh, well, I cannot do any more, I have been so misrepresented and misunderstood." Every time I insist upon my rights, I hurt the Son of God; whereas I can prevent Jesus from being hurt if I take the blow myself. That is the meaning of filling up that which is behind of the afflictions of Christ. The disciple realizes that it is his Lord's honour that is at stake in his life, not his own honour. Never look for right in the other man, but never cease to be right yourself. We are always looking for justice; the teaching of the Sermon on the Mount is - Never look for justice, but never cease to give it.

July 15
THE POINT OF SPIRITUAL HONOUR

"I am debtor both to the Greeks, and to the barbarians." Romans 1:14

Paul was overwhelmed with the sense of his indebtedness to Jesus Christ, and he spent himself to express it. The great inspiration in Paul's life was his view of Jesus Christ as his spiritual creditor. Do I feel that sense of indebtedness to Christ in regard to every unsaved soul? The spiritual honour of my life as a saint is to fulfil my debt to Christ in relation to them. Every bit of my life that is of value I owe to the Redemption of Jesus Christ; am I doing anything to enable Him to bring His Redemption into actual manifestation in other lives? I can only do it as the Spirit of God works in me this sense of indebtedness. I am not to be a superior person amongst men, but a bondslave of the Lord Jesus. "Ye are not your own." Paul sold himself to Jesus Christ. He says - I am a debtor to everyone on the face of the earth because of the Gospel of Jesus; I am free to be an absolute slave only. That is the characteristic of the life when once this point of spiritual honour is realized. Quit praying about yourself and be spent for others as the bondslave of Jesus. That is the meaning of being made broken bread and poured out wine in reality.

July 16
THE NOTION OF DIVINE CONTROL

"How much more shall your Father which is in heaven give good things to them that ask Him?" Matthew 7:11

Jesus is laying down rules of conduct for those who have His Spirit. By the simple argument of these verses He urges us to keep our minds filled with the notion of God's control behind everything, which means that the disciple must maintain an attitude of perfect trust and an eagerness to ask and to seek. Notion your mind with the idea that God is there. If once the mind is notioned along that line, then when you are in difficulties it is as easy as breathing to remember - Why, my Father knows all about it! It is not an effort, it comes naturally when perplexities press. Before, you used to go to this person and that, but now the notion of the Divine control is forming so powerfully in you that you go to God about it. Jesus is laying down the rules of conduct for those who have His Spirit, and it works on this principle - God is my Father, He loves me, I shall never think of anything He will forget, why should I worry? There are times, says Jesus, when God cannot lift the darkness from you, but trust Him. God will appear like an unkind friend, but He is not; He will appear like an unnatural Father, but He is not; He will appear like an unjust judge, but He is not. Keep the notion of the mind of God behind all things strong and growing. Nothing happens in any particular unless God's will is behind it, therefore you can rest in perfect confidence in Him. Prayer is not only asking, but an attitude of mind which produces the atmosphere in which asking is perfectly natural. "Ask, and it shall be given you."

July 17
THE MIRACLE OF BELIEF

My speech and my preaching was not with enticing words." 1 Corinthians 2:1-5

Paul was a scholar and an orator of the first rank; he is not speaking out of abject humility; but saying that he would veil the power of God if, when he preached the gospel, he impressed people with his "excellency of speech." Belief in Jesus is a miracle produced only by the efficacy of Redemption, not by impressiveness of speech, not by wooing and winning, but by the sheer unaided power of God. The creative power of the Redemption comes through the preaching of the Gospel, but never because of the personality of the preacher. The real fasting of the preacher is not from food, but rather from eloquence, from impressiveness and exquisite diction, from everything that might hinder the gospel of God being presented. The preacher is there as the representative of God - "as though God did beseech you by us." He is there to present the Gospel of God. If it is only because of my preaching that people desire to be better, they will never get anywhere near Jesus Christ. Anything that flatters me in my preaching of the Gospel will end in making me a traitor to Jesus; I prevent the creative power of His Redemption from doing its work. "I, if I be lifted up . . . , will draw all men unto Me."

July 18
THE MYSTERY OF BELIEVING

"And he said, Who art Thou, Lord?" Acts 9:5

By the miracle of Redemption Saul of Tarsus was turned in one second from a strong-willed, intense Pharisee into a humble, devoted slave of the Lord Jesus. There is nothing miraculous about the things we can explain. We command what we are able to explain, consequently it is natural to seek to explain. It is not natural to obey; nor is it necessarily sinful to disobey. There is no moral virtue in obedience unless there is a recognition of a higher authority in the one who dictates. It is possibly an emancipation to the other person if he does not obey. If one man says to another - 'You must,' and - 'You shall,' he breaks the human spirit and unfits it for God. A man is a slave for obeying unless behind his obedience there is a recognition of a holy God. Many a soul begins to come to God when he flings off being religious, because there is only one Master of the human heart, and that is not religion but Jesus Christ. But woe be to me if when I see Him I say - I will not. He will never insist that I do, but I have begun to sign the death warrant of the Son of God in my soul. When I stand face to face with Jesus Christ and say - I will not, He will never insist; but I am backing away from the recreating power of His Redemption. It is a matter of indifference to God's grace how abominable I am if I come to the light; but woe be to me if I refuse the light (see John 3:19-21).

July 19
MASTERY OVER THE BELIEVER

"Ye call Me Master and Lord: and ye say well; for so I am." John 13:13

Our Lord never insists on having authority; He never says - Thou shalt. He leaves us perfectly free - so free that we can spit in His face, as men did; so free that we can put Him to death, as men did; and He will never say a word. But when His life has been created in me by His Redemption I instantly recognize His right to absolute authority over me. It is a moral domination - "Thou art worthy . . ." It is only the unworthy in me that refuses to bow down to the worthy. If when I meet a man who is more holy than myself, I do not recognize his worthiness and obey what comes through him, it is a revelation of the unworthy in me. God educates us by means of people who are a little better than we are, not intellectually but "holily," until we get under the domination of the Lord

Himself, and then the whole attitude of the life is one of obedience to Him. If Our Lord insisted upon obedience He would become a taskmaster, and He would cease to have any authority. He never insists on obedience, but when we do see Him we obey Him instantly, He is easily Lord, and we live in adoration of Him from morning till night. The revelation of my growth in grace is the way in which I look upon obedience. We have to rescue the word "obedience" from the mire. Obedience is only possible between equals; it is the relationship between father and son, not between master and servant. "I and My Father are one." "Though He were a Son, yet learned He obedience by the things which He suffered." The Son's obedience was as Redeemer, because He was Son, not in order to be Son.

July 20
DEPENDENT ON GOD'S PRESENCE

"They that wait upon the Lord . . . shall walk and not faint." Isaiah 40:31

There is no thrill in walking; it is the test of all the stable qualities. To "walk and not faint" is the highest reach possible for strength. The word "walk" is used in the Bible to express the character - "John looking on Jesus as He walked, said, Behold the Lamb of God!" There is never any thing abstract in the Bible, it is always vivid and real. God does not say - Be spiritual, but - "Walk before Me." When we are in an unhealthy state physically or emotionally, we always want thrills. In the physical domain this will lead to counterfeiting the Holy Ghost; in the emotional life it leads to inordinate affection and the destruction of morality; and in the spiritual domain if we insist on getting thrills, on mounting up with wings, it will end in the destruction of spirituality. The reality of God's presence is not dependent on any place, but only dependent upon the determination to set the Lord always before us. Our problems come when we refuse to bank on the reality of His presence. The experience the Psalmist speaks of - "Therefore will we not fear, though . . ." will be ours when once we are based on Reality, not the consciousness of God's presence but the reality of it - Why, He has been here all the time! At critical moments it is necessary to ask guidance, but it ought to be unnecessary to be saying always - "O Lord, direct me here, and there." Of course He will! If our common-sense decisions are not His order, He will press through them and check; then we must be quiet and wait for the direction of His presence.

July 21
THE GATEWAY TO THE KINGDOM

"Blessed are the poor in spirit." Matthew 5:3

Beware of placing Our Lord as a Teacher first. If Jesus Christ is a Teacher only, then all He can do is tantalize me by erecting a standard I can not attain. What is the use of presenting me with an ideal I cannot possibly come near? I am happier without knowing it. What is the good of telling me to be what I never can be - to be pure in heart, to do more than my duty, to be perfectly devoted to God? I must know Jesus Christ as Saviour before His teaching has any meaning for me other than that of an ideal which leads to despair. But when I am born again of the Spirit of God, I know that Jesus Christ did not come to teach only: He came to make me what He teaches I should be. The Redemption means that Jesus Christ can put into any man the disposition that ruled His own life, and all the standards God gives are based on that disposition. The teaching of the Sermon on the Mount produces despair in the natural man - the very thing Jesus means it to do. As long as we have a self-righteous, conceited notion that we can carry out Our Lord's teaching, God will allow us to go on until we break our ignorance over some obstacle, then we are willing to come to Him as paupers and receive from Him. "Blessed are the paupers in spirit," that is the first principle in the Kingdom of God. The bedrock in Jesus Christ's kingdom is poverty, not possession; not decisions for Jesus Christ, but a sense of absolute futility - I cannot begin to do it. Then Jesus says - Blessed are you. That is the entrance, and it does take us a long while to believe we are poor! The knowledge of our own poverty brings us to the moral frontier where Jesus Christ works.

July 22
SANCTIFICATION

"This is the will of God, even your sanctification." 1 Thessalonians 4:3

The Death Side. In sanctification God has to deal with us on the death side as well as on the life side. Many of us spend so much time in the place of death that we get sepulchral. There is always a battle royal before sanctification, always something that tugs with resentment against the demands of Jesus Christ. Immediately the Spirit of God begins to show us what sanctification means, the struggle begins. "If any man come to Me and hate not . . his own life, he cannot be My disciple." The Spirit of God in the process of sanctification will strip me until I am nothing but "myself," that is the place of death. Am I willing to be "myself," and nothing more - no friends, no father, no brother, no self-interest - simply ready for death? That is the condition of sanctification.

No wonder Jesus said: "I came not to send peace, but a sword." This is where the battle comes, and where so many of us faint. We refuse to be identified with the death of Jesus on this point. "But it is so stern," we say; "He cannot wish me to do that." Our Lord is stern; and He does wish us to do that. Am I willing to reduce myself simply to "me," determinedly to strip myself of all my friends think of me, of all I think of myself, and to hand that simple naked self over to God? Immediately I am, He will sanctify me wholly, and my life will be free from earnestness in connection with every thing but God. When I pray - "Lord, show me what sanctification means for me," He will show me. It means being made one with Jesus. Sanctification is not something Jesus Christ puts into me: it is Himself in me. (1 Cor. 1:30.)

July 23
SANCTIFICATION

"Of Him are ye in Christ Jesus, who of God is made unto us . . . sanctification." 1 Corinthians 1:30

The Life Side. The mystery of sanctification is that the perfections of Jesus Christ are imparted to me, not gradually, but instantly when by faith I enter into the realization that Jesus Christ is made unto me sanctification. Sanctification does not mean anything less than the holiness of Jesus being made mine manifestly. The one marvellous secret of a holy life lies not in imitating Jesus, but in letting the perfections of Jesus manifest themselves in my mortal flesh. Sanctification is "Christ in you." It is His wonderful life that is imparted to me in sanctification, and imparted by faith as a sovereign gift of God's grace. Am I willing for God to make sanctification as real in me as it is in His word? Sanctification means the impartation of the Holy qualities of Jesus Christ. It is His patience, His love, His holiness, His faith, His purity, His godliness, that is manifested in and through every sanctified soul. Sanctification is not drawing from Jesus the power to be holy; it is drawing from Jesus the holiness that was manifested in Him, and He manifests it in me. Sanctification is an impartation, not an imitation. Imitation is on a different line. In Jesus Christ is the perfection of everything, and the mystery of sanctification is that all the perfections of Jesus are at my disposal, and slowly and surely I begin to live a life of ineffable order and sanity and holiness: "Kept by the power of God."

July 24
DISPOSITION AND DEEDS

"Except your righteousness shall exceed the righteousness of the scribes and Pharisees, ye shall in no case enter into the kingdom of heaven." Matthew 5:20

The characteristic of a disciple is not that he does good things, but that he is good in motive because he has been made good by the supernatural grace of God. The only thing that exceeds right-doing is right-being. Jesus Christ came to put into any man who would let Him a new heredity which would exceed the righteousness of the scribes and Pharisees. Jesus says - If you are My disciple you must be right not only in your living, but in your motives, in your dreams, in the recesses of your mind. You must be so pure in your motives that God Almighty can see nothing to censure. Who can stand in the Eternal Light of God and have nothing for God to censure? Only the Son of God, and Jesus Christ claims that by His Redemption He can put into any man His own disposition, and make him as unsullied and as simple as a child. The purity which God demands is impossible unless I can be remade within, and that is what Jesus has undertaken to do by His Redemption. No man can make himself pure by obeying laws. Jesus Christ does not give us rules and regulations; His teachings are truths that can only be interpreted by the disposition He puts in. The great marvel of Jesus Christ's salvation is that He alters heredity. He does not alter human nature; He alters its mainspring.

July 25
AM I BLESSED LIKE THIS?

Blessed are . . ." Matthew 5:3-10

When we first read the statements of Jesus they seem wonderfully simple and unstartling, and they sink unobserved into our unconscious minds. For instance, the Beatitudes seem merely mild and beautiful precepts for all unworldly and useless people, but of very little practical use in the stern workaday world in which we live. We soon find, however, that the Beatitudes contain the dynamite of the Holy Ghost. They explode, as it were, when the circumstances of our lives cause them to do so. When the Holy Spirit brings to our remembrance one of these Beatitudes we say - 'What a startling statement that is!' and we have to decide whether we will accept the tremendous spiritual upheaval that will be produced in our circumstances if we obey His words. That is the way the Spirit of God works. We do not need to be born again to apply the Sermon on the Mount literally. The literal interpretation of the Sermon on the Mount is child's play; the interpretation by the Spirit of God as He applies Our Lord's statements to our circumstances is the stern work of a saint. The teaching of Jesus is out of all proportion to our natural way of looking at things and it comes with astonishing discomfort to begin with. We have slowly to form our walk and conversation on the line of the precepts of Jesus Christ as the Holy Spirit applies them to our circumstances. The Sermon on the Mount is not a set of rules and regulations: it is a statement of the life we will live when the Holy Spirit is getting His way with us.

July 26
THE ACCOUNT WITH PURITY

"Out of the heart proceed . . ." Matthew 15:18-20

We begin by trusting our ignorance and calling it innocence, by trusting our innocence and calling it purity; and when we hear these rugged statements of Our Lord's, we shrink and say - But I never felt any of those awful things in my heart. We resent what Jesus Christ reveals. Either Jesus Christ is the supreme Authority on the human heart, or He is not worth paying any attention to. Am I prepared to trust His penetration, or do I prefer to trust my innocent ignorance? If I make conscious innocence the test, I am likely to come to a place where I find with a shuddering awakening that what Jesus Christ said is true, and I shall be appalled at the possibility of evil and wrong in me. As long as I remain under the refuge of innocence I am living in a fool's paradise. If I have never been a blackguard, the reason is a mixture of cowardice and the protection of civilized life; but when I am undressed before God, I find that Jesus Christ is right in His diagnosis. The only thing that safeguards is the Redemption of Jesus Christ. If I will hand myself over to Him, I need never experience the terrible possibilities that are in my heart. Purity is too deep down for me to get to naturally: but when the Holy Spirit comes in, He brings into the centre of my personal life the very Spirit that was manifested in the life of Jesus Christ, viz., Holy Spirit, which is unsullied purity.

July 27
THE WAY TO KNOW

"If any man will do His will, he shall know of the doctrine . . ." John 7:17

The golden rule for understanding spiritually is not intellect, but obedience. If a man wants scientific knowledge, intellectual curiosity is his guide; but if he wants insight into what Jesus Christ teaches, he can only get it by obedience. If things are dark to me, then I may be sure there is something I will not do. Intellectual darkness comes through ignorance; spiritual darkness comes because of something I do not intend to obey. No man ever receives a word from God without instantly being put to the test over it. We disobey and then wonder why we don't go on spiritually. 'If when you come to the altar,' said Jesus, 'there you remember your brother hath ought against you . . . don't say another word to Me, but first go and put that thing right.' The teaching of Jesus hits us where we live. We cannot stand as humbugs before Him for one second. He educates us down to the scruple. The Spirit of God unearths the spirit of self-vindication; He makes us sensitive to things we never thought of before. When Jesus brings a thing home by His word, don't shirk it. If you do, you will become a religious humbug. Watch the things you shrug your shoulders over, and you will know why you do not go on spiritually. First go - at the risk of being thought fanatical you must obey what God tells you.

July 28
AFTER OBEDIENCE - WHAT?

And straightway He constrained His disciples to get into the ship, and to go to the other side. . . ." Mark 6:45-52

We are apt to imagine that if Jesus Christ constrains us, and we obey Him, He will lead us to great success. We must never put our dreams of success as God's purpose for us; His purpose may be exactly the opposite. We have an idea that God is leading us to a particular end, a desired goal; He is not. The question of getting to a particular end is a mere incident. What we call the process, God calls the end. What is my dream of God's purpose? His purpose is that I depend on Him and on His power now. If I can stay in the middle of the turmoil calm and unperplexed, that is the end of the purpose of God. God is not working towards a particular finish; His end is the process - that I see Him walking on the waves, no shore in sight, no success, no goal, just the absolute certainty that it is all right because I see Him walking on the sea. It is the process, not the end, which is glorifying to God. God's training is for now, not presently. His purpose is for this minute, not for something in the future. We have nothing to do with the afterwards of obedience; we get wrong when we think of the afterwards. What men call training and preparation, God calls the end. God's end is to enable me to see that He can walk on the chaos of my life just now. If we have a further end in view, we do not pay sufficient attention to the immediate present: if we realize that obedience is the end, then each moment as it comes is precious.

July 29
WHAT DO YOU SEE IN YOUR CLOUDS?

"Behold, He cometh with clouds." Revelation 1:7

In the Bible clouds are always connected with God. Clouds are those sorrows or sufferings or providences, within or without our personal lives, which seem to dispute the rule of God. It is by those very clouds that the Spirit of God is teaching us how to walk by faith. If there were no clouds, we should have no faith. "The clouds are but the dust of our Father's feet." The clouds are a sign that He is there. What a revelation it is to know that sorrow and bereavement and suffering are the clouds that come along with God! God cannot come near without clouds, He does not come in clear shining. It is not true to say that God wants to teach us something in our trials: through every cloud He brings, He wants us to unlearn something. His purpose in the cloud is to simplify our belief until our relationship to Him is exactly that of a child - God and my own soul, other people are shadows. Until other people become shadows, clouds and darkness will be mine every now and again. Is the relationship between myself and God getting simpler than ever it has been? There is a connection between the strange providences of God and what we know of Him, and we have to learn to interpret the mysteries of life in the light of our knowledge of God. Unless we can look the darkest, blackest fact full in the face without damaging God's character, we do not yet know Him. "They feared as they entered the cloud . . ." - Is there anyone "save Jesus only" in your cloud? If so, it will get darker; you must get to the place where there is "no one any more save Jesus only."

July 30
THE DISCIPLINE OF DISILLUSIONMENT

"Jesus did not commit Himself unto them for He knew what was in man." John 2:24-25

Disillusionment means that there are no more false judgments in life. To be undeceived by disillusionment may leave us cynical and unkindly severe in our judgment of others, but the disillusionment which comes from God brings us to the place where we see men and women as they really are, and yet there is no cynicism, we have no stinging, bitter things to say. Many of the cruel things in life spring from the fact that we suffer from illusions. We are not true to one another as facts; we are true only to our ideas of one another. Everything is either delightful and fine, or mean and dastardly, according to our idea. The refusal to be disillusioned is the cause of much of the suffering in human life. It works in this way - if we love a human being and do not love God, we demand of him every perfection and every rectitude, and when we do not get it we become cruel and vindictive; we are demanding of a human being that which he or she cannot give. There is only one Being Who can satisfy the last aching abyss of the human heart, and that is the Lord Jesus Christ. Why Our Lord is apparently so severe regarding every human relationship is because He knows that every relationship not based on loyalty to Himself will end in disaster. Our Lord trusted no man, yet He was never suspicious, never bitter. Our Lord's confidence in God and in what His grace could do for any man, was so perfect that He despaired of no one. If our trust is placed in human beings, we shall end in despairing of everyone.

July 31
TILL YOU ARE ENTIRELY HIS

"Let your endurance be a finished product, so that you may be finished and complete, with never a defect." James 1:4 (MOFFATT)

Many of us are all right in the main, but there are some domains in which we are slovenly. It is not a question of sin, but of the remnants of the carnal life which are apt to make us slovenly. Slovenliness is an insult to the Holy Ghost. There should be nothing slovenly, whether it be in the way we eat and drink, or in the way we worship God. Not only must our relationship to God be right, but the external expression of that relationship must be right. Ultimately God will let nothing escape, every detail is under His scrutiny. In numberless ways God will bring us back to the same point over and over again. He never tires of bringing us to the one point until we learn the lesson, because He is producing the finished product. It may be a question of impulse, and again and again, with the most persistent patience, God has brought us back to the one particular point; or it may be mental wool-gathering, or independent individuality. God is trying to impress upon us the one thing that is not entirely right. We have been having a wonderful time this Session over the revelation of God's Redemption, our hearts are perfect towards Him; His wonderful work in us makes us know that in the main we are right with Him. "Now," says the Spirit, through St. James, "let your endurance be a finished product." Watch the slipshod bits - "Oh, that will have to do for now." Whatever it is, God will point it out with persistence until we are entirely His.

August 1
SOMETHING MORE ABOUT HIS WAYS

He comes where He commands us to leave. "When Jesus had made an end of commanding his disciples, he departed thence to teach and to preach in their cities." Matthew 11:1.

If when God said "Go," you stayed because you were so concerned about your people at home, you robbed them of the teaching and preaching of Jesus Christ Himself. When you obeyed and left all consequences to God, the Lord went into your city to teach; as long as you would not obey, you were in the way. Watch where you begin to debate and to put what you call duty in competition with your Lord's commands "I know He told me to go, but then my duty was here;" that means you do not believe that Jesus means what He says. He teaches where He instructs us not to. "Master, . . . let us make three tabernacles." Are we playing the spiritual amateur providence in other lives? Are we so noisy in our instruction of others that God cannot get anywhere near them? We have to keep our mouths shut and our spirits alert. God wants to instruct us in regard to His Son, He wants to turn our times of prayer into mounts of transfiguration, and we will not let Him. When we are certain of the way God is going to work, He will never work in that way any more. He works where He sends us to wait. "Tarry ye . . . until . . ." Wait on God and He will work, but don't wait in spiritual sulks because you cannot see an inch in front of you! Are we detached enough from our own spiritual hysterics to wait on God? To wait is not to sit with folded hands, but to learn to do what we are told. These are phases of His ways we rarely recognize.

August 2
THE DISCIPLINE OF DIFFICULTY

"In the world ye shall have tribulation: but be of good cheer; I have overcome the world." John 16:33

An average view of the Christian life is that it means deliverance from trouble. It is deliverance in trouble, which is very different. "He that dwelleth in the secret place of the Most High . . . there shall no evil befall thee" - no plague can come nigh the place where you are at one with God. If you are a child of God, there certainly will be troubles to meet, but Jesus says do not be surprised when they come. "In the world ye shall have tribulation: but be of good cheer, I have overcome the world, there is nothing for you to fear." Men who before they were saved would scorn to talk about troubles, often become "fushionless" after being born again because they have a wrong idea of a saint. God does not give us overcoming life: He gives us life as we overcome. The strain is the strength. If there is no strain, there is no strength. Are you asking God to give you life and liberty and joy? He cannot, unless you will accept the strain. Immediately you face the strain, you will get the strength. Overcome your own timidity and take the step, and God will give you to eat of the tree of life and you will get nourishment. If you spend yourself out physically, you become exhausted; but spend yourself spiritually, and you get more strength. God never gives strength for to-morrow, or for the next hour, but only for the strain of the minute. The temptation is to face difficulties from a common-sense standpoint. The saint is hilarious when he is crushed with difficulties because the thing is so ludicrously impossible to anyone but God.

August 3
THE BIG COMPELLING OF GOD

"Behold, we go up to Jerusalem." Luke 18:31

Jerusalem stands in the life of Our Lord as the place where He reached the climax of His Father's will. "I seek not Mine own will, but the will of the Father which hath sent Me." That was the one dominating interest all through our Lord's life, and the things He met with on the way, joy or sorrow, success or failure, never deterred Him from His purpose. "He steadfastly set His face to go to Jerusalem." The great thing to remember is that we go up to Jerusalem to fulfil God's purpose, not our own. Naturally, our ambitions are our own; in the Christian life we have no aim of our own. There is so much said to-day about our decisions for Christ, our determination to be Christians, our decisions for this and that, but in the New Testament it is the aspect of God's compelling that is brought out. "Ye have not chosen Me, but I have chosen you." We are not taken up into conscious agreement with God's purpose, we are taken up into God's purpose without any consciousness at all. We have no conception of what God is aiming at, and as we go on it gets more and more vague. God's aim looks like missing the mark because we are too short sighted to see what He is aiming at. At the beginning of the Christian life we have our own ideas as to what God's purpose is - 'I am meant to go here or there,' 'God has called me to do this special work'; and we go and do the thing, and still the big compelling of God remains. The work we do is of no account, it is so much scaffolding compared with the big compelling of God. "He took unto Him the twelve," He takes us all the time. There is more than we have got at as yet.

August 4
THE BRAVE COMRADESHIP OF GOD

"Then He took unto Him the twelve." Luke 18:31

The bravery of God in trusting us! You say - "But He has been unwise to choose me, because there is nothing in me; I am not of any value." That is why He chose you. As long as you think there is something in you, He cannot choose you because you have ends of your own to serve; but if you have let Him bring you to the end of your self-sufficiency then He can choose you to go with Him to Jerusalem, and that will mean the fulfilment of purposes which He does not discuss with you. We are apt to say that because a man has natural ability, therefore he will make a good Christian. It is not a question of our equipment but of our poverty, not of what we bring with us, but of what God puts into us; not a question of natural virtues of strength of character, knowledge, and experience - all that is of no avail in this matter. The only thing that avails is that we are taken up into the big compelling of God and made His comrades (cf. 1 Cor. 1:26-30). The comradeship of God is made up out of men who know their poverty. He can do nothing with the man who thinks that he is of use to God. As Christians we are not out for our own cause at all, we are out for the cause of God, which can never be our cause. We do not know what God is after, but we have to maintain our relationship with Him whatever happens. We must never allow anything to injure our relationship with God; if it does get injured we must take time and get it put right. The main thing about Christianity is not the work we do, but the relationship we maintain and the atmosphere produced by that relationship. That is all God asks us to look after, and it is the one thing that is being continually assailed.

August 5
THE BAFFLING CALL OF GOD

And all things that are written by the prophets concerning the Son of Man shall be accomplished . . . And they understood none of these things." Luke 18:31, 34

God called Jesus Christ to what seemed unmitigated disaster. Jesus Christ called His disciples to see Him put to death; He led every one of them to the place where their hearts were broken. Jesus Christ's life was an absolute failure from every standpoint but God's. But what seemed failure from man's standpoint was a tremendous triumph from God's, because God's purpose is never man's purpose. There comes the baffling call of God in our lives also. The call of God can never be stated explicitly; it is implicit. The call of God is like the call of the sea, no one hears it but the one who has the nature of the sea in him. It cannot be stated definitely what the call of God is to, because His call is to be in comradeship with Himself for His own purposes, and the test is to believe that God knows what He is after. The things that happen do not happen by chance, they happen entirely in the decree of God. God is working out His purposes. If we are in communion with God and recognize that He is taking us into His purposes, we shall no longer try to find out what His purposes are. As we go on in the Christian life it gets simpler, because we are less inclined to say - Now why did God allow this and that? Behind the whole thing lies the compelling of God. "There's a divinity that shapes our ends." A Christian is one who trusts the wits and the wisdom of God, and not his own wits. If we have a purpose of our own, it destroys the simplicity and the leisureliness which ought to characterize the children of God.

August 6
THE CROSS IN PRAYER

"At that day ye shall ask in My name." John 16:26

We are too much given to thinking of the Cross as something we have to get through; we get through it only in order to get into it. The Cross stands for one thing only for us - a complete and entire and absolute identification with the Lord Jesus Christ, and there is nothing in which this identification is realized more than in prayer. "Your Father knoweth what things ye have need of, before ye ask Him." Then why ask? The idea of prayer is not in order to get answers from God; prayer is perfect and complete oneness with God. If we pray because we want answers, we will get huffed with God. The answers come every time, but not always in the way we expect, and our spiritual huff shows a refusal to identify ourselves with Our Lord in prayer. We are not here to prove God answers prayer; we are here to be living monuments of God's grace. "I say not that I will pray the Father for you: for the Father Himself loveth you." Have you reached such an intimacy with God that the Lord Jesus Christ's life of prayer is the only explanation of your life of prayer? Has Our Lord's vicarious life become your vital life? "At that day" you will be so identified with Jesus that there will be no distinction. When prayer seems to be unanswered, beware of trying to fix the blame on someone else. That is always a snare of Satan. You will find there is a reason which is a deep instruction to you, not to anyone else.

August 7

PRAYER IN THE FATHER'S HOUSE

"Wist ye not that I must be in My Father's house?" Luke 2:49 (R.V.)

Our Lord's childhood was not immature man-hood; our Lord's childhood is an eternal fact. Am I a holy innocent child of God by identification with my Lord and Saviour? Do I look upon life as being in my Father's house? Is the Son of God living in His Father's house in me? The abiding Reality is God, and His order comes through the moments. Am I always in contact with Reality, or do I only pray when things have gone wrong, when there is a disturbance in the moments of my life? I have to learn to identify myself with my Lord in holy communion in ways some of us have not begun to learn as yet. "I must be about My Father's business" - live the moments in My Father's house. Narrow it down to your individual circumstances - are you so identified with the Lord's life that you are simply a child of God, continually talking to Him and realizing that all things come from His hands? Is the Eternal Child in you living in the Father's house? Are the graces of His ministering life working out through you in your home, in your business, in your domestic circle? Have you been wondering why you are going through the things you are? It is not that you have to go through them, it is because of the relation into which the Son of God has come in His Father's providence in your particular sainthood. Let Him have His way, keep in perfect union with Him. The vicarious life of your Lord is to become your vital simple life; the way He worked and lived among men must be the way He lives in you.

August 8
PRAYER IN THE FATHER'S HONOUR

"That holy thing which shall be born of thee shall be called the Son of God." Luke 1:35

If the Son of God is born into my mortal flesh, is His holy innocence and simplicity and oneness with the Father getting a chance to manifest itself in me? What was true of the Virgin Mary in the historic introduction of God's Son into this earth is true in every saint. The Son of God is born into me by the direct act of God; then I as a child of God have to exercise the right of a child, the right of being always face to face with my Father. Am I continually saying with amazement to my common-sense life - why do you want to turn me off here? Don't you know that I must be about my Father's business? Whatever the circumstances may be, that Holy Innocent Eternal Child must be in contact with His Father. Am I simple enough to identify myself with my Lord in this way? Is He getting his wonderful way in me? Is God realizing that His Son is formed in me, or have I carefully put Him on one side? Oh, the clamour of these days! Everyone is clamouring - for what? For the Son of God to be put to death. There is no room here for the Son of God just now, no room for quiet holy communion with the Father. Is the Son of God praying in me or am I dictating to Him? Is He ministering in me as He did in the days of His flesh? Is the Son of God in me going through His passion for His own purposes? The more one knows of the inner life of God's ripest saints, the more one sees what God's purpose is - "filling up that which is behind of the affliction of Christ." There is always something to be done in the sense of "filling up."

August 9
PRAYER IN THE FATHER'S HEARING

"Father, I thank Thee that Thou hast heard Me." John 11:41

When the Son of God prays, He has only one consciousness, and that consciousness is of His Father. God always hears the prayers of His Son, and if the Son of God is formed in me the Father will always hear my prayers. I have to see that the Son of God is manifested in my mortal flesh. "Your body is the temple of the Holy Ghost," i.e., the Bethlehem of the Son of God. Is the Son of God getting His chance in me? Is the direct simplicity of the life of God's Son being worked out exactly as it was worked out in His historic life? When I come in contact with the occurrences of life as an ordinary human being, is the prayer of God's Eternal Son to His Father being prayed in me? "In that day ye shall ask in My name. . . ." What day? The day when the Holy Ghost has come to me and made me effectually one with my Lord. Is the Lord Jesus Christ being abundantly satisfied in your life or have you got a spiritual strut on? Never let common sense obtrude and push the Son of God on one side. Common sense is a gift which God gave to human nature; but common sense is not the gift of His Son. Supernatural sense is the gift of His Son; never enthrone common sense. The Son detects the Father; common sense never yet detected the Father and never will. Our ordinary wits never worship God unless they are transfigured by the indwelling Son of God. We have to see that this mortal flesh is kept in perfect subjection to Him and that He works through it moment by moment. Are we living in such human dependence upon Jesus Christ that His life is being manifested moment by moment?

August 10
THE SACRAMENT OF THE SAINT

"Let them that suffer according to the will of God, commit the keeping of their souls to Him in well-doing." 1 Peter 4:19

To choose to suffer means that there is something wrong; to choose God's Will even if it means suffering is a very different thing. No healthy saint ever chooses suffering; he chooses God's will, as Jesus did, whether it means suffering or not. No saint dare interfere with the discipline of suffering in another saint. The saint who satisfies the heart of Jesus will make other saints strong and mature for God. The people who do us good are never those who sympathize with us, they always hinder, because sympathy enervates. No one understands a saint but the saint who is nearest to the Saviour. If we accept the sympathy of a saint, the reflex feeling is - Well, God is dealing hardly with me. That is why Jesus said self-pity was of the devil (see Matt. 16:23). Be merciful to God's reputation. It is easy to blacken God's character because God never answers back, He never vindicates Himself. Beware of the thought that Jesus needed sympathy in His earthly life; He refused sympathy from man because He knew far too wisely that no one on earth understood what He was after. He took sympathy from His Father only, and from the angels in heaven. (Cf. Luke 15:10.) Notice God's unutterable waste of saints, according to the judgment of the world. God plants His saints in the most useless places. We say - God intends me to be here because I am so useful. Jesus never estimated His life along the line of the greatest use. God puts His saints where they will glorify Him, and we are no judges at all of where that is.

August 11
THIS EXPERIENCE MUST COME

"And he saw him no more." 2 Kings 2:12

It is not wrong to depend upon Elijah as long as God gives him to you, but remember the time will come when he will have to go; when he stands no more to you as your guide and leader, because God does not intend he should. You say - "I cannot go on without Elijah." God says you must. Alone at your Jordan. v.14. Jordan is the type of separation where there is no fellowship with anyone else, and where no one can take the responsibility for you. You have to put to the test now what you learned when you were with your Elijah. You have been to Jordan over and over again with Elijah, but now you are up against it alone. It is no use saying you cannot go, and you must go. If you want to know whether God is the God you have faith to believe Him to be, then go through your Jordan alone. Alone at your Jericho. v.15. Jericho is the place where you have seen your Elijah do great things. When you come to your Jericho you have a strong disinclination to take the initiative and trust in God, you want someone else to take it for you. If you remain true to what you learned with Elijah, you will get the sign that God is with you. Alone at your Bethel. v.23. At your Bethel you will find yourself at your wits' end and at the beginning of God's wisdom. When you get to your wits' end and feel inclined to succumb to panic, don't; stand true to God and He will bring His truth out in a way that will make your life a sacrament. Put into practice what you learned with your Elijah, use his cloak and pray. Determine to trust in God and do not look for Elijah any more.

August 12
THE THEOLOGY OF REST

"Why are ye fearful, O ye of little faith?" Matthew 8:26

When we are in fear we can do nothing less than pray to God, but Our Lord has a right to expect that those who name His Name should have an understanding confidence in Him. God expects His children to be so confident in Him that in any crisis they are the reliable ones. Our trust is in God up to a certain point, then we go back to the elementary panic prayers of those who do not know God. We get to our wits' end, showing that we have not the slightest confidence in Him and His government of the world; He seems to be asleep, and we see nothing but breakers ahead. "O ye of little faith!" What a pang must have shot through the disciples - 'Missed it again!' And what a pang will go through us when we suddenly realize that we might have produced down right joy in the heart of Jesus by remaining absolutely confident in Him, no matter what was ahead. There are stages in life when there is no storm, no crisis, when we do our human best; it is when a crisis arises that we instantly reveal upon whom we rely. If we have been learning to worship God and to trust Him, the crisis will reveal that we will go to the breaking point and not break in our confidence in Him. We have been talking a great deal about sanctification - what is it all going to amount to? It should work out into rest in God which means oneness with God, a oneness which will make us not only blameless in His sight, but a deep joy to Him.

August 13
QUENCH NOT THE SPIRIT

"Quench not the Spirit." 1 Thessalonians 5:19

The voice of the Spirit is as gentle as a zephyr, so gentle that unless you are living in perfect communion with God, you never hear it. The checks of the Spirit come in the most extraordinarily gentle ways, and if you are not sensitive enough to detect His voice you will quench it, and your personal spiritual life will be impaired. His checks always come as a still small voice, so small that no one but the saint notices them. Beware if in personal testimony you have to hark back and say - "Once, so many years ago, I was saved." If you are walking in the light, there is no harking back, the past is transfused into the present wonder of communion with God. If you get out of the light you become a sentimental Christian and live on memories, your testimony has a hard, metallic note. Beware of trying to patch up a present refusal to walk in the light by recalling past experiences when you did walk in the light. Whenever the Spirit checks, call a halt and get the thing right, or you will go on grieving Him without knowing it. Suppose God has brought you up to a crisis and you nearly go through but not quite, He will engineer the crisis again, but it will not be so keen as it was before. There will be less discernment of God and more humiliation at not having obeyed; and if you go on grieving the Spirit, there will come a time when that crisis cannot be repeated, you have grieved Him away. But if you go through the crisis, there will be the pæan of praise to God. Never sympathize with the thing that is stabbing God all the time. God has to hurt the thing that must go.

August 14
CHASTENING

"Despise not the chastening of the Lord, nor faint when thou art rebuked of Him." Hebrews 12:5

It is very easy to quench the Spirit; we do it by despising the chastening of the Lord, by fainting when we are rebuked by Him. If we have only a shallow experience of sanctification, we mistake the shadow for the reality, and when the Spirit of God begins to check, we say - oh, that must be the devil. Never quench the Spirit, and do not despise Him when He says to you - "Don't be blind on this point any more; you are not where you thought you were. Up to the present I have not been able to reveal it to you, but I reveal it now." When the Lord chastens you like that, let Him have His way. Let Him relate you rightly to God. "Nor faint when thou art rebuked of Him." We get into sulks with God and say - "Oh, well, I can't help it; I did pray and things did not turn out right, and I am going to give it all up." Think what would happen if we talked like this in any other domain of life! Am I prepared to let God grip me by His power and do a work in me that is worthy of Himself? Sanctification is not my idea of what I want God to do for me; sanctification is God's idea of what He wants to do for me, and He has to get me into the attitude of mind and spirit where at any cost I will let Him sanctify me wholly.

August 15
SIGNS OF THE NEW BIRTH

"Ye must be born again." John 3:7

The answer to the question "How can a man be born when he is old?" is - When he is old enough to die - to die right out to his "rag rights," to his virtues, to his religion, to everything, and to receive into himself the life which never was there before. The new life manifests itself in conscious repentance and unconscious holiness. "As many as received Him." (John 1:12.) Is my knowledge of Jesus born of internal spiritual perception, or is it only what I have learned by listening to others? Have I something in my life that connects me with the Lord Jesus as my personal Saviour? All spiritual history must have a personal knowledge for its bedrock. To be born again means that I see Jesus. "Except a man be born again, he cannot see the kingdom of God." (John 3:3.) Do I seek for signs of the Kingdom, or do I perceive God's rule? The new birth gives a new power of vision whereby I begin to discern God's rule. His rule was there all the time, but true to His nature; now that I have received His nature I can see His rule. "Whosoever is born of God doth not commit sin." (1 John 3:9.) Do I seek to stop sinning or have I stopped sinning? To be born of God means that I have the supernatural power of God to stop sinning. In the Bible it is never - Should a Christian sin? The Bible puts it emphatically - A Christian must not sin. The effective working of the new birth life in us is that we do not commit sin, not merely that we have the power not to sin, but that we have stopped sinning. 1 John 3:9 does not mean that we cannot sin; it means that if we obey the life of God in us, we need not sin.

August 16
DOES HE KNOW ME

"He calleth . . . by name." John 10:3

When I have sadly misunderstood Him? (John 10:17.) It is possible to know all about doctrine and yet not know Jesus. The soul is in danger when knowledge of doctrine outsteps intimate touch with Jesus. Why was Mary weeping? Doctrine was no more to Mary than the grass under her feet. Any Pharisee could have made a fool of Mary doctrinally, but one thing they could not ridicule out of her was the fact that Jesus had cast seven demons out of her; yet His blessings were nothing in comparison to Himself. Mary "saw Jesus standing and knew not that it was Jesus . . ;" immediately she heard the voice, she knew she had a past history with the One who spoke. "Master!" When I have stubbornly doubted? (John 10:27.) Have I been doubting something about Jesus - an experience to which others testify but which I have not had? The other disciples told Thomas that they had seen Jesus, but Thomas doubted - "Except I shall see . . , I will not believe." Thomas needed the personal touch of Jesus. When His touches come, or how they come, we do not know; but when they do come they are indescribably precious. "My Lord and my God!" When I have selfishly denied Him? (John 21:15-17.) Peter had denied Jesus Christ with oaths and curses, and yet after the Resurrection Jesus appeared to Peter alone. He restored him in private, then He restored him before the others. "Lord, Thou knowest that I love Thee." Have I a personal history with Jesus Christ? The one sign of discipleship is intimate connection with Him, a knowledge of Jesus Christ which nothing can shake.

August 17
ARE YOU DISCOURAGED IN DEVOTION?

"Yet lackest thou one thing; sell all that thou hast . . and come, follow Me." Luke 18:22

"And when he heard this . . ." Have you ever heard the Master say a hard word? If you have not, I question whether you have heard Him say anything. Jesus Christ says a great deal that we listen to, but do not hear; when we do hear, His words are amazingly hard. Jesus did not seem in the least solicitous that this man should do what He told him, He made no attempt to keep him with Him. He simply said - Sell all you have, and come, follow Me. Our Lord never pleaded, He never cajoled, He never entrapped; He simply spoke the sternest words mortal ears ever listened to, and then left it alone. Have I ever heard Jesus say a hard word? Has He said something personally to me to which I have deliberately listened? Not something I can expound or say this and that about, but something I have heard Him say to me? This man did understand what Jesus said, he heard it and he sized up what it meant, and it broke his heart. He did not go away defiant; he went away sorrowful, thoroughly discouraged. He had come to Jesus full of the fire of earnest desire, and the word of Jesus simply froze him; instead of producing an enthusiastic devotion, it produced a heart-breaking discouragement. And Jesus did not go after him, He let him go. Our Lord knows perfectly that when once His word is heard, it will bear fruit sooner or later. The terrible thing is that some of us prevent it bearing fruit in actual life. I wonder what we will say when we do make up our minds to be devoted to Him on that particular point? One thing is certain, He will never cast anything up at us.

August 18
HAVE YOU EVER BEEN EXPRESSIONLESS WITH SORROW?

"And when he heard this, he was very sorrowful: for he was very rich." Luke 18:23

The rich young ruler went away expressionless with sorrow; he had not a word to say. He had no doubt as to what Jesus said, no debate as to what it meant, and it produced in him a sorrow that had not any words. Have you ever been there? Has God's word come to you about something you are very rich in - temperament, personal affinity, relationships of heart and mind? Then you have often been expressionless with sorrow. The Lord will not go after you, He will not plead, but every time He meets you on that point He will simply repeat - If you mean what you say, those are the conditions. "Sell all that thou hast," undress yourself morally before God of everything that might be a possession until you are a mere conscious human being, and then give God that. That is where the battle is fought - in the domain of the will before God. Are you more devoted to your idea of what Jesus wants than to Himself? If so, you are likely to hear one of His hard sayings that will produce sorrow in you. What Jesus says is hard, it is only easy when it is heard by those who have His disposition. Beware of allowing anything to soften a hard word of Jesus Christ's. I can be so rich in poverty, so rich in the consciousness that I am nobody, that I shall never be a disciple of Jesus; and I can be so rich in the consciousness that I am somebody that I shall never be a disciple. Am I willing to be destitute of the sense that I am destitute? This is where discouragement comes in. Discouragement is disenchanted self-love, and self-love may be love of my devotion to Jesus.

August 19
SELF-CONSCIOUSNESS

Come unto Me." Matthew 11:28

God means us to live a fully-orbed life in Christ Jesus, but there are times when that life is attacked from the outside, and we tumble into a way of introspection which we thought had gone. Selfconsciousness is the first thing that will upset the completeness of the life in God, and self-consciousness continually produces wrestling. Self-consciousness is not sin; it may be produced by a nervous temperament or by a sudden dumping down into new circumstances. It is never God's will that we should be anything less than absolutely complete in Him. Anything that disturbs rest in Him must be cured at once, and it is not cured by being ignored, but by coming to Jesus Christ. If we come to Him and ask Him to produce Christconsciousness, He will always do it until we learn to abide in Him. Never allow the dividing up of your life in Christ to remain without facing it. Beware of leakage, of the dividing up of your life by the influence of friends or of circumstances; beware of anything that is going to split up your oneness with Him and make you see yourself separately. Nothing is so important as to keep right spiritually. The great solution is the simple one - "Come unto Me." The depth of our reality, intellectually, morally and spiritually, is tested by these words. In every degree in which we are not real, we will dispute rather than come.

August 20
COMPLETENESS

"And I will give you rest." Matthew 11:28

Whenever anything begins to disintegrate your life with Jesus Christ, turn to Him at once and ask Him to establish rest. Never allow anything to remain which is making the dis-peace. Take every element of disintegration as something to wrestle against, and not to suffer. Say - Lord, prove Thy consciousness in me, and selfconsciousness will go and He will be all in all. Beware of allowing self-consciousness to continue because by slow degrees it will awaken self-pity, and self-pity is Satanic. Well, I am not understood; this is a thing they ought to apologize for; that is a point I really must have cleared up. Leave others alone and ask the Lord to give you Christ-consciousness, and He will poise you until the completeness is absolute. The complete life is the life of a child. When I am consciously conscious, there is something wrong. It is the sick man who knows what health is. The child of God is not conscious of the will of God because he is the will of God. When there has been the slightest deviation from the will of God, we begin to ask - What is Thy will? A child of God never prays to be conscious that God answers prayer, he is so restfully certain that God always does answer prayer. If we try to overcome self-consciousness by any common-sense method, we will develop it tremendously. Jesus says, "Come unto Me and I will give you rest," i.e., Christ-consciousness will take the place of self-consciousness.

Wherever Jesus comes He establishes rest, the rest of the perfection of activity that is never conscious of itself.

August 21
THE MINISTRY OF THE UNNOTICED

"Blessed are the poor in spirit." Matthew 5:3

The New Testament notices things which from our standards do not seem to count. "Blessed are the poor in spirit," literally - Blessed are the paupers - an exceedingly commonplace thing! The preaching of to-day is apt to emphasize strength of will, beauty of character - the things that are easily noticed. The phrase we hear so often, Decide for Christ, is an emphasis on something Our Lord never trusted. He never asks us to decide for Him, but to yield to Him - a very different thing. At the basis of Jesus Christ's Kingdom is the unaffected loveliness of the commonplace. The thing I am blessed in is my poverty. If I know I have no strength of will, no nobility of disposition, then Jesus says - Blessed are you, because it is through this poverty that I enter His Kingdom. I cannot enter His Kingdom as a good man or woman, I can only enter it as a complete pauper. The true character of the loveliness that tells for God is always unconscious. Conscious influence is priggish and un-Christian. If I say - I wonder if I am of any use - I instantly lose the bloom of the touch of the Lord. "He that believeth in me, out of him shall flow rivers of living water." If I examine the outflow, I lose the touch of the Lord. Which are the people who have influenced us most? Not the ones who thought they did, but those who had not the remotest notion that they were influencing us. In the Christian life the implicit is never conscious, if it is conscious it ceases to have this unaffected loveliness which is the characteristic of the touch of Jesus. We always know when Jesus is at work because He produces in the commonplace something that is inspiring.

August 22
"I INDEED... BUT HE"

I indeed baptize you with water . . but He shall baptize you with the Holy Ghost and fire." Matthew 3:11

Have I ever come to a place in my experience where I can say - "I indeed - but He"? Until that moment does come, I will never know what the baptism of the Holy Ghost means. I indeed am at an end, I cannot do a thing: but He begins just there - He does the things no one else can ever do. Am I prepared for His coming? Jesus cannot come as long as there is anything in the way either of goodness or badness. When He comes am I prepared for Him to drag into the light every wrong thing I have done? It is just there that He comes. Wherever I know I am unclean, He will put His feet; wherever I think I am clean, He will withdraw them.

Repentance does not bring a sense of sin, but a sense of unutterable unworthiness. When I repent, I realize that I am utterly helpless; I know all through me that I am not worthy even to bear His shoes. Have I repented like that? Or is there a lingering suggestion of standing up for myself? The reason God cannot come into my life is because I am not through into repentance. "He shall baptize you with the Holy Ghost and fire." John does not speak of the baptism of the Holy Ghost as an experience, but as a work performed by Jesus Christ. "He shall baptize you." The only conscious experience those who are baptized with the Holy Ghost ever have is a sense of absolute unworthiness. I indeed was this and that; but He came, and a marvellous thing happened. Get to the margin where He does everything.

August 23
PRAYER CHOICE AND PRAYER CONFLICT

"When thou prayest, enter into thy closet, and pray to thy Father which is in secret." Matthew 6:6

Jesus did not say - Dream about thy Father in secret, but pray to thy Father in secret. Prayer is an effort of will. After we have entered our secret place and have shut the door, the most difficult thing to do is to pray; we cannot get our minds into working order, and the first thing that conflicts is wandering thoughts. The great battle in private prayer is the overcoming of mental wool-gathering. We have to discipline our minds and concentrate on wilful prayer. We must have a selected place for prayer and when we get there the plague of flies begins - This must be done, and that. "Shut thy door." A secret silence means to shut the door deliberately on emotions and remember God. God is in secret, and He sees us from the secret place; He does not see us as other people see us, or as we see ourselves. When we live in the secret place it becomes impossible for us to doubt God, we become more sure of Him than of anything else. Your Father, Jesus says, is in secret and nowhere else. Enter the secret place, and right in the centre of the common round you find God there all the time. Get into the habit of dealing with God about everything. Unless in the first waking moment of the day you learn to fling the door wide back and let God in, you will work on a wrong level all day; but swing the door wide open and pray to your Father in secret, and every public thing will be stamped with the presence of God.

August 24
THE SPIRITUAL INDEX

"Or what man is there of you, whom if his son ask bread, will he give him a stone?" Matthew 7:9

The illustration of prayer that Our Lord uses here is that of a good child asking for a good thing. We talk about prayer as if God heard us irrespective of the fact of our relationship to Him (cf. Matthew 5:45). Never say it is not God's will to give you what you ask, don't sit down and faint, but find out the reason, turn up the index. Are you rightly related to your wife, to your husband, to your children, to your fellow-students - are you a "good child" there? "O Lord, I have been irritable and cross, but I do want spiritual blessing." You cannot have it, you will have to do without until you come into the attitude of a good child. We mistake defiance for devotion; arguing with God for abandonment. We will not look at the index. Have I been asking God to give me money for something I want when there is something I have not paid for? Have I been asking God for liberty while I am withholding it from someone who belongs to me? I have not forgiven someone his trespasses; I have not been kind to him; I have not been living as God's child among my relatives and friends. (v.12.) I am a child of God only by regeneration, and as a child of God I am good only as I walk in the light. Prayer with most of us is turned into pious platitude, it is a matter of emotion, mystical communion with God. Spiritually we are all good at producing fogs. If we turn up the index, we will see very clearly what is wrong - that friendship, that debt, that temper of mind. It is no use praying unless we are living as children of God. Then, Jesus says - "Everyone that asketh receiveth."

August 25
THE FRUITFULNESS OF FRIENDSHIP

"I have called you friends." John 15:15

We never know the joy of self-sacrifice until we abandon in every particular. Self-surrender is the most difficult thing - I will if . . . ! Oh, well, I suppose I must devote my life to God. There is none of the joy of self-sacrifice in that. As soon as we do abandon, the Holy Ghost gives us an intimation of the joy of Jesus. The final aim of self-sacrifice is laying down our lives for our Friend. When the Holy Ghost comes in, the great desire is to lay down the life for Jesus, and the thought of sacrifice never touches us because sacrifice is the love passion of the Holy Ghost. Our Lord is our example in the life of self-sacrifice - "I delight to do Thy will, O my God." He went on with His sacrifice with exuberant joy. Have I ever yielded in absolute submission to Jesus Christ? If Jesus Christ is not the lodestar, there is no benefit in the sacrifice; but when the sacrifice is made with the eyes on Him, slowly and surely the moulding influence begins to tell. Beware of letting natural affinities hinder your walk in love. One of the most cruel ways of killing natural love is by disdain built on natural affinities. The affinity of the saint is the Lord Jesus. Love for God is not sentimental, for the saint to love as God loves is the most practical thing. "I have called you friends." It is a friendship based on the new life created in us which has no affinity with our old life, but only with the life of God. It is unutterably humble, unsulliedly pure, and absolutely devoted to God.

August 26
ARE YOU EVER DISTURBED?

Peace I leave with you, My peace I give unto you." John 14:27

There are times when our peace is based upon ignorance, but when we awaken to the facts of life, inner peace is impossible unless it is received from Jesus. When Our Lord speaks peace, He makes peace, His words are ever "spirit and life." Have I ever received what Jesus speaks? "My peace I give unto you" - it is a peace which comes from looking into His face and realizing His undisturbedness. Are you painfully disturbed just now, distracted by the waves and billows of God's providential permission, and having, as it were, turned over the boulders of your belief, are you still finding no well of peace or joy or comfort; is all barren? Then look up and receive the undisturbedness of the Lord Jesus. Reflected peace is the proof that you are right with God because you are at liberty to turn your mind to Him. If you are not right with God, you can never turn your mind anywhere but on yourself. If you allow anything to hide the face of Jesus Christ from you, you are either disturbed or you have a false security. Are you looking unto Jesus now, in the immediate matter that is pressing and receiving from Him peace? If so, He will be a gracious benediction of peace in and through you. But if you try to worry it out, you obliterate Him and deserve all you get. We get disturbed because we have not been considering Him. When one confers with Jesus Christ the perplexity goes, because He has no perplexity, and our only concern is to abide in Him. Lay it all out before Him, and in the face of difficulty, bereavement and sorrow, hear Him say, "Let not your heart be troubled."

August 27
THEOLOGY ALIVE

"Walk while ye have the light lest darkness come upon you." John 12:35

Beware of not acting upon what you see in your moments on the mount with God. If you do not obey the light, it will turn into darkness. "If therefore the light that is in thee be darkness, how great is that darkness!" The second you waive the question of sanctification or any other thing upon which God gave you light, you begin to get dry rot in your spiritual life. Continually bring the truth out into actuality; work it out in every domain, or the very light you have will prove a curse. The most difficult person to deal with is the one who has the smug satisfaction of an experience to which he can refer back, but who is not working it out in practical life. If you say you are sanctified, show it. The experience must be so genuine that it is shown in the life. Beware of any belief that makes you self-indulgent; it came from the pit, no matter how beautiful it sounds. Theology must work itself out in the most practical relationships. "Except your righteousness shall exceed the righteousness of the scribes and Pharisees . . ." said Our Lord, i.e., you must be more moral than the most moral being you know. You may know all about the doctrine of sanctification, but are you running it out into the practical issues of your life? Every bit of your life, physical, moral and spiritual, is to be judged by the standard of the Atonement.

August 28
WHAT'S THE GOOD OF PRAYER?

"Lord, teach us to pray." Luke 11:1

It is not part of the life of a natural man to pray. We hear it said that a man will suffer in his life if he does not pray; I question it. What will suffer is the life of the Son of God in him, which is nourished not by food, but by prayer. When a man is born from above, the life of the Son of God is born in him, and he can either starve that life or nourish it. Prayer is the way the life of God is nourished. Our ordinary views of prayer are not found in the New Testament. We look upon prayer as a means of getting things for ourselves; the Bible idea of prayer is that we may get to know God Himself. "Ask and ye shall receive." We grouse before God, we are apologetic or apathetic, but we ask very few things. Yet what a splendid audacity a childlike child has! Our Lord says - "Except ye become as little children." Ask, and God will do. Give Jesus Christ a chance, give Him elbow room, and no man will ever do this unless he is at his wits' end. When a man is at his wits' end it is not a cowardly thing to pray, it is the only way he can get into touch with Reality. Be yourself before God and present your problems, the things you know you have come to your wits' end over. As long as you are self-sufficient, you do not need to ask God for anything. It is not so true that "prayer changes things" as that prayer changes me and I change things. God has so constituted things that prayer on the basis of Redemption alters the way in which a man looks at things. Prayer is not a question of altering things externally, but of working wonders in a man's disposition.

August 29
SUBLIME INTIMACY

Said I not unto thee, that, if thou wouldest believe, thou shouldest see the glory of God?" John 11:40

Every time you venture out in the life of faith, you will find something in your common-sense circumstances that flatly contradicts your faith. Common sense is not faith, and faith is not common sense; they stand in the relation of the natural and the spiritual. Can you trust Jesus Christ where your common sense cannot trust Him? Can you venture heroically on Jesus Christ's statements when the facts of your common-sense life shout - "It's a lie?" On the mount it is easy to say - 'Oh, yes, I believe God can do it'; but you have to come down into the demon-possessed valley and meet with facts that laugh ironically at the whole of your mount-oftransfiguration belief. Every time my programme of belief is clear to my own mind, I come across something that contradicts it. Let me say I believe God will supply all my need, and then let me run dry, with no outlook, and see whether I will go through the trial of faith, or whether I will sink back to something lower. Faith must be tested, because it can be turned into a personal possession only through conflict. What is your faith up against just now? The test will either prove that your faith is right, or it will kill it. "Blessed is he whosoever shall not be offended in Me." The final thing is confidence in Jesus. Believe steadfastly on Him and all you come up against will develop your faith. There is continual testing in the life of faith, and the last great test is death. May God keep us in fighting trim! Faith is unutterable trust in God, trust which never dreams that He will not stand by us.

August 30
AM I CONVINCED BY CHRIST?

"Notwithstanding in this rejoice not . . . , but rather rejoice because your names are written in heaven." Luke 10:19, 20

Jesus Christ says, in effect, Don't rejoice in successful service, but rejoice because you are rightly related to Me. The snare in Christian work is to rejoice in successful service, to rejoice in the fact that God has used you. You never can measure what God will do through you if you are rightly related to Jesus Christ. Keep your relationship right with Him, then whatever circumstances you are in, and whoever you meet day by day, He is pouring rivers of living water through you, and it is of His mercy that He does not let you know it. When once you are rightly related to God by salvation and sanctification, remember that wherever you are, you are put there by God; and by the reaction of your life on the circumstances around you, you will fulfil God's purpose, as long as you keep in the light as God is in the light. The tendency to-day is to put the emphasis on service. Beware of the people who make usefulness their ground of appeal. If you make usefulness the test, then Jesus Christ was the greatest failure that ever lived. The lodestar of the saint is God Himself, not estimated usefulness. It is the work that God does through us that counts, not what we do for Him. All that Our Lord heeds in a man's life is the relationship of worth to His Father. Jesus is bringing many sons to glory.

August 31
MY JOY . . . YOUR JOY

"That My joy might remain in you, and that your joy might be full." John 15:11

What was the joy that Jesus had? It is an insult to use the word happiness in connection with Jesus Christ. The joy of Jesus was the absolute self-surrender and self-sacrifice of Himself to His Father, the joy of doing that which the Father sent Him to do. "I delight to do Thy will." Jesus prayed that our joy might go on fulfilling itself until it was the same joy as His. Have I allowed Jesus Christ to introduce His joy to me? The full flood of my life is not in bodily health, not in external happenings, not in seeing God's work succeed, but in the perfect understanding of God, and in the communion with Him that Jesus Himself had. The first thing that will hinder this joy is the captious irritation of thinking out circumstances. The cares of this world, said Jesus, will choke God's word. Before we know where we are, we are caught up in the shows of things. All that God has done for us is the mere threshold; He wants to get us to the place where we will be His witnesses and proclaim Who Jesus is. Be rightly related to God, find your joy there, and out of you will flow rivers of living water. Be a centre for Jesus Christ to pour living water through. Stop being self-conscious, stop being a sanctified prig, and live the life hid with Christ. The life that is rightly related to God is as natural as breathing wherever it goes. The lives that have been of most blessing to you are those who were unconscious of it.

September 1
DESTINY OF HOLINESS

"Ye shall be holy; for I am holy." 1 Peter 1:16 (R.V.)

Continually restate to yourself what the purpose of your life is. The destined end of man is not happiness, nor health, but holiness. Nowadays we have far too many affinities, we are dissipated with them; right, good, noble affinities which will yet have their fulfilment, but in the meantime God has to atrophy them. The one thing that matters is whether a man will accept the God Who will make him holy. At all costs a man must be rightly related to God. Do I believe I need to be holy? Do I believe God can come into me and make me holy? If by your preaching you convince me that I am unholy, I resent your preaching. The preaching of the gospel awakens an intense resentment because it must reveal that I am unholy; but it also awakens an intense craving. God has one destined end for mankind, viz., holiness. His one aim is the production of saints. God is not an eternal blessing-machine for men; He did not come to save men out of pity: He came to save men because He had created them to be holy. The Atonement means that God can put me back into perfect union with Himself, without a shadow between, through the Death of Jesus Christ. Never tolerate through sympathy with yourself or with others any practice that is not in keeping with a holy God. Holiness means unsullied walking with the feet, unsullied talking with the tongue, unsullied thinking with the mind - every detail of the life under the scrutiny of God. Holiness is not only what God gives me, but what I manifest that God has given me.

September 2
THE SACRAMENT OF SACRIFICE

"He that believeth in Me . . out of him shall flow. . . ." John 7:38

Jesus did not say - "he that believeth in Me shall realize the blessing of the fulness of God," but - "he that believeth in Me out of him shall escape everything he receives." Our Lord's teaching is always antiself-realization. His purpose is not the development of a man; His purpose is to make a man exactly like Himself, and the characteristic of the Son of God is self-expenditure. If we believe in Jesus, it is not what we gain, but what He pours through us that counts. It is not that God makes us beautifully rounded grapes, but that He squeezes the sweetness out of us. Spiritually, we cannot measure our life by success, but only by what God pours through us, and we cannot measure that at all. When Mary of Bethany broke the box of precious ointment and poured it on Jesus' head, it was an act for which no one else saw any occasion; the disciples said it was a waste. But Jesus commended Mary for her extravagant act of devotion, and said that wherever His gospel was preached "this also that she hath done shall be spoken of for a memorial of her." Our Lord is carried beyond Himself with joy when He sees any of us doing what Mary did, not being set on this or that economy, but being abandoned to Him. God spilt the life of His Son that the world might be saved; are we prepared to spill out our lives for Him? "He that believeth in Me out of him shall flow rivers of living water" - hundreds of other lives will be continually refreshed. It is time now to break the life, to cease craving for satisfaction, and to spill the thing out. Our Lord is asking who of us will do it for Him?

September 3
THE WATERS OF SATISFACTION SCATTERED

"Nevertheless he would not drink thereof, but poured it out unto the Lord." 2 Samuel 23:16

What has been like water from the well of Bethlehem to you recently - love, friendship, spiritual blessing? Then at the peril of your soul, you take it to satisfy yourself. If you do, you cannot pour it out before the Lord. You can never sanctify to God that with which you long to satisfy yourself. If you satisfy yourself with a blessing from God, it will corrupt you; you must sacrifice it, pour it out, do with it what common sense says is an absurd waste. How am I to pour it out unto the Lord natural love or spiritual blessing? In one way only - in the determination of my mind. There are certain acts of other people which one could never accept if one did not know God, because it is not within human power to repay them. But immediately I say - This is too great and worthy for me, it is not meant for a human being at all, I must pour it out unto the Lord, then these things pour out in rivers of living water all around. Until I do pour these things out before the Lord, they endanger those I love as well as myself because they will turn to lust. We can be lustful in things which are not sordid and vile. Love has to get to its transfiguration point of being poured out unto the Lord. If you have become bitter and sour, it is because when God gave you a blessing you clutched it for yourself;

whereas if you had poured it out unto the Lord, you would have been the sweetest person out of heaven. If you are always taking blessings to yourself and never learn to pour out anything unto the Lord, other people do not get their horizon enlarged through you.

September 4
HIS!

Thine they were, and Thou gavest them Me." John 17:6

The missionary is one in whom the Holy Ghost has wrought this realization - "Ye are not your own." To say, "I am not my own" is to have reached a great point in spiritual nobility. The true nature of the life in the actual whirl is the deliberate giving up of myself to another in sovereign preference, and that other is Jesus Christ. The Holy Spirit expounds the nature of Jesus to me in order to make me one with my Lord, not that I might go off as a showroom exhibit. Our Lord never sent any of the disciples out on the ground of what He had done for them. It was not until after the Resurrection, when the disciples had perceived by the power of the Holy Spirit Whom He was, that Jesus said "Go." "If any man come to me and hate not . . . , he cannot be My disciple," not, he cannot be good and upright, but, he cannot be one over whom Jesus writes the word "Mine." Any one of the relationships Our Lord mentions may be a competitive relationship. I may prefer to belong to my mother, or to my wife, or to myself; then, says Jesus, you cannot be My disciple. This does not mean I will not be saved, but it does mean that I cannot be "His." Our Lord makes a disciple His own possession, He becomes responsible for him. "Ye shall be witnesses unto Me." The spirit that comes in is not that of doing anything for Jesus, but of being a perfect delight to Him. The secret of the missionary is - I am His, and He is carrying out His enterprises through me.

September 5
THE MISSIONARY WATCHING

"Watch with Me." Matthew 26:40

"Watch with Me" - with no private point of view of your own at all, but watch entirely with Me. In the early stages we do not watch with Jesus, we watch for Him. We do not watch with Him through the revelation of the Bible; in the circumstances of our lives. Our Lord is trying to introduce us to identification with Himself in a particular Gethsemane, and we will not go; we say - "No, Lord, I cannot see the meaning of this, it is bitter." How can we possibly watch with Someone Who is inscrutable? How are we going to understand Jesus sufficiently to watch with Him in His Gethsemane, when we do not know even what His suffering is for? We do not know how to watch with Him; we are only used to the idea of Jesus watching with us. The disciples loved Jesus Christ to the limit of their natural capacity, but they did not understand what He was after. In the Garden of Gethsemane they slept for their own sorrow, and at the end of three years of the closest intimacy they "all forsook Him and fled." "They were all filled with the Holy Ghost" - the same "they," but something wonderful has happened in between - Our Lord's Death and Resurrection and Ascension; and the disciples have been invaded by the Holy Spirit. Our Lord had said - "Ye shall receive power after that the Holy Ghost is come upon you," and this meant that they learned to watch with Him all the rest of their lives.

September 6
DIFFUSIVENESS OF LIFE

"Rivers of living water." John 7:38

A river touches places of which its source knows nothing, and Jesus says if we have received of His fulness, however small the visible measure of our lives, out of us will flow the rivers that will bless to the uttermost parts of the earth. We have nothing to do with the outflow - "This is the work of God that ye believe. . . ." God rarely allows a soul to see how great a blessing he is. A river is victoriously persistent, it overcomes all barriers. For a while it goes steadily on its course, then it comes to an obstacle and for a while it is baulked, but it soon makes a pathway round the obstacle. Or a river will drop out of sight for miles, and presently emerge again broader and grander than ever. You can see God using some lives, but into your life an obstacle has come and you do not seem to be of any use. Keep paying attention to the Source, and God will either take you round the obstacle or remove it. The river of the Spirit of God overcomes all obstacles. Never get your eyes on the obstacle or on the difficulty. The obstacle is a matter of indifference to the river which will flow steadily through you if you remember to keep right at the Source. Never allow anything to come between yourself and Jesus Christ, no emotion, or experience; nothing must keep you from the one great sovereign Source. Think of the healing and far-flung rivers nursing themselves in our souls! God has been opening up marvellous truths to our minds, and every point He has opened up is an indication of the wider power of the river He will flow through us. If you believe in Jesus, you will find that God has nourished in you mighty torrents of blessing for others.

September 7
SPRINGS OF BENIGNITY

"The water that I shall give him shall be in him a well of water." John 4:14

The picture Our Lord gives is not that of a channel but a fountain. "Be being filled," and the sweetness of vital relationship to Jesus will flow out of the saint as lavishly as it is imparted to him. If you find your life is not flowing out as it should, you are to blame; something has obstructed the flow. Keep right at the Source, and - you will be blessed personally? No, out of you will flow rivers of living water, irrepressible life. We are to be centres through which Jesus can flow as rivers of living water in blessing to every one. Some of us are like the Dead Sea, always taking in but never giving out, because we are not rightly related to the Lord Jesus. As surely as we receive from Him, He will pour out through us, and in the measure He is not pouring out, there is a defect in our relationship to Him. Is there anything between you and Jesus Christ? Is there anything that hinders your belief in Him? If not, Jesus says, out of you will flow rivers of living water. It is not a blessing passed on, not an experience stated, but a river continually flowing. Keep at the Source, guard well your belief in Jesus Christ and your relationship to Him, and there will be a steady flow for other lives, no dryness and no deadness. Is it not too extravagant to say that out of an individual believer rivers are going to flow? "I do not see the rivers," you say. Never look at yourself from the standpoint of - Who am I? In the history of God's work you will nearly always find that it has started from the obscure, the unknown, the ignored, but the steadfastly true to Jesus Christ.

September 8
DO IT YOURSELF

"Casting down imaginations and every high thing that exalteth itself against the knowledge of God." 2 Corinthians 10:5

Deliverance from sin is not deliverance from human nature. There are things in human nature, such as prejudices, which the saint has to destroy by neglect; and other things which have to be destroyed by violence, i.e., by the Divine strength imparted by God's Spirit. There are some things over which we are not to fight, but to stand still in and see the salvation of God; but every theory or conception which erects itself as a rampart against the knowledge of God is to be determinedly

281

demolished by drawing on God's power, not by fleshly endeavour or compromise (v. 4). It is only when God has altered our disposition and we have entered into the experience of sanctification that the fight begins. The warfare is not against sin; we can never fight against sin: Jesus Christ deals with sin in Redemption. The conflict is along the line of turning our natural life into a spiritual life, and this is never done easily, nor does God intend it to be done easily. It is done only by a series of moral choices. God does not make us holy in the sense of character; He makes us holy in the sense of innocence, and we have to turn that innocence into holy character by a series of moral choices. These choices are continually in antagonism to the entrenchments of our natural life, the things which erect themselves as ramparts against the knowledge of God. We can either go back and make ourselves of no account in the Kingdom of God, or we can determinedly demolish these things and let Jesus bring another son to glory.

September 9
DO IT YOURSELF

"Bringing into captivity every thought to the obedience of Christ." 2 Corinthians 10:5

This is another aspect of the strenuous nature of sainthood. Paul says, "I take every project prisoner to make it obey Christ." (Moffatt.) How much Christian work there is to-day which has never been disciplined, but has simply sprung into being by impulse! In Our Lord's life every project was disciplined to the will of His Father. There was not a movement of an impulse of His own will as distinct from His Father's - "The Son can do nothing of Himself." Then take ourselves - a vivid religious experience, and every project born of impulse put into action immediately, instead of being imprisoned and disciplined to obey Christ. This is a day when practical work is overemphasized, and the saints who are bringing every project into captivity are criticized and told that they are not in earnest for God or for souls. True earnestness is found in obeying God, not in the inclination to serve Him that is born of undisciplined human nature. It is inconceivable, but true nevertheless, that saints are not bringing every project into captivity, but are doing work for God at the instigation of their own human nature which has not been spiritualized by determined discipline. We are apt to forget that a man is not only committed to Jesus Christ for salvation; he is committed to Jesus Christ's view of God, of the world, of sin and of the devil, and this will mean that he must recognize the responsibility of being transformed by the renewing of his mind.

September 10
MISSIONARY MUNITIONS

"When thou wast under the fig tree, I saw thee." John 1:48

We imagine we would be all right if a big crisis arose; but the big crisis will only reveal the stuff we are made of, it will not put anything into us. "If God gives the call, of course I will rise to the occasion." You will not unless you have risen to the occasion in the workshop, unless you have been the real thing before God there. If you are not doing the thing that lies nearest, because God has engineered it; when the crisis comes instead of being revealed as fit, you will be revealed as unfit. Crises always reveal character. The private relationship of worshipping God is the great essential of fitness. The time comes when there is no more "fig-tree" life possible, when it is out into the open, out into the glare and into the work, and you will find yourself of no value there if you have not been worshipping as occasion serves you in your home. Worship aright in your private relationships, then when God sets you free you will be ready, because in the unseen life which no one saw but God you have become perfectly fit, and when the strain comes you can be relied upon by God. "I can't be expected to live the sanctified life in the circumstances I am in; I have no time for praying just now, no time for Bible reading, my opportunity hasn't come yet; when it does, of course I shall be all right." No, you will not. If you have not been worshipping as occasion serves, when you get into work you will not only be useless yourself, but a tremendous hindrance to those who are associated with you. The workshop of missionary munitions is the hidden, personal, worshipping life of the saint.

September 11
MISSIONARY MUNITIONS

"If I then, your Lord and Master, have washed your feet, ye also ought to wash one another's feet." John 13:14

Ministering as opportunity surrounds us does not mean selecting our surroundings, it means being very selectly God's in any haphazard surroundings which He engineers for us. The characteristics we manifest in our immediate surroundings are indications of what we will be like in other surroundings. The things that Jesus did were of the most menial and commonplace order, and this is an indication that it takes all God's power in me to do the most commonplace things in His way. Can I use a towel as He did? Towels and dishes and sandals, all the ordinary sordid things of our lives, reveal more quickly than anything what we are made of. It takes God Almighty Incarnate in us to do the meanest duty as it ought to be done. "I have given you an example that ye should do as I have done to you." Watch the kind of people God brings around you, and you will be humiliated to find that this is His way of revealing to you the kind of person you have been to Him. Now, He says, exhibit to that one exactly what I have shown to you. "Oh," you say, "I will do all that when I get out into the foreign field." To talk in this way is like trying to produce the munitions of war in the trenches - you will be killed while you are doing it. We have to go the "second mile" with God. Some of us get played out in the first ten yards, because God compels us to go where we cannot see the way, and we say - "I will wait till I get nearer the big crisis." If we do not do the running steadily in the little ways, we shall do nothing in the crisis.

September 12
BY SPIRITUAL CONFUSION

"Ye know not what ye ask." Matthew 20:22

There are times in spiritual life when there is confusion, and it is no way out to say that there ought not to be confusion. It is not a question of right and wrong, but a question of God taking you by a way which in the meantime you do not understand, and it is only by going through the confusion that you will get at what God wants. The Shrouding of His Friendship. Luke 11:5-8. Jesus gave the illustration of the man who looked as if he did not care for his friend, and He said that that is how the Heavenly Father will appear to you at times. You will think He is an unkind friend, but remember He is not; the time will come when everything will be explained. There is a cloud on the friendship of the heart, and often even love itself has to wait in pain and tears for the blessing of fuller communion. When God looks completely shrouded, will you hang on in confidence in Him? The Shadow on His Fatherhood. Luke 11:11-13. Jesus says there are times when your Father will appear as if He were an unnatural father, as if He were callous and indifferent, but remember He is not; I have told you - "Everyone that asketh receiveth." If there is a shadow on the face of the Father just now, hang onto it that He will ultimately give His clear revealing and justify Himself in all that He permitted. The Strangeness of His Faithfulness. Luke 18:1-8. "When the Son of Man cometh, shall He find faith on the earth?" Will He find the faith which banks on Him in spite of the confusion? Stand off in faith believing that what Jesus said is true, though in the meantime you do not under stand what God is doing. He has bigger issues at stake than the particular things you ask.

September 13
AFTER SURRENDER - WHAT?

"I have finished the work which Thou gavest Me to do." John 17:4

Surrender is not the surrender of the external life, but of the will; when that is done, all is done. There are very few crises in life; the great crisis is the surrender of the will. God never crushes a man's will into surrender, He never beseeches him, He waits until the man yields up his will to Him. That battle never needs to be re-fought Surrender for Deliverance. "Come unto Me and I will give you rest." It is after we have begun to experience what salvation means that we surrender our wills to Jesus for rest. Whatever is perplexing heart or mind is a call to the will - "Come unto Me." It is a voluntary coming. Surrender for Devotion. "If any man will come after Me, let him deny himself." The surrender here is of my self to Jesus, my self with His rest at the heart of it. "If you would be My disciple, give up your right to yourself to Me." Then the remainder of the life is nothing but the manifestation of this surrender. When once the surrender has taken place we never need "suppose" anything. We do not need to care what our circumstances are, Jesus is amply sufficient. Surrender for Death. John 21:18-19. ". . . another shall gird thee." Have you learned what it means to be bound for death? Beware of a surrender which you make to God in an ecstasy; you are apt to take it back again. It is a question of being united with Jesus in His death until nothing ever appeals to you that did not appeal to Him. After surrender - what? The whole of the life after surrender is an aspiration for unbroken communion with God.

September 14
IMAGINATION V. INSPIRATION

"The simplicity that is in Christ." 2 Corinthians 11:3

Simplicity is the secret of seeing things clearly. A saint does not think clearly for a long while, but a saint ought to see clearly without any difficulty. You cannot think a spiritual muddle clear, you have to obey it clear. In intellectual matters you can think things out, but in spiritual matters you will think yourself into cotton wool. If there is something upon which God has put His pressure, obey in that matter, bring your imagination into captivity to the obedience of Christ with regard to it and everything will become as clear as daylight. The reasoning capacity comes afterwards, but we never see along that line, we see like children;

when we try to be wise we see nothing (Matthew 11:25). The tiniest thing we allow in our lives that is not under the control of the Holy Spirit is quite sufficient to account for spiritual muddle, and all the thinking we like to spend on it will never make it clear. Spiritual muddle is only made plain by obedience. Immediately we obey, we discern. This is humiliating, because when we are muddled we know the reason is in the temper of our mind. When the natural power of vision is devoted to the Holy Spirit, it becomes the power of perceiving God's will and the whole life is kept in simplicity.

September 15
WHAT TO RENOUNCE

"But have renounced the hidden things of dishonesty." 2 Corinthians 4:2

Have you "renounced the hidden things of dishonesty" - the things that your sense of honour will not allow to come to the light? You can easily hide them. Is there a thought in your heart about anyone which you would not like to be dragged into the light? Renounce it as soon as it springs up; renounce the whole thing until there is no hidden thing of dishonesty or craftiness about you. Envy, jealousy, strife - these things arise not necessarily from the disposition of sin, but from the make-up of your body which was used for this kind of thing in days gone by (see Romans 6:19 and 1 Peter 4:1-2). Maintain a continual watchfulness so that nothing of which you would be ashamed arises in your life. "Not walking in craftiness," that is, resorting to what will carry your point. This is a great snare. You know that God will only let you work in one way, then be careful never to catch people the other way; God's blight will be upon you if you do. Others are doing things which to you would be walking in craftiness, but it may not be so with them: God has given you another standpoint. Never blunt the sense of your Utmost for His Highest. For you to do a certain thing would mean the incoming of craftiness for an end other than the highest, and the blunting of the motive God has given you. Many have gone back because they are afraid of looking at things from God's standpoint. The great crisis comes spiritually when a man has to emerge a bit farther on than the creed he has accepted.

September 16
THE DIVINE REGION OF RELIGION

"But thou, when thou prayest, enter into thy closet, and when thou hast shut thy door, pray to thy Father which is in secret." Matthew 6:6 The main idea in the region of religion is - Your eyes upon God, not on men. Do not have as your motive the desire to be known as a praying man. Get an inner chamber in which to pray where no one knows you are praying, shut the door and talk to God in secret. Have no other motive than to know your Father in heaven. It is impossible to conduct your life as a disciple without definite times of secret prayer. But when ye pray use not vain repetitions . . . (v.7). God does not hear us because we are in earnest, but only on the ground of Redemption. God is never impressed by our earnestness. Prayer is not simply getting things from God, that is a most initial form of prayer; prayer is getting into perfect communion with God. If the Son of God is formed in us by regeneration He will press forward in front of our common sense and change our attitude to the things about which we pray. "Everyone that asketh receiveth." We pray pious blether, our will is not in it, and then we say God does not answer; we never asked for anything. "Ye shall ask what ye will," said Jesus. Asking means our will is in it. Whenever Jesus talked about prayer, He put it with the grand simplicity of a child: we bring in our critical temper and say - Yes, but . . . Jesus said "Ask." But remember that we have to ask of God things that are in keeping with the God Whom Jesus Christ revealed.

September 17
WHAT'S THE GOOD OF TEMPTATION?

"There hath no temptation taken you but such as is common to man." 1 Corinthians 10:13

The word "temptation" has come down in the world; we are apt to use it wrongly. Temptation is not sin, it is the thing we are bound to meet if we are men. Not to be tempted would be to be beneath contempt. Many of us, however, suffer from temptations from which we have no business to suffer, simply because we have refused to let God lift us to a higher plane where we would face temptations of another order. A man's disposition on the inside, i.e., what he possesses in his personality, determines what he is tempted by on the outside. The temptation fits the nature of the one tempted, and reveals the possibilities of the nature. Every man has the setting of his own temptation, and the temptation will come along the line of the ruling disposition. Temptation is a suggested short cut to the realization of the highest at which I aim - not towards what I understand as evil, but towards what I understand as good. Temptation is something that completely baffles me for a while, I do not know whether the thing is right or wrong. Temptation yielded to is lust deified, and is a proof that it was timidity that prevented the sin before. Temptation is not something we may escape, it is essential to the fullorbed life of a man. Beware lest you think you are tempted as no one else is tempted; what you go through is the common inheritance of the race, not something no one ever went through before. God does not save us from temptations; He succours us in the midst of them (Heb. 2:18).

September 18
HIS TEMPTATION AND OURS

For we have not an high priest which cannot be touched with the feeling of our infirmities; but was in all points tempted like as we are, yet without sin." Hebrews 4:15

Until we are born again, the only kind of temptation we understand is that mentioned by St. James - "Every man is tempted, when he is drawn away of his own lust, and enticed." But by regeneration we are lifted into another realm where there are other temptations to face, viz., the kind of temptations Our Lord faced. The temptations of Jesus do not appeal to us, they have no home at all in our human nature. Our Lord's temptations and ours move in different spheres until we are born again and become His brethren. The temptations of Jesus are not those of a man, but the temptations of God as Man. By regeneration the Son of God is formed in us, and in our physical life He has the same setting that He had on earth. Satan does not tempt us to do wrong things; he tempts us in order to make us lose what God has put into us by regeneration, viz., the possibility of being of value to God. He does not come on the line of tempting us to sin, but on the line of shifting the point of view, and only the Spirit of God can detect this as a temptation of the devil. Temptation means the test by an alien power of the possessions held by a personality. This makes the temptation of Our Lord explainable. After Jesus in His baptism had accepted the vocation of bearing away the sin of the world, He was immediately put by God's Spirit into the testing machine of the devil, but He did not tire, He went through the temptation "without sin," and He retained the possessions of His personality intact.

September 19
DO YOU CONTINUE TO GO WITH JESUS?

"Ye are they which have continued with Me in My temptations." Luke 22:28

It is true that Jesus Christ is with us in our temptations, but are we going with Him in His temptations? Many of us cease to go with Jesus from the moment we have an experience of what He can do. Watch when God shifts your circumstances, and see whether you are going with Jesus, or siding with the world, the flesh and the devil. We wear His badge, but are we going with Him? "From that time many of His disciples went back and walked no more with Him." The temptations of Jesus continued throughout His earthly life, and they will continue throughout the life of the Son of God in us. Are we going with Jesus in the life we are living now? We have the idea that we ought to shield ourselves from some of the things God brings round us. Never! God engineers circumstances and whatever they may be like we have to see that we face them while abiding continually with Him in His temptations. They are His temptations, not temptations to us, but temptations to the life of the Son of God in us. The honour of Jesus Christ is at stake in your bodily life. Are you remaining loyal to the Son of God in the things which beset His life in you? Do you continue to go with Jesus? The way lies through Gethsemane, through the city gate, outside the camp; the way lies alone, and the way lies until there is no trace of a footstep left, only the voice, "Follow Me."

September 20
THE DIVINE RULE OF LIFE

"Be ye therefore perfect, even as your Father in heaven is perfect." Matthew 5:48

Our Lord's exhortation in these verses is to be generous in our behaviour to all men. In the spiritual life beware of walking according to natural affinities. Everyone has natural affinities; some people we like and others we do not like. We must never let those likes and dislikes rule in our Christian life. "If we walk in the light as God is in the light," God will give us communion with people for whom we have no natural affinity. The Example Our Lord gives us is not that of a good man, or even of a good Christian, but of God Himself. "Be ye therefore perfect even as your Father in heaven is perfect," show to the other man what God has shown to you; and God will give us ample opportunities in actual life to prove whether we are perfect as our Father in heaven is perfect. To be a disciple means that we deliberately identify ourselves with God's interests in other people. "That ye love one another; as I have loved you . . ." The expression of Christian character is not good doing, but Godlikeness. If the Spirit of God has transformed you within, you will exhibit Divine characteristics in your life, not good human characteristics. God's life in us expresses itself as God's life, not as human life trying to be godly. The secret of a Christian is that the supernatural is made natural in him by the grace of God, and the experience of this works out in the practical details of life, not in times of communion with God. When we come in contact with things that create a buzz, we find to our amazement that we have power to keep wonderfully poised in the centre of it all.

September 21
MISSIONARY PREDESTINATIONS

"And now, saith the Lord, that formed me from the womb to be His servant." Isaiah 49:5

The first thing that happens after we have realized our election to God in Christ Jesus is the destruction of our prejudices and our parochial notions and our patriotisms; we are turned into servants of God's own purpose. The whole human race was created to glorify God and enjoy Him for ever. Sin has switched the human race on to another tack, but it has not altered God's purpose in the tiniest degree; and when we are born again we are brought into the realization of God's great purpose for the human race, viz., I am created for God, He made me. This realization of the election of God is the most joyful realization on earth, and we have to learn to rely on the tremendous creative purpose of God. The first thing God will do with us is to "force through the channels of a single heart" the interests of the whole world. The love of God, the very nature of God, is introduced into us, and the nature of Almighty God is focused in John 3:16 - "God so loved the world. . ." We have to maintain our soul open to the fact of God's creative purpose, and not muddle it with our own intentions. If we do, God will have to crush our intentions on one side however much it may hurt. The purpose for which the missionary is created is that he may be God's servant, one in whom God is glorified. When once we realize that through the salvation of Jesus Christ we are made perfectly fit for God, we shall understand why Jesus Christ is so ruthless in His demands. He demands absolute rectitude from His servants, because He has put into them the very nature of God. Beware lest you forget God's purpose for your life.

September 22
THE MISSIONARY'S MASTER

"Ye call me Master and Lord: and ye say well; for so I am." John 13:13

To have a master and to be mastered is not the same thing. To have a master means that there is one who knows me better than I know myself, one who is closer than a friend, one who fathoms the remotest abyss of my heart and satisfies it, one who has brought me into the secure sense that he has met and solved every perplexity and problem of my mind. To have a master is this and nothing less - "One is your Master, even Christ." Our Lord never enforces obedience; He does not take means to make me do what He wants. At certain times I wish God would master me and make me do the thing, but He will not; in other moods I wish He would leave me alone, but He does not. "Ye call me Master and Lord" - but is He? Master and Lord have little place in our vocabulary, we prefer the words Saviour, Sanctifier, Healer. The only word to describe mastership in experience is love and we know very little about love as God reveals it. This is proved by the way we use the word obey. In the Bible obedience is based on the relationship of equals, that of a son with his father. Our Lord was not God's servant, He was His Son. "Though He were a Son, yet learned He obedience . . ." If our idea is that we are being mastered, it is a proof that we have no master; if that is our attitude to Jesus, we are far away from the relationship He wants. He wants us in the relationship in which He is easily Master without our conscious knowledge of it, all we know is that we are His to obey.

September 23
THE MISSIONARY'S GOAL

"Behold, we go up to Jerusalem." Luke 18:31

In the natural life our ambitions alter as we develop; in the Christian life the goal is given at the beginning, the beginning and the end are the same, viz., Our Lord Himself. We start with Christ and we end with Him - "until we all attain to the stature of the manhood of Christ Jesus," not to our idea of what the Christian life should be. The aim of the missionary is to do God's will, not to be useful, not to win the heathen; he is useful and he does win the heathen, but that is not his aim. His aim is to do the will of his Lord. In Our Lord's life Jerusalem was the place where He reached the climax of His Father's will upon the Cross, and unless we go with Jesus there we will have no companionship with Him. Nothing ever discouraged Our Lord on His way to Jerusalem. He never hurried through certain villages where He was persecuted, or lingered in others where He was blessed. Neither gratitude nor ingratitude turned Our Lord one hair's breadth away from His purpose to go up to Jerusalem. "The disciple is not above his Master." The same things will happen to us on our way to our Jerusalem. There will be the works of God manifested through us, people will get blessed, and one or two will show gratitude and the rest will show gross ingratitude, but nothing must deflect us from going up to our Jerusalem. "There they crucified Him." That is what happened when Our Lord reached Jerusalem, and that happening is the gateway to our salvation. The saints do not end in crucifixion: by the Lord's grace they end in glory. In the meantime our watchword is - I, too, go up to Jerusalem.

September 24
THE "GO" OF PREPARATION

"Therefore if thou bring thy gift to the altar, and there thou rememberest that thy brother hath ought against thee; leave there thy gift before the altar, and go thy way; first be reconciled to thy brother, and then come and offer thy gift." Matthew 5:23, 2

It is easy to imagine that we will get to a place where we are complete and ready, but preparation is not suddenly accomplished, it is a process steadily maintained. It is dangerous to get into a settled state of experience. It is preparation and preparation. The sense of sacrifice appeals readily to a young Christian. Humanly speaking, the one thing that attracts to Jesus Christ is our sense of the heroic, and the scrutiny of Our Lord's words suddenly brings this tide of enthusiasm to the test. "First be reconciled to thy brother." The "go" of preparation is to let the word of God scrutinize. The sense of heroic sacrifice is not good enough. The thing the Holy Spirit is detecting in you is the disposition that will never work in His service. No one but God can detect that disposition in you. Have you anything to hide from God? If you have, then let God search you with His light. If there is sin, confess it, not admit it. Are you willing to obey your Lord and Master whatever the humiliation to your right to yourself may be? Never discard a conviction. If it is important enough for the Spirit of God to have brought it to your mind, it is that thing He is detecting. You were looking for a great thing to give up. God is telling you of some tiny thing; but at the back of it there lies the central citadel of obstinacy: I will not give up my right to myself - the thing God intends you to give up if ever you are going to be a disciple of Jesus Christ.

September 25
THE "GO" OF RELATIONSHIP

"And whosoever shall compel thee to go a mile, go with him twain."
Matthew 5:41

The summing up of Our Lord's teaching is that the relationship which He demands is an impossible one unless He has done a supernatural work in us. Jesus Christ demands that there be not the slightest trace of resentment even suppressed in the heart of a disciple when he meets with tyranny and injustice. No enthusiasm will ever stand the strain that Jesus Christ will put upon His worker, only one thing will, and that is a personal relationship to Himself which has gone through the mill of His spring-cleaning until there is only one purpose left - I am here for God to send me where He will. Every other thing may get fogged, but this relationship to Jesus Christ must never be. The Sermon on the Mount is not an ideal, it is a statement of what will happen in me when Jesus Christ has altered my disposition and put in a disposition like His own. Jesus Christ is the only One Who can fulfil the Sermon on the Mount. If we are to be disciples of Jesus, we must be made disciples supernaturally; as long as we have the dead set purpose of being disciples we may be sure we are not. "I have chosen you." That is the way the grace of God begins. It is a constraint we cannot get away from; we can disobey it, but we cannot generate it. The drawing is done by the supernatural grace of God, and we never can trace where His work begins. Our Lord's making of a disciple is supernatural. He does not build on any natural capacity at all. God does not ask us to do the things that are easy to us naturally; He only asks us to do the things we are perfectly fitted to do by His grace, and the cross will come along that line always.

September 26
THE UNBLAMEABLE ATTITUDE

"If . . thou rememberest that thy brother hath ought against thee. . . ." Matthew 5:23

If when you come to the altar, there you remember that your brother has anything against you, not - If you rake up something by a morbid sensitiveness, but - "If thou rememberest," that is, if it is brought to your conscious mind by the Spirit of God: "first be reconciled to thy brother, and then come and offer thy gift." Never object to the intense sensitiveness of the Spirit of God in you when He is educating you down to the scruple. "First be reconciled to thy brother . . ." Our Lord's direction is simple, "first be reconciled." Go back the way you came, go the way indicated to you by the conviction given at the altar; have an attitude of mind and a temper of soul to the one who has something against you that makes reconciliation as natural as breathing. Jesus does not mention the other person, He says - you go. There is no question of your rights. The stamp of the saint is that he can waive his own rights and obey the Lord Jesus. "And then come and offer thy gift." The process is clearly marked. First, the heroic spirit of self-sacrifice, then the sudden checking by the sensitiveness of the Holy Spirit, and the stoppage at the point of conviction, then the way of obedience to the word of God, constructing an unblameable attitude of mind and temper to the one with whom you have been in the wrong; then the glad, simple, unhindered offering of your gift to God.

September 27
THE "GO" OF RENUNCIATION

"Lord, I will follow Thee whithersoever Thou goest." Luke 9:57

Our Lord's attitude to this man is one of severe discouragement because He knew what was in man. We would have said - "Fancy losing the opportunity of winning that man!" Fancy bringing about him a north wind that froze him and "turned him away discouraged!" Never apologize for your Lord. The words of the Lord hurt and offend until there is nothing left to hurt or offend. Jesus Christ has no tenderness whatever toward anything that is ultimately going to ruin a man in the service of God. Our Lord's answers are based not on caprice, but on a knowledge of what is in man. If the Spirit of God brings to your mind a word of the Lord that hurts you, you may be sure that there is something He wants to hurt to death. V. 58. These words knock the heart out of serving Jesus Christ because it is pleasing to me. The rigour of rejection leaves nothing but my Lord, and myself, and a forlorn hope. "Let the hundredfold come or go, your lodestar must be your relationship to Me, and I have nowhere to lay My head." v. 59. This man did not want to disappoint Jesus, nor to hurt his father. We put sensitive loyalty to relatives in place of loyalty to Jesus Christ and Jesus has to take the last place. In a conflict of loyalty, obey Jesus Christ at all costs. V. 61. The one who says - "Yes, Lord, but . . ." is the one who is fiercely ready, but never goes. This man had one or two reservations. The exacting call of Jesus Christ has no margin of good-byes, because good-bye, as it is often used, is pagan, not Christian. When once the call of God comes, begin to go and never stop going.

September 28
THE "GO" OF UNCONDITIONAL IDENTIFICATION

"One thing thou lackest: . . come, take up the cross, and follow Me." Mark 10:21

The rich young ruler had the master passion to be perfect. When he saw Jesus Christ, he wanted to be like Him. Our Lord never puts personal holiness to the fore when He calls a disciple; He puts absolute annihilation of my right to myself and identification with Himself - a relationship with Himself in which there is no other relationship. Luke 14:26 has nothing to do with salvation or sanctification, but with unconditional identification with Jesus Christ. Very few of us know the absolute "go" of abandonment to Jesus. "Then Jesus beholding him loved him." The look of Jesus will mean a heart broken for ever from allegiance to any other person or thing. Has Jesus ever looked at you? The look of Jesus transforms and transfixes. Where you are "soft" with God is where the Lord has looked at you. If you are hard and vindictive, insistent on your own way, certain that the other person is more likely to be in the wrong than you are, it is an indication that there are whole tracts of your nature that have never been transformed by His gaze. "One thing thou lackest . . ." The only "good thing" from Jesus Christ's point of view is union with Himself and nothing in between. "Sell whatsoever thou hast . ." I must reduce myself until I am a mere conscious man, I must fundamentally renounce possessions of all kinds, not to save my soul (only one thing saves a man - absolute reliance upon Jesus Christ) - but in order to follow Jesus. "Come, and follow Me." And the road is the way He went.

September 29
THE CONSCIOUSNESS OF THE CALL

"For necessity is laid upon me: yea, woe is unto me, if I preach not the gospel!" 1 Corinthians 9:16

We are apt to forget the mystical, supernatural touch of God. If you can tell where you got the call of God and all about it, I question whether you have ever had a call. The call of God does not come like that, it is much more supernatural. The realization of it in a man's life may come with a sudden thunder-clap or with a gradual dawning, but in whatever way it comes, it comes with the undercurrent of the supernatural, something that cannot be put into words, it is always accompanied with a glow. At any moment there may break the sudden consciousness of this incalculable, supernatural, surprising call that has taken hold of your life - "I have chosen you." The call of God has nothing to do with salvation and sanctification. It is not because you are sanctified that you are therefore called to preach the gospel; the call to preach the gospel is infinitely different. Paul describes it as a necessity laid upon him. If you have been obliterating the great super natural call of God in your life, take a review of your circumstances and see where God has not been first, but your ideas of service, or your temperamental abilities. Paul said - "Woe is unto me, if I preach not the gospel!" He had realized the call of God, and there was no competitor for his strength. If a man or woman is called of God, it does not matter how untoward circumstances are, every force that has been at work will tell for God's purpose in the end. If you agree with God's purpose He will bring not only your conscious life, but all the deeper regions of your life which you cannot get at, into harmony.

September 30
THE COMMISSION OF THE CALL

"Who now rejoice in my sufferings for you, and fill up that which is behind of the afflictions of Christ in my flesh for His body's sake." Colossians 1:24

We make calls out of our own spiritual consecration, but when we get right with God He brushes all these aside, and rivets us with a pain that is terrific to one thing we never dreamed of, and for one radiant flashing moment we see what He is after, and we say - "Here am I, send me." This call has nothing to do with personal sanctification, but with being made broken bread and poured-out wine. God can never make us wine if we object to the fingers He uses to crush us with. If God would only use His own fingers, and make me broken bread and poured-out wine in a special way! But when He uses someone whom we dislike, or some set of circumstances to which we said we would never submit, and makes those the crushers, we object. We must never choose the scene of our own martyrdom. If ever we are going to be made into wine, we will have to be crushed; you cannot drink grapes. Grapes become wine only when they have been squeezed. I wonder what kind of finger and thumb God has been using to squeeze you, and you have been like a marble and escaped? You are not ripe yet, and if God had squeezed you, the wine would have been remarkably bitter. To be a sacramental personality means that the elements of the natural life are presenced by God as they are broken providentially in His service. We have to be adjusted into God before we can be broken bread in His hands. Keep right with God and let Him do what He likes, and you will find that He is producing the kind of bread and wine that will benefit His other children.

October 1
THE SPHERE OF EXALTATION

"Jesus leadeth them up into a high mountain apart by themselves."
Mark 9:2

We have all had times on the mount, when we have seen things from God's standpoint and have wanted to stay there; but God will never allow us to stay there. The test of our spiritual life is the power to descend; if we have power to rise only, something is wrong. It is a great thing to be on the mount with God, but a man only gets there in order that afterwards he may get down among the devil-possessed and lift them up. We are not built for the mountains and the dawns and aesthetic affinities, those are for moments of inspiration, that is all. We are built for the valley, for the ordinary stuff we are in, and that is where we have to prove our mettle. Spiritual selfishness always wants repeated moments on the mount. We feel we could talk like angels and live like angels, if only we could stay on the mount. The times of exaltation are exceptional, they have their meaning in our life with God, but we must beware lest our spiritual selfishness wants to make them the only time. We are apt to think that everything that happens is to be turned into useful teaching, it is to be turned into something better than teaching, viz., into character. The mount is not meant to teach us anything, it is meant to make us something. There is a great snare in asking - What is the use of it? In spiritual matters we can never calculate on that line. The moments on the mountain tops are rare moments, and they are meant for something in God's purpose.

October 2
THE SPHERE OF HUMILIATION

"If Thou canst do any thing, have compassion on us, and help us." Mark 9:22

After every time of exaltation we are brought down with a sudden rush into things as they are where it is neither beautiful nor poetic nor thrilling. The height of the mountain top is measured by the drab drudgery of the valley; but it is in the valley that we have to live for the glory of God. We see His glory on the mount, but we never live for His glory there. It is in the sphere of humiliation that we find our true worth to God, that is where our faithfulness is revealed. Most of us can do things if we are always at the heroic pitch because of the natural selfishness of our hearts, but God wants us at the drab commonplace pitch, where we live in the valley according to our personal relationship to Him. Peter thought it would be a fine thing for them to remain on the mount, but Jesus Christ took the disciples down from the mount into the valley, the place where the meaning of the vision is explained. "If Thou canst do any thing . . ." It takes the valley of humiliation to root the scepticism out of us. Look back at your own experience, and you will find that until you learned Who Jesus was, you were a cunning sceptic about His power. When you were on the mount, you could believe anything, but what about the time when you were up against facts in the valley? You may be able to give a testimony to sanctification, but what about the thing that is a humiliation to you just now? The last time you were on the mount with God, you saw that all power in heaven and in earth belonged to Jesus - will you be sceptical now in the valley of humiliation?

October 3
THE SPHERE OF MINISTRATION

"This kind can come forth by nothing, but by prayer and fasting." Mark 9:29

"Why could not we cast him out?" The answer lies in a personal relationship to Jesus Christ. This kind can come forth by nothing but by concentration and redoubled concentration on Him. We can ever remain powerless, as were the disciples, by trying to do God's work not in concentration on His power, but by ideas drawn from our own temperament. We slander God by our very eagerness to work for Him without knowing Him. You are brought face to face with a difficult case and nothing happens externally, and yet you know that emancipation will be given because you are concentrated on Jesus Christ. This is your line of service - to see that there is nothing between Jesus and yourself. Is there? If there is, you must get through it, not by ignoring it in irritation, or by mounting up, but by facing it and getting through it into the presence of Jesus Christ, then that very thing, and all you have been through in connection with it, will glorify Jesus Christ in a way you will never know till you see Him face to face. We must be able to mount up with wings as eagles; but we must also know how to come down. The power of the saint lies in the coming down and the living down. "I can do all things through Christ which strengtheneth me," said Paul, and the things he referred to were mostly humiliating things. It is in our power to refuse to be humiliated and to say - "No, thank you, I much prefer to be on the mountain top with God." Can I face things as they actually are in the light of the reality of Jesus Christ, or do things as they are efface altogether my faith in Him, and put me into a panic?

October 4
THE VISION AND THE VERITY

"Called to be saints." 1 Corinthians 1:2

Thank God for the sight of all you have never yet been. You have had the vision, but you are not there yet by any means. It is when we are in the valley, where we prove whether we will be the choice ones, that most of us turn back. We are not quite prepared for the blows which must come if we are going to be turned into the shape of the vision. We have seen what we are not, and what God wants us to be, but are we willing to have the vision "batter'd to shape and use" by God? The batterings always come in commonplace ways and through commonplace people. There are times when we do know what God's purpose is; whether we will let the vision be turned into actual character depends upon us, not upon God. If we prefer to loll on the mount and live in the memory of the vision, we will be of no use actually in the ordinary stuff of which human life is made up. We have to learn to live in reliance on what we saw in the vision, not in ecstasies and conscious contemplation of God, but to live in actualities in the light of the vision until we get to the veritable reality. Every bit of our training is in that direction. Learn to thank God for making known His demands. The little "I am" always sulks when God says do. Let the little "I am" be shrivelled up in God's indignation - "I AM THAT I AM hath sent thee." He must dominate. Is it not penetrating to realize that God knows where we live, and the kennels we crawl into! He will hunt us up like a lightning flash. No human being knows human beings as God does.

October 5
THE BIAS OF DEGENERATION

"Wherefore as by one man sin entered into the world, and death by sin; and so death passed upon all men, for that all have sinned." Romans 5:12

The Bible does not say that God punished the human race for one man's sin; but that the disposition of sin, viz., my claim to my right to myself, entered into the human race by one man, and that another Man took on Him the sin of the human race and put it away (Heb. 9:26) - an infinitely profounder revelation. The disposition of sin is not immorality and wrong-doing, but the disposition of self- realization - I am my own god. This disposition may work out in decorous morality or in indecorous immorality, but it has the one basis, my claim to my right to myself. When Our Lord faced men with all the forces of evil in them, and men who were clean living and moral and up right, He did not pay any attention to the moral degradation of the one or to the moral attainment of the other; He looked at something we do not see, viz., the disposition. Sin is a thing I am born with and I cannot touch it; God touches sin in Redemption. In the Cross of Jesus Christ God redeemed the whole human race from the possibility of damnation through the heredity of sin. God nowhere holds a man responsible for having the heredity of sin. The condemnation is not that I am born with a heredity of sin, but if when I realize Jesus Christ came to deliver me from it, I refuse to let Him do so, from that moment I begin to get the seal of damnation. "And this is the judgment" (the critical moment), "that the light is come into the world, and men loved the darkness rather than the light."

October 6
THE BENT OF REGENERATION

"When it pleased God . . to reveal His Son in me." Galatians 1:15, 16

If Jesus Christ is to regenerate me, what is the problem He is up against? I have a heredity I had no say in; I am not holy, nor likely to be; and if all Jesus Christ can do is to tell me I must be holy, His teaching plants despair. But if Jesus Christ is a Regenerator, One Who can put into me His own heredity of holiness, then I begin to see what He is driving at when He says that I have to be holy. Redemption means that Jesus Christ can put into any man the hereditary disposition that was in Himself, and all the standards He gives are based on that disposition: His teaching is for the life He puts in. The moral transaction on my part is agreement with God's verdict on sin in the Cross of Jesus Christ. The New Testament teaching about regeneration is that when a man is struck by a sense of need, God will put the Holy Spirit into his spirit, and his personal spirit will be energized by the Spirit of the Son of God, "until Christ be formed in you." The moral miracle of Redemption is that God can put into me a new disposition whereby I can live a totally new life. When I reach the frontier of need and know my limitations, Jesus says - "Blessed are you." But I have to get there. God cannot put into me, a responsible moral being, the disposition that was in Jesus Christ unless I am conscious I need it. Just as the disposition of sin entered into the human race by one man, so the Holy Spirit entered the human race by another Man; and Redemption means that I can be delivered from the heredity of sin and through Jesus Christ can receive an unsullied heredity, viz., the Holy Spirit.

October 7
RECONCILIATION

"For He hath made Him to be sin for us, who knew no sin; that we might be made the righteousness of God in Him." 2 Corinthians 5:21

Sin is a fundamental relationship; it is not wrong doing, it is wrong being, deliberate and emphatic independence of God. The Christian religion bases everything on the positive, radical nature of sin. Other religions deal with sins; the Bible alone deals with sin. The first thing Jesus Christ faced in men was the heredity of sin, and it is because we have ignored this in our presentation of the Gospel that the message of the Gospel has lost its sting and its blasting power. The revelation of the Bible is not that Jesus Christ took upon Himself our fleshly sins, but that He took upon Himself the heredity of sin which no man can touch. God made His own Son to be sin that He might make the sinner a saint. All through the Bible it is revealed that Our Lord bore the sin of the world by identification, not by sympathy. He deliberately took upon His own shoulders, and bore in His own Person, the whole massed sin of the human race - "He hath made Him to be sin for us, who knew no sin," and by so doing He put the whole human race on the basis of Redemption. Jesus Christ rehabilitated the human race; He put it back to where God designed it to be, and anyone can enter into union with God on the ground of what Our Lord has done on the Cross. A man cannot redeem himself; Redemption is God's "bit," it is absolutely finished and complete; its reference to individual men is a question of their individual action. A distinction must always be made between the revelation of Redemption and the conscious experience of salvation in a man's life.

October 8
THE EXCLUSIVENESS OF CHRIST

"Come unto Me." Matthew 11:28

Is it not humiliating to be told that we must come to Jesus! Think of the things we will not come to Jesus Christ about. If you want to know how real you are, test yourself by these words - "Come unto Me." In every degree in which you are not real, you will dispute rather than come, you will quibble rather than come, you will go through sorrow rather than come, you will do anything rather than come the last lap of unutterable foolishness - "Just as I am." As long as you have the tiniest bit of spiritual impertinence, it will always reveal itself in the fact that you are expecting God to tell you to do a big thing, and all He is telling you to do is to "come." "Come unto Me." When you hear those words you will know that something must happen in you before you can come. The Holy Spirit will show you what you have to do, anything at all that will put the axe at the root of the thing which is preventing you from getting through. You will never get further until you are willing to do that one thing. The Holy Spirit will locate the one impregnable thing in you, but He cannot budge it unless you are willing to let Him. How often have you come to God with your requests and gone away with the feeling - Oh, well, I have done it this time! And yet you go away with nothing, whilst all the time God has stood with outstretched hands not only to take you, but for you to take Him. Think of the invincible, unconquerable, unwearying patience of Jesus - "Come unto Me."

October 9
PULL YOURSELF TOGETHER

"Yield your members servants to righteousness unto holiness." Romans 6:13-22

I cannot save and sanctify myself; I cannot atone for sin; I cannot redeem the world; I can not make right what is wrong, pure what is impure, holy what is unholy. That is all the sovereign work of God. Have I faith in what Jesus Christ has done? He has made a perfect Atonement, am I in the habit of constantly realizing it? The great need is not to do things, but to believe things. The Redemption of Christ is not an experience, it is the great act of God which He has performed through Christ, and I have to build my faith upon it. If I construct my faith on my experience, I produce that most unscriptural type, an isolated life, my eyes fixed on my own whiteness. Beware of the piety that has no pre-supposition in the Atonement of the Lord. It is of no use for anything but a sequestered life; it is useless to God and a nuisance to man. Measure every type of experience by our Lord Himself. We cannot do anything pleasing to God unless we deliberately build on the pre-supposition of the Atonement. The Atonement of Jesus has to work out in practical, unobtrusive ways in my life. Every time I obey, absolute Deity is on my side, so that the grace of God and natural obedience coincide. Obedience means that I have banked everything on the Atonement, and my obedience is met immediately by the delight of the supernatural grace of God. Beware of the piety that denies the natural life, it is a fraud. Continually bring yourself to the bar of the Atonement - where is the discernment of the Atonement in this thing, and in that?

October 10
WHEREBY SHALL I KNOW?

"I thank Thee, O Father . . . because Thou hast hid these things from the wise and prudent, and hast revealed them unto babes." Matthew 11:25

In spiritual relationship we do not grow step by step; we are either there or we are not. God does not cleanse us more and more from sin, but when we are in the light, walking in the light, we are cleansed from all sin. It is a question of obedience, and instantly the relationship is perfected. Turn away for one second out of obedience, and darkness and death are at work at once. All God's revelations are sealed until they are opened to us by obedience. You will never get them open by philosophy or thinking. Immediately you obey, a flash of light comes. Let God's truth work in you by soaking in it, not by worrying into it. The only way you can get to know is to stop trying to find out and by being born again. Obey God in the thing He shows you, and instantly the next thing is opened up. One reads tomes on the work of the Holy Spirit, when one five minutes of drastic obedience would make things as clear as a sunbeam. "I suppose I shall understand these things some day!" You can understand them now. It is not study that does it, but obedience. The tiniest fragment of obedience, and heaven opens and the profoundest truths of God are yours straight away. God will never reveal more truth about Himself until you have obeyed what you know already. Beware of becoming "wise and prudent."

October 11
AFTER GOD'S SILENCE - WHAT?

"When He had heard therefore that he was sick, He abode two days in the same place where he was." John 11:6

Has God trusted you with a silence - a silence that is big with meaning? God's silences are His answers. Think of those days of absolute silence in the home at Bethany! Is there anything analogous to those days in your life? Can God trust you like that, or are you still asking for a visible answer? God will give you the blessings you ask if you will not go any further without them; but His silence is the sign that He is bringing you into a marvellous understanding of Himself. Are you mourning before God because you have not had an audible response? You will find that God has trusted you in the most intimate way possible, with an absolute silence, not of despair, but of pleasure, because He saw that you could stand a bigger revelation. If God has given you a silence, praise Him, He is bringing you into the great run of His purposes. The manifestation of the answer in time is a matter of God's sovereignty. Time is nothing to God. For a while you said - "I asked God to give me bread, and He gave me a stone." He did not, and to-day you find He gave you the bread of life. A wonderful thing about God's silence is that the contagion of His stillness gets into you and you become perfectly confident - "I know God

303

has heard me." His silence is the proof that He has. As long as you have the idea that God will bless you in answer to prayer, He will do it, but He will never give you the grace of silence. If Jesus Christ is bringing you into the understanding that prayer is for the glorifying of His Father, He will give you the first sign of His intimacy - silence.

October 12
GETTING INTO GOD'S STRIDE

"Enoch walked with God." Genesis 5:24

The test of a man's religious life and character is not what he does in the exceptional moments of life, but what he does in the ordinary times, when there is nothing tremendous or exciting on. The worth of a man is revealed in his attitude to ordinary things when he is not before the footlights (cf. John 1:36). It is a painful business to get through into the stride of God, it means getting your second wind spiritually. In learning to walk with God there is always the difficulty of getting into His stride; but when we have got into it, the only characteristic that manifests itself is the life of God. The individual man is lost sight of in his personal union with God, and the stride and the power of God alone are manifested. It is difficult to get into stride with God, because when we start walking with Him we find He has outstripped us before we have taken three steps. He has different ways of doing things, and we have to be trained and disciplined into His ways. It was said of Jesus - "He shall not fail nor be discouraged," because He never worked from His own individual standpoint but always from the standpoint of His Father, and we have to learn to do the same. Spiritual truth is learned by atmosphere, not by intellectual reasoning. God's Spirit alters the atmosphere of our way of looking at things, and things begin to be possible which never were possible before. Getting into the stride of God means nothing less than union with Himself. It takes a long time to get there, but keep at it. Don't give in because the pain is bad just now, get on with it, and before long you will find you have a new vision and a new purpose.

October 13
INDIVIDUAL DISCOURAGEMENT AND PERSONAL ENLARGEMENT

"Moses went out unto his brethren, and looked on their burdens." Exodus 2:11

Moses saw the oppression of his people and felt certain that he was the one to deliver them, and in the righteous indignation of his own spirit he started to right their wrongs. After the first strike for God and for the right, God allowed Moses to be driven into blank discouragement, He sent him into the desert to feed sheep for forty years. At the end of that time, God appeared and told Moses to go and bring forth His people, and Moses said - "Who am I, that I should go?" In the beginning Moses realized that he was the man to deliver the people, but he had to be trained and disciplined by God first. He was right in the individual aspect, but he was not the man for the work until he had learned communion with God. We may have the vision of God and a very clear understanding of what God wants, and we start to do the thing, then comes something equivalent to the forty years in the wilderness, as if God had ignored the whole thing, and when we are thoroughly discouraged God comes back and revives the call, and we get the quaver in and say - "Oh, who am I?" We have to learn the first great stride of God - "I AM THAT I AM hath sent thee." We have to learn that our individual effort for God is an impertinence; our individuality is to be rendered incandescent by a personal relationship to God (see Matthew 3:17). We fix on the individual aspect of things; we have the vision - "This is what God wants me to do;" but we have not got into God's stride. If you are going through a time of discouragement, there is a big personal enlargement ahead.

October 14
THE KEY TO THE MISSIONARY

"All power is given unto Me in heaven and in earth. Go ye therefore, and teach all nations." Matthew 28:18-20

The basis of missionary appeals is the authority of Jesus Christ, not the needs of the heathen. We are apt to look upon Our Lord as One Who assists us in our enterprises for God. Our Lord puts Himself as the absolute sovereign supreme Lord over His disciples. He does not say the heathen will be lost if we do not go; He simply says - "Go ye therefore and teach all nations." Go on the revelation of My sovereignty; teach and preach out of a living experience of Me. "Then the eleven disciples went . . unto a mountain where Jesus had appointed them." v. 16. If I want to know the universal sovereignty of Christ, I must know Him for myself, and how to get alone with Him; I must take time to worship the Being Whose Name I bear. "Come unto Me" - that is the place to meet Jesus. Are you weary and heavy laden? How many missionaries are! We banish those marvellous words of the universal Sovereign of the world to the threshold of an after-meeting; they are the words of Jesus to His disciples. "Go ye therefore. . . ." Go simply means live. Acts 1:8 is the description of how to go. Jesus did not say - Go into Jerusalem and

Judea and Samaria, but, "Ye shall be witnesses unto Me" in all these places. He undertakes to establish the goings. "If ye abide in Me, and My words abide in you. . . " - that is the way to keep going in our personal lives. Where we are placed is a matter of indifference; God engineers the goings. "None of these things move me, neither count I my life dear unto myself . . ." That is how to keep going till we're gone.

October 15
THE KEY TO THE MISSIONARY MESSAGE

And He is the propitiation for our sins: and not for ours only, but also for the sins of the whole world." 1 John 2:2

The key to the missionary message is the propitiation of Christ Jesus. Take any phase of Christ's work - the healing phase, the saving and sanctifying phase; there is nothing limitless about those. "The Lamb of God which taketh away the sin of the world! " - that is limitless. The missionary message is the limitless significance of Jesus Christ as the propitiation for our sins, and a missionary is one who is soaked in that revelation. The key to the missionary message is the remissionary aspect of Christ's life, not His kindness and His goodness, and His revealing of the Fatherhood of God; the great limitless significance is that He is the propitiation for our sins. The missionary message is not patriotic, it is irrespective of nations and of individuals, it is for the whole world. When the Holy Ghost comes in He does not consider my predilections, He brings me into union with the Lord Jesus. A missionary is one who is wedded to the charter of his Lord and Master, he has not to proclaim his own point of view, but to proclaim the Lamb of God. It is easier to belong to a coterie which tells what Jesus Christ has done for me, easier to become a devotee to Divine healing, or to a special type of sanctification, or to the baptism of the Holy Ghost. Paul did not say - "Woe is unto me, if I do not preach what Christ has done for me," but - "Woe is unto me, if I preach not the gospel." This is the Gospel - "The Lamb of God, which taketh away the sin of the world!"

October 16
THE KEY TO THE MASTER'S ORDERS

"Pray ye therefore the Lord of the harvest, that He will send forth labourers into His harvest." Matthew 9:38

The key to the missionary problem is in the hand of God, and that key is prayer not work, that is, not work as the word is popularly understood to-day because that may mean the evasion of concentration on God. The key to the missionary problem is not the key of common sense, nor the medical key, nor the key of civilization or education or even evangelization. The key is prayer. "Pray ye therefore the Lord of the harvest." Naturally, prayer is not practical, it is absurd; we have to realize that prayer is stupid from the ordinary common-sense point of view. There are no nations in Jesus Christ's outlook, but the world. How many of us pray without respect of persons, and with respect to only one Person, Jesus Christ? He owns the harvest that is produced by distress and conviction of sin, and this is the harvest we have to pray that labourers may be thrust out to reap. We are taken up with active work while people all round are ripe to harvest, and we do not reap one of them, but waste our Lord's time in over-energized activities. Suppose the crisis comes in your father's life, in your brother's life, are you there as a labourer to reap the harvest for Jesus Christ? "Oh, but I have a special work to do!" No Christian has a special work to do. A Christian is called to be Jesus Christ's own, one who is not above his Master, one who does not dictate to Jesus Christ what he intends to do. Our Lord calls to no special work: He calls to Himself. "Pray ye therefore the Lord of the harvest," and He will engineer circumstances and thrust you out.

October 17
GREATER WORKS

"And greater works than these shall he do; because I go unto My Father." John 14:12

Prayer does not fit us for the greater works; prayer is the greater work. We think of prayer as a common-sense exercise of our higher powers in order to prepare us for God's work. In the teaching of Jesus Christ prayer is the working of the miracle of Redemption in me which produces the miracle of Redemption in others by the power of God. The way fruit remains is by prayer, but remember it is prayer based on the agony of Redemption, not on my agony. Only a child gets prayer answered; a wise man does not. Prayer is the battle; it is a matter of indifference where you are. Whichever way God engineers circumstances, the duty is to pray. Never allow the thought - "I am of no use where I am;" because you certainly can be of no use where you are not. Wherever God has dumped you down in circumstances pray, ejaculate to Him all the time. "Whatsoever ye ask in My name, that will I do." We won't pray unless we get thrills, that is the intensest form of spiritual selfishness. We have to labour along the line of God's direction, and He says pray. "Pray ye therefore the Lord of the harvest, that He will send forth labourers into His harvest." There is nothing thrilling about a labouring man's work, but it is the labouring man who makes the conceptions of the genius possible; and it is the labouring saint who makes the conceptions of his Master possible. You labour at prayer and results happen all the time from His standpoint. What an astonishment it will be to find, when the veil is lifted, the souls that have been reaped by you, simply because you had been in the habit of taking your orders from Jesus Christ.

October 18
THE KEY TO MISSIONARY DEVOTION

"For His name's sake they went forth." 3 John 7

Our Lord has told us how love to Him is to manifest itself. "Lovest thou Me?" "Feed My sheep" - identify yourself with My interests in other people, not, identify Me with your interests in other people. 1 Corinthians 13:4-8 gives the character of this love, it is the love of God expressing itself. The test of my love for Jesus is the practical one, all the rest is sentimental jargon. Loyalty to Jesus Christ is the supernatural work of Redemption wrought in me by the Holy Ghost Who sheds abroad the love of God in my heart, and that love works efficaciously through me in contact with everyone I meet. I remain loyal to His Name although every common-sense fact gives the lie to Him, and declares that He has no more power than a morning mist. The key to missionary devotion means being attached to nothing and no one saving Our Lord Himself, not being detached from things externally. Our Lord was amazingly in and out among ordinary things; His detachment was on the inside towards God. External detachment is often an indication of a secret vital attachment to the things we keep away from externally. The loyalty of a missionary is to keep his soul concentratedly open to the nature of the Lord Jesus Christ. The men and women Our Lord sends out on His enterprises are the ordinary human stuff, plus dominating devotion to Himself wrought by the Holy Ghost.

October 19
THE UNHEEDED SECRET

"My kingdom is not of this world." John 18:36

The great enemy to the Lord Jesus Christ in the present day is the conception of practical work that has not come from the New Testament, but from the Systems of the world in which endless energy and activities are insisted upon, but no private life with God. The emphasis is put on the wrong thing. Jesus said, "The kingdom of God cometh not with observation, for lo the kingdom of God is within you," a hidden, obscure thing. An active Christian worker too often lives in the shop window. It is the innermost of the innermost that reveals the power of the life. We have to get rid of the plague of the spirit of the religious age in which we live. In Our Lord's life there was none of the press and rush of tremendous activity that we regard so highly, and the disciple is to be as His Master. The central thing about the kingdom of Jesus Christ is a personal relationship to Himself, not public usefulness to men. It is not its practical activities that are the strength of this Bible Training College, its whole strength lies in the fact that here you are put into soak before God. You have no idea of where God is going to engineer your circumstances, no knowledge of what strain is going to be put on you either at home or abroad, and if you waste your time in over-active energies instead of getting into soak on the great fundamental truths of God's Redemption, you will snap when the strain comes; but if this time of soaking before God is being spent in getting rooted and grounded in God on the unpractical line, you will remain true to Him what ever happens.

October 20
IS GOD'S WILL MY WILL?

"This is the will of God, even your sanctification." 1 Thessalonians 4:3

It is not a question of whether God is willing to sanctify me; is it my will? Am I willing to let God do in me all that has been made possible by the Atonement? Am I willing to let Jesus be made sanctification to me, and to let the life of Jesus be manifested in my mortal flesh? Beware of saying - Oh, I am longing to be sanctified. You are not, stop longing and make it a matter of transaction - "Nothing in my hands I bring." Receive Jesus Christ to be made sanctification to you in implicit faith, and the great marvel of the Atonement of Jesus will be made real in you. All that Jesus made possible is made mine by the free loving gift of God on the ground of what He performed, my attitude as a saved and sanctified soul is that of profound humble holiness (there is no such thing as proud holiness), a holiness based on agonizing repentance and a sense of unspeakable shame and degradation; and also on the amazing realization that the love of God commended itself to me in that while I cared nothing about Him, He completed everything for my salvation and sanctification (see Rom. 5:8. R.V.). No wonder Paul says nothing is "able to separate us from the love of God, which is in Christ Jesus our Lord." Sanctification makes me one with Jesus Christ, and in Him one with God, and it is done only through the superb Atonement of Christ. Never put the effect as the cause. The effect in me is obedience and service and prayer, and is the out come of speechless thanks and adoration for the marvellous sanctification wrought out in me because of the Atonement.

October 21
DIRECTION BY IMPULSE

"Building up yourselves on your most holy faith." Jude 20

There was nothing either of the nature of impulse or of coldbloodedness about Our Lord, but only a calm strength that never got into panic. Most of us develop our Christianity along the line of our temperament, not along the line of God. Impulse is a trait in natural life, but Our Lord always ignores it, because it hinders the development of the life of a disciple. Watch how the Spirit of God checks impulse, His checks bring a rush of self-conscious foolishness which makes us instantly want to vindicate ourselves. Impulse is all right in a child, but it is disastrous in a man or woman; an impulsive man is always a petted man. Impulse has to be trained into intuition by discipline. Discipleship is built entirely on the supernatural grace of God. Walking on the water is easy to impulsive pluck, but walking on dry land as a disciple of Jesus Christ is a different thing. Peter walked on the water to go to Jesus, but he followed Him afar off on the land. We do not need the grace of God to stand crises, human nature and pride are sufficient, we can face the strain magnificently; but it does require the supernatural grace of God to live twenty-four hours in every day as a saint, to go through drudgery as a disciple, to live an ordinary, unobserved, ignored existence as a disciple of Jesus. It is inbred in us that we have to do exceptional things for God; but we have not. We have to be exceptional in the ordinary things, to be holy in mean streets, among mean people, and this is not learned in five minutes.

October 22
THE WITNESS OF THE SPIRIT

"The Spirit Himself beareth witness with our spirit. . ." Romans 8:16 (R.V.)

We are in danger of getting the barter spirit when we come to God, we want the witness before we have done what God tells us to do. "Why does not God reveal Himself to me?" He cannot, it is not that He will not, but He cannot, because you are in the road as long as you won't abandon absolutely to Him. Immediately you do, God witnesses to Himself, He cannot witness to you, but He witnesses instantly to His own nature in you. If you had the witness before the reality, it would end in sentimental emotion. Immediately you transact on the Redemption, and stop the impertinence of debate, God gives on the witness. As soon as you abandon reasoning and argument, God witnesses to what He has done, and we are amazed at our impertinence in having kept Him waiting. If you are in debate as to whether God can deliver from sin, either let Him do it, or tell Him He cannot. Do not quote this and that person, try Matthew 11:28 - "Come unto Me." Come, if you are weary and heavy laden; ask, if you know you are evil (Luke 11:13). The Spirit of God witnesses to the Redemption of Our Lord, He does not witness to anything else; He cannot witness to our reason. The simplicity that comes from our natural common-sense decisions is apt to be mistaken for the witness of the Spirit, but the Spirit witnesses only to His own nature, and to the work of Redemption, never to our reason. If we try to make Him witness to our reason, it is no wonder we are in darkness and perplexity. Fling it all overboard, trust in Him, and He will give the witness.

October 23
NOT A BIT OF IT!

"If any man be in Christ, he is a new creature: old things are passed away." 2 Corinthians 5:17

Our Lord never nurses our prejudices, He mortifies them, runs clean athwart them. We imagine that God has a special interest in our particular prejudices; we are quite sure that God will never deal with us as He has to deal with other people. "God must deal with other people in a very stern way, but of course He knows that my prejudices are all right." We have to learn - "Not a bit of it!" Instead of God being on the side of our prejudices, He is deliberately wiping them out. It is part of our moral education to have our prejudices run straight across by His providence, and to watch how He does it. God pays no respect to anything we bring to Him. There is only one thing God wants of us, and that is our unconditional surrender. When we are born again, the Holy Spirit begins to work His new creation in us, and there will come a time when there is not a bit of the old order left, the old solemnity goes, the old attitude to things goes, and "all things are of God." How are we going to get the life that has no lust, no self-interest, no sensitiveness to pokes, the love that is not provoked, that thinketh no evil, that is always kind? The only way is by allowing not a bit of the old life to be left; but only simple perfect trust in God, such trust that we no longer want God's blessings, but only want Himself. Have we come to the place where God can withdraw His blessings and it does not affect our trust in Him? When once we see God at work, we will never bother our heads about things that happen, because we are actually trusting in our Father in Heaven Whom the world cannot see.

October 24
THE VIEWPOINT

"Now thanks be to God, which always causeth us to triumph in Christ." 2 Corinthians 2:14

The viewpoint of a worker for God must not be as near the highest as he can get, it must be the highest. Be careful to maintain strenuously God's point of view, it has to be done every day, bit by bit; don't think on the finite. No outside power can touch the viewpoint. The viewpoint to maintain is that we are here for one purpose only, viz., to be captives in the train of Christ's triumphs. We are not in God's showroom, we are here to exhibit one thing - the absolute captivity of our lives to Jesus Christ. How small the other points of view are - I am standing alone battling for Jesus; I have to maintain the cause of Christ and hold this fort for Him. Paul says - I am in the train of a conqueror, and it does not matter what the difficulties are, I am always led in triumph. Is this idea being worked out practically in us? Paul's secret joy was that God took him, a red-handed rebel against Jesus Christ, and made him a captive, and now that is all he is here for. Paul's joy was to be a captive of the Lord, he had no other interest in heaven or in earth. It is a shameful thing for a Christian to talk about getting the victory. The Victor ought to have got us so completely that it is His victory all the time, and we are more than conquerors through Him. "For we are unto God a sweet savour of Christ." We are enwheeled with the odour of Jesus, and wherever we go we are a wonderful refreshment to God.

October 25
THE ETERNAL CRUSH OF THINGS

"I am made all things to all men, that I might by all means save some." 1 Corinthians 9:22

A Christian worker has to learn how to be God's noble man or woman amid a crowd of ignoble things. Never make this plea - If only I were somewhere else! All God's men are ordinary men made extraordinary by the matter He has given them. Unless we have the right matter in our minds intellectually and in our hearts affectionately, we will be hustled out of usefulness to God. We are not workers for God by choice. Many people deliberately choose to be workers, but they have no matter in them of God's almighty grace, no matter of His mighty word. Paul's whole heart and mind and soul were taken up with the great matter of what Jesus Christ came to do, he never lost sight of that one thing. We have to face ourselves with the one central fact - Jesus Christ and Him crucified. "I have chosen you." Keep that note of greatness in your creed. It is not that you have got God but that He has got you. Here, in this College, God is at work, bending, breaking, moulding, doing just as He chooses. Why He is doing it, we do not know; He is doing it for one purpose only - that He may be able to say, This is My man, My woman. We have to be in God's hand so that He can plant men on the Rock as He has planted us. Never choose to be a worker, but when God has put His call on you, woe be to you if you turn to the right hand or to the left. He will do with you what He never did with you before the call came; He will do with you what He is not doing with other people. Let Him have His way.

October 26
WHAT IS A MISSIONARY?

"As My Father hath sent Me, even so send I you." John 20:21

A missionary is one sent by Jesus Christ as He was sent by God. The great dominant note is not the needs of men, but the command of Jesus. The source of our inspiration in work for God is behind, not before. The tendency to-day is to put the inspiration ahead, to sweep everything in front of us and bring it all out to our conception of success. In the New Testament the inspiration is put behind us, the Lord Jesus. The ideal is to be true to Him, to carry out His enterprises. Personal attachment to the Lord Jesus and His point of view is the one thing that must not be overlooked. In missionary enterprise the great danger is that God's call is effaced by the needs of the people until human sympathy absolutely overwhelms the meaning of being sent by Jesus. The needs are so enormous, the conditions so perplexing, that every power of mind falters and fails. We forget that the one great reason underneath all missionary enterprise is not first the elevation of the people, nor the education of the people, nor their needs; but first and foremost the command of Jesus Christ - "Go ye therefore, and teach all nations." When looking back on the lives of men and women of God the tendency is to say - What wonderfully astute wisdom they had! How perfectly they understood all God wanted! The astute mind behind is the Mind of God, not human wisdom at all. We give credit to human wisdom when we should give credit to the Divine guidance of God through childlike people who were foolish enough to trust God's wisdom and the supernatural equipment of God.

October 27
THE METHOD OF MISSIONS

"Go ye therefore, and teach (disciple) all nations." Matthew 28:19

Jesus Christ did not say - Go and save souls (the salvation of souls is the supernatural work of God), but - "Go and teach," i.e., disciple, "all nations," and you cannot make disciples unless you are a disciple yourself. When the disciples came back from their first mission they were filled with joy because the devils were subject to them, and Jesus said - Don't rejoice in successful service; the great secret of joy is that you are rightly related to Me. The great essential of the missionary is that he remains true to the call of God, and realizes that his one purpose is to disciple men and women to Jesus. There is a passion for souls that does not spring from God, but from the desire to make converts to our point of view. The challenge to the missionary does not come on the line that people are difficult to get saved, that backsliders are difficult to reclaim, that there is a wadge of callous indifference; but along the line of his own personal relationship to Jesus Christ. "Believe ye that I am able to do this?" Our Lord puts that question steadily, it faces us in every individual case we meet. The one great challenge is - Do I know my Risen Lord? Do I know the power of His indwelling Spirit? Am I wise enough in God's sight, and foolish enough according to the world, to bank on what Jesus Christ has said, or am I abandoning the great supernatural position, which is the only call for a missionary, viz., boundless confidence in Christ Jesus? If I take up any other method I depart altogether from the methods laid down by Our Lord - "All power is given unto Me . . , therefore go ye."

October 28
JUSTIFICATION BY FAITH

"For if, when we were enemies, we were reconciled to God by the death of His Son, much more, being reconciled, we shall be saved by His life." Romans 5:10

I am not saved by believing; I realize I am saved by believing. It is not repentance that saves me, repentance is the sign that I realize what God has done in Christ Jesus. The danger is to put the emphasis on the effect instead of on the cause. It is my obedience that puts me right with God, my consecration. Never! I am put right with God because prior to all, Christ died. When I turn to God and by belief accept what God reveals I can accept, instantly the stupendous Atonement of Jesus Christ rushes me into a right relationship with God; and by the supernatural miracle of God's grace I stand justified, not because I am sorry for my sin, not because I have repented, but because of what Jesus has done. The Spirit of God brings it with a breaking, all-over light, and I know, though I do not know how, that I am saved. The salvation of God does not stand on human logic, it stands on the sacrificial Death of Jesus. We can be born again because of the Atonement of Our Lord. Sinful men and women can be changed into new creatures, not by their repentance or their belief, but by the marvellous work of God in Christ Jesus which is prior to all experience. The impregnable safety of justification and sanctification is God Himself. We have not to work out these things ourselves; they have been worked out by the Atonement. The supernatural becomes natural by the miracle of God; there is the realization of what Jesus Christ has already done - "It is finished."

October 29
SUBSTITUTION

"He hath made Him to be sin for us . . . that we might be made the righteousness of God. . ." 2 Corinthians 5:.21

The modern view of the death of Jesus is that He died for our sins out of sympathy. The New Testament view is that He bore our sin not by sympathy, but by identification. He was made to be sin. Our sins are removed because of the death of Jesus, and the explanation of His death is His obedience to His Father, not His sympathy with us. We are acceptable with God not because we have obeyed, or because we have promised to give up things, but because of the death of Christ, and in no other way. We say that Jesus Christ came to reveal the Fatherhood of God, the loving-kindness of God; the New Testament says He came to bear away the sin of the world. The revelation of His Father is to those to whom He has been introduced as Saviour. Jesus Christ never spoke of Himself to the world as one Who revealed the Father, but as a stumbling block (see John 15:22- 24). John 14:9 was spoken to His disciples. That Christ died for me, therefore I go scot free, is never taught in the New Testament. What is taught in the New Testament is that "He died for all" (not - He died my death), and that by identification with His death I can be freed from sin, and have imparted to me His very righteousness. The substitution taught in the New Testament is twofold: "He hath made Him to be sin for us, who knew no sin; that we might be made the righteousness of God in Him." It is not Christ for me unless I am determined to have Christ formed in me.

October 30
FAITH

"Without faith it is impossible to please Him." Hebrews 11:6

Faith in antagonism to common sense is fanaticism, and common sense in antagonism to faith is rationalism. The life of faith brings the two into a right relation. Common sense is not faith, and faith is not common sense; they stand in the relation of the natural and the spiritual; of impulse and inspiration. Nothing Jesus Christ ever said is common sense, it is revelation sense, and it reaches the shores where common sense fails. Faith must be tried before the reality of faith is actual. "We know that all things work together for good," then no matter what happens, the alchemy of God's providence transfigures the ideal faith into actual reality. Faith always works on the personal line, the whole purpose of God being to see that the ideal faith is made real in His children. For every detail of the common-sense life, there is a revelation fact of God whereby we can prove in practical experience what we believe God to be. Faith is a tremendously active principle which always puts Jesus Christ first - Lord, Thou hast said so and so (e.g., Matthew 6:33), it looks mad, but I am going to venture on Thy word. To turn head faith into a personal possession is a fight always, not sometimes. God brings us into circumstances in order to educate our faith, because the nature of faith is to make its object real. Until we know Jesus, God is a mere abstraction, we can not have faith in Him; but immediately we hear Jesus say - "He that hath seen Me hath seen the Father," we have something that is real, and faith is boundless. Faith is the whole man rightly related to God by the power of the Spirit of Jesus Christ.

October 31
DISCERNMENT OF FAITH

"Faith as a grain of mustard seed. . ." Matthew 17:20

We have the idea that God rewards us for our faith, it may be so in the initial stages; but we do not earn anything by faith, faith brings us into right relationship with God and gives God His opportunity. God has frequently to knock the bottom board out of your experience if you are a saint in order to get you into contact with Himself. God wants you to understand that it is a life of faith, not a life of sentimental enjoyment of His blessings. Your earlier life of faith was narrow and intense, settled around a little sun-spot of experience that had as much of sense as of faith in it, full of light and sweetness; then God withdrew His conscious blessings in order to teach you to walk by faith. You are worth far more to Him now than you were in your days of conscious delight and thrilling testimony. Faith by its very nature must be tried, and the real trial of faith is not that we find it difficult to trust God, but that God's character has to be cleared in our own minds. Faith in its actual working out has to go through spells of unsyllabled isolation. Never confound the trial of faith with the ordinary discipline of life, much that we call the trial of faith is the inevitable result of being alive. Faith in the Bible is faith in God against everything that contradicts Him - I will remain true to God's character whatever He may do. "Though He slay me, yet will I trust Him" - this is the most sublime utterance of faith in the whole of the Bible.

November 1
YE ARE NOT YOUR OWN

"Know ye not that . . ye are not your own?" 1 Corinthians 6:19

There is no such thing as a private life - "a world within the world" - for a man or woman who is brought into fellowship with Jesus Christ's sufferings. God breaks up the private life of His saints, and makes it a thoroughfare for the world on the one hand and for Himself on the other. No human being can stand that unless he is identified with Jesus Christ. We are not sanctified for ourselves, we are called into the fellowship of the Gospel, and things happen which have nothing to do with us, God is getting us into fellowship with Himself. Let Him have His way, if you do not, instead of being of the slightest use to God in His Redemptive work in the world, you will be a hindrance and a clog. The first thing God does with us is to get us based on rugged Reality until we do not care what becomes of us individually as long as He gets His way for the purpose of His Redemption. Why shouldn't we go through heartbreaks? Through those doorways God is opening up ways of fellowship with His Son. Most of us fall and collapse at the first grip of pain; we sit down on the threshold of God's purpose and die away of self-pity, and all so called Christian sympathy will aid us to our death bed. But God will not. He comes with the grip of the pierced hand of His Son, and says - "Enter into fellowship with Me; arise and shine." If through a broken heart God can bring His purposes to pass in the world, then thank Him for breaking your heart.

November 2
AUTHORITY AND INDEPENDENCE

"If ye love Me, ye will keep My commandments." John 14:15 (R.V.)

Our Lord never insists upon obedience; He tells us very emphatically what we ought to do, but He never takes means to make us do it. We have to obey Him out of a oneness of spirit. That is why whenever Our Lord talked about discipleship, He prefaced it with an IF - you do not need to unless you like. "If any man will be My disciple, let him deny himself," let him give up his right to himself to Me. Our Lord is not talking of eternal positions, but of being of value to Himself in this order of things, that is why He sounds so stern (cf. Luke 14:26). Never interpret these words apart from the One Who uttered them. The Lord does not give me rules, He makes His standard very clear, and if my relationship to Him is that of love, I will do what He says without any hesitation. If I hesitate, it is because I love some one else in competition with Him, viz., myself. Jesus Christ will not help me to obey Him, I must obey Him; and when I do obey Him, I fulfil my spiritual destiny. My personal life may be crowded with small petty incidents, altogether unnoticeable and mean; but if I obey Jesus Christ in the haphazard circumstances, they become pinholes through which I see the face of God, and when I stand face to face with God I will discover that through my obedience thousands were blessed. When once God's Redemption comes to the point of obedience in a human soul, it always creates. If I obey Jesus Christ, the Redemption of God will rush through me to other lives, because behind the deed of obedience is the Reality of Almighty God.

November 3
A BOND-SLAVE OF JESUS

"I am crucified with Christ; nevertheless I live; yet not I, but Christ liveth in me." Galatians 2:20

These words mean the breaking of my independence with my own hand and surrendering to the supremacy of the Lord Jesus. No one can do this for me, I must do it myself. God may bring me up to the point three hundred and sixty-five times a year, but He cannot put me through it. It means breaking the husk of my individual independence of God, and the emancipating of my personality into oneness with Himself, not for my own ideas, but for absolute loyalty to Jesus. There is no possibility of dispute when once I am there. Very few of us know anything about loyalty to Christ - "For My sake." It is that which makes the iron saint. Has that break come? All the rest is pious fraud. The one point to decide is - Will I give up, will I surrender to Jesus Christ, and make no conditions whatever as to how the break comes? I must be broken from my self-realization, and immediately that point is reached, the reality of the supernatural identification takes place at once, and the witness of the

Spirit of God is unmistakable - "I have been crucified with Christ." The passion of Christianity is that I deliberately sign away my own rights and become a bond-slave of Jesus Christ. Until I do that, I do not begin to be a saint. One student a year who hears God's call would be sufficient for God to have called this College into existence. This College as an organization is not worth anything, it is not academic; it is for nothing else but for God to help Himself to lives. Is He going to help Himself to us, or are we taken up with our conception of what we are going to be?

November 4
THE AUTHORITY OF REALITY

"Draw nigh to God, and He will draw nigh to you." James 4:8

It is essential to give people a chance of acting on the truth of God. The responsibility must be left with the individual, you cannot act for him, it must be his own deliberate act, but the evangelical message ought always to lead a man to act. The paralysis of refusing to act leaves a man exactly where he was before; when once he acts, he is never the same. It is the foolishness of it that stands in the way of hundreds who have been convicted by the Spirit of God. Immediately I precipitate myself over into an act, that second I live; all the rest is existence. The moments when I truly live are the moments when I act with my whole will. Never allow a truth of God that is brought home to your soul to pass without acting on it, not necessarily physically, but in will. Record it, with ink or with blood. The feeblest saint who transacts business with Jesus Christ is emancipated the second he acts; all the almighty power of God is on his behalf. We come up to the truth of God, we confess we are wrong, but go back again; then we come up to it again, and go back; until we learn that we have no business to go back. We have to go clean over on some word of our redeeming Lord and transact business with Him. His word "come" means "transact." "Come unto Me." The last thing we do is to come; but everyone who does come knows that that second the supernatural rush of the life of God invades him instantly. The dominating power of the world, the flesh and the devil is paralysed, not by your act, but because your act has linked you on to God and His redemptive power.

November 5
PARTAKERS OF HIS SUFFERINGS

"Rejoice, inasmuch as ye are partakers of Christ's sufferings." 1 Peter 4:13

If you are going to be used by God, He will take you through a multitude of experiences that are not meant for you at all, they are meant to make you useful in His hands, and to enable you to understand what transpires in other souls so that you will never be surprised at what you come across. Oh, I can't deal with that person. Why not? God gave you ample opportunity to soak before Him on that line, and you barged off because it seemed stupid to spend time in that way. The sufferings of Christ are not those of ordinary men. He suffered "according to the will of God," not from the point of view we suffer from as individuals. It is only when we are related to Jesus Christ that we can understand what God is after in His dealings with us. It is part of Christian culture to know what God's aim is. In the history of the Christian Church the tendency has been to evade being identified with the sufferings of Jesus Christ; men have sought to procure the carrying out of God's order by a short cut of their own. God's way is always the way of suffering, the way of the "long, long trail." Are we partakers of Christ's sufferings? Are we prepared for God to stamp our personal ambitions right out? Are we prepared for God to destroy by transfiguration our individual determinations? It will not mean that we know exactly why God is taking us that way, that would make us spiritual prigs. We never realize at the time what God is putting us through; we go through it more or less misunderstandingly; then we come to a luminous place, and say - ' 'Why, God has girded me, though I did not know it!"

November 6
PROGRAMME OF BELIEF

"Believest thou this?" John 11:26

Martha believed in the power at the disposal of Jesus Christ, she believed that if He had been present He could have healed her brother; she also believed that Jesus had a peculiar intimacy with God and that whatever He asked of God, God would do; but she needed a closer personal intimacy with Jesus. Martha's programme of belief had its fulfilment in the future; Jesus led her on until her belief became a personal possession, and then slowly emerged into a particular inheritance - "Yea, Lord, I believe that Thou art the Christ. . . " Is there something like that in the Lord's dealings with you? Is Jesus educating you into a personal intimacy with Himself? Let Him press home His question to you - "Believest thou this?" What is your ordeal of doubt? Have you come, like Martha, to some overwhelming passage in your circumstances where your programme of belief is about to emerge into a personal belief? This can never be until a personal need arises out of a personal problem. To believe is to commit. In the programme of mental belief I commit myself, and abandon all that is not related to that commitment. In personal belief I commit myself morally to this way of confidence and refuse to compromise with any other; and in particular belief I commit myself spiritually to Jesus Christ, and determine in that thing to be dominated by the Lord alone. When I stand face to face with Jesus Christ and He says to me – "Believest thou this?" I find that faith is as natural as breathing, and I am staggered that I was so stupid as not to trust Him before.

November 7
THE UNDETECTED SACREDNESS OF CIRCUMSTANCES

All things work together for good to them that love God." Romans 8:28

The circumstances of a saint's life are ordained of God. In the life of a saint there is no such thing as chance. God by His providence brings you into circumstances that you cannot understand at all, but the Spirit of God understands. God is bringing you into places and among people and into conditions in order that the intercession of the Spirit in you may take a particular line. Never put your hand in front of the circumstances and say – I am going to be my own providence here, I must watch this, and guard that. All your circumstances are in the hand of God, therefore never think it strange concerning the circumstances you are in. Your part in intercessory prayer is not to enter into the agony of intercession, but to utilize the common-sense circumstances God puts you in, and the common- sense people He puts you amongst by His providence, to bring them before God's throne and give the Spirit in you a chance to intercede for them. In this way God is going to sweep the whole world with His saints. Am I making the Holy Spirit's work difficult by being indefinite, or by trying to do His work for Him? I must do the human side of intercession, and the human side is the circumstances I am in and the people I am in contact with. I have to keep my conscious life as a shrine of the Holy Ghost, then as I bring the different ones before God, the Holy Spirit makes intercession for them. Your intercessions can never be mine, and my intercessions can never be yours, but the Holy Ghost makes intercession in our particular lives, without which intercession someone will be impoverished.

November 8
THE UNRIVALLED POWER OF PRAYER

"We know not what we should pray for as we ought: but the Spirit itself maketh intercession for us with groanings which cannot be uttered." Romans 8:26

We realize that we are energized by the Holy Spirit for prayer; we know what it is to pray in the Spirit; but we do not so often realize that the Holy Spirit Himself prays in us prayers which we cannot utter. When we are born again of God and are indwelt by the Spirit of God, He expresses for us the unutterable. "He," the Spirit in you, "maketh intercession for the saints according to the will of God," and God searches your heart not to know what your conscious prayers are, but to find out what is the prayer of the Holy Spirit. The Spirit of God needs the nature of the believer as a shrine in which to offer His intercession. "Your body is the temple of the Holy Ghost." When Jesus Christ cleansed the temple, He "would not suffer that any man should carry any vessel through the temple." The Spirit of God will not allow you to use your body for your own convenience. Jesus ruthlessly cast out all them that sold and bought in the temple, and said - "My house shall be called the house of prayer; but ye have made it a den of thieves." Have we recognized that our body is the temple of the Holy Ghost? If so, we must be careful to keep it undefiled for Him. We have to remember that our conscious life, though it is only a tiny bit of our personality, is to be regarded by us as a shrine of the Holy Ghost. He will look after the unconscious part that we know nothing of; but we must see that we guard the conscious part for which we are responsible.

November 9
SACRAMENTAL SERVICE

"Who now rejoice in my sufferings for you, and fill up that which is behind of the afflictions of Christ. . . ." Colossians 1:24

The Christian worker has to be a sacramental "go-between," to be so identified with his Lord and the reality of His Redemption that He can continually bring His creating life through him. It is not the strength of one man's personality being superimposed on another, but the real presence of Christ coming through the elements of the worker's life. When we preach the historic facts of the life and death of Our Lord as they are conveyed in the New Testament, our words are made sacramental, God uses them on the ground of His Redemption to create in those who listen that which is not created otherwise. If we preach the effects of Redemption in human life instead of the revelation regarding Jesus, the result in those who listen is not new birth, but refined spiritual culture, and the Spirit of God cannot witness to it because such preaching is in another domain. We have to see that we are in such living sympathy with God that as we proclaim His truth He can create in souls the things which He alone can do. What a wonderful personality! What a fascinating man! Such marvellous insight! What chance has the Gospel of God through all that? It cannot get through, because the line of attraction is always the line of appeal. If a man attracts by his personality, his appeal is along that line; if he is identified with his Lord's personality, then the appeal is along the line of what Jesus Christ can do. The danger is to glory in men; Jesus says we are to lift Him up.

November 10
FELLOWSHIP IN THE GOSPEL

"Fellow labourer in the gospel of Christ." 1 Thessalonians 3:2

After sanctification it is difficult to state what your aim in life is, because God has taken you up into His purpose by the Holy Ghost; He is using you now for His purposes throughout the world as He used His Son for the purpose of our salvation. If you seek great things for yourself - God has called me for this and that; you are putting a barrier to God's use of you. As long as you have a personal interest in your own character, or any set ambition, you cannot get through into identification with God's interests. You can only get there by losing for ever any idea of yourself and by letting God take you right out into His purpose for the world, and because your goings are of the Lord, you can never understand your ways. I have to learn that the aim in life is God's, not mine. God is using me from His great personal standpoint, and all He asks of me is that I trust Him, and never say - Lord, this gives me such heart-ache. To talk in that way makes me a clog. When I stop telling God what I want, He can catch me up for what He wants without let or hindrance. He can crumple me up or exalt me, He can do anything He chooses. He simply asks me to have implicit faith in Himself and in His goodness. Self pity is of the devil, if I go off on that line I cannot be used by God for His purpose in the world. I have "a world within the world" in which I live, and God will never be able to get me outside it because I am afraid of being frost-bitten.

November 11
THE SUPREME CLIMB

"Take now thy son ." Genesis 22:2

God's command is - Take now, not presently. It is extraordinary how we debate! We know a thing is right, but we try to find excuses for not doing it at once. To climb to the height God shows can never be done presently, it must be done now. The sacrifice is gone through in will before it is performed actually. "And Abraham rose up early in the morning and went unto the place of which God had told him" (v. 3). The wonderful simplicity of Abraham! When God spoke, he did not confer with flesh and blood. Beware when you want to confer with flesh and blood, i.e., your own sympathies, your own insight, anything that is not based on your personal relationship to God. These are the things that compete with and hinder obedience to God. Abraham did not choose the sacrifice. Always guard against self- chosen service for God; self-sacrifice may be a disease. If God has made your cup sweet, drink it with grace; if He has made it bitter, drink it in communion with Him. If the providential order of God for you is a hard time of difficulty, go through with it, but never choose the scene of your martyrdom. God chose the crucible for Abraham, and Abraham made no demur; he went steadily through. If you are not living in touch with Him, it is easy to pass a crude verdict on God. You must go through the crucible before you have any right to pronounce a verdict, because in the crucible you learn to know God better. God is working for His highest ends until His purpose and man's purpose become one.

November 12
THE TRANSFIGURED LIFE

"If any man be in Christ, he is a new creature; old things are passed away; behold, all things are become new." 2 Corinthians 5:17

What idea have you of the salvation of your soul? The experience of salvation means that in your actual life things are really altered, you no longer look at things as you used to; your desires are new, old things have lost their power. One of the touchstones of experience is - Has God altered the thing that matters? If you still hanker after the old things, it is absurd to talk about being born from above, you are juggling with yourself. If you are born again, the Spirit of God makes the alteration manifest in your actual life and reasoning, and when the crisis comes you are the most amazed person on earth at the wonderful difference there is in you. There is no possibility of imagining that you did it. It is this complete and amazing alteration that is the evidence that you are a saved soul. What difference has my salvation and sanctification made? For instance, can I stand in the light of 1 Corinthians 13, or do I have to shuffle? The salvation that is worked out in me by the Holy Ghost emancipates me entirely, and as long as I walk in the light as God is in the light, He sees nothing to censure because His life is working out in every particular, not to my consciousness, but deeper than my consciousness.

November 13
FAITH AND EXPERIENCE

"The Son of God, who loved me, and gave Himself for me." Galatians 2:20

We have to battle through our moods into absolute devotion to the Lord Jesus, to get out of the hole-and-corner business of our experience into abandoned devotion to Him. Think Who the New Testament says that Jesus Christ is, and then think of the despicable meanness of the miserable faith we have - I haven't had this and that experience! Think what faith in Jesus Christ claims - that He can present us faultless before the throne of God, unutterably pure, absolutely rectified and profoundly justified. Stand in implicit adoring faith in Him, He is made unto us "wisdom, and righteousness, and sanctification, and redemption." How can we talk of making a sacrifice for the Son of God! Our salvation is from hell and perdition, and then we talk about making sacrifices! We have to get out into faith in Jesus Christ continually; not a prayer meeting Jesus Christ, nor a book Jesus Christ, but the New Testament Jesus Christ, Who is God Incarnate, and Who ought to strike us to His feet as dead. Our faith must be in the One from Whom our experience springs. Jesus Christ wants our absolute abandon of devotion to Himself. We never can experience Jesus Christ, nor ever hold Him within the compass of our own hearts, but our faith must be built in strong emphatic confidence in Him. It is along this line that we see the rugged impatience of the Holy Ghost against unbelief. All our fears are wicked, and we fear because we will not nourish ourselves in our faith. How can any one who is identified with Jesus Christ suffer from doubt or fear! It ought to be an absolute pæan of perfectly irrepressible, triumphant belief.

November 14
DISCOVERING DIVINE DESIGNS

"I being in the way, the Lord led me. . ." Genesis 24:27

We have to be so one with God that we do not continually need to ask for guidance. Sanctification means that we are made the children of God, and the natural life of a child is obedience - until he wishes to be disobedient, then instantly there is the intuitive jar. In the spiritual domain the intuitive jar is the monition of the Spirit of God. When He gives the check, we have to stop at once and be renewed in the spirit of our mind in order to make out what God's will is. If we are born again of the Spirit of God, it is the abortion of piety to ask God to guide us here and there. "The Lord led me," and on looking back we see the presence of an amazing design, which, if we are born of God, we will credit to God. We can all see God in exceptional things, but it requires the culture of spiritual discipline to see God in every detail. Never allow that the haphazard is anything less than God's appointed order, and be ready to discover the Divine designs any where. Beware of making a fetish of consistency to your convictions instead of being devoted to God. I shall never do that - in all probability you will have to, if you are a saint. There never was a more inconsistent Being on this earth than Our Lord, but He was never inconsistent to His Father. The one consistency of the saint is not to a principle, but to the Divine life. It is the Divine life which continually makes more and more discoveries about the Divine mind. It is easier to be a fanatic than a faithful soul, because there is something amazingly humbling, particularly to our religious conceit, in being loyal to God.

November 15
WHAT IS THAT TO THEE?

Lord, what shall this man do? . . What is that to thee? Follow thou Me." John 21:21,2

One of our severest lessons comes from the stubborn refusal to see that we must not interfere in other people's lives. It takes a long time to realize the danger of being an amateur providence, that is, interfering with God's order for others. You see a certain person suffering, and you say - He shall not suffer, and I will see that he does not. You put your hand straight in front of God's permissive will to prevent it, and God says - "What is that to thee?" If there is stagnation spiritually, never allow it to go on, but get into God's presence and find out the reason for it. Possibly you will find it is because you have been interfering in the life of another; proposing things you had no right to propose; advising when you had no right to advise. When you do have to give advice to another, God will advise through you with the direct understanding of His Spirit; your part is to be so rightly related to God that His discernment comes through you all the time for the blessing of another soul. Most of us live on the borders of consciousness - consciously serving, consciously devoted to God. All this is immature, it is not the real life yet. The mature stage is the life of a child which is never conscious; we become so abandoned to God that the consciousness of being used never enters in. When we are consciously being used as broken bread and poured-out wine, there is another stage to be reached, where all consciousness of ourselves and of what God is doing through us is eliminated. A saint is never consciously a saint; a saint is consciously dependent on God.

November 16
STILL HUMAN!

"Whatsoever ye do, do all to the glory of God." 1 Corinthians 10:31

The great marvel of the incarnation slips into ordinary childhood's life; the great marvel of the Transfiguration vanishes in the devilpossessed valley; the glory of the Resurrection descends into a breakfast on the sea-shore. This is not an anti-climax, but a great revelation of God. The tendency is to look for the marvellous in our experience; we mistake the sense of the heroic for being heroes. It is one thing to go through a crisis grandly, but another thing to go through every day glorifying God when there is no witness, no limelight, no one paying the remotest attention to us. If we do not want mediaeval haloes, we want something that will make people say - What a wonderful man of prayer he is! What a pious devoted woman she is! If you are rightly devoted to the Lord Jesus, you have reached the sublime height where no one ever thinks of noticing you, all that is noticed is that the power of God comes through you all the time. Oh, I have had a wonderful call from God! It takes Almighty God Incarnate in us to do the meanest duty to the glory of God. It takes God's Spirit in us to make us so absolutely humanly His that we are utterly unnoticeable. The test of the life of a saint is not success, but faithfulness in human life as it actually is. We will set up success in Christian work as the aim; the aim is to manifest the glory of God in human life, to live the life hid with Christ in God in human conditions. Our human relationships are the actual conditions in which the ideal life of God is to be exhibited.

November 17
THE ETERNAL GOAL

"By Myself have I sworn, saith the Lord, for because thou hast done this thing . . . that in blessing I will bless thee. . . ." Genesis 22:15-19

Abraham has reached the place where he is in touch with the very nature of God, he understands now the Reality of God. "My goal is God Himself . . . At any cost, dear Lord, by any road." "At any cost, by any road" means nothing self-chosen in the way God brings us to the goal. There is no possibility of questioning when God speaks if He speaks to His own nature in me; prompt obedience is the only result. When Jesus says - "Come," I simply come; when He says - "Let go," I let go; when He says - "Trust in God in this matter," I do trust. The whole working out is the evidence that the nature of God is in me. God's revelation of Himself to me is determined by my character, not by God's character. "'Tis because I am mean, Thy ways so oft look mean to me." By the discipline of obedience I get to the place where Abraham was and I see Who God is. I never have a real God until I have come face to face with Him in Jesus Christ, then I know that "in all the world, my God, there is none but Thee, there is none but Thee." The promises of God are of no value to us until by obedience we understand the nature of God. We read some things in the Bible three hundred and sixty-five times and they mean nothing to us, then all of a sudden we see what God means, because in some particular we have obeyed God, and instantly His nature is opened up. "All the promises of God in Him are yea, and in Him Amen." The "yea" must be born of obedience; when by the obedience of our lives we say "Amen" to a promise, then that promise is ours.

November 18
WINNING INTO FREEDOM

"If the Son therefore shall make you free, ye shall be free indeed." John 8:36

If there is any remnant of individual conceit left, it always says "I can't." Personality never says "I can't," but simply absorbs and absorbs. Personality always wants more and more. It is the way we are built. We are designed with a great capacity for God; and sin and our individuality are the things that keep us from getting at God. God delivers us from sin: we have to deliver our selves from individuality, i.e., to present our natural life to God and sacrifice it until it is transformed into a spiritual life by obedience. God does not pay any attention to our natural individuality in the development of our spiritual life. His order runs right across the natural life, and we have to see that we aid and abet God, not stand against Him and say - I can't do that. God will not discipline us, we must discipline ourselves. God will not bring every thought and imagination into captivity; we have to do it. Do not say - O Lord, I suffer from wandering thoughts. Don't suffer from wandering thoughts. Stop listening to the tyranny of your individuality and get emancipated out into personality. "If the Son shall make you free . ." Do not substitute 'Saviour' for 'Son.' The Saviour sets us free from sin; this is the freedom of being set free by the Son. It is what Paul means in Gal. 2:20 - "I have been crucified with Christ," his natural individuality has been broken and his personality united with his Lord, not merged but united. "Ye shall be free indeed," free in essence, free from the inside. We will insist on energy, instead of being energized into identification with Jesus.

November 19
WHEN HE IS COME

And when He is come, He will convict the world of sin. . . ." John 16:8 (R.V.)

Very few of us know anything about conviction of sin; we know the experience of being disturbed because of having done wrong things; but conviction of sin by the Holy Ghost blots out every relationship on earth and leaves one relationship only - "Against Thee, Thee only, have I sinned!" When a man is convicted of sin in this way, he knows with every power of his conscience that God dare not forgive him; if God did forgive him, the man would have a stronger sense of justice than God. God does forgive, but it cost the rending of His heart in the Death of Christ to enable Him to do so. The great miracle of the grace of God is that He forgives sin, and it is the death of Jesus Christ alone that enables the Divine nature to forgive and to remain true to itself in doing so. It is shallow nonsense to say that God forgives us because He is love. When we have been convicted of sin we will never say this again. The love of God means Calvary, and nothing less; the love of God is spelt on the Cross and nowhere else. The only ground on which God can forgive me is through the Cross of my Lord. There, His conscience is satisfied. Forgiveness means not merely that I am saved from hell and made right for heaven (no man would accept forgiveness on such a level); forgiveness means that I am forgiven into a recreated relationship, into identification with God in Christ. The miracle of Redemption is that God turns me, the unholy one, into the standard of Himself, the Holy One, by putting into me a new disposition, the disposition of Jesus Christ.

November 20
THE FORGIVENESS OF GOD

"In whom we have . . . the forgiveness of sins." Ephesians 1:7

Beware of the pleasant view of the Fatherhood of God - God is so kind and loving that of course He will forgive us. That sentiment has no place whatever in the New Testament. The only ground on which God can forgive us is the tremendous tragedy of the Cross of Christ; to put forgiveness on any other ground is unconscious blasphemy. The only ground on which God can forgive sin and reinstate us in His favour is through the Cross of Christ, and in no other way. Forgiveness, which is so easy for us to accept, cost the agony of Calvary. It is possible to take the forgiveness of sin, the gift of the Holy Ghost, and our sanctification with the simplicity of faith, and to forget at what enormous cost to God it was all made ours. Forgiveness is the divine miracle of grace; it cost God the Cross of Jesus Christ before He could forgive sin and remain a holy God. Never accept a view of the Fatherhood of God if it blots out the Atonement. The revelation of God is that He cannot forgive; He would contradict His nature if He did. The only way we can be forgiven is by being brought back to God by the Atonement. God's forgiveness is only natural in the supernatural domain. Compared with the miracle of the forgiveness of sin, the experience of sanctification is slight. Sanctification is simply the marvellous expression of the forgiveness of sins in a human life, but the thing that awakens the deepest well of gratitude in a human being is that God has forgiven sin. Paul never got away from this. When once you realize all that it cost God to forgive you, you will be held as in a vice, constrained by the love of God.

November 21
IT IS FINISHED

"I have finished the work which Thou gavest Me to do." John 17:4

The Death of Jesus Christ is the performance in history of the very Mind of God. There is no room for looking on Jesus Christ as a martyr; His death was not something that happened to Him which might have been prevented: His death was the very reason why He came. Never build your preaching of forgiveness on the fact that God is our Father and He will forgive us because He loves us. It is untrue to Jesus Christ's revelation of God; it makes the Cross unnecessary, and the Redemption "much ado about nothing." If God does forgive sin, it is because of the Death of Christ. God could forgive men in no other way than by the death of His Son, and Jesus is exalted to be Saviour because of His death. "We see Jesus because of the suffering of death, crowned with glory and honour." The greatest note of triumph that ever sounded in the ears of a startled universe was that sounded on the Cross of Christ - "It is finished." That is the last word in the Redemption of man. Anything that belittles or obliterates the holiness of God by a false view of the love of God, is untrue to the revelation of God given by Jesus Christ. Never allow the thought that Jesus Christ stands with us against God out of pity and compassion; that He became a curse for us out of sympathy with us. Jesus Christ became a curse for us by the Divine decree. Our portion of realizing the terrific meaning of the curse is conviction of sin, the gift of shame and penitence is given us - this is the great mercy of God. Jesus Christ hates the wrong in man, and Calvary is the estimate of His hatred.

November 22
SHALLOW AND PROFOUND

"Whether therefore ye eat, or drink, or whatsoever ye do, do all to the glory of God." 1 Corinthians 10:31

Beware of allowing yourself to think that the shallow concerns of life are not ordained of God; they are as much of God as the profound. It is not your devotion to God that makes you refuse to be shallow, but your wish to impress other people with the fact that you are not shallow, which is a sure sign that you are a spiritual prig. Be careful of the production of contempt in yourself, it always comes along this line, and causes you to go about as a walking rebuke to other people because they are more shallow than you are. Beware of posing as a profound person; God became a Baby. To be shallow is not a sign of being wicked, nor is shallowness a sign that there are no deeps: the ocean has a shore. The shallow amenities of life, eating and drinking, walking and talking, are all ordained by God. These are the things in which Our Lord lived. He lived in them as the Son of God, and He said that "the disciple is not above his Master." Our safeguard is in the shallow things. We have to live the surface common-sense life in a common-sense way; when the deeper things come, God gives them to us apart from the shallow concerns. Never show the deeps to anyone but God. We are so abominably serious, so desperately interested in our own characters, that we refuse to behave like Christians in the shallow concerns of life. Determinedly take no one seriously but God, and the first person you find you have to leave severely alone as being the greatest fraud you have ever known, is yourself.

November 23
DISTRACTION OF ANTIPATHY

"Have mercy upon us, O Lord, have mercy upon us: for we are exceedingly piled with contempt." Psalm 123:3

The thing of which we have to beware is not so much damage to our belief in God as damage to our Christian temper. "Therefore take heed to thy spirit, that ye deal not treacherously." The temper of mind is tremendous in its effects, it is the enemy that penetrates right into the

331

soul and distracts the mind from God. There are certain tempers of mind in which we never dare indulge; if we do, we find they have distracted us from faith in God, and until we get back to the quiet mood before God, our faith in Him is nil, and our confidence in the flesh and in human ingenuity is the thing that rules. Beware of "the cares of this world," because they are the things that produce a wrong temper of soul. It is extraordinary what an enormous power there is in simple things to distract our attention from God. Refuse to be swamped with the cares of this life. Another thing that distracts us is the lust of vindication. St. Augustine prayed - "O Lord, deliver me from this lust of always vindicating myself." That temper of mind destroys the soul's faith in God. "I must explain myself; I must get people to understand." Our Lord never explained anything; He left mistakes to correct themselves. When we discern that people are not going on spiritually and allow the discernment to turn to criticism, we block our way to God. God never gives us discernment in order that we may criticize, but that we may intercede.

November 24
DIRECTION OF ASPIRATION

"Behold, as the eyes of servants look unto the hand of their masters . . . so our eyes wait upon the Lord our God." Psalm 123:2

This verse is a description of entire reliance upon God. Just as the eyes of the servant are riveted on his master, so our eyes are up unto God and our knowledge of His countenance is gained (cf. Isaiah 53:1. R.V). Spiritual leakage begins when we cease to lift up our eyes unto Him. The leakage comes not so much through trouble on the outside as in the imagination; when we begin to say - "I expect I have been stretching myself a bit too much, standing on tiptoe and trying to look like God instead of being an ordinary humble person." We have to realize that no effort can be too high. For instance, you came to a crisis when you made a stand for God and had the witness of the Spirit that all was right, but the weeks have gone by, and the years maybe, and you are slowly coming to the conclusion - 'Well, after all, was I not a bit too pretentious? Was I not taking a stand a bit too high?' Your rational friends come and say - Don't be a fool, we knew when you talked about this spiritual awakening, that it was a passing impulse, you can't keep up the strain, God does not expect you to. And you say - Well, I suppose I was expecting too much. It sounds humble to say it, but it means that reliance on God has gone and reliance on worldly opinion has come in. The danger is lest no longer relying on God you ignore the lifting up of your eyes to Him. Only when God brings you to a sudden halt, will you realize how you have been losing out. Whenever there is a leakage, remedy it immediately. Recognize that something has been coming between you and God, and get it readjusted at once.

November 25
THE SECRET OF SPIRITUAL COHERENCE

But God forbid that I should glory, save in the cross of our Lord Jesus Christ." Galatians 6:14

When a man is first born again, he becomes incoherent, there is an amount of unrelated emotion about him, unrelated phases of external things. In the apostle Paul there was a strong steady coherence underneath, consequently he could let his external life change as it liked and it did not distress him because he was rooted and grounded in God. Most of us are not spiritually coherent because we are more concerned about being coherent externally. Paul lived in the basement; the coherent critics live in the upper storey of the external statement of things, and the two do not begin to touch each other. Paul's consistency was down in the fundamentals. The great basis of his coherence was the agony of God in the Redemption of the world, viz., the Cross of Jesus Christ. Re-state to yourself what you believe, then do away with as much of it as possible, and get back to the bedrock of the Cross of Christ. In external history the Cross is an infinitesimal thing; from the Bible point of view it is of more importance than all the empires of the world. If we get away from brooding on the tragedy of God upon the Cross in our preaching, it produces nothing. It does not convey the energy of God to man; it may be interesting but it has no power. But preach the Cross, and the energy of God is let loose. "It pleased God by the foolishness of preaching to save them that believe." "We preach Christ crucified."

November 26
THE CONCENTRATION OF SPIRITUAL ENERGY

". . . save in the cross of our Lord Jesus Christ." Galatians 6:14

If you want to know the energy of God (i.e., the resurrection life of Jesus) in your mortal flesh, you must brood on the tragedy of God. Cut yourself off from prying personal interest in your own spiritual symptoms and consider bare-spirited the tragedy of God, and instantly the energy of God will be in you. "Look unto Me," pay attention to the objective Source and the subjective energy will be there. We lose power if we do not concentrate on the right thing. The effect of the Cross is salvation, sanctification, healing, etc., but we are not to preach any of these, we are to preach Jesus Christ and Him crucified. The proclaiming of Jesus will do its own work. Concentrate on God's centre in your preaching, and though your crowd may apparently pay no attention, they can never be the same again. If I talk my own talk, it is of no more importance to you than your talk is to me; but if I talk the truth of God, you will meet it again and so will I. We have to concentrate on the great point of spiritual energy - the Cross, to keep in contact with that centre where all the power lies, and the energy will be let loose. In holiness movements and spiritual experience meetings the concentration is apt to be put not on the Cross of Christ, but on the effects of the Cross. The feebleness of the churches is being criticized to-day, and the criticism is justified. One reason for the feebleness is that there has not been this concentration of spiritual energy; we have not brooded enough on the tragedy of Calvary or on the meaning of Redemption.

November 27
THE CONSECRATION OF SPIRITUAL ENERGY

"By whom the world is crucified unto me, and I unto the world."
Galatians 6:14

If I brood on the Cross of Christ, I do not become a subjective pietist, interested in my own whiteness; I become dominantly concentrated on Jesus Christ's interests. Our Lord was not a recluse nor an ascetic, He did not cut Himself off from society, but He was inwardly disconnected all the time. He was not aloof, but He lived in an other world. He was so much in the ordinary world that the religious people of His day called Him a glutton and a wine-bibber. Our Lord never allowed anything to interfere with His consecration of spiritual energy. The counterfeit of consecration is the conscious cutting off of things with the idea of storing spiritual power for use later on, but that is a hopeless mistake. The Spirit of God has spoiled the sin of a great many, yet there is no emancipation, no fullness in their lives. The kind of religious life we see abroad to-day is entirely different from the robust holiness of the life of Jesus Christ. "I pray not that Thou shouldest take them out of the world, but that Thou shouldest keep them from the evil." We are to be in the world but not of it; to be disconnected fundamentally, not externally. We must never allow anything to interfere with the consecration of our spiritual energy. Consecration is our part, sanctification is God's part; and we have deliberately to determine to be interested only in that in which God is interested. The way to solve perplexing problems is to ask - Is this the kind of thing in which Jesus Christ is interested, or the kind of thing in which the spirit that is the antipodes of Jesus is interested?

November 28
THE BOUNTY OF THE DESTITUTE

"Being justified freely by His grace. . ." Romans 3:24

The Gospel of the grace of God awakens an intense longing in human souls and an equally intense resentment, because the revelation which it brings is not palatable. There is a certain pride in man that will give and give, but to come and accept is another thing. I will give my life to martyrdom, I will give myself in consecration, I will do anything, but do not humiliate me to the level of the most hell-deserving sinner and tell me that all I have to do is to accept the gift of salvation through Jesus Christ. We have to realize that we cannot earn or win anything from God; we must either receive it as a gift or do without it. The greatest blessing spiritually is the knowledge that we are destitute; until we get there Our Lord is powerless. He can do nothing for us if we think we are sufficient of ourselves, we have to enter into His Kingdom through the door of destitution. As long as we are rich, possessed of anything in the way of pride or independence, God cannot do anything for us. It is only when we get hungry spiritually that we receive the Holy Spirit. The gift of the essential nature of God is made effectual in us by the Holy Spirit, He imparts to us the quickening life of Jesus, which puts "the beyond" within, and immediately "the beyond" has come within, it rises up to "the above," and we are lifted into the domain where Jesus lives. (John 3:5.)

November 29
THE ABSOLUTENESS OF JESUS CHRIST

"He shall glorify Me." John 16:14

The pietistic movements of to-day have none of the rugged reality of the New Testament about them; there is nothing about them that needs the Death of Jesus Christ; all that is required is a pious atmosphere, and prayer and devotion. This type of experience is not supernatural nor miraculous, it did not cost the passion of God, it is not dyed in the blood of the Lamb, not stamped with the hall-mark of the Holy Ghost; it has not that mark on it which makes men say, as they look with awe and wonder - "That is the work of God Almighty." That and nothing else is what the New Testament talks about. The type of Christian experience in the New Testament is that of personal passionate devotion to the Person of Jesus Christ. Every other type of Christian experience, so called, is detached from the Person of Jesus. There is no regeneration, no being born again into the Kingdom in which Christ lives, but only the idea that He is our Pattern. In the New Testament Jesus Christ is Saviour long before He is Pattern. To-day He is being despatched as the Figurehead of a Religion, a mere Example. He is that, but He is infinitely more; He is salvation itself, He is the Gospel of God. Jesus said, "When He the Spirit of truth is come . . . He shall glorify Me." When I commit myself to the revelation made in the New Testament, I receive from God the gift of the Holy Spirit Who begins to interpret to me what Jesus did and does in me subjectively all that Jesus Christ did for me objectively.

November 30
BY THE GRACE OF GOD I AM WHAT I AM

"His grace which was bestowed upon me was not in vain." 1 Corinthians 15:10

The way we continually talk about our own inability is an insult to the Creator. The deploring of our own incompetence is a slander against God for having overlooked us. Get into the habit of examining in the sight of God the things that sound humble before men, and you will be amazed at how staggeringly impertinent they are. "Oh, I shouldn't like to say I am sanctified; I'm not a saint." Say that before God; and it means - "No, Lord, it is impossible for You to save and sanctify me; there are chances I have not had; so many imperfections in my brain and body; no, Lord, it isn't possible." That may sound wonderfully humble before men, but before God it is an attitude of defiance. Again, the things that sound humble before God may sound the opposite before men. To say Thank God, I know I am saved and sanctified is in the sight of God the acme of humility, it means you have so completely abandoned yourself to God that you know He is true. Never bother your head as to whether what you say sounds humble before men or not, but always be humble before God, and let Him be all in all. There is only one relationship that matters, and that is your personal relationship to a personal Redeemer and Lord. Let everything else go, but maintain that at all costs, and God will fulfil His purpose through your life. One individual life may be of priceless value to God's purposes, and yours may be that life.

December 1
THE LAW AND THE GOSPEL

"For whosoever shall keep the whole law, and yet offend in one point, he is guilty of all" James 2:10

The moral law does not consider us as weak human beings at all, it takes no account of our heredity and infirmities, it demands that we be absolutely moral. The moral law never alters, either for the noblest or for the weakest, it is eternally and abidingly the same. The moral law ordained by God does not make itself weak to the weak, it does not palliate our shortcomings, it remains absolute for all time and eternity. If we do not realize this, it is because we are less than alive; immediately we are alive, life becomes a tragedy. "I was alive without the law once: but when the commandment came, sin revived, and I died." When we realize this, then the Spirit of God convicts us of sin. Until a man gets there and sees that there is no hope, the Cross of Jesus Christ is a farce to him. Conviction of sin always brings a fearful binding sense of the law, it makes a man hopeless - "sold under sin." I, a guilty sinner, can never get right with God, it is impossible. There is only one way in which I can get right with God, and that is by the Death of Jesus Christ. I must get rid of the lurking idea that I can ever be right with God because of my obedience - which of us could ever obey God to absolute perfection! We only realize the power of the moral law when it comes with an "if." God never coerces us. In one mood we wish He would make us do the thing, and in another mood we wish He would leave us alone. Whenever God's will is in the ascendant, all compulsion is gone. When we choose deliberately to obey Him, then He will tax the remotest star and the last grain of sand to assist us with all His almighty power.

December 2
CHRISTIAN PERFECTION

"Not as though I had already attained, either were already perfect. . . ." Philippians 3:12

It is a snare to imagine that God wants to make us perfect specimens of what He can do; God's purpose is to make us one with Himself. The emphasis of holiness movements is apt to be that God is producing specimens of holiness to put in His museum. If you go off on this idea of personal holiness, the dead-set of your life will not be for God, but for what you call the manifestation of God in your life. "It can never be God's will that I should be sick." If it was God's will to bruise His own Son, why should He not bruise you? The thing that tells for God is not your relevant consistency to an idea of what a saint should be, but your real vital relation to Jesus Christ, and your abandonment to Him whether you are well or ill. Christian perfection is not, and never can be, human perfection. Christian perfection is the perfection of a relationship to God which shows itself amid the irrelevancies of human life. When you obey the call of Jesus Christ, the first thing that strikes you is the irrelevancy of the things you have to do, and the next thing that strikes you is the fact that other people seem to be living perfectly consistent lives. Such lives are apt to leave you with the idea that God is unnecessary, by human effort and devotion we can reach the standard God wants. In a fallen world this can never be done. I am called to live in perfect relation to God so that my life produces a longing after God in other lives, not admiration for myself. Thoughts about myself hinder my usefulness to God. God is not after perfecting me to be a specimen in His show-room; He is getting me to the place where He can use me. Let Him do what He likes.

December 3
NOT BY MIGHT NOR BY POWER

"And my speech and my preaching was not with enticing words of man's wisdom, but in demonstration of the Spirit and of power." 1 Corinthians 2:4

If in preaching the Gospel you substitute your clear knowledge of the way of salvation for confidence in the power of the Gospel, you hinder people getting to Reality. You have to see that while you proclaim your knowledge of the way of salvation, you yourself are rooted and grounded in faith in God. Never rely on the clearness of your exposition, but as you give your exposition see that you are relying on the Holy Spirit. Rely on the certainty of God's redemptive power, and He will create His own life in souls. When once you are rooted in Reality, nothing can shake you. If your faith is in experiences, any thing that happens is likely to upset that faith; but nothing can ever upset God or the almighty Reality of Redemption; base your faith on that, and you are as eternally secure as God. When once you get into personal contact with Jesus Christ, you will never be moved again. That is the meaning of sanctification. God puts His disapproval on human experience when we begin to adhere to the conception that sanctification is merely an experience, and forget that sanctification itself has to be sanctified (see John 17:19). I have deliberately to give my sanctified life to God for His service, so that He can use me as His hands and His feet.

December 4
THE LAW OF ANTAGONISM

"To him that overcometh. . . ." Revelation 2:7

Life without war is impossible either in nature or in grace. The basis of physical, mental, moral, and spiritual life is antagonism. This is the open fact of life. Health is the balance between physical life and external nature, and it is maintained only by sufficient vitality on the inside against things on the outside. Everything outside my physical life is designed to put me to death. Things which keep me going when I am alive, disintegrate me when I am dead. If I have enough fighting power, I produce the balance of health. The same is true of the mental life. If I want to maintain a vigorous mental life, I have to fight, and in that way the mental balance called thought is produced. Morally it is the same. Everything that does not partake of the nature of virtue is the enemy of virtue in me, and it depends on what moral calibre I have whether I overcome and produce virtue. Immediately I fight, I am moral in that particular. No man is virtuous because he cannot help it; virtue is acquired. And spiritually it is the same. Jesus said, "In the world ye shall have tribulation," i.e., every thing that is not spiritual makes for my undoing, but - "Be of good cheer, I have overcome the world." I have to learn to score off the things that come against me, and in that way produce the balance of holiness; then it becomes a delight to meet opposition. Holiness is the balance between my disposition and the law of God as expressed in Jesus Christ.

December 5
THE TEMPLE OF THE HOLY GHOST

"Only in the throne will I be greater than thou." Genesis 41:40

I have to account to God for the way in which I rule my body under His domination. Paul said he did not "frustrate the grace of God" - make it of no effect. The grace of God is absolute, the salvation of Jesus is perfect, it is done for ever. I am not being saved, I am saved; salvation is as eternal as God's throne; the thing for me to do is to work out what God works in. "Work out your own salvation," I am responsible for doing it. It means that I have to manifest in this body the life of the Lord Jesus, not mystically, but really and emphatically. "I keep under my body, and bring it into subjection." Every saint can have his body under absolute control for God. God has made us to have government over all the temple of the Holy Spirit, over imaginations and affections. We are responsible for these, and we must never give way to inordinate affections. Most of us are much sterner with others than we are in regard to ourselves; we make excuses for things in ourselves whilst we condemn in others things to which we are not naturally inclined. "I beseech you," says Paul, "present your bodies a living sacrifice." The point to decide is this - "Do I agree with my Lord and Master that my body shall be His temple?' If so, then for me the whole of the law for the body is summed up in this revelation, that my body is the temple of the Holy Ghost.

December 6
THE BOW IN THE CLOUD

"I do set my bow in the cloud, and it shall be for a token of a covenant between Me and the earth." Genesis 9:13

It is the Will of God that human beings should get into moral relationship with Him, and His covenants are for this purpose. Why does not God save me? He has saved me, but I have not entered into relationship with Him. Why does not God do this and that? He has done it, the point is - Will I step into covenant relationship? All the great blessings of God are finished and complete, but they are not mine until I enter into relationship with Him on the basis of His covenant. Waiting for God is incarnate unbelief, it means that I have no faith in Him; I wait for Him to do something in me that I may trust in that. God will not do it, because that is not the basis of the God-and-man relationship. Man has to go out of himself in his covenant with God as God goes out of Himself in His covenant with man. It is a question of faith in God - the rarest thing; we have faith only in our feelings. I do not believe God unless He will give me something in my hand whereby I may know I have it, then I say - "Now I believe." There is no faith there. "Look unto Me, and be ye saved." When I have really transacted business with God on His covenant and have let go entirely, there is no sense of merit, no human ingredient in it at all, but a complete overwhelming sense of being brought into union with God, and the whole thing is transfigured with peace and joy.

December 7
REPENTANCE

"For godly sorrow worketh repentance to salvation." 2 Corinthians 7:10

Conviction of sin is best portrayed in the words - "My sins, my sins, my Saviour, How sad on Thee they fall." Conviction of sin is one of the rarest things that ever strikes a man. It is the threshold of an understanding of God. Jesus Christ said that when the Holy Spirit came He would convict of sin, and when the Holy Spirit rouses a man's conscience and brings him into the presence of God, it is not his relationship with men that bothers him, but his relationship with God - "against Thee, Thee only, have I sinned, and done this evil in Thy sight." The marvels of conviction of sin, forgiveness, and holiness are so interwoven that it is only the forgiven man who is the holy man, he proves he is forgiven by being the opposite to what he was, by God's grace. Repentance always brings a man to this point: I have sinned. The surest sign that God is at work is when a man says that and means it. Anything less than this is remorse for having made blunders, the reflex action of disgust at himself. The entrance into the Kingdom is through the panging pains of repentance crashing into a man's respectable goodness; then the Holy Ghost, Who produces these agonies, begins the formation of the Son of God in the life. The new life will manifest itself in conscious repentance and unconscious holiness, never the other way about. The bedrock of Christianity is repentance. Strictly speaking, a man cannot repent when he chooses; repentance is a gift of God. The old Puritans used to pray for "the gift of tears." If ever you cease to know the virtue of repentance, you are in darkness. Examine yourself and see if you have forgotten how to be sorry.

December 8
THE IMPARTIAL POWER OF GOD

"For by one offering he hath perfected for ever them that are sanctified." Hebrews 10:14

We trample the blood of the Son of God under foot if we think we are forgiven because we are sorry for our sins. The only explanation of the forgiveness of God and of the unfathomable depth of His forgetting is the Death of Jesus Christ. Our repentance is merely the outcome of our personal realization of the Atonement which He has worked out for us. "Christ Jesus . . . is made unto us wisdom, and righteousness, and sanctification, and redemption." When we realize that Christ is made all this to us, the boundless joy of God begins; wherever the joy of God is not present, the death sentence is at work. It does not matter who or what we are, there is absolute reinstatement into God by the death of Jesus Christ and by no other way, not because Jesus Christ pleads, but because He died. It is not earned, but accepted. All the pleading which deliberately refuses to recognize the Cross is of no avail; it is battering at another door than the one which Jesus has opened. I don't want to come that way, it is too humiliating to be received as a sinner. "There is none other Name . . ." The apparent heartlessness of God is the expression of His real heart, there is boundless entrance in His way. "We have forgiveness through His blood." Identification with the death of Jesus Christ means identification with Him to the death of everything that never was in Him. God is justified in saving bad men only as He makes them good. Our Lord does not pretend we are all right when we are all wrong. The Atonement is a propitiation whereby God through the death of Jesus makes an unholy man holy.

December 9
THE OFFENCE OF THE NATURAL

"And they that are Christ's have crucified the flesh with the affections and lusts." Galatians 5:24

The natural life is not sinful; we must be apostatized from sin, have nothing to do with sin in any shape or form. Sin belongs to hell and the devil; I, as a child of God, belong to heaven and God. It is not a question of giving up sin, but of giving up my right to myself, my natural independence and self-assertiveness, and this is where the battle has to be fought. It is the things that are right and noble and good from the natural stand point that keep us back from God's best. To discern that natural virtues antagonize surrender to God, is to bring our soul into the centre of its greatest battle. Very few of us debate with the sordid and evil and wrong, but we do debate with the good. It is the good that hates the best, and the higher up you get in the scale of the natural virtues, the more intense is the opposition to Jesus Christ. "They that are Christ's have crucified the flesh" - it is going to cost the natural in you everything, not something. Jesus said - "If any man will be My disciple, let him deny himself," i.e., his right to himself, and a man has to realize Who Jesus Christ is before he will do it. Beware of refusing to go to the funeral of your own independence. The natural life is not spiritual, and it can only be made spiritual by sacrifice. If we do not resolutely sacrifice the natural, the supernatural can never become natural in us. There is no royal road there; each of us has it entirely in his own hands. It is not a question of praying, but of performing.

December 10
THE OFFERING OF THE NATURAL

"Abraham had two sons, the one by a bondmaid, the other by a freewoman." Galatians 4:22

Paul is not dealing with sin in this chapter of Galatians, but with the relation of the natural to the spiritual. The natural must be turned into the spiritual by sacrifice, otherwise a tremendous divorce will be produced in the actual life. Why should God ordain the natural to be sacrificed? God did not. It is not God's order, but His permissive will. God's order was that the natural should be transformed into the spiritual by obedience; it is sin that made it necessary for the natural to be sacrificed. Abraham had to offer up Ishmael before he offered up Isaac. Some of us are trying to offer up spiritual sacrifices to God before we have sacrificed the natural. The only way in which we can offer a spiritual sacrifice to God is by presenting our bodies a living sacrifice. Sanctification means more than deliverance from sin, it means the deliberate commitment of myself whom God has saved to God, and that I do not care what it costs. If we do not sacrifice the natural to the spiritual, the natural life will mock at the life of the Son of God in us and produce a continual swither. This is always the result of an undisciplined spiritual nature. We go wrong because we stubbornly refuse to discipline ourselves, physically, morally or mentally. "I wasn't disciplined when I was a child." You must discipline yourself now. If you do not, you will ruin the whole of your personal life for God. God is not with our natural life while we pamper it; but when we put it out in the desert and resolutely keep it under, then God will be with it; and He will open up wells and oases, and fulfill all His promises for the natural.

December 11
INDIVIDUALITY

"If any man will come after Me, let him deny himself." Matthew 16:24

Individuality is the husk of the personal life. Individuality is all elbows, it separates and isolates. It is the characteristic of the child and rightly so; but if we mistake individuality for the personal life, we will remain isolated. The shell of individuality is God's created natural covering for the protection of the personal life; but individuality must go in order that the personal life may come out and be brought into fellowship with God. Individuality counterfeits personality as lust counterfeits love. God designed human nature for Himself; individuality debases human nature for itself. The characteristics of individuality are independence and selfassertiveness. It is the continual assertion of individuality that hinders our spiritual life more than anything else. If you say - "I cannot believe," it is because individuality is in the road; individuality never can believe. Personality cannot help believing. Watch yourself when the Spirit of God is at work. He pushes you to the margins of your individuality, and you have either to say - "I shan't," or to surrender, to break the husk of individuality and let the personal life emerge. The Holy Spirit narrows it down every time to one thing (cf. Matthew 5:23-24). The thing in you that will not be reconciled to your brother is your individuality. God wants to bring you into union with Himself, but unless you are willing to give up your right to yourself He cannot. "Let him deny

343

himself" - deny his independent right to himself, then the real life has a chance to grow.

December 12
PERSONALITY

"That they may be one, even as we are one." John 17:22

Personality is that peculiar, incalculable thing that is meant when we speak of ourselves as distinct from everyone else. Our personality is always too big for us to grasp. An island in the sea may be but the top of a great mountain. Personality is like an island, we know nothing about the great depths underneath, consequently we cannot estimate ourselves. We begin by thinking that we can, but we come to realize that there is only one Being Who understands us, and that is our Creator. Personality is the characteristic of the spiritual man as individuality is the characteristic of the natural man. Our Lord can never be defined in terms of individuality and independence, but only in terms of personality, "I and My Father are one." Personality merges, and you only reach your real identity when you are merged with another person. When love, or the Spirit of God strikes a man, he is transformed, he no longer insists upon his separate individuality. Our Lord never spoke in terms of individuality, of a man's "elbows" or his isolated position, but in terms of personality - "that they may be one, even as We are one." If you give up your right to yourself to God, the real true nature of your personality answers to God straight away. Jesus Christ emancipates the personality, and the individuality is transfigured; the transfiguring element is love, personal devotion to Jesus. Love is the outpouring of one personality in fellowship with another personality.

December 13
WHAT TO PRAY FOR

"Men ought always to pray, and not to faint" Luke 18:1

You cannot intercede if you do not believe in the reality of the Redemption; you will turn intercession into futile sympathy with human beings which will only increase their submissive content to being out of touch with God. In intercession you bring the person, or the circumstance that impinges on you before God until you are moved by His attitude towards that person or circumstance. Intercession means filling up "that which is behind of the afflictions of Christ," and that is why there are so few intercessors. Intercession is put on the line of -

"Put yourself in his place." Never! Try to put yourself in God's place. As a worker, be careful to keep pace with the communications of reality from God or you will be crushed. If you know too much, more than God has engineered for you to know, you cannot pray, the condition of the people is so crushing that you cannot get through to reality. Our work lies in coming into definite contact with God about everything, and we shirk it by becoming active workers. We do the things that can be tabulated but we will not intercede. Intercession is the one thing that has no snares, because it keeps our relationship with God completely open. The thing to watch in intercession is that no soul is patched up, a soul must get through into contact with the life of God. Think of the number of souls God has brought about our path and we have dropped them! When we pray on the ground of Redemption, God creates something He can create in no other way than through intercessory prayer.

December 14
THE GREAT LIFE

"Peace I leave with you, My peace I give unto you: . . Let not your heart be troubled." John 14:27

Whenever a thing becomes difficult in personal experience, we are in danger of blaming God, but it is we who are in the wrong, not God, there is some perversity somewhere that we will not let go. Immediately we do, everything becomes as clear as daylight. As long as we try to serve two ends, ourselves and God, there is perplexity. The attitude must be one of complete reliance on God. When once we get there, there is nothing easier than living the saintly life; difficulty comes in when we want to usurp the authority of the Holy Spirit for our own ends. Whenever you obey God, His seal is always that of peace, the witness of an unfathomable peace, which is not natural, but the peace of Jesus. Whenever peace does not come, tarry till it does or find out the reason why it does not. If you are acting on an impulse, or from a sense of the heroic, the peace of Jesus will not witness; there is no simplicity or confidence in God, because the spirit of simplicity is born of the Holy Ghost, not of your decisions. Every decision brings a reaction of simplicity. My questions come whenever I cease to obey. When I have obeyed God, the problems never come between me and God, they come as probes to keep the mind going on with amazement at the revelation of God. Any problem that comes between God and myself springs out of disobedience; any problem, and there are many, that is alongside me while I obey God, increases my ecstatic delight, because I know that my Father knows, and I am going to watch and see how He unravels this thing.

December 15
APPROVED UNTO GOD

"Study to show thyself approved unto God, a workman that needeth not to be ashamed, rightly dividing the word of truth." 2 Timothy 2:15

If you cannot express yourself on any subject, struggle until you can. If you do not, someone will be the poorer all the days of his life. Struggle to re-express some truth of God to yourself, and God will use that expression to someone else. Go through the winepress of God where the grapes are crushed. You must struggle to get expression experimentally, then there will come a time when that expression will become the very wine of strengthening to someone else; but if you say lazily - "I am not going to struggle to express this thing for myself, I will borrow what I say," the expression will not only be of no use to you, but of no use to anyone. Try to state to yourself what you feel implicitly to be God's truth, and you give God a chance to pass it on to someone else through you. Always make a practice of provoking your own mind to think out what it accepts easily. Our position is not ours until we make it ours by suffering. The author who benefits you most is not the one who tells you something you did not know before, but the one who gives expression to the truth that has been dumbly struggling in you for utterance.

December 16
WRESTLING BEFORE GOD

"Wherefore take unto you the whole armour of God . . . praying always . . ." Ephesians 6:13, 18

You have to wrestle against the things that prevent you from getting to God, and you wrestle in prayer for other souls; but never say that you wrestle with God in prayer, it is scripturally untrue. If you do wrestle with God, you will be crippled all the rest of your life. If, when God comes in some way you do not want, you take hold of Him as Jacob did and wrestle with Him, you compel Him to put you out of joint. Don't be a hirpler in God's ways, but be one who wrestles before God with things, becoming more than conqueror through Him. Wrestling before God tells in His Kingdom. If you ask me to pray for you and I am not complete in Christ, I may pray but it avails nothing; but if I am complete in Christ my prayer prevails all the time. Prayer is only effective when there is completeness - "Wherefore take unto you the whole armour of God." Always distinguish between God's order and His permissive will, i.e., His providential purpose towards us. God's order is unchangeable; His permissive will is that with which we must wrestle before Him. It is our reaction to the permissive will of God that enables us to get at His order. "All things work together for good to them that love God" - to those who remain true to God's order, to His calling in Christ Jesus. God's permissive will is the means whereby His sons and daughters are to be manifested. We are not to be like jelly-fish saying, "It's the Lord's will." We have not to put up a fight before God, not to wrestle with God, but to wrestle before God with things. Beware of squatting lazily before God instead of putting up a glorious fight so that you may lay hold of His strength.

December 17
REDEMPTION CREATES THE NEED IT SATISFIES

"But the natural man receiveth not the things of the Spirit of God: for they are foolishness unto him." 1 Corinthians 2:14

The Gospel of God creates a sense of need of the Gospel. Paul says - "If our gospel be hid, it is hid" - to those who are blackguards? No, "to them that are lost: in whom the god of this world hath blinded the minds of them which believe not." The majority of people have their morality well within their own grasp, they have no sense of need of the Gospel. It is God Who creates the need of which no human being is conscious until God manifests Himself. Jesus said - "Ask, and it shall be given you," but God cannot give until a man asks. It is not that He withholds, but that that is the way He has constituted things on the basis of Redemption. By means of our asking, God gets processes into work whereby He creates the thing that is not in existence until we do ask. The inner reality of Redemption is that it creates all the time. As the Redemption creates the life of God in us, so it creates the things belonging to that life. Nothing can satisfy the need but that which created the need. This is the meaning of Redemption - it creates and it satisfies. "I, if I be lifted up from the earth, will draw all men unto Me." We preach our own experiences and people are interested, but no sense of need is awakened by it. If once Jesus Christ is lifted up, the Spirit of God will create a conscious need of Him. Behind the preaching of the Gospel is the creative Redemption of God at work in the souls of men. It is never personal testimony that saves men. "The words that I speak unto you, they are spirit and they are life."

December 18
THE TEST OF LOYALTY

"And we know that all things work together for good to them that love God." Romans 8:28

It is only the loyal soul who believes that God engineers circumstances. We take such liberty with our circumstances, we do not believe God engineers them, although we say we do; we treat the things that happen as if they were engineered by men. To be faithful in every circumstance means that we have only one loyalty, and that is to our Lord. Suddenly God breaks up a particular set of circumstances, and the realization comes that we have been disloyal to Him by not recognizing that He had ordered them; we never saw what He was after, and that particular thing will never be repeated all the days of our life. The test of loyalty always comes just there. If we learn to worship God in the trying circumstances, He will alter them in two seconds when He chooses. Loyalty to Jesus Christ is the thing that we "stick at" to-day. We will be loyal to work, to service, to anything, but do not ask us to be loyal to Jesus Christ. Many Christians are intensely impatient of talking about loyalty to Jesus. Our Lord is dethroned more emphatically by Christian workers than by the world. God is made a machine for blessing men, and Jesus Christ is made a Worker among workers. The idea is not that we do work for God, but that we are so loyal to Him that He can do His work through us - "I reckon on you for extreme service, with no complaining on your part and no explanation on Mine." God wants to use us as He used His own Son.

December 19
WHAT TO CONCENTRATE ON

"I came not to send peace, but a sword." Matthew 10:34

Never be sympathetic with the soul whose case makes you come to the conclusion that God is hard. God is more tender than we can conceive, and every now and again He gives us the chance of being the rugged one that He may be the tender One. If a man cannot get through to God it is because there is a secret thing he does not intend to give up - I will admit I have done wrong, but I no more intend to give up that thing than fly. It is impossible to deal sympathetically with a case like that: we have to get right deep down to the root until there is antagonism and resentment against the message. People want the blessing of God, but they will not stand the thing that goes straight to the quick. If God has had His way with you, your message as His servant is merciless insistence on the one line, cut down to the very root, otherwise there will be no healing. Drive home the message until there is no possible refuge from its application. Begin to get at people where they are until you get them to realize what they lack, and then erect the standard of Jesus Christ for their lives - "We never can be that." Then drive it home - "Jesus Christ says you must." "But how can we be?" "You cannot, unless you have a new Spirit." (Luke 11:13.) There must be a sense of need before your message is of any use. Thousands of people are happy without God in this world. If I was happy and moral till Jesus came, why did He come? Because that kind of happiness and peace is on a wrong level; Jesus Christ came to send a sword through every peace that is not based on a personal relationship to Himself.

December 20
THE RIGHT LINES OF WORK

"I, if I be lifted up, will draw all men unto Me." John 12:32

Very few of us have any understanding of the reason why Jesus Christ died. If sympathy is all that human beings need, then the Cross of Christ is a farce, there was no need for it. What the world needs is not "a little bit of love," but a surgical operation. When you are face to face with a soul in difficulty spiritually, remind yourself of Jesus Christ on the Cross. If that soul can get to God on any other line, then the Cross of Jesus Christ is unnecessary. If you can help others by your sympathy or understanding, you are a traitor to Jesus Christ. You have to keep your soul rightly related to God and pour out for others on His line, not pour out on the human line and ignore God. The great note to-day is amiable religiosity. The one thing we have to do is to exhibit Jesus Christ crucified, to lift Him up all the time. Every doctrine that is not imbedded in the Cross of Jesus will lead astray. If the worker himself believes in Jesus Christ and is banking on the Reality of Redemption, the people he talks to must be concerned. The thing that remains and deepens is the worker's simple relationship to Jesus Christ; his usefulness to God depends on that and that alone. The calling of a New Testament worker is to uncover sin and to reveal Jesus Christ as Saviour, consequently he cannot be poetical, he must be sternly surgical. We are sent by God to lift up Jesus Christ, not to give wonderfully beautiful discourses. We have to probe straight down as deeply as God has probed us, to be keen in sensing the Scriptures which bring the truth straight home and to apply them fearlessly.

December 21
EXPERIENCE OR REVELATION

"We have received . . . the spirit which is of God; that we might know the things that are freely given to us of God." 1 Corinthians 2:12

Reality is Redemption, not my experience of Redemption; but Redemption has no meaning for me until it speaks the language of my conscious life. When I am born again, the Spirit of God takes me right out of myself and my experiences, and identifies me with Jesus Christ. If I am left with my experiences, my experiences have not been produced by Redemption. The proof that they are produced by Redemption is that I am led out of myself all the time, I no longer pay any attention to my experiences as the ground of Reality, but only to the Reality which produced the experiences. My experiences are not worth anything unless they keep me at the Source, Jesus Christ. If you try to dam up the Holy Spirit in you to produce subjective experiences, you will find that He will burst all bounds and take you back again to the historic Christ. Never nourish an experience which has not God as its Source and faith in God as its result. If you do, your experience is anti-Christian, no matter what visions you may have had. Is Jesus Christ Lord of your experiences, or do you try to lord it over Him? Is any experience dearer to you than your Lord? He must be Lord over you, and you must not pay attention to any experience over which He is not Lord. There comes a time when God will make you impatient with your own experience - I do not care what I experience; I am sure of Him. Be ruthless with yourself if you are given to talking about the experiences you have had. Faith that is sure of itself is not faith; faith that is sure of God is the only faith there is.

December 22
THE DRAWING OF THE FATHER

"No man can come to Me, except the Father which hath sent Me draw him." John 6:44

When God draws me, the issue of my will comes in at once - will I react on the revelation which God gives - will I come to Him? Discussion on spiritual matters is an impertinence. Never discuss with anyone when God speaks. Belief is not an intellectual act; belief is a moral act whereby I deliberately commit myself. Will I dump myself down absolutely on God and transact on what He says? If I will, I shall find I am based on Reality that is as sure as God's throne. In preaching the gospel, always push an issue of will. Belief must be the will to believe. There must be a surrender of the will, not a surrender to persuasive power, a deliberate launching forth on God and on what He says until I am no longer confident in what I have done, I am confident only in God. The hindrance is that I will not trust God, but only my mental understanding. As far as feelings go, I must stake all blindly. I must will to believe, and this can never be done without a violent effort on my part to disassociate myself from my old ways of looking at things, and by putting myself right over on to Him. Every man is made to reach out beyond his grasp. It is God who draws me, and my relationship to Him in the first place is a personal one, not an intellectual one. I am introduced into the relationship by the miracle of God and my own will to believe, then I begin to get an intelligent appreciation and understanding of the wonder of the transaction.

December 23
HOW CAN I PERSONALLY PARTAKE IN THE ATONEMENT?

"But God forbid that I should glory save in the cross of Our Lord Jesus Christ." Galatians 6:14

The Gospel of Jesus Christ always forces an issue of will. Do I accept God's verdict on sin in the Cross of Christ? Have I the slightest interest in the death of Jesus? Do I want to be identified with His death, to be killed right out to all interest in sin, in worldliness, in self - to be so identified with Jesus that I am spoilt for every thing else but Him? The great privilege of discipleship is that I can sign on under His Cross, and that means death to sin. Get alone with Jesus and either tell Him that you do not want sin to die out in you; or else tell Him that at all costs you want to be identified with His death. Immediately you transact in confident faith in what Our Lord did on the Cross, a supernatural identification with His death takes place, and you will know with a knowledge that passeth knowledge that your "old man" is crucified with Christ. The proof that your old man is crucified with Christ is the amazing ease with which the life of God in you enables you to obey the voice of Jesus Christ. Every now and again, Our Lord lets us see what we would be like if it were not for Himself; it is a justification of what He said - "Without Me ye can do nothing." That is why the bedrock of Christianity is personal, passionate devotion to the Lord Jesus. We mistake the ecstasy of our first introduction into the Kingdom for the purpose of God in getting us there; His purpose in getting us there is that we may realize all that identification with Jesus Christ means.

December 24
THE HIDDEN LIFE

"Your life is hid with Christ in God." Colossians 3:3

The Spirit of God witnesses to the simple almighty security of the life hid with Christ in God and this is continually brought out in the Epistles. We talk as if it were the most precarious thing to live the sanctified life; it is the most secure thing, because it has Almighty God in and behind it. The most precarious thing is to try and live without God. If we are born again it is the easiest thing to live in right relationship to God and the most difficult thing to go wrong, if only we will heed God's warnings and keep in the light. When we think of being delivered from sin, of being filled with the Spirit, and of walking in the light, we picture the peak of a great mountain, very high and wonderful, and we say - "Oh, but I could never live up there!" But when we do get there by God's grace, we find it is not a mountain peak, but a plateau where there is ample room to live and to grow. "Thou hast enlarged my steps under me." When you really see Jesus, I defy you to doubt Him. When He says - "Let not your heart be troubled," if you see Him I defy you to trouble your mind, it is a moral impossibility to doubt when He is there. Every time you get into personal contact with Jesus, His words are real. "My peace I give unto you," it is a peace all over from the crown of the head to the sole of the feet, an irrepressible confidence. "Your life is hid with Christ in God," and the imperturbable peace of Jesus Christ is imparted to you.

December 25
HIS BIRTH AND OUR NEW BIRTH

"Behold, a virgin shall bring forth a son, and they shall call His name Emanuel, which being interpreted is, God with us." Isaiah 7:14 (R.V.)

His Birth in History. "Therefore also that holy thing which shall be born of thee shall be called the Son of God." (Luke 1:35.) Jesus Christ was born into this world, not from it. He did not evolve out of history; He came into history from the outside. Jesus Christ is not the best human being, He is a Being Who cannot be accounted for by the human race at all. He is not man becoming God, but God Incarnate, God coming into human flesh, coming into it from outside. His life is the Highest and the Holiest entering in at the Lowliest door. Our Lord's birth was an advent.

His Birth in Me. "Of whom I travail in birth again until Christ be formed in you." (Gal. 4:19.) Just as Our Lord came into human history from outside, so He must come into me from outside. Have I allowed my personal human life to become a "Bethlehem" for the Son of God? I cannot enter into the realm of the Kingdom of God unless I am born from above by a birth totally unlike natural birth. "Ye must be born again." This is not a command, it is a foundation fact. The characteristic of the new birth is that I yield myself so completely to God that Christ is formed in me. Immediately Christ is formed in me, His nature begins to work through me. God manifest in the flesh - that is what is made profoundly possible for you and me by the Redemption.

December 26
PLACED IN THE LIGHT

"If we walk in the light, as He is in the light the blood of Jesus Christ His Son cleanseth us from all sin." 1 John 1:7 To mistake conscious freedom from sin for deliverance from sin by the Atonement is a great error. No man knows what sin is until he is born again. Sin is what Jesus Christ faced on Calvary. The evidence that I am delivered from sin is that I know the real nature of sin in me. It takes the last reach of the Atonement of Jesus Christ, that is, the impartation of His absolute perfection, to make a man know what sin is. The Holy Spirit applies the Atonement to us in the unconscious realm as well as in the realm of which we are conscious, and it is only when we get a grasp of the unrivalled power of the Spirit in us that we understand the meaning of 1 John 1:7, "the blood of Jesus Christ cleanseth us from all sin." This does not refer to conscious sin only, but to the tremendously profound understanding of sin which only the Holy Ghost in me realizes. If I walk in the light as God is in the light, not in the light of my conscience, but in the light of God - if I walk there, with nothing folded up, then there comes the amazing revelation, the blood of Jesus Christ cleanses me from all sin so that God Almighty can see nothing to censure in me. In my consciousness it works with a keen poignant knowledge of what sin is. The love of God at work in me makes me hate with the hatred of the Holy Ghost all that is not in keeping with God's holiness. To walk in the light means that everything that is of the darkness drives me closer into the centre of the light.

December 27
WHERE THE BATTLE'S LOST AND WON

"If thou wilt return, O Israel, saith the Lord. . . ." Jeremiah 4:1

The battle is lost or won in the secret places of the will before God, never first in the external world. The Spirit of God apprehends me and I am obliged to get alone with God and fight the battle out before Him. Until this is done, I lose every time. The battle may take one minute or a year, that will depend on me, not on God; but it must be wrestled out alone before God, and I must resolutely go through the hell of a renunciation before God. Nothing has any power over the man who has fought out the battle before God and won there. If I say, "I will wait till I get into the circumstances and then put God to the test," I shall find I cannot. I must get the thing settled between my self and God in the secret places of my soul where no stranger intermeddles, and then I can go forth with the certainty that the battle is won. Lose it there, and calamity and disaster and upset are as sure as God's decree. The reason the battle is not won is because I try to win it in the external world first. Get alone with God, fight it out before Him, settle the matter there once and for all. In dealing with other people, the line to take is to push them to an issue of will. That is the way abandonment begins. Every now and again, not often, but sometimes, God brings us to a point of climax. That is the Great Divide in the life; from that point we either go towards a more and more dilatory and useless type of Christian life, or we become more and more ablaze for the glory of God - My Utmost for His Highest.

December 28
CONTINUOUS CONVERSION

"Except ye be converted, and become as little children. . . ." Matthew 18:3

These words of Our Lord are true of our initial conversion, but we have to be continuously converted all the days of our lives, continually to turn to God as children. If we trust to our wits instead of to God, we produce consequences for which God will hold us responsible. Immediately our bodies are brought into new conditions by the providence of God, we have to see that our natural life obeys the dictates of the Spirit of God. Because we have done it once is no proof that we shall do it again. The relation of the natural to the spiritual is one of continuous conversion, and it is the one thing we object to. In every setting in which we are put, the Spirit of God remains unchanged and His salvation unaltered, but we have to "put on the new man." God holds us responsible every time we refuse to convert ourselves, our reason for refusing is wilful obstinacy. Our natural life must not rule, God must rule in us. The hindrance in our spiritual life is that we will not be continually converted, there are wadges of obstinacy where our pride spits at the throne of God and says - I won't. We deify independence and wilfulness and call them by the wrong name. What God looks on as obstinate weakness, we call strength. There are whole tracts of our lives which have not yet been brought into subjection, and it can only be done by this continuous conversion. Slowly but surely we can claim the whole territory for the Spirit of God.

December 29
DESERTER OR DISCIPLE?

"From that time many of His disciples went back, and walked no more with Him." John 6:66 When God gives a vision by His Spirit through His word of what He wants, and your mind and soul thrill to it, if you do not walk in the light of that vision, you will sink into servitude to a point of view which Our Lord never had. Disobedience in mind to the heavenly vision will make you a slave to points of view that are alien to Jesus Christ. Do not look at someone else and say - Well, if he can have those views and prosper, why cannot I? You have to walk in the light of the vision that has been given to you and not compare yourself with others or judge them, that is between them and God. When you find that a point of view in which you have been delighting clashes with the heavenly vision and you debate, certain things will begin to develop in you - a sense of property and a sense of personal right, things of which Jesus Christ made nothing. He was always against these things as being the root of everything alien to Himself. "A man's life consisteth not in the abundance of the things that he possesseth." If we do not recognize this, it is because we are ignoring the undercurrent of Our Lord's teaching. We are apt to lie back and bask in the memory of the wonderful experience we have had. If there is one standard in the New Testament revealed by the light of God and you do not come up to it, and do not feel inclined to come up to it, that is the beginning of backsliding, because it means your conscience does not answer to the truth. You can never be the same after the unveiling of a truth. That moment marks you for going on as a more true disciple of Jesus Christ or for going back as a deserter.

December 30
"AND EVERY VIRTUE WE POSSESS"

"All my fresh springs shall be in Thee." Psalm 87:7 (P.B.V.)

Our Lord never patches up our natural virtues, He re-makes the whole man on the inside. "Put on the new man," i.e., see that your natural human life puts on the garb that is in keeping with the new life. The life God plants in us develops its own virtues, not the virtues of Adam but of Jesus Christ. Watch how God will wither up your confidence in natural virtues after sanctification, and in any power you have, until you learn to draw your life from the reservoir of the resurrection life of Jesus. Thank God if you are going through a drying-up experience! The sign that God is at work in us is that He corrupts confidence in the natural virtues, because they are not promises of what we are going to be, but remnants of what God created man to be. We will cling to the natural virtues, while all the time God is trying to get us into contact with the life of Jesus Christ which can never be described in terms of the natural virtues. It is the saddest thing to see people in the service of God depending on that which the grace of God never gave them, depending on what they have by the accident of heredity. God does not build up our natural virtues and transfigure them, because our natural virtues can never come anywhere near what Jesus Christ wants. No natural love, no natural patience, no natural purity can ever come up to His demands. But as we bring every bit of our bodily life into harmony with the new life which God has put in us, He will exhibit in us the virtues that were characteristic of the Lord Jesus. "And every virtue we possess Is His alone."

December 31
YESTERDAY

"The God of Israel will be your rereward." Isaiah 52:12

Security from Yesterday. "God requireth that which is past." At the end of the year we turn with eagerness to all that God has for the future, and yet anxiety is apt to arise from remembering the yesterdays. Our present enjoyment of God's grace is apt to be checked by the memory of yesterday's sins and blunders. But God is the God of our yesterdays, and He allows the memory of them in order to turn the past into a ministry of spiritual culture for the future. God reminds us of the past lest we get into a shallow security in the present. Security for To-morrow. "For the Lord will go before you." This is a gracious revelation, that God will garrison where we have failed to. He will watch lest things trip us up again into like failure, as they assuredly would do if He were not our rereward. God's hand reaches back to the past and makes a clearing-house for conscience. Security for To-day. "For ye shall not go out with haste." As we go forth into the coming year, let it not be in the haste of impetuous, unremembering delight, nor with the flight of impulsive thoughtlessness, but with the patient power of knowing that the God of Israel will go before us. Our yesterdays present irreparable things to us; it is true that we have lost opportunities which will never return, but God can transform this destructive anxiety into a constructive thoughtfulness for the future. Let the past sleep, but let it sleep on the bosom of Christ. Leave the Irreparable Past in His hands, and step out into the Irresistible Future with Him

About the Author

Arlyn Satanek was radically saved by Christ in July of 1993. He was called by God to minister the Word just weeks later. He now holds a bachelor's degree in biblical studies (B.B.S). He is married with 3 children and serving as the pastor of Anchored Fellowship in Uniontown, PA. Pastor Arlyn teaches through the Bible, chapter by chapter and verse by verse. For free access to all of Pastor Arlyn's teachings, and other Anchored Fellowship resources, go to: anchoredfellowship.com.

Pastor Arlyn plans to release a Pastor's Edition of this book, which will also serve as a pastoral manual for all things pertaining to the work of ministry. He hopes to release the Pastor's Edition in 2025.

Made in the USA
Columbia, SC
27 September 2024